TURKISH FOREIGN POLICY
1774–2000

TURKISH
FOREIGN POLICY
1774–2000

William Hale

School of Oriental and African Studies, London

FRANK CASS
LONDON • PORTLAND, OR

First published in 2000 in Great Britain by
FRANK CASS PUBLISHERS
Crown House, 47 Chase Side, Southgate
London N14 5BP, England

and in the United States by
FRANK CASS PUBLISHERS
c/o ISBS, 5824 N.E. Hassalo Street
Portland, Oregon, 97213-3644

Website: www.frankcass.com

Copyright © 2000 W. Hale
Reprinted 2002

British Library Cataloguing in Publication Data

Hale, William M. (William Mathew), 1940–
  Turkish foreign policy, 1774–2000
  1. Turkey – Foreign relations 2. Turkey – Politics and
  government
  I. Title
  327.5'61

ISBN 0-7146-5071-4 (cloth)

Library of Congress Cataloging-in-Publication Data

Hale, William M.
  Turkish foreign policy, 1774–2000 / William Hale.
    p. cm.
  Includes bibliographical references and index.
  ISBN 0-7146-5071-4 (cloth)
  1. Turkey–Foreign relations 2. Turkey–Politics and government–
  19th century. 3. Turkey–Politics and government–20th century.
  I. Title.

  DR474 .H35 2000
  327.561'009'04–dc21
  00-031605

Typeset by Regent Typesetting, London
Printed in Great Britain by
MPG Books Ltd, Bodmin, Cornwall

Contents

Note on Spellings

Since 1928, Turkish has been written in a version of the Latin script, and this has been used for spelling all Turkish personal and place names when writing of the period after the First World War. In writing of the Ottoman period, when Turkish was written in Arabic characters, the transliterations normally used by writers at the time have been adhered to, although this has resulted in some inconsistencies. Similarly, non-Turkish names originally written in the Arabic, Cyrillic or Greek alphabets have been rendered in the way normally used by English-language writers, and the author must beg the forgiveness of specialists for any mistakes.

In the modern Turkish alphabet, the letters are pronounced roughly as in English, with the following exceptions:

a – short 'a', as in French, or the English 'u' in 'hut'.
c – 'j', as in English 'jam'.
ç – 'ch', as in English 'church'.
ğ – normally silent: lengthens preceding vowel.
ı – as in the first and last 'a's in 'banana'.
i – as in English 'bit': notice the upper case form İ.
ö – as in German, or the French 'eu' in 'leur'.
ş – 'sh', as in 'shut'.
ü – as in German, or the French 'u' in 'tu'.

Acknowledgements

The research for this book was originally carried out as part of a project on modern Turkish foreign policy under the auspices of the Royal Institute of International Affairs, London, and generously financed by the Lever-hulme Trust, in which the author collaborated with Dr Philip Robins. I must express my deep thanks to both the Institute and the Trust for their invaluable support. Dr Robins and I eventually decided to produce separate studies on the subject, but I benefited greatly from his advice in undertaking this project. I am also very grateful to the School of Oriental and African Studies (SOAS) in London for granting me study leave during 1999, and to its Research Committee for financial support, as well as to Professor Ersin Kalaycıoğlu and his colleagues in the Department of Political Science and International Relations at Boğaziçi University for their generous hospitality during my stay in Istanbul.

I also owe an immense debt to academic colleagues, as well as many others, who helped me greatly in my work. I benefited enormously from the advice and experience of Dr Andrew Mango and Professor Clement Dodd, besides that of my colleagues in SOAS, in particular Dr Ben Fortna and Dr Bhavna Dave. Unfortunately, Dr Mango's definitive biography, *Atatürk* (London, Murray, 1999), appeared too late to allow me to incorporate the wealth of information it contains in this book, but he has been an invaluable source of advice and ideas. Among overseas friends and colleagues, I am extremely grateful to George Harris, Professor Bruce Kuniholm, Dr Heinz Kramer and Dr Bill Harris, who generously shared advice and information, and allowed me to use unpublished material. My main debt is to many friends in Turkey, without whose help I could never have completed the book. Among many others, I must particularly thank Captain Gündüz and Professor Rona Aybay, Mr Candan Azer, Professor Gülnur Aybet, Professor Suha Bölükbaşı, Dr Ali Çarkoğlu, Professor Kemal Kirişci, Dr Nilüfer Oral, Ambassador Özdem Sanberk, Ambassador İsmail Soysal, Mr Seyfi Taşhan and Dr Gareth Winrow. To all of them, I am extremely grateful.

List of Abbreviations

AIOC	Azerbaijan International Oil Consortium
BP	British Petroleum company, later BP Amoco
BSEC	Black Sea Economic Cooperation project
CAP	Common Agricultural Policy
CENTO	Central Treaty Organisation
CFE	Conventional Forces in Europe treaty
CHP	Republican People's Party (*Cumhuriyet Halk Partisi*)
CIS	Commonwealth of Independent States
CSCE	Conference on Security and Cooperation in Europe (later OSCE)
DECA	Defence and Economic Cooperation Agreements
DEP	Democracy Party (*Demokrasi Partisi*)
DİSK	Reformist Trades Unions Confederation (*Devrimci İşçi Sendikaları Konfederasyonu*)
DSP	Democratic Left Party (*Demokratik Sol Partisi*)
DTP	Democratic Turkey Party (*Demokratik Türkiye Partisi*)
DYP	True Path Party (*Doğru Yol Partisi*)
EC	European Community
ECO	Economic Cooperation Organisation
EEC	European Economic Community
EIB	European Investment Bank
ESDI	European Security and Defence Identity
EU	European Union
GNP	Gross National Product
GUAM	Georgia–Ukraine–Azerbaijan–Moldova grouping
HADEP	People's Labour Party (*Halkın Demokrasi Partisi*)
HEP	People's Labour Party (*Halkın Emek Partisi*)
IDA	International Development Association
IFC	International Finance Corporation
IFOR	Implementation Force (in Bosnia-Herzegovina)
ILSA	Iran–Libya Sanctions Act
IMF	International Monetary Fund
IMO	International Maritime Organisation
JP	Justice Party

KDP	Kurdistan Democratic Party
KDPI	Kurdistan Democratic Party of Iran
KFOR	Kosovo international peace-keeping force
MHP	Nationalist Action Party (*Milliyetçi Hareket Partisi*)
MSP	National Salvation Party (*Milli Selamet Partisi*)
MÜSİAD	Independent Industrialists and Businessmen's Association (*Müstakil Sanayici ve İş Adamları Derneği*)
NATO	North Atlantic Treaty Organisation
OECD	Organisation for Economic Cooperation and Development
OEEC	Organisation for European Economic Cooperation (predecessor to OECD)
OIC	Organisation of the Islamic Conference
OSCE	Organisation for Security and Cooperation in Europe
PKK	Kurdistan Workers' Party (*Partiya Karkeren Kurdistan*)
PUK	Patriotic Union of Kurdistan
RCD	Regional Cooperation and Development
SACEUR	Supreme Allied Commander, Europe
SALT	Strategic Arms Limitation Talks
SFOR	Stabilisation Force (in Bosnia-Herzegovina)
SHP	Social Democrat People's Party (*Sosyaldemokrat Halkçı Parti*)
SOCAR	Azerbaijan state petroleum company
TICA	Turkish International Cooperation Agency
TPAO	Turkish Petroleum Company (*Türk Petrolleri Anonim Ortakliği*)
TRNC	Turkish Republic of Northern Cyprus
TTOBB	Turkish Union of Chambers (*Türkiye Ticaret Odalar ve Borsalar Birliği*)
TUDEV	Turkic States and Communities Friendship, Brotherhood and Cooperation Foundation
Türk-İs	Turkish Trades Unions Confederation (*Türkiye İşçi Sendikaları Konfederasyonu*)
TÜSİAD	Turkish Industrialists and Businessmen's Association (*Türkiye Sanayici ve İş Adamları Derneği*)
UNCLOS	United Nations Convention on the Law of the Sea
UNPROFOR	UN protection force in Bosnia
WEU	Western European Union

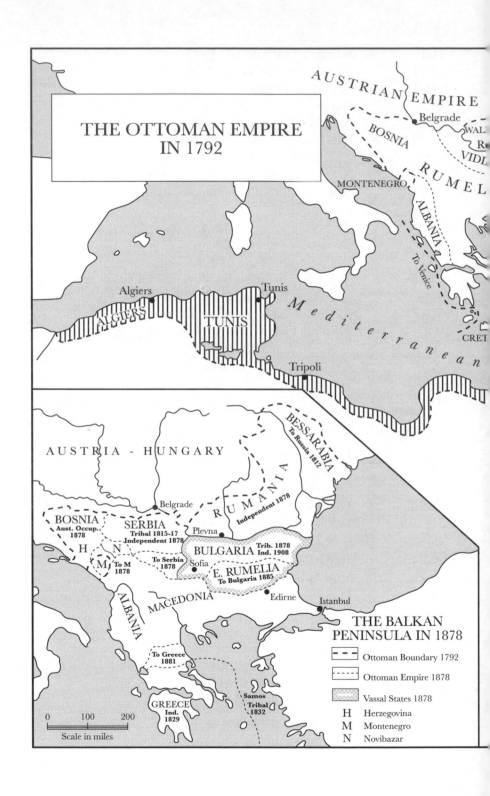

THE OTTOMAN EMPIRE
IN 1792

AUSTRIAN EMPIRE

Belgrade

BOSNIA

WAL

R

VIDI

MONTENEGRO

RUMEL

ALBANIA

To Venice

Algiers

Tunis

Mediterranean

ALGIERS

TUNIS

CRET

Tripoli

AUSTRIA - HUNGARY

BESSARABIA
To Russia 1812

Belgrade

RUMANIA
Independent 1878

BOSNIA
Aust. Occup.
1878

SERBIA
Tribal 1815-17
Independent 1878

Plevna

H   N

BULGARIA   Trib. 1878
            Ind. 1908

M
To M
1878

To Serbia
1878

Sofia

E. RUMELIA
To Bulgaria 1885

ALBANIA

MACEDONIA

Edirne

Istanbul

To Greece
1881

THE BALKAN
PENINSULA IN 1878

- - - Ottoman Boundary 1792

- - - - Ottoman Empire 1878

Vassal States 1878

GREECE
Ind.
1829

Samos
Tribal
1832

H   Herzegovina
M   Montenegro
N   Novibazar

0   100   200

Scale in miles

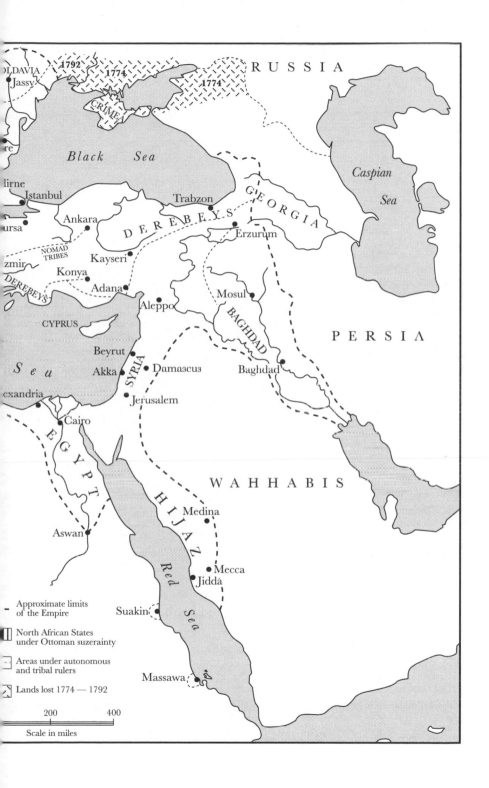

RUSSIA

1792
Jassy
OLDAVIA
1774
1774
CRIMEA

Black   Sea

*Caspian
Sea*

lirne
Istanbul
Trabzon
GEORGIA
Ankara
DEREBEYS
Erzurum
ursa
NOMAD
TRIBES
Kayseri
zmir
Konya
Adana
Mosul
DEREBEYS
Aleppo
PERSIA
CYPRUS
BAGHDAD
S e u
Beyrut
SYRIA
Akka
Damascus
Baghdad
exandria
Jerusalem
Cairo
EGYPT

WAHHABIS

HIJAZ
Aswan
Medina

Red   Sea
Mecca
Jiddá
Approximate limits
of the Empire
Suakin
North African States
under Ottoman suzerainty

Areas under autonomous
and tribal rulers
Massawa
Lands lost 1774 — 1792

200   400

Scale in miles

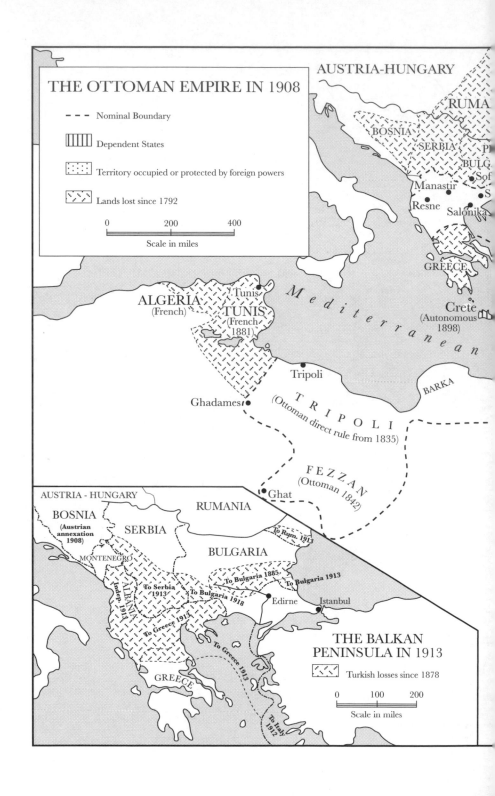

THE OTTOMAN EMPIRE IN 1908

- - - Nominal Boundary

▥ Dependent States

⣿ Territory occupied or protected by foreign powers

▧ Lands lost since 1792

```
0        200        400
```
Scale in miles

AUSTRIA-HUNGARY

RUMA

BOSNIA

SERBIA

P

BULG

Sof

Manastir

S

Resne

Salonika

GREECE

Crete
(Autonomous
1898)

Mediterranean

ALGERIA
(French)

Tunis

TUNIS
(French
1881)

Tripoli

BARKA

Ghadames

TRIPOLI
(Ottoman direct rule from 1835)

FEZZAN
(Ottoman 1842)

Ghat

AUSTRIA - HUNGARY

RUMANIA

BOSNIA
(Austrian
annexation
1908)

SERBIA

MONTENEGRO

BULGARIA

To Rum. 1913

To Bulgaria 1885

To Bulgaria 1913

ALBANIA Indep. 1913

To Serbia 1913

To Bulgaria 1918

Edirne

Istanbul

To Greece 1913

To Greece 1913

GREECE

To Italy 1912

THE BALKAN
PENINSULA IN 1913

▧ Turkish losses since 1878

```
0      100      200
```
Scale in miles

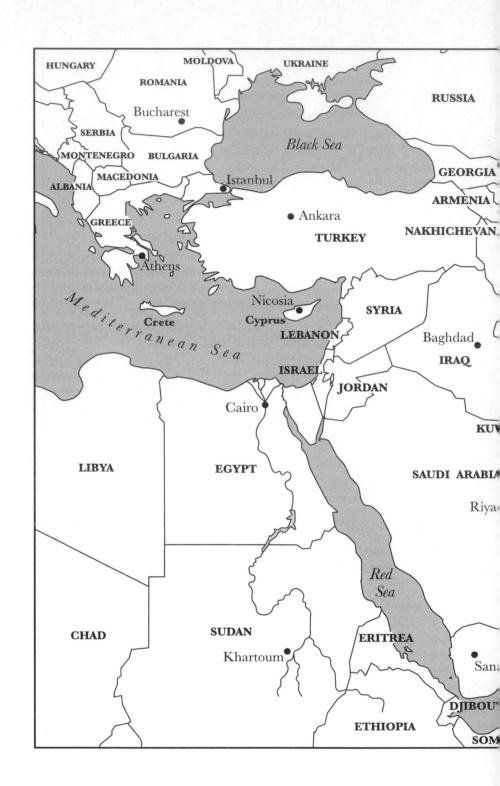

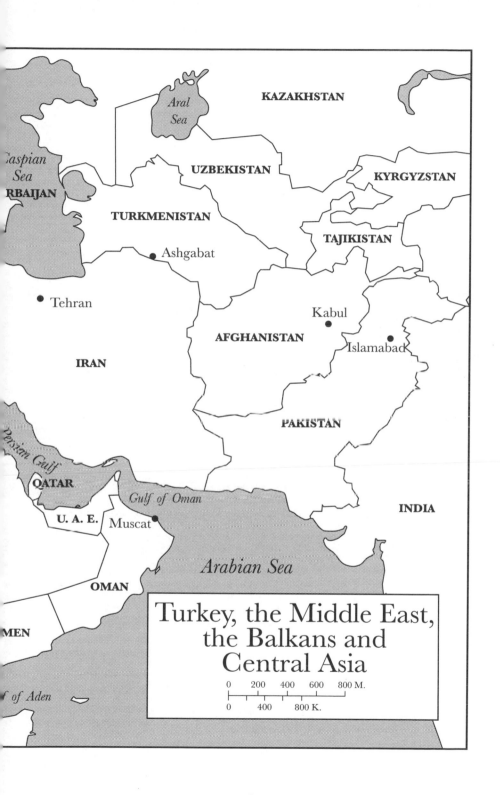

Turkey, the Middle East, the Balkans and Central Asia

Introduction

This book has been written with two broad objectives in mind. First, although Turkey's position in the international politics of south-eastern Europe and the Middle East has long been an important one, there are few overall studies of Turkish foreign policy. This book tries to fill the gap, by summarising the evolution of Turkey's external relations since the late eighteenth century, while concentrating on the period since the Second World War. For the statesmen of the nineteenth century, the Ottoman empire was 'the eastern question'. For their twentieth-century successors, Turkey is alternately seen as an emerging regional power, or a vexing problem in the construction of a new Europe. On their side, many Turks have felt that their growing economy as well as the continued strategic importance of their country entitled it to carry greater international weight. Taking the story back to the late eighteenth century illuminates the continuities, as well as the changes in external policies. Second, the Turkish example may also offer some interesting pointers as to how medium-sized states have acted in the changing international environments of the past 200 years.

What follows does not seek to offer any new general theories in the field of international politics. Nevertheless, the story it tells needs to be set in some sort of general framework. The fundamental assumption made here is that modern Turkey, and its predecessor state, the late Ottoman empire, can be fitted into the international system as a middle power – power being here defined as the ability to oblige other states to take actions which they would not otherwise have taken, and to resist pressure to do so from other states. This power depends on a mixture of the country's military strength (which in the nineteenth century depended quite largely on its population) and its economic resources and level of development. Small powers have little ability to act independently in the international system, especially when compared with what were referred to as the 'Great Powers' in the nineteenth century, or the superpowers during the Cold War era. Middle powers stand somewhere between the two extremes of the scale – that is to say, they have some ability to resist pressure from more powerful states, and may sometimes be able to influence the policies of weaker ones, especially if they are geographically contiguous. They may possess some regional power, but cannot expect to be able to influence global politics more than marginally. Most crucially, they cannot normally fight a successful war against a major power. Hence, if they are threatened by a major power, the solution to their security problem must come from outside, either through an alliance, or through the exploitation of a balance of forces between the great powers. Essentially, they are forced to adopt defensive strategies. In the Turkish case, the question of whether this could best be achieved by alliance or neutrality was a frequently recurring one, depending on the nature of the international system at the time, and the country's position in it.[1]

Within a defensive strategy, however, the decision as to whether to opt for an alliance is not an easy one. The advantage of an alliance is that it will help to deter an enemy, and that a small power may be able to use the alliance to influence its ally in a direction favourable to itself. However, dangers are also apparent. In Chapter 21 of *The Prince*, Machiavelli warns the ruler of a small state not to forge an alliance with a more powerful one, unless he is forced to do so, since he will end up being 'under the will and pleasure' of his ally. As Robert Rothstein puts it, 'the Small Power may move not from insecurity to security, but from insecurity to the status of a satellite'.[2] The choice of ally is also a critical one, since the interests of the allies should at least be complementary if not identical, though on some occasions each ally may be protecting a different set of interests. Alternatively, to avoid the dangers of an alliance with a more powerful state, a middle power may prefer to gamble on one with a weaker partner, or a number of small powers.

HISTORICAL PROCESSES

While these general proposals may be said to have affected the positions and policies of small or medium states through modern international history, it is also clear that both are influenced deeply by the nature of the international system at the time. These changes have been fundamentally important for the Ottoman and Turkish states during the period covered in this book – that is, from the last quarter of the eighteenth century until today. Essentially, the international order can be seen as having undergone four systemic changes, through five successive phases, during this time.

During the nineteenth century, international politics were dominated by the five indisputably 'great powers' of Europe – France, Prussia/ Germany, Austria, Russia and Britain – with no power in a hegemonic position. The preservation of peace, and the survival of small states, rested essentially on the preservation of a balance of power between the main European states. If one of them attempted to conquer a weaker power, then it ran the risk that another great power, or alliance of powers, might see this as an attempt to alter the balance of power to its disadvantage, and might launch a successful war against the aggressor. In this situation, alliances were normally short-term *ad hoc* accords, involving relatively little agreement on common political principles (as opposed to interests) between the participants. They could be overtaken by a new pattern of alliances, as circumstances changed. In general, states also preferred to negotiate rather than fight, and were prepared to stop fighting rather than eliminate an essential national actor. No one state was strong enough to conquer all the others, and the mutual jealousies of the major powers preserved even small or relatively weak states, which could not have done this by themselves.[3]

Between the early 1890s and 1914, the relationship between the European great powers began to move into a pattern of intense rivalry, with the emergence of two major alliances, between Germany and Austria–Hungary on the one side, and Russia and France, joined later by Britain, on the other. The cataclysm of the great war brought about the destruction of the nineteenth-century balance-of-power system and of the assumptions on which it was perceived to have rested. With the establishment of the League of Nations, the hope was that commitments to collective security could achieve the task of keeping the peace, in which the balance-of-power system had catastrophically failed. The most significant fact about the new order of the 1920s, however, was that one of the previous great powers, Austria-Hungary, had now ceased to exist, having been reduced to a number of small states, while Germany and Russia had been debilitated by war and revolution. The United States also withdrew from world politics after 1920. The resultant international system has been described as unique, and hard to categorise – it was not a balance-of-power system, nor a bipolar one, but perhaps a transition to bipolarity. After 1933, with the rise of Nazi Germany, it is argued that it developed into a quasi-bipolar system, similar to that of 1890–1914. What is also clear is that, after the great war, Europe saw a substantial increase in the number of small and medium powers, caused by the break up of the former German, Habsburg, Russian and Ottoman empires, and an apparent rise in their influence. However, the latter was illusory.

Collective security proved to be an unachievable dream, since advances in military technology left the small powers at a severe disadvantage, and the element of protection which the old balance-of-power system had formerly given them was now lost.

The period of the Second World War was clearly one of intense conflict and bipolarity, though the makeup of the two poles obviously altered at critical junctures – notably through the entry of the Soviet Union into the war following the Nazi invasion of Russia in June 1941, and that of the United States and Japan, subsequent to the attack on Pearl Harbour in December 1941. On the face of it, the position of the small or medium power in such a conflict seemed hopeless. If it tried to remain neutral, it could nevertheless still be invaded by one side or the other, depending on its geographical situation. If it joined an alliance, this might still be no effective defence against invasion by the opposing side. However, in certain fortunate circumstances, it could manage to stay out of the conflict, and might even gain from it. Apart from most of the Latin American republics, six European states – Sweden, Spain, Turkey, Switzerland, Republic of Ireland and Portugal – managed to preserve neutrality and independence. To achieve this, they were effectively able to convince the belligerents that the cost of trying to coerce them would outweigh the benefits – that the small power might be able to deny the belligerent access to essential supplies, that the opposing belligerent could retaliate so as to outweigh any advantage, or that, if pressed too hard, it might go over to the other camp. As a result, the small powers were not always helpless pawns in the international game.[4]

Normally, the period of the Cold War, between 1945 and the late 1980s, is taken as the archetype of a bipolar global system. Reduced to its essentials, it was a struggle between the United States and the Soviet Union, in which the role of other states was, at best, subsidiary. British and French power declined sharply after the Second World War, while German power was temporarily ended. Even after it recovered, Germany was understandably reluctant to take on an active or independent policy in world affairs. Moreover, all the European states, with the exception of neutral countries like Switzerland, Austria and Sweden, were bound into alliances in which the two superpowers played dominant (and in the Soviet case dictatorial) roles. Two other features of the Cold War provided important contrasts with the pre-1914 situation. First, after 1949, both sides possessed nuclear weapons, whose number and effectiveness they steadily developed over the next four decades. Hence, peace depended not just on a balance of power, but a balance of terror. This deterred each side from starting a conventional war, at least in Europe, for fear that it might develop into a nuclear one. However, it also placed a very high premium on crisis management, since a false move would be hard to correct, and liable to result in rapid escalation and mutual destruction. Second, the Cold War was seen as an ideological contest, in which political ideas and principles, and not just material interests, were declared to be at stake. Even if small states might rank security or economic interests above ideological commitments, the broad political preferences of their leaders were almost bound to have some effect on how they positioned themselves in the global contest.

Although, in retrospect, the Cold War era marks a distinct phase in international politics, there were important changes in the international system between 1945 and the late 1980s. Not all countries in the world were closely involved in the confrontation between the superpowers, and with the emergence of the so-called 'non-aligned bloc' in the 1950s, elements of multi-polarity began to slip into the system. Following the Cuban missile crisis of 1962, the superpowers set up a process of détente designed to lower the risk of another potentially disastrous collision between them. This effectively opened a new chapter in the history of the Cold War. In this environment, small or medium powers outside Europe found it easier to opt out of Cold War alignment, and even saw moral advantage in doing so. Some of these conditions altered again during the phase of what has been called the 'second Cold War' between 1979 and the mid-1980s. The most striking manifestation of this was the build-up in military expenditure, especially by the United States after 1978, in response to a steady increase on the Soviet side during the 1970s. The Soviet invasion of Afghanistan at the end of 1979 was also an important turning point, since it showed that the Soviet Union was prepared to use force against a neighbouring but non-aligned state. The ideological contest between the two blocs also intensified, especially after US President Ronald Reagan's inauguration in 1981. This phase was effectively ended by changes within the Soviet Union, following the death of Konstantin Chernenko and his succession by Mikhail Gorbachev as Secretary-General of the Soviet Communist Party, in 1985.[5]

The demise of the Cold War was marked by the collapse of communist rule in eastern Europe in 1989–90, and the signature of the Conventional Forces in Europe (CFE) treaty in November 1990, to be followed by that of the Strategic Arms Limitation Treaty (SALT) agreement which drastically reduced both sides' nuclear arsenals, in July 1991. The formal dissolution of the Soviet Union at the end of 1991 left the United States as the world's sole superpower, as previously defined. Nonetheless, it was hard to define the new order as simply unipolar, and it did not seem to have any clear historical precedent. There were some similarities with the situation which immediately followed the First World War, but the parallel was far from complete. Economically, the United States was still the world's most powerful state, but it had been rivalled by the dramatic growth of Japan since the 1960s, with China also likely to become an economic, and perhaps a military superpower by the twenty-first century. The emergence of the European Community (EC), later the European Union (EU), marked the rise of a major economic power which was not a state. Nor did the end of the Cold War bring an end to Western alliances, which (most notably, in the case of NATO [North Atlantic Treaty Organisation]) continued to exist, since they still had important utility for both the United States and their small- or medium-power members even after the Warsaw Pact ceased to exist.

For the middle powers, especially those which, like Turkey, had previously been threatened by the Soviet Union, the end of the Cold War had obvious benefits, since it removed the most immediate threat to their security. However, it did not by itself, end regional conflicts. In fact, new ones were created by the collapse of communist hegemony in eastern Europe and the former Soviet Union. Moreover, the emergence of an international coalition of the advanced industrialised nations, under US and European leadership, and a new emphasis on the international application of democratic norms, began to erode previous assumptions about unrestricted state sovereignty within national frontiers – a change most dramatically illustrated by the cases of Iraq in 1991, and the former Yugoslavia after 1995. Middle powers like Turkey were thus faced with as many problems as in previous eras, even if their character had been changed.

THE OTTOMAN AND TURKISH STATES AND THE INTERNATIONAL SYSTEM

In a recent book entitled *Turkey's Power*, Onur Öymen, a distinguished member of Turkey's diplomatic service, claims that 'from several angles, Turkey can be seen as one of the states in the front rank, not just in Europe, but in the world'.[6] His assessment may be inflated by an element of natural national pride, but it raises important questions about Turkey's position in the international state system. On the empirical evidence, most of the generalisations made about the position of small and medium powers in the international system fit the Turkish case quite aptly. On the one hand, in the world as it was before 1945, it was clearly weaker than the great powers of Europe. After 1945, it was still well behind the secondary powers, to say nothing of the two superpowers. On the other hand, it was not entirely powerless internationally, since it was often able to bargain with the great powers, to its own advantage, and it had some regional power, both in south-eastern Europe and the Middle East, especially if its neighbours were not satellites or colonies of a great power or superpower.

The main factors affecting Turkey's international position have been its geographical situation, its human and natural resources, and its economic development, especially since the 1950s. On the first score, Turkey is the only state, apart from Russia, with territory in both Europe and Asia, and is affected by and affects international politics in both south-eastern Europe and the eastern Mediterranean, in Transcaucasia and the southern regions of the former Soviet Union, and in the northern parts of the Middle East. Historically, Turkey's most strategically significant asset has been its control of the straits of the Dardanelles and Bosphorus, on which Russia has depended for direct maritime access to the Mediterranean, and the only route through which Britain, France and later the United States could challenge Russia in the Black Sea (or try to assist it, during the First World War).

Since the start of the Second World War, the development of air power, nuclear weapons, and later of intercontinental missiles has reduced the role of conventional naval forces. However, it has not eliminated Turkey's strategic importance, since the possession of air bases on Turkish soil, and access for ground forces in time of war, gives any of the major powers a crucial advantage for actual or potential action in the northern part of the Middle East, the Balkans and Transcaucasia, besides blocking any direct aggressive moves by Russia against the oil-producing countries of the Gulf. The fact that Turkey's geographical position is one in which the interests of several great powers intersect has also given its foreign policy-makers a degree of flexibility not open to states which are likely to be dominated by a single great power (the case of Mexico and the United States being an obvious example). While this means that Turkey can extract some 'strategic rent' from a great-power ally, it also means that it cannot usually back out of great-power conflicts, especially if they are centred on south-eastern Europe or the Middle East. In short, while its geographical situation increases Turkey's international weight, it also raises the prospect of an attack by any of the great powers with ambitions in these regions, making it quite unrealistic for Turkey to adopt a passive policy of opting out of international politics.

Turkey's natural and human resources also appear to put it in the middle-power category. At 780,000 square kilometres, its land area is slightly less than that of France and Britain combined. During the nineteenth and early twentieth centuries, the population of the Ottoman empire fluctuated erratically, owing to frontier changes, wars and migrations (scc p. 15) but it was still large enough to raise a respectably large army, by the standards of the day. At the time of the foundation of the Turkish republic in 1923, the population was probably somewhere around 12 million, but better health conditions and reduced infant mortality had raised this to about 64 million in 1999. Given what is now a declining birth rate, the population is expected to stabilise at around 95 million by the middle of the twenty-first century. Meanwhile, Turkey's international strength is not limited by a shortage of manpower – in fact, there is a surplus rather than shortage of labour, and the standing strength of the armed forces, at around 600,000, is the second highest in NATO. Over the past 70 years, Turkey has also made better use of its human resources. In 1927 (the earliest date for which statistics are available) the literacy rate stood at around 10 per cent, and only a tiny proportion of the population had received higher education. By 1997, the reported literacy rate had risen to risen to around 80–90 per cent, while the proportion of the student age group in higher education was about 18 per cent. In educational terms, this leaves Turkey behind western Europe, but still ahead of most of the rest of the world's population.[7]

The country's natural resources also put it in a fairly favourable position internationally. Normally, it can produce more than enough food to feed its population, and does not usually need to import more than a small quantity of agricultural products. It has sufficient deposits of most of the main industrial minerals, with the significant exceptions of oil, natural gas and hard coal. Nor is it dependent on the export of a single or limited range of products. Until the 1980s it relied mainly on agricultural exports, such as cotton, tobacco, dried fruits, nuts and cereals. Since then, industrial exports, notably textiles, clothing, iron and steel and light machinery, have come to account for around 90 per cent of total exports. On the other hand, Turkey is not a strategically important source of supply of any particular commodity in the world market (the sole exception being chromite, which was eagerly sought by both the Allies and Germany during the Second World War). Politically, its main resource liability, apart from its lack of significant deposits of oil and gas, is its dependence on the advanced industrial states for modern military hardware. A domestic arms industry has recently been established, including the manufacture of jet fighters, but this is still heavily dependent on imported know-how and components. As in the cases of other middle powers, complete self-sufficiency is an unrealistic dream.

The Ottoman empire was poor and backward, with virtually no modern industry and poor internal communications. Its dependence on foreign capital, both for economic development and for staving off government bankruptcy, left it vulnerable to pressure from the leading industrial states. With the establishment of the Turkish republic, there was better financial management and a sharp reduction in the external debt, followed by a state-sponsored industrialisation programme in the 1930s. Nonetheless, until the 1960s, Turkey remained a predominantly agricultural country, with low per capita incomes. Since then, there has been a rapid increase in the size and sophistication of Turkish industry, and of the economy as a whole, so that agriculture now accounts for only about 17 per cent of GNP, compared with around 29 per cent for industry and construction, and 54 per cent for services. Measured at current exchange rates, GNP has risen from US$18 billion in 1968 to around US$202 billion in 1998.[8]

Using the more realistic conversion by purchasing power parities, GNP now stands at around US$420 billion. This appears to give Turkey the world's seventeenth-biggest economy. By the same calculation, among the European states (excluding Russia) its economy is the sixth biggest, after that of Spain.[9] This relative economic strength has been offset by chronic economic mismanagement by successive governments, resulting in heavy government indebtedness, high inflation, and constant devaluations. The government's failure to control the economy has also resulted in periodic crises, signalled by large external deficits, and sharp falls in the value of the currency and foreign confidence. Hence, the government's ability to conduct an independent economic policy is seriously constrained by the prescriptions of the International Monetary Fund (IMF) and other international financial institutions. As the economy has grown, so has its dependence on foreign trade, which has risen from around 8 per cent of GNP in 1970 to 38 per cent in 1998. In this way, economic growth has increased rather then reduced external dependencies.

A state's ability to act effectively and independently on the international scene can also be seriously affected by the readiness of its people to accept sacrifices for the sake of national security, and, in the last analysis, to go to war. The homogeneity of the society, and the presence or absence of significant ethnic or religious cleavages are also significant factors affecting national strength. Although these indicators are impossible to measure accurately, Turkey almost certainly ranks highly on the first score. In spite of three open military interventions since the Second World War, none of which was entirely successful or uncontentious, the military still enjoys extraordinarily high respect in Turkish society, and it is very rare to hear complaints about the fact that almost all young men have to perform 18 months of virtually unpaid military service, in spite of the end of the Cold War. The military budget normally passes through parliament on the nod, and Turkey spends about 4 per cent of its GNP on defence – more than any other NATO member, but for Greece.[10]

Turkish nationalism also stresses the homogeneity and unity of the Turkish nation, but for substantial periods in Turkey's modern history this has been more of a wish than a reality. In the nineteenth century, the Ottoman empire embraced a patchwork of rival faiths and ethnic identities, in which the large Christian minorities in the Balkans and Anatolia were increasingly drawn towards the aim of achieving national independence. These movements constituted the most immediate threat to the empire's survival, and were frequently supported by the European great powers – notably by Russia but sometimes by the British and other governments. In effect, the empire's divided society, besides its economic backwardness, was its greatest weakness internationally. After the First World War, the new Turkish republic was left with a far more defensible block of territory and a far more homogeneous society, with the Kurds of south-eastern Anatolia the only sizeable ethnic minority, accounting for around 10–20 per cent of the total population. A serious rebellion by Kurdish tribes in 1925 was harshly suppressed, as were several subsequent Kurdish revolts between then and 1938. However, the conflicts were effectively contained within Turkey, and did not affect its foreign relations more than marginally. This situation changed radically during the 1990s as the campaign of violence launched by the Kurdistan Workers' Party (*Partiya Karkeren Kurdistan* – PKK) in 1984 resulted in some 30,000 deaths on both sides, the wrecking of the economy in the south-eastern provinces, and a serious cost to the government budget. It also had costly effects in Turkey's external relations. Until the 1990s, the outside world paid little attention to the problem, but with the end of the Cold War, the increased concern shown for universal adherence to democratic norms began to have a marked effect on foreign policies – especially those of the European Union (EU). In this way, the conventional distinction between internal politics and external relations seemed to have broken down, and the agenda of foreign policy-makers began to acquire new and challenging dimensions.

NOTES

1. These suggestions are based on the proposals of David Vital, *The Inequality of States: A Study of the Small Power in International Relations* (Oxford, Clarendon Press, 1967); Carsten Holbraad, *Middle Powers in International Politics* (London, Macmillan, 1984) and Robert L. Rothstein, *Alliances and Small Powers* (New York, NY, and London, Columbia University Press, 1968).
2. Rothstein, *Alliances*, p. 61.
3. See Morton A. Kaplan, *System and Process in International Politics* (New York, NY, Wiley, 1957), Preface and pp. 22–8, and A. J. P. Taylor, *The Struggle for Mastery in Europe, 1848–1918* (Oxford, Oxford University Press, 1954), pp. xix–xxiv.
4. Annette Baker Fox, *The Power of Small States: Diplomacy in World War II* (Chicago, IL, University of Chicago Press, 1959), pp. 1–4, 8–9.
5. Fred Halliday prefers a more complicated periodisation, seeing the period 1946–53 as 'Cold War I', that of 1953–69 as one of 'Oscillatory Antagonism', and starting the period of détente in 1969, running through to 1979: Fred Halliday, *The Making of the Second Cold War* (2nd edn, London, Verso, 1986), pp. 3, 10–11.
6. Onur Öymen, *Türkiye'nin Gücü* (Istanbul, AD Kitapçilik, 1998), p. 355.
7. Data from William Hale, *The Political and Economic Development of Modern Turkey* (London, Croom Helm, 1981), pp. 18–19, 67, and *Statistical Yearbook of Turkey 1998* (Ankara, State Institute of Statistics, 1999), pp. 71, 180. The population projection is from data issued by the Turkish Industrialists and Businessmen's Association (TUSIAD) quoted in *Hürriyet* newspaper, 14 January 1999.
8. *Statistical Yearbook of Turkey 1998*, p. 654: 1998 data from Economist Intelligence Unit, London.
9. Ibid., p. 688 (using OECD data).
10. *The Military Balance, 1998/99* (London, Oxford University Press for International Institute of Strategic Studies, 1998), pp. 55, 67.

1

Foreign Relations of the Late Ottoman Empire, 1774–1918

The Turkish republic was established in 1922–24, when the monarchy and the Islamic Caliphate were abolished, and Atatürk and his colleagues set out to create a new nation state on the ruins of the Ottoman empire. Constitutionally and territorially, the transformation marked a clean break with the Ottoman past. Nonetheless, the attitudes of the new state's rulers, as well as its citizens, were inevitably shaped by the experiences of the Ottoman period, or what they learnt of them either formally or informally. Rather than attempt a full history of the Ottoman empire's foreign relations during the last 150 years of its existence, this chapter attempts to summarise those aspects of the story which played an important role in shaping later attitudes. It starts by giving a brief sketch of the structure of the Ottoman state, as it affected its foreign policies, as well as the international system and the options available to late Ottoman policy-makers – some of which still affect their successors. A narrative section then attempts to illustrate these points by sketching in the main events in the foreign relations of the Ottoman empire during the period. The concluding discussion assesses the implications of these events in forming later attitudes and policies.

THE OTTOMAN STATE: DILEMMAS AND CHANGE

The central problem faced by the Ottoman empire in the nineteenth century was both an internal and an external one. At the zenith of its power in the sixteenth and seventeenth centuries, the Sultan's government had ruled over a vast territory stretching from Hungary to the Crimea and from Tunis to the Persian Gulf, and had been the hegemonic power in the eastern Mediterranean. By the 1770s, in the west, Hungary and Transylvania had been lost to the Habsburg empire, while north Africa was ruled by local dynasties over whom Ottoman control was normally not much more than nominal. Nonetheless, the Ottomans still had formal sovereignty over a huge territory. Unfortunately they lacked the power to control it effectively internally, or to protect it against external enemies. During the sixteenth century, the empire had been equal if not superior to any of the European states in military, technological, and economic advances, and administrative efficiency. By the last quarter of the eighteenth century it had fallen well behind all the major European powers in all these respects. In effect, it was neither a great power, nor a minor one, but a former great power in gradual eclipse, whose future became a continuing problem for both its own rulers and the leading European states.

In 1912, Count Johann von Pallavicini, the Austrian ambassador in Istanbul, suggested to his government that 'Turkey was not, and is not now, a state in the European sense of the word.'[1] Setting aside the counter-claim that the Habsburg monarchy was itself something of an anachronism, Pallavicini's judgement would certainly have been true a century earlier. The empire had been what is described as a 'tributary state', in the sense that the ruling class of army officers and state bureaucrats had no specific socio-economic foundation, but extracted surplus from all sectors of the economy – agriculture, trade and industry.[2] It was 'tributary' also in the sense that those who exercised power in most of the empire were tributaries, rather than the obedient servants, of the central government. While officially invested with power by the Sultan as governors or military commanders, they could often exercise it independently, and by process of bargaining and manoeuvre with other local power-holders. In effect, the empire could be seen as a series of local satrapies. In 1864, following a series of partial earlier reforms, and as part of a wide-ranging programme of reform known as the *Tanzimat* ('reorganisation') a new law on provincial administration introduced a centralised system on the Napoleonic model. This provided in theory for a hierarchy of trained officials taking their orders from the centre and remitting regular revenues to it.[3] Nevertheless, in practice, and until the end of the empire, state power remained dispersed and unreliable in outlying regions. In Istanbul and the other main port cities it was also limited by the capitulations – the special arrangements under which foreigners resident in the Ottoman empire enjoyed fiscal and legal privileges. Since the European consuls frequently gave out citizenship of their states to members of the Christian communities who were natives of the empire and were originally Ottoman citizens, these concessions came to have considerable importance: by the 1880s, resident 'foreigners' had come to account for as much as 15 per cent of the population of Istanbul.[4]

This administrative weakness was compounded by ethnic and religious heterogeneity. Westerners often referred to the Ottoman empire as 'Turkey', and its people as 'Turks', but the Turks themselves preferred to speak of their empire as the 'exalted Ottoman state' and its ruling class as 'Ottomans' (even if they were not of the imperial dynasty) reflecting its lack of ethnic identity. Population figures for the empire in the nineteenth century are often guesswork, since the government failed to carry out a population census in the accepted sense. However, from the 1830s, local officials were supposed to keep registers of the population in their districts, and calculations of the entire population were issued, based on these admittedly incomplete statistics. On this basis, it would appear that in 1844 (the first year for which we have remotely complete figures) the population of the territories actually, rather than nominally, controlled by the Sultan, was somewhere around 26 million. Of this about two-thirds was Muslim (Turks, followed by Arabs, Kurds, Muslim Slavs and Albanians) and the remainder Christian (Slavs, followed by Armenians, Greeks, Christian Arabs and Albanians) with a small Jewish community.[5] By 1885, following territorial losses to the empire in the Balkans, which reduced the total population while increasing the percentage of Muslims, the population had fallen to around 17–18 million, of which about 72 per cent was Muslim, but it then rose to around 21 million by 1906. In 1914, after the loss of virtually all the empire's territories in Europe during the Balkan wars, the population had dropped back to 18.5 million, of which about 81 per cent was Muslim. Since the Ottoman government classified its citizens by religion (that is, as Muslims or Jews, or adherents of the different Christian denominations) we have no breakdown of the population by ethnic groups, but it would appear that in the last quarter of the nineteenth century ethnic Turks accounted for only about 45–50 per cent of the population, and a lower proportion before that.[6]

The Ottoman state was largely non-assimilative, and lacked the technical, economic and institutional resources to integrate its diverse populations into a single political community, even if it had wanted to. Hence, its society remained highly fragmented. Its subject peoples retained their own languages and religions, with some degree of formal political autonomy. Non-Muslims could be seen as second-class citizens, in that they could not serve in the army and were subjected to special taxes, but were not subjected to forcible conversion. Each religiously defined community, or *millet*, had its own hierarchy, led in theory by its religious head, or *milletbaşı* (thus, the Patriarch of Constantinople for Orthodox Christians, the Chief Rabbi for Jews, and so on), and administered its own courts for personal status cases, as well as educational institutions.[7] Until the nineteenth century, this diversity did not pose too serious a challenge to the empire's territorial integrity, since the vast majority of Ottoman citizens accepted traditional authority, and identified primarily with local communities based on residence or kinship. If they saw themselves as part of a wider 'imagined community' then it was that of the religiously based *millet*, not the ethnic or territorially based nation.[8] However, modern ideas of ethnic nationalism began to affect the Greeks and Serbs in the early nineteenth century, and later spread to the Romanians, Bulgarian and Macedonian Slavs, and Armenians. Since Christianity and Islam were still the primary markers, most Muslims remained loyal to the Ottoman state until its end, although a successful nationalist revolt broke out among the mainly Muslim Albanians in 1910, and an embryonic nationalist movement had begun among the Ottoman Arabs just before the First World War. Left to itself, the Ottoman army could normally defeat a national rebellion by a single ethnic group, since the proto-nations were mostly geographically dispersed and often mutually hostile, but it could not do so if the rebellion was supported by one or more of the major European powers, or if a number of ethnic groups or emergent nations combined against it. Hence, the empire was subjected to a process of gradual territorial dismemberment and ethnic cleansing.

During the nineteenth and early twentieth centuries, rebellions by the Christian minorities sporadically triggered off ruthless and brutal reactions by the Ottoman authorities which naturally aroused righteous indignation on the part of European statesmen and writers – as on the occasion of the massacres on Chios in 1822, the 'Bulgarian horrors' denounced by Gladstone in 1876, and the massacres and deportation of virtually the entire Armenian population of Anatolia in 1915. What Western opinion almost entirely ignored was the fact that the Muslim populations of the Balkans, Crimea and the Caucasus suffered equally appalling atrocities at the hands of the emerging Balkan nations and advancing Russian armies, and in far greater numbers. Well-documented calculations by Justin McCarthy and others show that between 1827 and 1922 around five million Muslims in Greece, the Crimea, the Caucasus and the Balkans were killed, while about another 5.4 million were expelled and took refuge in the Ottoman empire. A large proportion of these victims of Greek and Balkan chauvinism and Russian imperialism were ethnic Turks, but their numbers also included millions of Slavic Muslims and Crimean Tatars, plus the Muslim minorities of the Caucasus (Muslim Circassians, Abkhazians, Chechens, Azeris and Muslim Georgians) many of whom had not been under Ottoman rule, but had fled to the Ottoman empire because they recognised it as a 'kin state'.[9]

Of course, two wrongs do not make a right, and atrocities by one side cannot justify counter-atrocities by the other. At the same time, it is clear that the massacres and expulsions of these Muslim communities had profound effects on the empire. First, the influx of refugees tended to enhance the effect of territorial contraction, by increasing the Muslim share in the total Ottoman population. Second, it created a profound sense of injustice and deep hostility towards those nations who had been responsible for it. By the 1920s, around one-third of the population of what became the Republic of Turkey was probably composed of refugees or their descendants, creating a strong sense of shared suffering and solidarity. Third, it had important effects on the attitudes of the Ottoman rulers. What looked to Europeans like an effort to prop up a crumbling, corrupt and sometimes brutal empire, was seen by Ottoman governments and their Muslim subjects as a perfectly legitimate attempt to protect their own people against slaughter and exile, in the face of indifference or outright hostility on the part of the European powers.

The primary aim of Ottoman Sultans and statesmen was to preserve their state and to protect its Muslim populations in these unpromising conditions, and this was almost the sole goal of the *Tanzimat* reforms. Apart from the attempted administrative modernisation referred to earlier, reform and strengthening of their armed forces was naturally a major focus of attention. After a false start between 1789 and 1807, the construction of an effective modern army which began with the destruction of the Janissary corps by Sultan Mahmud II in 1826, finally yielded results in the 1840s. Hence, as Feroze Yasamee suggests, after a period of pronounced decline between 1768 and 1839, Ottoman power began to revive after that date. After a system for conscription of Muslim males was introduced in 1869, the strength of the standing army had risen to around 200,000 by the 1870s, and to around 470,000 by 1897. During the First World War, some 2.7 million men were mobilised, although the maximum strength of the army probably failed to exceed 650,000 at any one time. Modern weapons and tactics, and an officer corps trained in both, also increased the empire's military strength. As a result, the Ottoman army could still win battles (especially defensive ones) and even wars. Its main deficiencies were its almost total reliance on imported weaponry, its lack of logistical backup and modern transport, the financial weakness of the state and, above all, the sheer number and strength of its potential enemies compared with the relatively small size of the Muslim population and the immense length of frontiers it had to defend. Hence, the government had to resort to diplomatic manoeuvring, rather than risk unaided military resistance to any major European power.[10]

OTTOMAN DIPLOMACY: AIMS, METHODS AND POLICIES

Careful diplomacy was thus the key to Ottoman survival. As has been suggested in the Introduction (pp. 2–3), it rested on exploiting the balance of power between the main European states – Russia, Britain, France and Austria, with Germany emerging as a major power in the last part of the nineteenth century – and their mutual fear that if either one or a coalition of powers destroyed the Ottoman empire, this would provoke a major war with their rivals.

Since 'the eastern question' was a major focus of concern in nineteenth-century diplomacy, the history of the policies of the major powers towards it has received a good deal of scholarly attention. Unfortunately, this has not been the case on the Ottoman side. Hence, while we have relatively abundant information on the diplomacy of the main European states, and the effects of Ottoman decline on their relations with one another, we have little direct information about what Ottoman governments thought or planned in the foreign policy field – and then only for the last quarter of the nineteenth century.[11] Most of what we know about the policies of Ottoman governments thus has to be inferred from their actions, or from what European diplomats believed and reported at the time.

Ottoman foreign policy was also affected by the institutional resources available to it. Until the last years of the eighteenth century, the empire had no permanent diplomatic representatives abroad, although temporary diplomatic missions were frequently sent abroad for specific purposes. This defect was remedied during 1793–96 as permanent embassies were established in London, Vienna, Berlin and Paris, to be followed in due course by other capitals. Besides representing their government, the staff of these embassies were also supposed to find out about Western technical and administrative advances, and thus came to play a major role in pushing forward the *Tanzimat* reforms. Originally, there was no separate foreign ministry: foreign policy was decided at the centre by the Grand Vizier (*Sadr-i Azam*) and its administration by the office of the 'Chief of the Scribes' (*Reisülküttab*) an assistant to the Grand Vizier, who also had responsibility for a variety of other functions. In 1835, however, his foreign-policy and diplomatic responsibilities were transferred to a new Ministry of Foreign Affairs (*Umur-i Hariciye Nezareti*). The ministry continued to handle relations with the non-Muslim *millets* within the empire until the 1880s. In the meantime, the post of foreign minister came to be one of the most important in the state, as leading statesmen of the *Tanzimat* interchanged this appointment with that of Grand Vizier (*Sadr-i Azam*). The Grand Vizier thus joined the foreign minister as an important deter-minant of foreign policy. At other times, a forceful and determined Sultan could take over the reins, reducing the foreign minister to relatively minor status: this was certainly the case during the reign of Abdul Hamid II (1876–1909).[12] Overall, however, the Ottoman empire seems to have built up a reasonably effective foreign-policy structure, not very different from those of other autocratic monarchies at the time, and probably more effective than other parts of the Ottoman state bureaucracy.

As an active foreign policy-maker, Abdul Hamid II evidently had a low opinion of the way it had been conducted. Having suggested that every state needed a 'fundamental goal' and a 'policy which accords with its circumstances and position',[13] he regretted that:

> The Ottoman empire has no definite and decided goal and policy: in every question the person in power acts in accordance with his own opinion, and in the event of failure successor blames predecessor and predecessor successor, and in the process the sacred interests of the state suffer.

In fact, the Sultan probably did his predecessors as well as himself some-thing of an injustice, since late Ottoman foreign policy was arguably more consistent and effective than he suggested. From around the beginning of the nineteenth century, Ottoman statesmen had evidently recognised that the empire could not win a war for territory with the major European powers unless it was supported by one or more of the others. They hoped that in the long run they could restore the empire to its former strength by modernising state structures and the economy, and by rebuilding its army and finances, but to do this they needed a fairly long breathing space, with sufficient external stability and security. They thus had to consider how to exploit the international situation to their advantage. Territorially, the principal threats arose in three main zones of conflict: first, in the Balkans, where emerging local nationalist movements, aided by Russia and some-times by other powers, threatened to end Ottoman rule; second, in the straits of the Bosphorus and Dardanelles, which it was assumed Russia aimed to dominate as a means of securing access to the Mediterranean and thus the world's oceans; third, in Egypt and to a lesser extent the rest of the Arab Middle East, where France and Britain had ambitions. Against this, it could be expected that, at least to some degree, Russia and Austria (aided later by Germany) could cancel one another out in the Balkans, Russia and Britain at the straits, and Britain and France in Egypt.

In this situation Ottoman statesmen had two broad options in policies towards the major powers. One would be to avoid both conflicts and firm alliances with any of them, meeting each crisis as it arose, and relying on the workings of the balance of power to preserve the status quo. This policy would also avoid the danger that excessively close relations with any one power or group of powers might mean the subordination of Ottoman interests to those of the partner or partners. As an alternative, the Ottoman government could try to negotiate a reasonably stable alliance with one or more of the European powers. This assumed that one power could definitely be identified as the enemy, intent on destroying the empire or reducing it to impotence, while another power or combination of powers could be potential allies, who were not capable of reaching an accommodation with the enemy, and were themselves genuinely committed to maintaining the Ottoman empire. Which of these two broad options was adopted depended on the circumstances at the time, the relative strength of the main powers, and their perceived intentions, besides the situation on the ground in the zone or zones of conflict. At the same time, the Ottoman empire had a clear interest in staying out of a war between the European powers, unless their conflict centred on its own territory: at most, it could hope to sell its friendly neutrality to whichever side offered it the most favourable terms.

If the second option were chosen, then Ottoman policy-makers obviously had to decide which power was the enemy, and which others were actual or potential allies. During the middle part of the century – that is, roughly between 1840 and 1878 – the answers to both these questions seemed fairly obvious. Russia was identified as the most serious foe, since it was best placed to launch a land invasion of Ottoman territory, had an assumed interest in gaining control of or at least free passage through the straits, and presented itself as the patron and protector of the Sultan's Orthodox Christian subjects. On the other hand, Britain, supported on occasion by France and Austria, appeared as the obvious ally, since the British had a (probably exaggerated) fear that if Russia achieved its assumed ambitions at the straits, or managed to conquer or subordinate the empire as a whole, then it could challenge British naval dominance in the Mediterranean and the sea route to India. However, this calculation could not be applied at all times or in all circumstances. In the first place, Russian power or ambitions might not be so far-reaching as the calculation assumed: faced with obstacles to the achievement of a maximalist and expansionist programme, Russia might be prepared to accept the status quo, or even to offer protection to the empire against other enemies. Equally, alliance with Britain was far from risk-free, or necessarily effective. In the first place, Britain had its own ambitions in Egypt and the Middle East, and might use an alliance with the empire to further its own interests at Ottoman expense. Second, Britain was a naval rather than a land power, and was poorly positioned to prevent Russian territorial advances in south-eastern Europe or along the empire's north-eastern border.[14] In effect, the British navy could not, by itself, reliably protect the empire against the Russian army, or vice versa. Hence in certain circumstances the Ottomans might do best to avoid any alliances – the first broad option – or to seek an alliance with another power, maybe even with Russia. By the end of the century, Germany was emerging as the most likely candidate for alliance, although this connection eventually led to the Ottoman empire's destruction in the First World War.[15]

DIPLOMACY IN ACTION: 1774–1918

These general observations about Ottoman foreign policy in the nine-teenth century need some illustration and expansion, by reference to the main relevant events during the period, and the way in which Ottoman statesmen coped with them. Needless to say, this exploration can only be introductory, and cannot do more than give a summary sketch of the full story, which is well covered by a substantial quantity of scholarly literature.[16]

For most of the eighteenth century, the Ottoman empire's main adversary had been Austria and its main ally, France. This pattern was radically altered in the 1770s by Russian expansion to the Black Sea, as a result of which Russia replaced Austria as the most immediate threat. After defeat by Russia in the war of 1768–74, the Ottomans were forced to sign the treaty of Küçük Kaynarca of 1774. This gave Russia a foothold on the northern shores of the Black Sea, recognised the independence of the Crimea (previously a vassal-state of the Ottoman empire) and allowed Russia navigation rights in the Black Sea as well as what was dubiously interpreted as a right of protection over Ottoman subjects of the Orthodox faith. Meanwhile, Austria helped itself to the formerly Ottoman territory of Bukovina in 1775. Russia annexed the Crimea in 1783 and, after another war of 1787–92, captured further territory between the rivers Dniestr and Bug. For the first time, Ottoman territory mainly inhabited by

Muslims, had been occupied by a Christian state. It had also become clear that the empire was no match for Russia unless the Ottomans were supported by one of the other European powers.[17]

France's internal turmoils after the revolution of 1789 temporarily removed it as a counterweight to Russia, and the Napoleonic wars brought constant shifts in the kaleidoscope of the Ottoman empire's alliances and enmities. Between 1799 and 1812 the Ottoman government was periodically either allied with or at war with all the main European protagonists. The traditional Ottoman entente with France was ended by Napoleon's invasion of Egypt in 1798. In response, the Ottomans signed a treaty with Russia in December 1798 which Britain adhered to in the following month. The British, aided by the Ottoman army, ousted the French from Egypt in 1801, but Russia did not want to carry on the war with France and signed peace with it in October 1801, to be followed by the British and Ottomans in May and June 1802. However, the re-opening of the war between Britain and France in 1803 led to an Anglo-Russian alliance in April 1805: this was followed by an Ottoman–Russian agreement in September, in which the two sides agreed to cooperate in case of an attack by a third party.

This resurrection of the alliance between the Ottomans, British and Russians was nonetheless to be very short-lived. The overwhelming victories by Napoleon at Ulm and Austerlitz persuaded the Ottoman leaders that they had joined the wrong side: they never ratified the agreement of September 1805, and entered into negotiations with France in the summer of 1806. In response, Russian forces occupied the nominally Ottoman principalities of Moldavia and Wallachia (modern Moldova and part of Romania) in November 1806, causing the Ottomans to declare war the following month. In effect, the empire had now joined France against Britain and Russia. In February–March 1807 the British and Russian fleets made an abortive attempt to capture the straits, but in July the tables were once again turned by Napoleon's peace agreement with the Tsar Alexander I at Tilsit. The Ottoman empire was now faced with the real danger that the French and Russians might partition its territory between them.

Fortunately for the Ottomans, Napoleon never decided what he wanted to achieve in the Balkans, since there was the danger that Austria and Britain would be the main gainers from an Ottoman collapse, and he was determined to prevent Russia from seizing the straits. Accordingly, the Russo-French partition plan was abandoned in 1808 – a good example of the balance-of-power system in operation. The position was strengthened by an Ottoman–British peace treaty of January 1809, under which the two sides confirmed the traditional rule that the straits would be closed in peacetime to all non-Ottoman warships. Meanwhile, the Russo-Ottoman war over the principalities dragged on, with periodic armistices, until early 1812, when the imminent attack by France forced Russia to come to terms. Under the treaty of Bucharest of May 1812, Russia held on to the formerly Ottoman territory of Bessarabia, but the Ottoman state regained sovereignty over Wallachia and Moldavia. Thereafter, the Ottoman state effectively dropped out of the Napoleonic wars. In spite of internal turbulence, and the fact that its military power was almost at rock bottom, it had managed to come through the conflict with relatively little loss of territory, by forming flexible alliances and exploiting the mutual rivalries of the European powers.[18]

During the complex crises of 1798–1812, the empire's survival had mainly been threatened by direct territorial expansion by the major European powers: after this period, the main challenge came indirectly, from European support for rebellions by the Balkan Christian communities and its own vassals. A rebellion had begun in Serbia in 1804–05 under the Serb leader, Karageorge, but this was crushed by the Ottomans in 1813 after the treaty of Bucharest allowed them to re-direct their forces against Serbia. However, in 1815 the revolt was re-started by Milos Obrenovich, who had Karageorge murdered in 1817. Meanwhile, Obrenovich had reached an agreement with the Ottomans under which Serbia remained within the empire, but power was shared between him and the Turkish governor in Belgrade.

During the 1820s, two new players appeared on the Ottoman and Balkan scene, in the shape of Mehmet Ali Pasha, the Sultan's governor in Egypt, and a rising Greek resistance movement. A native of Kavala (now in Greek Macedonia) Mehmet Ali had arrived in Egypt after the expulsion of the French as a member of the Albanian contingent of the Ottoman army, and became governor of Egypt in 1805. Over the next 40 years, with the help of European (mainly French) professionals, he launched an impressive programme of modernisation and strengthening of his armed forces, and Egypt's economy and administrative structures. This achievement acted as a model for the Ottoman *Tanzimat* and converted him from a servant into a rival of the Ottoman Sultan. When a Greek uprising began in earnest in 1821, the Ottoman army was so weak that it was unable to defeat even the divided rebels. The task was left to Mehmet Ali, who landed his forces in southern Greece in February 1825, and had defeated the Greeks by the spring of 1826. This brought about naval intervention by the European powers. The combined fleets of Britain, France and Russia destroyed the Egyptian-cum-Ottoman fleet in the port of Navarino in September 1827, and Mehmet Ali's army withdrew. Eventually, Greece was established as an independent state in the southern part of its modern territory, and recognised as such by the Ottoman government in 1832.[19]

For Sultan Mahmud II, the success of the Greek revolt had pointed up the urgent need to modernise his army, and to dissolve the Janissary corps, which was the main obstacle to military reform. To achieve this, however, he needed a breathing space, and a settlement with Russia, which in 1825 had threatened unilateral action on behalf of the Greeks. Accordingly, in October of that year, his government accepted the Convention of Akerman with Russia. This established the autonomy of Moldavia and Wallachia as well as Serbia within the Ottoman empire, recognised Russian conquests in the Caucasus, and allowed Russian merchant ships freedom of navigation throughout the empire. Later, however, the defeat at Navarino hardened Mahmud's policy, and he refused to implement these provisions. In response, Russia declared war on the empire in April 1828. By the summer of 1829 the Ottoman forces had collapsed: the Russians had captured Edirne (Adrianople) which is only some 270 kilometres north-west of Istanbul, and had advanced along the Black Sea coast as far as Trabzon. Nonetheless, the Russian army was also ravaged by disease. Correctly fearful that a total destruction of the Ottoman empire might provoke a major war with France and Britain, Tsar Nicholas I decided to sue for peace. In the last analysis, Russia preferred to preserve a weak Ottoman empire along its southern border, rather than risk its total dissolution. Under the treaty of Edirne of September 1829, the Russian hold over Armenia and Georgia (much of which had not been Ottoman territory anyway) was confirmed, and Russia only made small territorial gains at the mouth of the Danube. Once again, the balance of power, and cautious Russian policy, had prevented the general disintegration of the empire.

This pattern repeated itself in the case of the next challenge to the Ottoman state, which came from Mehmet Ali. Frustrated by his failure to hold on to his conquests in the Greek peninsula, the Egyptian governor sent his armies into Palestine and Syria in October 1831. By February 1833 they had reached Kütahya, in western Anatolia, and Mehmet Ali seemed poised to succeed the Ottomans on the throne of Istanbul. Bereft of other support, Mahmud II turned to Russia, and in April 1833, 14,000 Russian troops arrived in the Bosphorus with naval support. Under the treaty of Hünkâr İskelesi, signed in July, Russia and the Ottoman empire agreed to help one another in case of outside attack. In a secret clause, Russia conceded that it would not call for Ottoman military and naval support if it were attacked by a third party, and in return the Ottoman government agreed to close the straits to foreign warships. Meanwhile, the Ottomans also agreed to recognise Mehmet Ali as governor of Syria, to which the Egyptian army withdrew. Britain had hitherto stood aside in the crisis, but the Hünkâr İskelesi treaty eventually stung the British Foreign Secretary, Lord Palmerston, into action, since he mistakenly believed that its secret clause had given Russian warships free passage through the straits. He also appreciated the risk that the Ottoman empire might be turned into a Russian protectorate. During the 1830s, France emerged as Mehmet Ali's main supporter, further complicating the situation for Britain. This danger was put to the test in 1839 when Mahmud decided to try to eject Mehmet Ali from Syria, but was decisively defeated at the battle of Nezib (Nizip in Turkish) in June. Before news of the defeat had reached Istanbul, Mahmud had died, to be succeeded by his 16-year-old son, Abdul Mejid, and the empire was again dependent for its survival on European support. Fortunately for the Ottomans, the apparent indirect challenge from France, through Mehmet Ali, produced a Russo-British *rapprochement*. Under a convention signed with the Ottoman government in July 1840, Britain, Austria, Prussia and Russia agreed to protect the Sultan's government against Mehmet Ali, in return for an Ottoman declaration that the straits would be closed to all non-Ottoman warships in peacetime. The following September, the British fleet bombarded Beirut, and by February 1841 the Egyptian army had returned to its country, defeated by British and Ottoman forces and with no effective help from France. Under an agreement of June 1841, Mehmet Ali accepted the limitation of his army, in return for the hereditary governorship of Egypt, vested in his family.[20]

The defeat of Mehmet Ali marked the emergence of Britain as a more active player in the Near Eastern power game, and the Ottoman empire's main ally for the next 37 years. Under the treaty of Balta Limanı of 1838 Britain also acquired a dominant position in the empire's foreign trade. This was strengthened by British support for the principles of the *Tanzimat*, and those Ottoman statesmen who promoted it, such as Mustafa Reshid Pasha, Ali Pasha and Fuad Pasha. In September 1841 the new British Ambassador, Stratford Canning, was instructed by the Foreign Secretary, Lord Aberdeen, that '[T]he policy of Great Britain in the Levant has long been distinguished by a sincere desire to support the Turkish Power; and to avert the dissolution [of the empire], either from the effects of internal convulsion or of Foreign aggression'. Britain hoped 'by promoting judicious and well considered reform, to impart some degree of consistency and stability to the government which is threatened by so many causes of dissolution'.[21] There is some room for doubt as to how influential British policy was in furthering the cause of reform. Ottoman internal policies were almost certainly more autonomous than foreign commentators supposed and, as Frank Edgar Bailey remarks, the *Tanzimat* reforms were 'essentially Turkish in origin'.[22] Admittedly, the imperial rescript (*Hatt-i Şerif*) of Gülhane of 1839, which promised an end to tax farming, and pledged that all Ottoman subjects regardless of their religion would be treated equally and justly by the courts, was an important turning point, and was introduced more than partly as a means of winning foreign (particularly British) support against Mehmet Ali. However, the programme of modernisation of the administration, the army and education had begun well before then, and continued for many years after Britain and the Ottoman empire had drifted apart diplomatically. At the same time, the fact that British policy-makers believed that they were playing an important role in the *Tanzimat* almost certainly helped to stiffen British policy. For their part, Ottoman statesmen realised that they needed Western support against Russia, although they did not necessarily favour Britain as their sole ally.

The policy of allying with the other European powers against Russia reached its apogee at the time of the Crimean war of 1854–55. The conflict began with a dispute between France and Russia in 1851–52 over the respective rights of the Orthodox and Latin churches in the Christian shrines of Jerusalem, but escalated in 1853 when the Russian General, Prince Menshikov, was sent to Istanbul as a personal representative of the Tsar. Menshikov demanded the restoration of all Orthodox privileges in Jerusalem, and that Russia be given the right to protect all Orthodox Christians in the Ottoman empire. This demand was quite unacceptable to both the Ottoman government and the Western powers. In June 1853, Russia threatened to occupy the principalities of Moldavia and Wallachia, British and French warships were sent in response to the Dardanelles, and Russia carried out its threat at the end of the month. In the ensuing war with Russia, the Ottoman fleet was destroyed in the Black Sea port of Sinop in November 1853, but in March 1854 Britain and France signed a treaty with the Ottomans committing themselves to defend Ottoman territory against Russia, and formally declared war. Meanwhile, Austria refused to support the Russian advance into Moldavia and Wallachia, and in June 1854 concluded a treaty with the Ottoman government in which the latter transferred its sovereign rights in the principalities to Austria until the conclusion of peace. With great reluctance, the Russians backed down: the Russian troops in Moldavia and Wallachia were replaced by Austrians in July–August 1854.

Having lost their original *casus belli*, the allies decided to replace it with an attack on the Crimea, with the aim of destroying Russian naval power in the Black Sea. The Crimean war began in September 1854, when British, French and Ottoman troops were landed in the peninsula, and was ended after the allies captured Sebastopol in September 1855. Under the treaty of Paris, signed in March 1856, the Black Sea was closed to warships of all nations, but for small vessels for coastal protection: effectively, it had now ceased to be an Ottoman lake, and had become a neutral one. The principalities were restored to Turkish suzerainty, but were to enjoy autonomous rights guaranteed by the powers. Similarly, the signatories agreed to respect the independence and integrity of the Ottoman empire, and any state in conflict with it was to seek the mediation of a third power before resorting to force. In return, the Sultan's government agreed to give guarantees of good treatment of its Christian subjects: this was enacted by the issue of a new imperial decree, the *Hatt-i Hümayun*, in February 1856. Under the treaty, the Ottoman government was also invited to 'participate in the public law and concert of Europe'. To the uninitiated, this might seem a vague and pointless provision. For the Ottoman government, however, it had a great deal of significance, since it was treated as recognition of the empire's status as a European power. The continuation of this recognition has since remained one of the Turkish state's main foreign-policy goals.[23]

The treaty of Paris ushered in a period of relative calm in the empire's relations with the European powers which lasted until 1875: the Ottomans were affected by further upsets in the Balkans and the Lebanon,[24] but there were no international crises affecting their territories on the scale of those of 1831–33, 1839–41, or 1853–55. In 1871 an international agreement allowed Russia to resume its sovereign rights in the Black Sea, and thus reversed the neutralisation provisions of the treaty of Paris. This concession had no immediate practical effect, since for many years afterwards poverty and the lack of a consistent Near Eastern policy prevented Russia from building a Black Sea fleet of any consequence. However, in 1874 a revolt began in Bosnia-Herzegovina which spread to Bulgaria in 1876 and set off shock waves which nearly proved fatal for the empire. In 1875, as Anatolia was gripped by drought and famine, the Ottoman government announced that it was suspending payment on the huge foreign debt of £191 million sterling which Sultan Abdul Aziz had accumulated, inviting intervention by the Western governments to protect their bondholders. The financial problem was eventually settled in 1881 with the establishment of the international Council of the Ottoman Debt, but the political crisis was far more difficult to solve. The brutality with which the Ottoman forces suppressed the Bulgarian uprising alienated Western liberal opinion, especially in Britain, and Russia threatened to intervene on behalf of its Orthodox Slavic brethren. Istanbul was further affected by internal turmoil, as Abdul Aziz was deposed by a virtual *coup d'état* in May 1876, to be succeeded by his nephew Murad. The hope of Midhat Pasha and other reformist Ottoman statesmen was that the new Sultan would agree to a constitution, with a representative parliament in which all the communities of the empire would assent to Ottoman rule. However, Murad proved to be mentally unstable, and it was not until December 1876, after he had been replaced by his brother Abdul Hamid, that the empire's first and only constitution was proclaimed.[25]

Meanwhile, the European powers, who were generally unimpressed by the constitution, proposed governmental reforms and some territorial changes in the Balkans. In April 1877, Abdul Hamid rejected their reform proposals and declared war on Russia. Opinions on the Russian side were divided between pan-Slavists, led by the Tsar's ambassador in Istanbul, General Ignatiev, who wished to end Ottoman rule in the Balkans by setting up a chain of Russian-protected states, and the more cautious policies pursued by the foreign minister, Prince Gorchakov. Owing to stout resistance by the Ottomans, who held out in the fortress of Plevna (Pleven) in northern Bulgaria until December 1877, the Ottoman–Russian war of 1877–78 was far from a one-sided match, but the Ottoman forces were eventually defeated. In the east, the Russians captured the vital fortress of Kars in November 1877. In the west, they took Edirne in January 1878, and advanced to the Ottomans' final defence lines at Çatalca the following month. These victories allowed the pan-Slavist school of thought to gain the upper hand in Russia. Under a treaty signed at San Stefano (now Yeşilköy, a suburb of Istanbul) in March 1878, Abdul Hamid's government agreed to the creation of a 'Greater Bulgaria', with a southern coastline on the Aegean, which was to be nominally tributary to the Sultan, but in fact under Russian military occupation for the next two years. Russia would gain territorial advances in Bessarabia (or northern Romania) and on the Ottoman empire's north-eastern frontier. Serbia and Montenegro would gain further territory at Ottoman expense. In brief, had the treaty of San Stefano been implemented, Russia would have become the dominant power in the Balkans.

The main weakness of Russia – and an advantage for the Ottomans – was that the Tsar's government was diplomatically isolated. None of the Western powers wished to preserve the Ottoman empire unaltered, but Britain opposed any settlement which would leave Russia in a strong position to take over the straits. With Germany now emerging as an important power-broker, Bismarck also wished to prevent a war between Russia and Austria over the Balkans. There was thus a good deal of coincidence between British, German and Austrian aims. At the height of the crisis in February 1878 the British fleet passed through the Dardanelles to Istanbul, and a war between Russia and Britain seemed a possibility. The outcome was settled at the congress of Berlin of June–July 1878, which ended with a treaty signed on 13 July. Under its terms the 'Greater Bulgaria' foreseen at San Stefano was dismantled. Bulgaria north and west of the Balkan mountains was established as an autonomous state under nominal Ottoman suzerainty and a Christian prince. The region to the south and east of this, known as 'eastern Rumelia', was to remain under Ottoman rule, but with a Christian governor and a Christian militia as well as some Ottoman garrisons (in fact, the Sultan never exercised this last right). The remainder of 'Greater Bulgaria' was returned to Ottoman government. However, Serbia, Romania and Montenegro were recognised as independent states, and Russia gained some territory from Romania, as well as the formerly Ottoman districts of Kars, Ardahan and Batum in the east. Austria was allowed to occupy Bosnia-Herzegovina (though it remained nominally under Ottoman suzerainty until 1908) while Britain also took a share of the spoils by occupying Cyprus.[26] In effect, the treaty had bought the Ottoman empire another uncertain lease of life, albeit at a very heavy price. Apart from its territorial losses in the east, it had lost all direct control of south-east Europe, except for a long and strategically indefensible arm of territory stretching from the present Greek–Turkish frontier into northern Greece, Macedonia and Albania. In terms of population, from a previous total of somewhere around 25 million, the Sultan had lost about 5.5 million subjects, almost half of whom were Muslims.[27]

With the Berlin settlement, the 'eastern question' moved off the top of the agenda for the main European powers for the next 40 years. However, this did not solve the central problems faced by Ottoman statesmen. Abdul Hamid had prorogued the Ottoman parliament indefinitely in February 1878, and virtually monopolised decision-making until

1908, both domestically and in foreign policy. The main problems he encountered were that his territory, especially that remaining in Europe, was very hard to defend, that the entente with Britain was fading, and that France's power in the Near East had also waned. By occupying Egypt in 1882, Britain secured a vital stepping stone on the route to India which did not depend on Ottoman goodwill and it thus had less need to prop up the empire in south-east Europe. At the same time, Abdul Hamid became very suspicious that Britain meant to break off the Arab provinces of his empire, and establish a British sponsored Armenian state in eastern Anatolia. In fact, the Sultan had no way of preventing the British occupation of Egypt, nor could he prevent the union of the two halves of Bulgaria in 1885–86, and its emergence as a virtually independent state. His only consolation was that, thanks to internal upheavals and diplomatic pressure from Britain and Austria, the new Bulgaria was, for a time at least, anti- rather than pro-Russian. Abdul Hamid was a pious Muslim and, unlike his predecessors, emphasised his position as Caliph, or nominal head of all the world's Muslims. Politically, this may have been of some value, by promoting Islamic unity against incipient Arab or Albanian nationalism. Though it depended on bluff, it may also have provided some leverage against those European powers, such as Britain, France and Russia, with large subject Muslim populations. However, the Sultan was pro-European in culture, and there is no evidence that he ever regarded a pan-Islamic state as a practical project. As an alternative, he continued the policy of modernising the empire's administrative and military machine, though with the objective of strengthening the empire against the European powers, rather than improving the position of the Christian minorities, which was what the Europeans normally meant by 'reforms'.[28]

Initially, Abdul Hamid attempted to tackle his security problem by seeking a defensive alliance with Germany, as the one power which was too far away to threaten his empire directly, but could offer him some protection against Britain and Russia. However, Bismarck turned down the Ottoman approaches in 1881–82: he had only recently constructed the 'League of the Three Emperors' between Germany, Russia and Austria in June 1881 and did not want to arouse Russian suspicions, though he did agree to the despatch of a German military mission to modernise the Ottoman army in March 1882. In 1886, at the prompting of the Grand Vizier Kâmil Pasha, there was some discussion of a renewed Anglo-Ottoman alliance. However, the British government backed off since it feared that an alliance with the Sultan might allow Bismarck to embroil Britain with Russia, and thus free Germany to attack France – a good example of the complexities of the balance-of-power system. The failure provoked some consideration of a Russian–Ottoman alliance, for which the Ottoman officials even drew up a draft treaty, but this project also came to nothing. Hence, after 1886, the Sultan moved back to the alternative option of trying to preserve friendly neutrality towards all the main powers, without forming an alliance with any of them.[29]

During the 1890s, European economic penetration into the empire became a major focus of international attention – most notably, the proposal to construct a railway from Istanbul to Baghdad. After much trumpeted visits to the Ottoman empire by Kaiser Wilhelm II in 1889 and 1898, a largely German-backed company received a concession for the project in 1903. This, combined with growing German trade with the empire and the German role in modernising the Ottoman army, convinced some later observers that the empire was being converted into a satellite of Germany. In fact, in the years before 1914, Germany's share of the Ottoman empire's foreign trade was still well behind those of Britain, Austria and France, and Germany only accounted for about 21 per cent of the total foreign capital invested in the empire, compared with France's share of 49 per cent. In the event, the Baghdad line was not completed in its entirety until 1940, and Britain settled its differences with Germany over the railway in 1913–14.[30] Hence, it seems that there was nothing inevitable or economic about the Ottoman–German alliance in the First World War.

Meanwhile, the main problem faced by the empire was still the rising tide of Balkan nationalism and the European powers' entanglement with it. A rebellion in Crete led to a brief war with Greece in 1897 in which the Ottoman armies won an easy victory, but pressure from the powers forced the Sultan's government to withdraw from the island and recognise it as an autonomous province under Ottoman suzerainty. By the early years of the twentieth century attention had switched to turmoils in Macedonia, in which the Ottomans tried to play off Greek against Bulgarian nationalists. The European powers sponsored reform schemes, but these had little effect. Eventually, the struggle in Macedonia provided the background for a revolution in the Ottoman army itself. In July 1908 a group of officers in the Third Ottoman Army, based in Salonika, rose in rebellion, and demanded that the Sultan reactivate the 1876 constitution by reconvening the parliament which had been closed since 1878. Unable to resist his own army, Abdul Hamid rapidly capitulated. Free debate and a free press began again after the long years of royal autocracy, elections were held and the new parliament was duly inaugurated in December 1908. For the optimists, a new era seemed to have dawned in which all the diverse communities of the empire would unite behind the principle of constitutional and representative government, under the banner of 'Union and Progress'.[31]

Unfortunately for the empire, the brave hopes of 1908 proved stillborn. Before long the 'Young Turk' regime fell apart through internal struggles between liberals and 'unionists', resulting by 1914 in the establishment of an autocratic triumvirate of Enver, Mehmet Talat and Ahmed Jemal, three of the leaders of the original revolution. Austria seized the opportunity to annex Bosnia-Herzegovina in October 1908, while Bulgaria proclaimed its independence and Greece annexed Crete.[32] Without the shadow of an excuse, Italy invaded the Ottoman provinces of Tripoli and Cyrenaica (modern Libya) in September 1911, forcing the Ottoman government to cede the territory in October 1912.[33] The Albanians, a majority of whom were Muslims, rose in revolt in 1910, seeking a measure of self-government within the empire, and achieved this in September 1912. Elsewhere in the Balkans, the Christians of the empire pushed forward for independent statehood rather than a civic or supra-ethnic identity within the Ottoman state, strengthening the tendency towards a defensive Turkish nationalism on the other side. Hence, it is only at this point that one can begin to speak of 'the Turks' as a political rather than just an ethnic category.[34]

In foreign policy, it has frequently been assumed that the Young Turks initially favoured an alliance with Britain, as the supposed progenitor of democratic government. However, research by Hasan Ünal suggests that, at best, their ideas were very vague, ill formed and inconsistent. Turkish diplomacy was also constrained by the fact that, by the late nineteenth and early twentieth centuries, it was becoming more difficult to play off one European power against another, since the main European states were becoming divided into two camps, with France, Russia and later Britain on the one side, and Germany and Austria on the other. Before coming to power, the Young Turks' debates had shown a general hostility towards all the European powers, while after the revolution they switched to the opposite policy of trying to establish friendship with all of them. Initially, the picture was further confused by a division of power in Istanbul where the Grand Vizier, Kâmil Pasha, adhered to careful diplomacy, while some of the Young Turk leaders tried to follow an independent and more adventurous line. During October 1908 they made approaches to both the British and the French, as well as the Germans and Austrians, although this blunderbuss approach lacked logic, given the mutual hostilities of the European states.[35] Hence, their hopes were disappointed, and not just because relations with the empire were badly handled, notably by Britain. Admittedly, the British government was extraordinarily badly served at the time by Sir Gerard Lowther, its ambassador in Istanbul between 1908 and 1913, and his staff, who had a deep hostility to the Young Turks and all their works, intrigued constantly against their government, and harboured outrageous and absurd prejudices against Jews, Freemasons, Turks and Muslims in general.[36] However, this was not the sole or the most important reason for the failure of the projected alliance with Britain. In London, the Foreign Secretary, Sir Edward Grey, was working for an entente with France and Russia, in an effort to preserve the continental balance of power against Germany, and was anxious not to provoke Russia by entering into an alliance with the Ottoman empire. Hence, when an Ottoman delegation arrived in London in November 1908 to propose an alliance, it was told by Grey that Britain wished to keep its hands free. After the outbreak of war with Italy, the Ottoman government again proposed a formal alliance, either bilateral or with the triple entente as a whole, but again learnt that Britain favoured neutrality.[37]

The Ottoman state was thus left without an alliance with any of the European powers when it faced its final trial of strength in the Balkans in 1912–13. In October 1912, the four states of the 'Balkan League' – Bulgaria, Serbia, Greece and Montenegro – launched an all-out attack on the remaining Ottoman territories in Europe. By itself, the Ottoman army could probably have defeated any of the Balkan nations individually, but it could not overcome an alliance of all of them. The Bulgarians, who bore the brunt of the fighting on the alliance side, had reached the Çatalca lines by November 1912, and captured Edirne in the following March. Under the treaty of London of April 1913, the Ottoman empire ceded all of its territory west of the Enez–Midye line, including Edirne. In June 1913, the Istanbul government again approached the British for a defensive alliance, but this was rejected on the grounds that it would unite 'all Europe' against Britain. However, the Ottomans were meanwhile able to save some face, as well as territory, when Bulgaria fell out with its erstwhile allies, Greece and Serbia, over the division of their territorial spoils in Macedonia. Since the Bulgarians were forced to transfer most of their forces to their western front to fight the Serbs, Edirne was left virtually undefended. Turkish troops entered the city on 21 July, with Enver hogging the limelight – an advantage which he then used to project himself into a position of almost total power by his appointment as minister of war on 1 January 1914.

Meanwhile, the treaty of Bucharest of August 1913 brought the war to a close, and the Turks' western frontier was fixed along its present line.[38]

The Balkan wars set the stage for the final drama in the Ottoman empire's long history, when it entered the First World War on the German side. This fatal decision was preceded by negotiations with both sides, and apparently not regarded as inevitable by either of them. On the Ottoman side, the majority of the public and the government initially favoured neutrality, with Enver the only consistent advocate of an alliance with Germany. In May 1914, Mehmet Talat approached the Russians with an offer of alliance, but was turned down: the furthest Russia was willing to go was to ensure Ottoman neutrality. Ahmed Jemal was similarly rebuffed by France when he visited Paris in July. On 2 August, the day after the war had begun in Europe, Enver negotiated a secret treaty with Germany, promising Ottoman support for the central powers if Germany's assistance to Austria led to war with Russia – a condition which was fulfilled four days later. However, Jemal and the other cabinet members were not informed of the agreement until after it was signed, and for some time it was not certain that the Ottoman government would act on it.

A turning-point was reached on 3 August when the British government – apparently unaware of the secret Ottoman–German agreement – commandeered two dreadnoughts which had just been built in England for the Ottoman navy, and been paid for by public subscription. This arbitrary decision turned public opinion against the British as few other steps could have done. Even at this late stage, however, Enver was still negotiating with the Russian ambassador, N. K. Giers, for an alliance with Russia in return for the restoration of western Thrace and the Aegean islands which had been lost to Bulgaria and Greece in the Balkan wars. The most Giers offered was a joint guarantee by Britain, France and Russia of Turkish neutrality and territorial integrity. Enver continued to insist on the return of the Aegean islands, as well as the abolition of the capitulations and the return of the commandeered warships, but France and Britain refused the last two conditions, and the negotiations broke down.

The problem for the entente powers was, as Grey put it, that 'Turkey's decision will not be influenced by the value of the offers made to her, but by her opinion which side will probably win and which is in a position to make the offers good.'[39] On this score, the Germans had the advantage. On 10 August the German battle cruisers, *Goeben* and *Breslau*, arrived in Istanbul, and were transferred to the Ottoman navy by a bogus sale. Germany had thus demonstrated a clear material commitment to aid the empire, and exploited the advantage created by Britain's mistake in impounding the two dreadnoughts. On 11 October the German ambassador secretly promised delivery of £T2 million (£1.8 million sterling) in gold if war was declared; the arrival of the gold on 16 and 21 October sealed the deal. Without consulting the rest of the cabinet, Enver ordered the German admiral Souchon, now commanding the Ottoman fleet in the Black Sea, to attack the Russians. Souchon carried out his orders on 29 October. Russia declared war on the Ottoman empire on 2 November and Britain and France followed suit three days later. Enver's decision appears to have been formed by the expectation that the central powers would win a rapid victory in the war, that Russia would attempt to exploit Armenian resistance in eastern Anatolia to take territory from the empire, and that alliance with Germany was the best way of preventing this. On the other hand, he appeared to have broken one of the ground rules of earlier Ottoman diplomacy, that the empire should not join a war between the European powers unless its own territories were directly involved (which they were not). Previously, the Ottoman government had compensated for its internal weakness by playing off one European power against another, but Enver now threw away this advantage. Some later writers, like Feroz Ahmad, admit that the Young Turks backed the wrong horse in 1914, but claim that 'events had shown that they had no other horse to back'.[40] Against this, it can be argued that they would have done better to have stayed away from the race track.[41]

During the war, the future disposition of the Ottoman empire's territories was the subject of intense and complicated negotiations between the entente powers. These were inconsistent with one another, and many of them later became dead letters after Russia's withdrawal from the war: moreover, the Ottoman government obviously had nothing to do with them. Three events during the war did, however, have a powerful effect on the post-war Turkish state's foreign policy and relations. Of these, the first was certainly tragic, and is still bitterly contested. In January 1915 the Turkish forces fighting the Russians on the eastern front were devastatingly defeated at Sarıkamış, and the way opened for a large-scale Russian advance. In response, the Ottoman government ordered the deportation of the Armenian population of the region, which it rightly suspected of siding with the enemy. What happened then is strongly disputed. According to Armenian accounts, over a million of their people were massacred, in a planned genocide. Turkish or pro-Turkish accounts argue that the number who died during the transportation, or from conditions of famine or disease which also killed around two million Muslims, was only about 200,000, and that a genocide was not ordered or carried out. What is indisputable is that by the end of the war, the Armenian population of Anatolia, which had formerly numbered about 1.3 million, had been wiped out – either through flight, massacre or disease. Whatever the historical truth may be, the events of 1915 undoubtedly created a source of deep mistrust between Turks and Armenians which survives to this day.[42]

The second event had an equally important long-term effect on the Turks' relations with their Arab neighbours. The British-sponsored Arab revolt, led by the Hashemite family who had been the rulers of Mecca under the Ottomans, which began in the Hijaz in 1916 was a turning point in the history of Arab nationalism, though of disputable military value to the British. For the Turks, it also represented a treacherous stab in the back, after the official Ottoman declaration in 1914 that the war was a *jihad*, in which all good Muslims should join the fight against the infidel. The third event was further away, and the Ottomans played no part in it. Nevertheless, the Bolshevik revolution had profound effects on the empire, as on all Russia's neighbours. In the short run, it relieved the Ottoman army on a vital front, allowing the empire to regain the territories lost to Russia in 1878, under the treaty of Brest-Litovsk of December 1917. As a result, in 1918 Turkish forces advanced into Transcaucasia in a pointless campaign. This was the only practical expression of the idea of pan-Turkish nationalism, or the union of the Turkic peoples of central Asia with those of Turkey, which was fashionable in Young Turk intellectual circles, but it soon came adrift. In the longer run, the revolution and the consequent turmoil in Russia severely reduced Russian power until the late 1930s, and even converted what had been regarded as the hereditary enemy into an ally, at least for a few years.

During 1915–16 two of the Young Turk leaders – Ahmed Jemal, now Commander of the Ottoman Fourth Army in Syria, and Rahmi Evranos, the governor of the Aegean province of Aydın – were not above trying to make side deals with the Russians and the British, in the hope of establishing themselves in power by taking the Ottoman empire out of the war, but nothing came of these approaches.[43] As a result, the Ottoman government stayed in the war much longer than it should have done. During 1917 it could probably have arranged a separate peace with the British which would have left much of the empire intact, if it had made a serious effort to do so. However, Enver did not lose confidence in a final victory for the central powers until June 1918. By September 1918, total defeat was staring him in the face. With the withdrawal of Bulgaria from the list of Germany's allies, the empire was cut off from Germany, and faced with the serious danger of an advance on Istanbul from the west by entente troops. In Palestine and Syria, the Ottoman army expected almost certain destruction by vastly stronger British forces. Even then, Enver kept the truth from the cabinet, and it was not until he was removed from power through the installation of a new government under Izzet Pasha on 14 October that peace feelers were put out to the British.[44] These resulted in the signature of an armistice on the British battleship, HMS *Agamemnon*, anchored off Mudros, on the island of Lemnos, on 30 October. Under its terms, all Ottoman troops were to lay down their arms, and the straits were opened to the navies of the entente. The critical clause 7 of the armistice agreement also gave the entente powers 'the right to occupy any strategic points in the event of a situation arising which threatens the security of the allies'.[45] The war was finally ended, but the Ottoman state faced a very uncertain future.

IMPLICATIONS AND LEGACIES

For subsequent Turkish policy-makers, as well as the Turkish people, the most obvious and important lesson of the Ottoman state's long period of struggle and decline since the late eighteenth century was that, territorially and structurally, the empire was not sustainable and could not be recreated. In effect, the late Ottoman rulers had been engaged in a long project of damage limitation, which had ultimately failed. Through careful diplomacy, they had been able to slow down the decline, but they had never been able to create a long enough breathing space to reconstruct and modernise the empire effectively, and might well have been unable to do so even if they had managed to secure external stability. The European powers had paid lip service to the principle of Ottoman sovereignty, and had frequently repeated the claim that they respected the empire's territorial integrity, but in reality this respect was usually a fiction, and not always a polite one. The process of dismemberment of the empire had been a long and gradual one, rather than a single and cataclysmic collapse, as many had predicted. Most commonly, a subject community would rise in revolt, would be defeated by the Ottomans, but would then win autonomy within the empire thanks to support by one or more of the European powers. Autonomy would eventually be converted into full independence, after the next Ottoman defeat and a respectable length of time. This story had been repeated in the case of Serbia, Greece, Romania, Bulgaria and, finally, Albania. Even when the Ottoman armies won a clear victory against an enemy state – as in the case of Greece in

1897 – political pressure by the European powers had reversed the verdict of the battlefield. In effect the late Ottoman empire had apparently been locked into a no-win situation.

This experience did not mean that the tactic of exploiting the balance of power had been wrong. The greatest mistake made by Ottoman foreign policy had been in 1914, when Enver had abandoned it (though how long the Ottoman empire might have survived if it had remained neutral in 1914 is still an unanswerable question). At the same time, there were certain inescapable conclusions to be drawn from the late Ottoman experience. First, the future Turkish state would have to draw a firm line round those territories which it could reasonably expect to defend, either by itself or, if absolutely necessary, with the support of allies whose long-term interests were very close to its own. For the most part, this meant the territory inhabited by ethnic Turks, or other Muslims who were willing to integrate into or cooperate with the Turkish state. Ethnic Turks outside these boundaries could not be protected, except in rare circumstances where Turkish military force could be brought to bear.[46] Second, the nineteenth-century experience encouraged a highly suspicious attitude towards any expressions of religious or ethnic separatism by non-Muslim or non-Turkish minorities remaining in Turkish territory. This derived not from innate prejudice, but from the perception that, in the past, such movements had been used by rapacious foreign powers as a mask to hide their own imperialist ambitions. This reaction ignored the genuine humanitarian sympathies which might exist abroad for such minorities, but was nonetheless real for all that. The huge influx of refugees resulting from the empire's contraction reinforced this feeling of betrayal by the West, and led to a high degree of integration of the newcomers into the existing Turkish population of Anatolia. The modern Turkish nation was born in this melting pot.[47]

In other circumstances, this might have produced a nation of xeno-phobes, determined to cut themselves off from the outside world. That this was not so in the Turkish case was primarily due to the fact that, for the political élite, the Western nation state and its values still retained a power-ful attraction as the sole practical model for national reconstruction – political, economic and cultural. As Atatürk was later to put it : 'The West has always been prejudiced against the Turks ... but we Turks have always consistently moved towards the West ... In order to be a civilised nation, there is no alternative.'[48] Those outside the élite might still prefer tradi-tional or Islamic values – as they were perfectly entitled to do – but only the most eccentrically conservative could deny the importance of Western economic and technical achievements, or refuse to emulate them. The result was something of a love–hate relationship with the West. There was a natural desire to emulate the West in technical, economic and military terms, and to be recognised as a respected member of the Western community of nations. This was balanced by a suspicion of Western motives, and a fierce resentment of any sign of patronising or dictatorial behaviour by Western governments, which was not unjustified by past experiences.

Perhaps the most complicated and problematic element in the resulting political culture was its attitude to Islam. On the one hand, there can be little doubt that, even at the end of the empire, most Turkish and Kurdish inhabitants of Anatolia still identified themselves in primarily religious terms, and continued to do so for many years. The Ottoman state had been defeated, but the idea that political authority should have a religious basis still remained common. On the other hand, most of the original Islamic political project lay in ruins. Muslims were not united in a single state, and had not been for centuries. Abdul Hamid had appealed for Islamic unity as a general principle, but even he had never treated it as a real political blueprint. Above all, Ottoman rule over the Arab Middle East and its holy places had been decisively ended, both by superior British military strength and what the Turks saw as Arab betrayal during the First World War. Hence, the idea of rooting the legitimacy of the state in Islam was greatly weakened and that of continuing the empire as a geographical entity almost entirely destroyed. Yet Islam as a cultural and social system as well as a religious faith still commanded mass respect. How to integrate it into the structures and values of a modern state, with its concomitant foreign-policy assumptions, still remains a problem for many Muslim Turks.

NOTES

1. Quoted in F.R. Bridge, 'The Hapsburg Monarchy and the Ottoman Empire, 1900–18', in Marian Kent, ed., *The Great Powers and the End of the Ottoman Empire* (London, Cass, 2nd edn, 1996), p. 42. Officially, Austria became 'Austria–Hungary' with the establishment of the Dual Monarchy in 1867. (Hereafter referred to throughout simply as 'Austria'.)
2. Feroz Ahmad, 'The Late Ottoman Empire', in ibid., p. 6.
3. See Roderic H. Davison, *Reform in the Ottoman Empire, 1856–1876* (Princeton, NJ, Princeton University Press, 1963), pp. 136–71. For shorter accounts, see, Bernard Lewis, *The Emergence of Modern Turkey* (London, Oxford University Press, 1961), pp. 381–4, and Stanford J. Shaw and Ezel Kural Shaw, *History of the Ottoman Empire and Modern Turkey* (Cambridge, Cambridge University Press, 1977), Vol. 2, pp. 83–91.
4. Shaw and Shaw, *History,* Vol. 2, p. 242.

5. This calculation excludes Serbia, the Danubian principalities, Egypt, and the rest of north Africa, which were only nominally under Ottoman rule at the time. Data from Nuri Akbayar, 'Tanzimat'tan Sonra Osmanlı Devleti Nüfusu', *Tanzimat'tan Cumhuriyet'e Türkiye Ansiklopedisi* (Istanbul, İletişim Yayınları, 1985), Vol. 5, pp. 1239–40.

6. Stanford J. Shaw, 'The Ottoman Census System and Population, 1831–1914', *International Journal of Middle East Studies*, Vol. 9 (1978), pp. 325–38: Meir Zamir, 'Population Statistics of the Ottoman Empire in 1914 and 1918', *Middle Eastern Studies*, Vol. 17 (1981), p. 100.

7. Erik J. Zürcher, *Turkey: A Modern History* (London, I.B. Tauris, 1993), pp. 12–13, disputes the idea that the *milletbaşıs* actually commanded their religious communities: instead, power was dispersed, with local communities enjoying some autonomy vis-à-vis local representatives of the Ottoman government. For an account of the *millet* system, and its reform in the nineteenth century, see Davison, *Reform*, Ch. 4.

8. For an excellent summary, see Hugh Poulton, *Top Hat, Grey Wolf and Crescent: Turkish Nationalism and the Turkish Republic* (London, Hurst, 1997) Ch. 2.

9. Akbayar, 'Tanzimat'tan Sonra', pp. 1242–3: Justin McCarthy, *Death and Exile: The Ethnic Cleansing of Ottoman Muslims, 1821–1922* (Princeton, NJ, Darwin Press, 1995) esp. pp. 1–5, 333–40.

10. F.A.K. Yasamee, *Ottoman Diplomacy: Abdülhamid II and the Great Powers, 1878–1888* (Istanbul, Isis, 1996), pp. 2–4, 45–6, and 'Abdülhamid II and the Ottoman Defence Problem', *Diplomacy and Statecraft*, Vol. 4 (1993), pp. 22–3. For a summary of Ottoman military reforms in the nineteenth century, see William Hale, *Turkish Politics and the Military* (London, Routledge, 1994), pp. 15–24, 28–9.

11. Notably, from Yasamee, *Ottoman Diplomacy*.

12. Ibid., pp. 30–9: Kemal Girgin, *Osmanlı ve Cumhuriyet Dönemleri Hariciye Tarihimiz (Teşkilat ve Protokol)* (Ankara, Türk Tarih Kurumu, 1992), pp. 15–18, 40–8: J.C. Hurewitz, 'Ottoman Diplomacy and the European State System', *Middle East Journal*, Vol. 15 (1961), pp. 141–52: Lewis, *Emergence*, pp. 60–1: Shaw and Shaw, *History*, Vol. 2, pp. 62, 72–3: İlber Ortaylı, 'Osmanlı Diplomasisi ve Dışişleri Örgütü', *Tanzimat'tan Cumhuriyet'e Türkiye Ansiklopedisi* (see note 4), Vol. 1, pp. 278–81. Girgin points out that in the earlier period, the *Reis-ül Küttab* was not really a Foreign Minister in the modern sense, but rather a sort of Chief Secretary dealing with the administration of foreign affairs: the actual determination of policy was left in the hands of the Grand Vizier: Girgin, *Hariciye Tarihimiz*, p. 15.

13. Quoted in Yasamee, *Ottoman Diplomacy*, p. 43.

14. This generalisation needs some qualification, since it applied particularly to the latter half of the nineteenth century rather than the first. Until the 1860s Britain's relatively small but professional army was roughly comparable in effectiveness with those of the main continental powers (thus, for instance, the British army made a relatively respectable showing in the Crimean war): after that, it fell well behind them, as first Prussia and then the other continental powers built up mass armies based on universal conscription. Britain failed to follow suit, preferring to concentrate expenditure on its navy, which was clearly of greater relevance to an island state with a large colonial empire. See A.J.P. Taylor, *The Struggle for Mastery in Europe, 1848–1918* (Oxford, Oxford University Press, 1954), pp. xix–xxiv.

15. Yasamee, *Ottoman Diplomacy*, pp. 43–5, 107–9, 184–5 and 'Abdülhamid', pp. 20–1, 26–9: Selim Deringil, 'Aspects of Continuity in Turkish Foreign Policy: Abdülhamid II

and İsmet İnönü', *International Journal of Turkish Studies*, Vol. 4 (1987), pp. 39–43.

16. See, in particular, M.S. Anderson, *The Eastern Question, 1774–1923: A Study in International Relations* (London, Macmillan, 1966) and J.A.R. Marriott, *The Eastern Question: An Historical Study in European Diplomacy* (Oxford, Clarendon Press, 4th edn, 1940). More Turkish-centred studies are those of Yasamee, *Ottoman Diplomacy*; Shaw and Shaw, *History*, Vol. 2, Chs 1–4, and Zürcher, *Turkey*, Chs 1–8.

17. Anderson, *Eastern Question*, pp. xi–xii, 1–9, 13–20 and Marriott, *Eastern Question*, pp. 151–4, 158, 163–4.

18. Anderson, *Eastern Question*, pp. 26–47 and Marriott, *Eastern Question*, pp. 167–73.

19. Anderson, *Eastern Question*, pp. 48–50, 53–7, 67–8, 73–6 and J.C.B. Richmond, *Egypt, 1798–1952* (London, Methuen, 1977), pp. 36–8, 47–9, 62–9.

20. Anderson, *Eastern Question*, pp. 65–73, 77–87, 95–107; Marriott, *Eastern Question*, pp. 183, 221–45 and Richmond, *Egypt*, pp. 50–62. On Russia's rights at the straits under the 1833 and previous treaties, see J.C. Hurewitz, 'Russia and the Turkish Straits: A Revaluation of the Origins of the Problem', *World Politics*, Vol. 14 (1961–62), pp. 607–32.

21. Quoted in Frank Edgar Bailey, *British Policy and the Turkish Reform Movement: A Study in Anglo-Turkish Relations, 1826–1853* (Cambridge, MA, Harvard University Press, 1942), p. 209. It can be argued that Aberdeen was exaggerating in suggesting that Britain had 'long' been supporting the Ottoman empire, but as a statement of British policy between the 1840s and the mid-1870s his claim seems important.

22. Ibid., p. 228. Bailey's argument is confirmed by the work of other scholars, working from Ottoman sources – notably, Lewis, *Emergence*; Shaw and Shaw, *History*, and Davison, *Reform*.

23. Anderson, *Eastern Question*, pp. 116–43; Marriott, *Eastern Question*, pp. 256–78 and Shaw and Shaw, *History*, Vol. 2, pp. 140–1. On the last point, see Hurewitz, 'Ottoman Diplomacy', pp. 151–2. For the texts of the *Hatt-i Şerif* and the *Hatt-i Hümayun*, see Bailey, *British Policy*, pp. 277–9, 287–91.

24. In 1866, Ottoman suzerainty in Moldavia and Wallachia became a pure formality, following internal upheavals. Serbia also became virtually independent, though under strong Austrian influence, following the withdrawal of the last Ottoman garrisons in 1867. Conflict between the Druzes and Maronites in the Lebanon had meanwhile led to French intervention and the establishment of the autonomous district (*sancak*) of Mount Lebanon in 1861. See Anderson, *Eastern Question*, pp. 152–8, 164–6 and Shaw and Shaw, *History*, Vol. 2, pp. 141–4, 147–9.

25. For details, see Robert Devereux, *The First Ottoman Constitutional Period* (Baltimore, MD, Johns Hopkins University Press, 1963). Following his deposition, Abdul Aziz committed suicide in June 1876.

26. Strictly speaking, this was not part of the treaty of Berlin, but agreed to by a separate convention between the British and Ottoman governments signed in June 1878. In return, Britain was supposed to aid the Ottoman empire if Russia attacked it in the east. The British did not officially annex Cyprus until 1914.

27. Anderson, *Eastern Question*, pp. 169–73, 178–217, 226 and Shaw and Shaw, *History*, Vol. 2, pp. 158–67, 172–4, 182–4, 186–91.

28. Yasamee, *Ottoman Diplomacy*: pp. 24–30, 89–90.

29. Ibid., pp. 51, 80–81, 84, 184–86, 189–91, 255–9.

30. E.M. Earle, *Turkey, the Great Powers and the Baghdad Railway* (New York, NY, Macmillan,

1923), pp. 40, 43, 53, 68–70, 104–06: Charles Issawi, *An Economic History of the Middle East and North Africa* (London, Methuen, 1982), p. 69; H.C. Meyer, 'German Economic Relations with South-Eastern Europe, 1870–1914', *American Historical Review*, Vol. 62 (1951–52), p. 85 and Anderson, *Eastern Question*, pp. 263–7.

31. Feroz Ahmad, *The Young Turks: The Committee of Union and Progress in Turkish Politics, 1908–1914* (Oxford, Oxford University Press, 1969), pp. 1–13; Shaw and Shaw, *History*, Vol. 2, pp. 206–11, 266–7, 273–9 and Anderson, *Eastern Question*, pp. 262–3, 268–78.

32. Although the annexation of Bosnia-Herzegovina provoked the most serious concerns among the European powers, the clash with Bulgaria was a more immediate worry for the Ottoman government, since Bulgaria was well-armed and could have launched an assault on Ottoman territory before the Turks could have mobilised in response. In the event, war was avoided, and the Ottoman parliament recognised Bulgaria's independence in April–May 1909. For details, see Hasan Ünal, 'Ottoman Policy during the Bulgarian Independence Crisis, 1908–9: Ottoman Empire and Bulgaria at the Outset of the Young Turk Revolution', *Middle Eastern Studies*, Vol. 34 (1998), pp. 140, 147, 165–6.

33. Under the treaty of Ouchy of 15 October 1912. Under the treaty Italy also gained 'temporary' possession of the Dodecanese islands, in the southern Aegean.

34. Shaw and Shaw, *History*, Vol. 2, pp. 279–87, 290–2, 298–305.

35. Hasan Unal, 'Young Turks Assessments of International Politics, 1906–9', *Middle Eastern Studies* Vol. 32 (1996), pp. 30–44, reprinted in Sylvia Kedourie, ed., *Turkey; Identity, Democracy, Politics* (London and Portland, OR, Cass, 1996) and 'Ottoman Policy', pp. 135, 137–9, 167.

36. Joseph Heller, *British Policy towards the Ottoman Empire, 1908–1914* (London, Cass, 1983), pp. 13, 23–6, 29–31, 78, 98–100; Feroz Ahmad, 'Great Britain's Relations with the Young Turks, 1908–1914', *Middle Eastern Studies*, Vol. 2 (1965–66), pp. 309–15 and Elie Kedourie, 'Young Turks, Freemasons and Jews', *Middle Eastern Studies*, Vol. 7 (1971), pp. 89–104.

37. Heller, *British Policy*, pp. 11, 16, 35, 53, 63–4, 74–5, 80 and Ahmad, 'Great Britain's Relations', pp. 309, 319–21.

38. Heller, *British Policy*, pp. 78–80 and Shaw and Shaw, *History*, Vol. 2, pp. 292–8. To be strictly accurate, the empire recovered Edirne by a separate treaty signed in Istanbul in September 1913. Since Albania was now cut off from the rest of Ottoman territory, it received formal independence in July 1913. Elsewhere, the treaty of Bucharest divided Macedonia between Greece, Serbia and Montenegro, and gave Bulgaria a short stretch of Aegean coastline, including the port of Dedeağaç (Alexandroupolis); this was transferred to Greece in 1920.

39. Quoted in Taylor, *Struggle for Mastery*, p. 534.

40. Ahmad, 'Great Britain's Relations', p. 325.

41. Ibid., pp. 324–5; Anderson, *Eastern Question*, pp. 311–14; Shaw and Shaw, *History*, Vol. 2, pp. 310–12, and Ulrich Trumpener, 'Turkey's Entry into World War I: An Assessment of Responsibilities', *Journal of Modern History*, Vol. 34 (1962), pp. 369–80. For a statement by Enver of July 1914 that he expected the central powers to win the war, see Ulrich Trumpener, 'Germany and the End of the Ottoman Empire', in Kent, ed., *Great Powers*, p. 124 and Ulrich Trumpener, *Germany and the Ottoman Empire, 1914–1918* (Princeton, NJ, Princeton University Press, 1968), p. 20.

42. Shaw and Shaw, *History*, Vol. 2, pp. 315–17, adhere to the Turkish account, whereas Zürcher, *Turkey*, p. 121, believes that there was a centrally controlled policy of extermination, ordered by Talat and an inner circle within the Young Turk regime. For a review of the dispute, see Gwynne Dyer, 'Turkish "Falsifiers" and Armenian "Deceivers": Historiography and the Armenian Massacres', *Middle Eastern Studies*, Vol. 12 (1976), pp. 99–107.

43. See Frank Weber, *Eagles on the Crescent: Germany, Austria and the Diplomacy of the Turkish Alliance, 1914–1918* (Ithaca, NY, and London, Cornell University Press, 1970), pp. 135–6, 153–4.

44. Gwynne Dyer, 'The Turkish Armistice of 1918: 1 – The Turkish Decision for a Separate Peace, Autumn 1918', *Middle Eastern Studies*, Vol. 8 (1972), pp. 143–6, 150 1, 158–69.

45. Full text in Gwynne Dyer, 'The Turkish Armistice of 1918: 2 – A lost Opportunity: The Armistice Negotiations of Moudros', *Middle Eastern Studies*, Vol. 8 (1972), pp. 340–1.

46. The only such case which springs to mind is that of the Turkish Cypriots.

47. See Poulton, *Top Hat*, pp. 265–9. This process was not completed until some time after the First World War, under the population exchanges provided for by the treaty of Lausanne, see below, pp. 55–6.

48. Quoted in Altemur Kılıç, *Turkey and the World* (Washington, DC, Public Affairs Press, 1959), p. 49.

2

Resistance, Reconstruction and Diplomacy, 1918–39

Between 1919 and 1923 the Turks passed through the most critical turning point in their modern history. With the defeat of the Ottoman empire in 1918, the victorious entente powers seemed poised to divide up almost all its remaining territory, thus practically extinguishing the Turkish state as an independent international actor. After the Russian revolution, the Bolshevik government withdrew the Tsarist regime's claims to Turkish territory, making Britain the dominant power in the Near East. Once the war was over, the British prime minister, David Lloyd George, tried to give effect to this, by establishing British rule in Iraq and Palestine, and by using Greece as Britain's surrogate in Asia Minor. Since Greece had been coerced into the war by Britain and France in July 1917, the Greek premier, Eleutherios Venizelos, was accorded a place at the Versailles peace conference in February 1919. On the basis of bogus population statistics claiming that the majority of the population was Greek, he put forward a grandiose claim to the whole of western Asia Minor, eastern Thrace and all the Aegean islands. These claims were broadly supported by Britain and France, but opposed by Italy. What the entente powers failed to anticipate was the emergence of a powerful movement of national resistance which decisively defeated the partition project. Eventually, in 1923, this forced the Turks' former enemies to recognise an independent Turkey within what are virtually its present frontiers. The leader of the resistance movement, Mustafa Kemal Atatürk,[1] then used his traditionally derived authority as a 'Ghazi', the victor in a war against the infidel, to reconstruct the Turkish state on quite untraditional lines – as a secular republic, committed to modernism and a Turkish–ethnic rather than Muslim identity, with himself as president. This outcome was basically determined on the battlefield, not at the conference table. Nonetheless, the military victory would probably have been impossible without adroit diplomacy by Atatürk and his colleagues – in effect, the exploitation of the balance of power, and rivalries between the main European states, on which their Ottoman predecessors had relied. After the victory, their over-whelming aim was to secure peace and national security, following years of struggle and loss, by avoiding expansionary projects, and limiting their objectives to what they could achieve by relying on their own resources.

DIPLOMACY, WAR AND PEACE, 1918–23

While the First World War had still been raging, the entente powers had, in effect, written themselves vague and sometimes contradictory promissory notes for the territories of the Ottoman empire. In 1915, reversing a century of policy, the British promised to hand over Istanbul and the whole straits region to Russia if the entente won the war, and secured French acquiescence to this. After the Russian revolution, the Bolshevik government renounced all claims to Turkish territory, but this still left open the fate of the straits as well as territories in eastern Anatolia which the Tsarist government had occupied or claimed. After much nego-tiation, the entente powers' plans were eventually formulated as the treaty of Sèvres, which was reluctantly accepted by the government of the last Sultan Vahdettin (Mehmet VI) in August 1920. Under this stillborn treaty, Ottoman rule in Istanbul would be maintained, but control over the straits placed under an international commission, on which the Ottoman govern-ment would have only minor representation. İzmir and the surrounding territory would be administered by Greece for the following five years, after which it could be attached to Greece, subject to a plebiscite. Eastern Thrace was separately allotted to the Greeks. In eastern Anatolia, Armenia would be established as an independent state in the provinces of Erzurum, Trabzon, Van and Bitlis (of which only a minority of the population had ever been Armenian). A scheme for 'local autonomy' for the Kurds, possibly leading to full independence, would be worked out by a commission composed of British, French and Italian delegates. The treaty provided for the severance of the Arab provinces of the empire, which the Turkish nationalists broadly accepted, but a separate agreement between Britain, France and Italy recognised the 'special interests' of Italy in southern Anatolia, and of France in Cilicia (that is, Adana and the area to its north-east). In effect, the treaty envisaged that the future Turkish state would be reduced to a rump including only Istanbul and central and northern Anatolia, with very few resources and practically no freedom of action in the economic sphere.[2] Legally, the treaty of Sèvres was quite invalid, since it was never ratified by the Ottoman or any other

Turkish parliament. Nonetheless, it was important as a statement of the entente's plans, and its failure was a striking defeat for allied, especially British, policy.

Although these plans were not formalised until the Sèvres treaty was prepared in 1920, several of the states involved had moved to create *faits accomplis* for some time before. On 15 May 1919, Greek troops were landed in İzmir, primarily to pre-empt the Italians, who had been promised the region in separate inter-allied agreements of 1915 and 1917.[3] Meanwhile, in the spring of 1919, Italy landed troops in Antalya, while the French occupied Cilicia, and British, French and Italian forces were stationed in the straits. In response, huge protest meetings were held in Istanbul, and local resistance movements organised in Anatolia. They were coordinated by Mustafa Kemal, the Turks' most distinguished general in the great war, who had been sent by the Istanbul government to the Black Sea port of Samsun in May 1919, nominally to suppress attacks by the local Turks on Greek settlements in the area. Exploiting the underground organisation known as Karakol ('The Guard') set up by Enver towards the end of the great war, local resistance leaders in the 'Eastern Provinces Society for the Defence of National Rights', whose core was drawn from army officers and the middle ranking echelons of the old Union and Progress organisation, met in Erzurum during July–August 1919. Here they elected Mustafa Kemal as chairman of their Representative Committee. The Erzurum congress also issued a proclamation declaring that 'the entire country within its [undefined] national frontiers is an undivided whole',[4] and that any foreign occupation of it would be resisted by force. These commitments were repeated at a second congress held in Sivas on 4–11 September, which established a national organisation, known as the Society for the Defence of Rights of Anatolia and Rumelia ('Rumelia' referred to Turkey's remaining European territory in Thrace). In effect, Mustafa Kemal, who moved his headquarters to Ankara on 27 December, had now been made head of an embryonic government over most of Anatolia, which was effectively outside the Sultan's control.

The ensuing struggle for Anatolia – or, as the Turks call it, the 'National Struggle' (*Milli Mücadele*) – was effectively divided into two phases. During the first of these, between June 1919 and March 1920, the nationalist resistance movement, which was still building up its military and political structure, evidently hoped that it might achieve its aims without facing a military showdown with the entente powers, and in collaboration with sympathetic members of the Sultan's government. It is suggested that at this stage Kemal planned to capture control of the imperial government rather than overthrow it.[5] A possible opportunity to do this occurred at the end of September, when the Sultan dismissed his subservient Grand Vizier and brother-in-law, Ferid Pasha, replacing him with Ali Riza Pasha. The new Grand Vizier then sent his Navy Minister, Salih Pasha, to meet Mustafa Kemal in the town of Amasya, near the Black Sea. Under the resulting 'Amasya protocol' of 23 October 1919, the two sides agreed that a new Chamber of Deputies, under the Ottoman constitution, would be elected and convened outside Istanbul, and that the declarations of the Sivas congress would be accepted by the Sultan's government, assuming they were passed by the Chamber. The elections, in which nationalist sympathisers won a handsome majority, were held during October–November, and the Chamber convened in Istanbul (in spite of the Amasya agreement) on 12 January 1920. On 28 January it voted through the 'National Pact' (*Misak-i Milli*) which effectively became the official statement of the nationalist aims. This accepted the loss of the 'portions of the Ottoman State which are populated exclusively by an Arab majority', and which were under occupation by the entente powers at the time of the Mudros armistice of October 1918, with which most Turks were apparently happy to cut their links. In effect, the nationalist resistance had decided not to try to re-build Turkish power in the Middle East. However, the Pact declared that:

> The whole of those parts [of the Ottoman empire] whether within or outside the said armistice lines which are inhabited by an Ottoman Muslim [in effect, Turkish and Kurdish] majority, united in religion, in race and in aim … form a whole which does not of division for any reason.[6]

In reaction to the Chamber's defiance, and because they apparently feared some sort of link between the Turkish resistance and the Bolshevik regime in Russia,[7] the entente forces subjected Istanbul to a full military occupation beginning on 16 March 1920, allowing the Sultan to restore Ferid Pasha to power, and arresting all the nationalist deputies whom they could lay their hands on. However, 92 deputies managed to escape arrest and assembled in Ankara, where they were joined by 232 new members elected by local branches of the Defence of Rights movement. On 23 April they opened their first session as the Grand National Assembly of Turkey, proclaiming their sovereignty in the name of the nation, though leaving open the question as to whether the Sultanate could be continued.[8]

The publication of the Sèvres terms in April 1920, and their acceptance by the Sultan's government in August, effectively dashed hopes that the

Turkish nationalists might be able to negotiate their way out of the partition plan, or could do so in collaboration with the Istanbul government.
This opened the second phase in the struggle. For the nationalists, the
prospects must at first have seemed daunting. After centuries of decline,
the Ottoman empire had just been defeated by the most powerful armies
of the day. On the ground, the Turks had been unable to stem the advance
of the Greek forces, which had captured Bursa and most of the Aegean
region by the summer of 1920. Moreover, the nationalist movement could
not make an undisputed claim to sovereignty, since the Sultan's government continued its existence until November 1922. Most foreign states
continued to recognise it, maintaining their diplomatic missions in
Istanbul rather than Ankara. The nationalists had difficulty in finding the
personnel for their embryonic foreign ministry, which originally consisted
of just three officials and a secretary. According to one story, passengers
alighting from the train from Istanbul who were wearing neckties (an
assumed sign of Western culture) were asked whether they spoke any
French. Those who did were immediately invited to join the foreign
ministry, where they were given jobs regardless of their qualifications or
profession. As time went on, officials from the old Istanbul government
transferred themselves to the new ministry. It was not until after the
proclamation of the republic in October 1923 that a regular ministerial
and diplomatic structure was established, and it was only in the late 1920s
that most foreign diplomatic missions in Turkey transferred their
embassies to Ankara. By this stage, Turkey had started to build up an
impressive cadre of trained diplomats who helped to maintain a fairly high
degree of consistency and independence in the execution of policy.[9]

However, events were to show that the odds were less stacked against
the Turks than might have appeared. The entente governments could not
enforce their partition scheme without a massive military commitment,
but neither they nor their peoples were prepared for this. In April 1920
Marshal Foch, the French wartime commander, reported that an army of
27 divisions would be needed to force the Turks to accept the proposed
peace terms, but such forces were simply not available.[10] British or French
conscripts who had just been told that they had won 'the war to end wars'
would not now be prepared to go back to fight another one, in a remote
region where no obvious national interests could be identified. The only
entente state with a clear national and territorial interest in Anatolia was
Greece, but in the long run Greece was too weak to defeat the Turks without effective military support from Britain, which was not forthcoming.
The French and Italians soon made it clear that they had no stomach for

another bitter war with the Turks, and sought separate peace deals with them. The Sèvres scheme also excluded Russia, where the Bolshevik government had established effective control by the end of 1920, and aligned with the Turkish nationalists against the entente. Finally, the entente states were not only at odds with one another, they were also internally divided. Italy, always the weakest of the major European powers, was further weakened by internal convulsions, culminating in the Fascist takeover of October 1922. In Britain, Lloyd George's policy of full support for the Greeks, and the reduction of Turkey to impotence, was not supported by his foreign secretary, Lord Curzon who, while far from pro-Turkish, believed that peace would be impossible if the Greeks were allowed to take over large parts of Anatolia. Winston Churchill, the secretary of state for war, took a more explicitly pro-Turkish line, since he wished to preserve a friendly and relatively strong Turkey as a barrier against the Bolsheviks.[11]

For their part, Mustafa Kemal and his colleagues were evidently aware of these weaknesses and divisions on the entente side, and fully prepared to exploit them. During 1920–21, the first occasion to put these policies to the test occurred on Turkey's disputed north-eastern border, where the collapse of Tsardom and the consequent struggle between the Bolsheviks, their pro-Tsarist opponents and local nationalist forces, created a constantly changing and unpredictable situation, but one which turned out to be to the Turks' advantage. In September 1918, just before the end of the great war and as part of Enver Pasha's eleventh-hour Caucasian campaign, Ottoman troops had briefly tried to fill the power vacuum in Transcaucasia, and occupied Baku, the oil centre and chief city of Azerbaijan, but had then withdrawn under the Mudros armistice. Baku and Batum were occupied by the British in November 1918. The three Transcaucasian republics – Georgia, Armenia and Azerbaijan – had all declared their independence the previous May, and now moved to assert it, but were locked in mutual struggles over disputed territory. Meanwhile, General Denikin, the local leader of the anti-Bolshevik Russian forces, who was supported by Britain, refused to countenance any independence for the Transcaucasian republics, insisting on the aim of 'Great Russia, One and Indivisible'. By March 1919, realising that they could not maintain substantial military forces in both Transcaucasia and the Turkish straits, the British decided to withdraw virtually all their troops from Transcaucasia by the end of the year. Denikin's forces had collapsed by December 1919.[12]

Mustafa Kemal had first struck up contact with the Soviets in May

1919, and broadly favoured their cause in Transcaucasia, primarily because he looked to Moscow for arms supplies to aid him against the entente, whereas the independent republics, especially Armenia, blocked the land bridge between Turkey and Soviet-controlled territory. He strictly abjured Enver's pan-Turkist ideas, declaring that 'neither Islamic union nor Turanism may constitute a doctrine, or logical policy, for us'.[13] In effect, vague ideology was far less important than strategic considerations. In April 1920, Bolshevik forces made their first major step into Transcaucasia by taking over power in Azerbaijan, with Turkish support. Mustafa Kemal simultaneously wrote to the Soviet government promising support for the Bolshevik campaign. Turkey's biggest obstacle in Transcaucasia was Armenia, since the Armenians, unlike the other Transcaucasian nations, had substantial territorial claims against Turkey, and had occupied the disputed provinces of Kars and Ardahan, which the Turkish nationalists regarded as legitimately theirs.[14] In September 1920, the Ankara government decided to take matters into its own hands by launching an invasion of Armenia. Left to themselves, the Armenians collapsed. By 30 October, Turkish forces led by General Kâzim Karabekir had swept through Kars to the frontier town of Alexandropol (later Leninakan – in Turkish, Gümrü). Under the treaty of Alexandropol signed on 2 December, the Armenians agreed to the present Turkish–Armenian frontier, and denounced the treaty of Sèvres. However, the Bolsheviks simultaneously took over Armenia, and rejected the Alexandropol treaty.

Until early in 1921, the Soviet leaders seem to have believed that pro-communist forces could take over in Turkey, and that there was therefore no need to reach an agreement with Kemal. They were rapidly disillusioned, however. On 28 January 1921 Mustafa Suphi and the leaders of the tiny Turkish communist party were drowned – almost certainly murdered – in the Black Sea off Trabzon. In the same month, the so-called 'Green Army ' led by the guerrilla warlord, Çerkes Ethem, in western Anatolia, which was attached to a bizarre mixture of Islamism and socialism, was decisively defeated by the Kemalist forces. Kemal meanwhile outflanked the Bolsheviks by setting up his own 'official' communist party, which included leading members of his government, and even suggested that it would seek affiliation with the Third International. On the western front, on 10 January 1921, nationalist forces commanded by İsmet Pasha defeated a Greek attempt to break out from Bursa at İnönü, from which İsmet later took his surname. These events persuaded the Soviet government that they would do best to seek an accommodation with the Turkish nationalists, and aid them against the entente. A communist takeover in Turkey could be postponed to an indefinite future. In the meantime, it was far more realistic to reach an agreement with Ankara. After a brief clash over the Georgian port of Batum, which had been occupied by the Turks on 5 March 1921, the two sides signed a Treaty of Friendship in Moscow on 16 March which fixed the northeastern frontier of Turkey along its present line. Significantly, under Article 8 of the treaty, they agreed 'to forbid the formation or presence on their territory of organisations or groups claiming to be the government of the other country or part of the territory and also the presence of groups that have hostile intentions to the other country'.[15] Although this was not specifically provided for in the treaty, the Soviets also gave substantial financial aid to the nationalists, probably amounting to around 10 million gold roubles, plus large amounts of arms and ammunition.[16] As Bülent Gökay suggests, the Turkish–Soviet accord resembled 'a business partnership rather than a unity of principles'.[17] Nonetheless, it was of undoubted value to the Kemalists, since it strengthened their material resources, freed them to concentrate their military efforts on their western front against the Greeks, and helped to convince the entente powers that they would be a permanent force to be reckoned with.

While these agreements with the Bolsheviks were being worked out, the Ankara government was also negotiating with the entente. At a conference convened in London in February–March 1921, concessions were offered on the Sèvres terms, but the Greeks refused any modification of their own claims, and thus saved the Ankara government from the need to accept anything short of the conditions of the National Pact. As its foreign minister and the head of the nationalist delegation, Bekir Sami also secured the secret agreement of France and Italy to withdraw their forces from Anatolia in return for economic concessions. This solution was rejected by the Grand National Assembly, evidently with Kemal's assent, and Bekir Sami was forced to resign as foreign minister. However, the possibility of separate agreements with France and Italy, which would detach them from Britain and Greece, was clearly on the table. A further sign of this came in June, when the Italians began to evacuate their forces from Antalya. After some false starts, the French Senator, Henri Franklin-Bouillon, signed an agreement with the Ankara government on 20 October 1921 under which the French withdrew their forces from Cilicia, leaving substantial military supplies to the Turkish nationalists.[18] In effect, Kemal had neutralised France and Italy, leaving the war in Anatolia as a straight fight between the Greeks and Turks, with the British in an uncertain position at the straits.

These diplomatic moves were both accompanied and affected by the changing military fortunes of the two sides in Anatolia. On 1 April 1921 İsmet Pasha inflicted another defeat on the Greeks at a second battle of İnönü, but the Greeks then regrouped and on 10 July began a general advance in which they captured Eskişehir, Kütahya and Afyon, obliging the Turks to withdraw to the line of the Sakarya river, only 50 miles west of Ankara. The biggest battle of the war then ensued along the Sakarya between 23 August and 13 September, stopping the Greeks in their tracks and forcing them to retire to Eskişehir. This was the turning point in the war, since the Greeks had needed to gain a decisive victory over the Turks at the Sakarya if they were to win the struggle in the long run. With a lull in the fighting during the winter of 1921–22, Yusuf Kemal (Tengirşenk), Bekir Sami's successor as foreign minister, spent fruitless weeks in March 1922 in London and Paris trying to persuade the entente governments to accept peace on the basis of the National Pact. The furthest the British, French and Italian governments were now prepared to go was outlined in a statement of 27 March, accepting the restoration of Turkish sovereignty throughout Anatolia, an armistice and a Greek withdrawal once a peace treaty were signed. This was accepted by Greece, but rejected by the Kemalists who feared that the Greeks would use the armistice to recover, and instead demanded an immediate evacuation. In July 1922, Kemal sent his trusted friend Fethi [Okyar] to London for renewed talks with the British, but this was just a device to gain time, pending the launch of a military offensive. This was opened on 26 August, and resulted in a decisive Turkish victory at Dumlupınar, near Afyon, and the capture of İzmir on 11 September.[19]

Flushed by victory, the Turks then turned north to deal with remaining Greek forces in eastern Thrace, but found their way blocked by a small allied garrison at Çanakkale, guarding the straits. The French and Italians withdrew their contingents, leaving the British to face the Turks unaided. In the last resort, the Lloyd George government was prepared to re-start a war against the Turks, but it was also ready to make important concessions to prevent this. This realism was reciprocated on the Turkish side. On 3 October, British, Turkish, Greek, French and Italian military representatives gathered in the town of Mudanya, on the southern shores of the Sea of Marmara, where they signed an armistice agreement on 10 October 1922. Under its terms, the Greeks were to evacuate eastern Thrace up to the river Maritsa (Meriç) within 30 days, and Turkish sovereignty over the region, as well as the straits and Istanbul, was recognised. In return the

Turks promised to respect a neutral zone around the straits, pending the signature of a definitive peace treaty. To this end, invitations to a peace conference to be held in the Swiss city of Lausanne had been issued on 20 September to the governments of Britain, France, Italy, Romania, Yugoslavia, Japan, Greece, Turkey and the United States.[20]

The Lausanne conference opened on 21 November 1922, but only after encountering serious problems as to who was to attend. When the original invitations had been issued, the Soviet government had pointedly been left off the list, but this caused predictable protests from Moscow, as well as from Ankara, where the Kemalists were anxious to avoid being isolated against the Western powers. As a result, on 27 October, an invitation was issued to the Soviets, but on condition that they could only participate in those discussions which had to do with the future of the straits. Equally crucially, separate invitations were issued to the Ankara government and to that of the Sultan in Istanbul, although by this stage Vahdettin only exercised vestigial power. Kemal and his colleagues were naturally anxious to prevent a divided Turkish representation at Lausanne. Almost certainly, Kemal had had it in mind to end the rule of the Ottoman dynasty for some time, but this diplomatic accident forced his hand. The Assembly dealt with the problem by the abrupt step of abolishing the Sultanate on 1 November. Sultan Vahdettin, the last of his line, went into exile on a British warship on 17 November 1922, leaving his cousin Abdul Mejid to carry on as Caliph, or nominal head of the world's Muslims, for another 16 months.

In the event, it was not until 24 July 1923 that a peace treaty between Turkey and the wartime entente was eventually signed at Lausanne. In the negotiations, the British, Turks and Soviets were the main players, with France and Italy principally concerned with the economic aspects of the eventual treaty, and Greece too weak to have any effect on the outcome. In Britain, the Lloyd George government had fallen on 19 October 1922 – partly, but not entirely, as the result of the collapse of his policy in the Near East – and Lord Curzon, as foreign secretary, was free to set the course of British diplomatic strategy. This essentially consisted of aiding the establishment of an independent Turkey as an anti-Soviet barrier, while protecting British interests. Such a policy had long been Curzon's preference, and it had in any case been made virtually inevitable by the startling revival of Turkish power between 1920 and 1922. As a memorandum by the British General Staff of October 1922 put it, 'we can no longer treat the Turks as a conquered nation to whom it is possible to dictate any terms we wish'.[21] From the British viewpoint, there was no further point in assisting the Greeks, who lost their claims to eastern Thrace and any territory in Anatolia. The river Maritsa was thus fixed as the land frontier between Greece and Turkey, where it remains to this day, though the treaty also established demilitarised zones along the Turkish–Greek and Turkish–Bulgarian frontiers. Under the treaty, the Aegean islands were granted to Greece, but for the Dodecanese (principally Rhodes), which were confirmed as Italian territory, and the islands of Tenedos (Bozcaada) and Imbros (Gökçeada), close to the entrance to the Dardanelles, which remained under Turkish sovereignty. The islands attached to Greece were also to be demilitarised.[22]

Britain's main interests, as Curzon saw them, were to secure freedom of passage for British warships through the straits, and the attachment of the disputed province of Mosul to British-ruled Iraq, rather than to Turkey. On the first score, Britain's interests were fairly consistent with those of the Turks, though inconsistent with those of the Soviets. British and Soviet policies on the straits at this time represented a striking reversal of the positions adopted during the nineteenth century, in which the Tsarist government had sought to gain passage for its warships into the Mediterranean, whereas the British sought to keep the straits closed, under Turkish control. Instead, the British now sought to have the straits opened to warships, while the Soviets aimed to keep them closed. The main reason for the change was the fact that the Russian Black Sea fleet had been completely destroyed in the civil war, leaving the Soviet government anxious to keep the British fleet out of the Black Sea, rather than gain access to the Mediterranean for its own navy. Meanwhile, the British wished to prevent the Turks from closing the straits to Western navies, as Enver Pasha had done in 1914. The Turks, for their part, were prepared to allow limited access to the Black Sea for the navies of non-Black Sea states, so as to maintain a balance of power against Russia. The result was a compromise under which non-Black Sea powers gained limited access to that sea, and both sides of the straits were demilitarised. These arrangements were to be supervised by an international commission.[23]

The second issue proved more difficult to settle, since British and Turkish interests directly clashed. The Turks based their claim to the province of Mosul on the grounds that it was part of the 'non-Arab' territories which were included within the putative Turkish state under the National Pact, and had not been under British occupation at the time of the Mudros armistice. The fact that most of the population was ethnically Kurdish rather than Turkish did not persuade them to drop their claim, since İsmet [İnönü], the chief Turkish delegate at Lausanne, maintained that there were no differences between Turks and Kurds, and that 'the Government of the Grand National Assembly of Turkey is the Government of the Kurds just as much as the Government of the Turks'.[24] This claim had some justification at the time, in that the Turkish Kurds had in general supported the nationalist cause against the Greeks. However, it was hotly disputed by the British, who were anxious to attach the Mosul province to Iraq as a defensive barrier against Turkey. Moreover, although they both denied it, both sides were keen to gain control of the rich oil resources of the province, which were suspected, but not proven, at this stage.[25] Although Atatürk had privately suggested to Turkish journalists in April 1922 that Turkey would not be prepared to go to war with Britain for the sake of Mosul,[26] İsmet refused to abandon the Turkish claim, and the question was left unsettled when the treaty was signed, with an undertaking that both sides would come to an agreement within nine months.[27]

What were referred to as the 'economic' clauses of the treaty also proved to be extremely difficult to settle, and led to a long intermission in the negotiations during February–April 1923. For the Turkish side, the major objective was to secure international recognition of the abolition of the capitulations, which were regarded as a quite unacceptable limitation of the powers of a modern sovereign state.[28] The entente powers fought hard to maintain some special legal rights for foreign citizens living in Turkey, but were eventually forced to concede the 'complete abolition' of the capitulations, under Article 28 of the treaty. In return, the Turkish government undertook to respect all concessionary contracts given to foreign firms before October 1914, and to maintain its import tariff at the relatively low levels established by the Ottoman customs tariff of September 1916, until 1929.[29] The Ottoman empire's huge war debt to the central powers, put at £170 million sterling, was written off. Turkey's share of the Ottoman debt was fixed at TL gold 84.8 million (or £78 million sterling), with the remainder distributed to those parts of the Ottoman empire, as of 1914, which had now become independent states. The foreign-controlled Public Debt administration, established in 1881 (see p. 28), was also wound up.[30]

Finally, in human and political terms, one of the most significant provisions of the Lausanne settlement was a Greek–Turkish convention on the exchange of populations, under which the Greek (or at least, Greek Orthodox) population of Anatolia, which apparently numbered around 900,000, was exchanged for the Muslim community of Greece, of around 400,000. While these massive movements of population helped to homogenise the population of both countries, the gain was bought at appalling human cost, and ended centuries of generally peaceful co-existence between the two communities. An exception was also made in the case of the Greeks of Istanbul (then numbering about 120,000) and the Turks and other Muslims of western Thrace. As recognised 'non-Muslim minorities', Christians and Jews remaining in Turkey were given the right to maintain their own educational and religious institutions, using their own languages, and the Orthodox Ecumenical Patriarchate was maintained in Istanbul. No such rights were accorded to the Turkish Kurds, who probably accounted for about 10–15 per cent of the population at the time, since they represented an ethnic rather than religious minority. At the same time, the draconian exchange of populations, combined with the massacres and deportation of virtually all the former Armenian community of Anatolia during the great war (see pp. 35–6) had a transformatory effect on the cultural and political landscape of the country. The population of Anatolia, of which about 20 per cent had been non-Muslim before the war, was now about 98 per cent Muslim, completing a long process which had begun in the nineteenth century.[31]

SETTLEMENTS AND CHALLENGES, 1923–39

With the signature of the treaty of Lausanne of 1923, the new Turkish state passed its most critical test. It had at last achieved a degree of security and international recognition which its Ottoman predecessor had lacked ever since the last quarter of the eighteenth century. As a result, foreign policy could take second place to internal reconstruction. During the 1920s, Atatürk and his colleagues used this breathing space to transform the political institutions of their country, and to try to reorient its society and culture, on the basis of their secular–nationalist and modernist beliefs. On 29 October 1923 a republic was formally declared, with Atatürk as its president and İsmet İnönü its prime minister. The Caliphate – separated from the Sultanate since November 1922 – was abolished on 3 March 1924, and Abdul Mejid, the last Caliph, sent into exile. These changes were embodied in a new constitution, enacted on 20 April 1924, which confirmed the Grand National Assembly as 'sole rightful representative of the nation' and, among other things, fixed Ankara as the capital of the new state. The institutional reforms were continued into the social, legal and cultural spheres during the rest of the 1920s, notably by the abandonment of the old Islamic-based civil and penal codes in 1926, in favour of secular codes based on those of Switzerland and Italy respectively, and the compulsory change from the Arabic to the Latin script for written Turkish, in 1928. In the same year, the clause in the 1924 constitution declaring Islam to be the official religion of the state, was withdrawn, although it was not until 1937 that 'secularism' was officially written into the constitution as one of the six guiding principles of the republic.

In domestic politics, Atatürk faced some serious challenges to his authority during the first half of the 1920s. Once the war against the Greeks had been won, many of the leaders of the nationalist movement, both civilian and military, assumed that Turkey could now be established as a parliamentary democracy, on Western lines, and were anxious to prevent Atatürk from making himself a dictator. In November 1924, they formed a Progressive Republican Party, in opposition to the ruling People's Party (later re-named the Republican People's Party). Atatürk's government was also opposed by those who refused to accept the abolition of the Caliphate and the establishment of a secular state, as well as sections of the Kurdish minority. In February 1925, the opposition took a violent turn, when a major rebellion was raised in the eastern provinces by a Kurdish tribal and religious leader, Sheikh Saiyid of Palu. The insurrection was rapidly suppressed in draconian fashion, and Atatürk and İsmet seized the opportunity to close down the Progressive Party and muzzle all potential opposition. An attempt on Atatürk's life in İzmir in 1926 produced another round of arrests and executions. Henceforth, and with only a brief interlude of limited pluralism in 1930, Turkey was run as a single-party state until 1945.[32]

For Atatürk and his supporters, the constantly repeated objective was to raise Turkey to the 'level of contemporary civilisation', and to reinforce the power of the state and its rulers. State power, both internally and externally, was the central focus of their concern. In foreign policy, their primary aim was to see their country recognised as a respected European power, and to safeguard the hard-won security which they had achieved in 1923. This had left them in a position of greater relative strength than their Ottoman predecessors had enjoyed, since they did not try to rule over territories which they could not defend, and because Turkey now had virtually no non-Muslim minorities, which foreign powers could exploit to undermine its territorial integrity. They were also aided by the external environment, since Russia, the traditional enemy, was too isolated, and too convulsed by internal upheavals, to represent a serious threat to Turkish security until the end of the 1930s. Instead, it had actually been converted into a friend. Unlike the other defeated states of the First World War, Turkey had reversed the defeat of 1918 by 1923, and thus acted as a generally conservative and anti-revisionist, rather than revisionist force in European politics.

Between 1923 and 1926 the main item on Turkey's foreign policy agenda was the Mosul dispute with Britain, the principal piece of unfinished business left over from the Lausanne conference. For the Turks, giving the province to Iraq could be seen as a failure to achieve part of the objectives of the National Pact. On the other side, the British believed that the state of Iraq would not be viable, either militarily or economically, without Mosul, thanks to its important strategic position and expected oil resources. The Kurds were the biggest single ethnic group in the province, accounting for an estimated three-quarters of the population, but the city of Mosul itself was Arab, and there was also a substantial Turkish-speaking (or 'Turcoman') minority. Hence, neither Britain or Turkey had a strong moral case in ethnic terms. Nor was the idea of an independent Kurdish state a realistic option, given the political and economic circumstances of the time.

In accordance with their undertakings at Lausanne, Britain and Turkey engaged in bilateral negotiations during May–June 1924, but these failed to make any progress, and in August 1924 Britain referred the question to the League of Nations, of which Turkey was not a member. In the following month, the Council of the League decided to establish a commission of enquiry, to investigate the position on the ground. Not surprisingly, the commission failed to find a clear-cut case for an award to either Turkey or Iraq, but it rejected the idea that most of the local population preferred Turkey. Hence, its report, issued in July 1925, awarded the province to Iraq. The British government accepted this decision, but it was predictably opposed by Turkey, which questioned its assumptions and opposed the Council's right of jurisdiction. This led to a referral to the Permanent Court of International Justice, which on 21 November 1925 decided that a decision by the Council would be binding on both parties. On 16 December, the Council then made a unanimous decision in favour of Iraq. For a time there was speculation that Turkey might defy the League and all the main Western powers on this issue, fuelled by the fact that in December 1925 it signed a new Treaty of Neutrality and Friendship with the Soviet Union. The British prepared plans to blockade the Dardanelles, though they were reluctant to resort to force. On the other side, the battle-weary Turks were ultimately not prepared to go to war over Mosul, after their years of struggle, as Atatürk had predicted in 1922. Hence, after bilateral negotiations were re-opened in Ankara in April 1926, they accepted the League's decision, subject to a face-saving formula under which Turkey was to receive 10 per cent of the oil royalties payable in the Mosul province for the next 25 years.[33] The agreement was formalised in a treaty signed in Ankara on 5 June 1926. The settlement did not bring about an instant friendship between Turkey and Britain – memories of the wars of 1914–18 and of 1920–22 were too recent and bitter for that – but it did at least prepare the ground for a *rapprochement* with Britain and the other Western powers.[34]

Its relations with Greece were Turkey's other main foreign policy concern during the late 1920s. The population exchanges created complicated disputes over the disposition of properties left in each country by the emigrants, and these were only partially settled by an agreement reached between the two governments in 1926. The expulsion of the Ecumenical Patriarch Constantine by the Turkish authorities at the end of 1924 provoked further ill-will on both sides, which was only defused when Constantine was succeeded by Patriarch Basil Georgiadis in May 1925. This allowed normal diplomatic relations, and the exchange of ambassadors, to begin in the summer of that year. The dispute over properties continued until 1929, by which stage it even appeared that the two countries might resort to force to settle the issue. However, in February 1930, Eleutherios Venizelos, who had now returned to the premiership in Greece, launched an unexpected initiative, telling the Greek parliament that he believed that Turkey was a peace-loving country, which would not attack Greece. The Turkish government rapidly reciprocated, paving the way for another agreement, signed in June 1930, in which the dispute over properties was finally settled. At İsmet İnönü's invitation, the Greek premier, Turkey's former arch-enemy, visited Ankara and Istanbul in October 1930, to an enthusiastic public reception. On 30 October the two countries signed a Treaty of Friendship, Neutrality, Mediation and Arbitration, together with commercial and other agreements. The reconciliation was completed by a return visit by İnönü to Athens in October 1931, and effectively continued up to the time of the outbreak of the Cyprus dispute in the mid-1950s. It is frequently cited in Turkey as an example of what could be achieved again in Greek–Turkish relations, given the right circumstances.[35]

The *rapprochement* with Greece was part of a general shift in Turkish foreign policy, in which Turkey sought to steer itself back into a position of equality and cooperation with the main Western powers, without breaking its links with Moscow. The most conspicuous evidence of this was its decision to join the League of Nations in 1932. As one of the defeated powers, Turkey had been left out of the League when it had been founded

in 1919. During the Mosul dispute it had continued to view the organisation with grave suspicion, as a body controlled by the imperialist powers,
primarily Britain and France. This view was reinforced by Turkey's links
with Soviet Russia, which took a similar view until the 1930s. Under a
protocol of 1929 which renewed the Turkish–Soviet treaty of 1925, both
sides had pledged not to acccpt any undertakings to third parties without
obtaining approval from the other. By 1931, the Turks had changed their
position, seeing membership of the League as a necessary step to restoring
their relations with the Western powers. Hence, when they accepted an
invitation to join the organisation in 1932, they were careful to obtain
Soviet approval and informed the Soviet government that they would not
allow their obligations to the League to damage their relations with the
Soviet Union, assuming the latter did not attack a third state.[36] The
position was naturally eased in 1934 when the Soviet Union itself joined
the League. Henceforth, Turkey was a strong supporter of its principles.
As the foreign minister, Tevfik Rüştü Aras, told the British ambassador,
Sir Percy Loraine, in 1935, 'the integral maintenance of the covenant of
the League' was the foundation of Turkey's foreign policy.[37] More
practically, Turkey was an outspoken advocate of sanctions against Italy,
after Mussolini invaded Ethiopia in 1935. Unfortunately, however, the
Turks turned out to have joined the League at the point when it lost what
little power it had ever had, marked by the withdrawal from the League of
Germany and Japan in 1933 and Italy in 1935. In attempting to preserve
peace, Turkey, like other nations, had to look for alternative forms of
security.[38]

As Europe moved towards war during the 1930s, the main focus of
Turkey's security concerns lay in the Balkans – the traditional zone of
danger for the Ottoman empire – and the Mediterranean. With the
removal of the threat from Russia, Italy initially emerged as the most
powerful potential enemy, followed later by Germany. As in the past, the
danger from the Balkans was complicated by internecine disputes between
the Balkan states themselves, and their individual weakness. Turkey's
relationship with Italy was also an unstable one. During the 1920s, in spite
of the Italian annexation of the Dodecanese, Italian approaches to Ankara
appeared to be friendly, and there was no immediate reason to rebuff
them. Hence, in 1928, Turkey signed a Treaty of Neutrality, Mediation
and Judicial Settlement with Mussolini's government. This acted as a
model for the similar treaty signed with Greece in 1930, which was
encouraged by Rome, as part of an eastern Mediterranean alliance which
would protect Italy's flank in its contest with Yugoslavia over Albania. The

treaty with Italy was renewed in 1932.[39] Apparently, it was not until 1933–34 that the tables clearly turned, and Italy began to be seen as a potential threat to Turkey as well as most of the Balkan states.

Turkish policy was also affected by divisions within the Balkans at this time. On the one hand, Greece, Yugoslavia and Romania, which had been on the winning side in the First World War and gained territory from it, took a pro-status quo, or anti-revisionist position, while on the other Bulgaria and Hungary, which had lost it, were in the revisionist camp. Italy had also been on the winning side, but was at odds with Yugoslavia, and hence a leading revisionist. In the military sphere, thanks to the demilitarisation of the straits and the Thracian border under the treaty of Lausanne, Turkey was at a serious disadvantage in seeking to defend its western frontier against an attack by Greece or Bulgaria, especially if the two states combined, or were supported by Italy. Hence, a major objective of Turkish policy was to form an entente with at least one, or preferably both of its two Balkan neighbours. More broadly, Turkey wished to keep war out of the Balkans, to prevent the Balkan states from squabbling among themselves and, as Loraine put it, to 'deprive [the] Balkans of their former character of a kind of Tom Tiddle's ground for the ambitions of great powers'.[40]

Although it does not seem to have been originally envisaged as an anti-Italian alliance, the *rapprochement* with Greece was a first step towards the realisation of this strategy. It was extended in September 1933 by what was called an 'Entente Cordiale' under which Greece and Turkey mutually guaranteed their common frontier in Thrace and agreed to consult with one another on all questions of common interest. In its wake, Turkey signed separate non-aggression pacts with Romania and Yugoslavia. Meanwhile, a series of four conferences was held of all the Balkan states between October 1930 and November 1933. This resulted in the conclusion of the Balkan Pact between Greece, Romania, Turkey and Yugoslavia in February–March 1934. Under the pact, the four states agreed that in the event of aggression against any of them, they would each guarantee the frontiers of the signatory state against the aggressor, and would consult with one another in the event of any threat to peace in the region. The pact was a notable achievement, but it still fell far short of the original objectives of Turkish policy which, according to Aras, included the idea of a much broader pact under which Britain, France, Italy, the Balkan states and the Soviet Union would all bind themselves together for mutual assistance. More specifically, the exclusion of Bulgaria was a serious disadvantage from the Turkish viewpoint. Turkish diplomacy had put considerable effort into trying to bring in the Bulgarians, but Bulgaria was unwilling to drop its territorial claims in Macedonia (against Yugoslavia) or western Thrace (against Greece). Hence, the pact still left Turkey vulnerable to an attack by Bulgaria, possibly supported by Mussolini. Greece also insisted that its commitments under the Pact should not involve it in a war against Italy. This reservation was accepted, together with the general provision that none of the signatories were under an obligation to assist if one of them were attacked by Italy alone. Ironically, this was just the situation which eventually arose when Italy attacked Greece in 1940.[41] During the late 1930s, the Balkan pact became even weaker, as Yugoslavia and Romania drifted into the German orbit. Nor did it suffice to deflate Italian ambitions – indeed, Mussolini's most overt threats against Turkey came just afterwards, in March 1934, when he told the Fascist Congress that Italy's 'historical ambitions' lay in Asia and Africa, and later in 1934–36, when he refortified the Dodecanese.[42] Needless to say, both these moves were seen by Turkey as a threat, and provoked a sharp reaction, but still left it with the task of finding a credible way of deterring Italy.

In July 1937 the Turks extended the principle of regional security pacts eastward, when Iraq, Iran, Turkey and Afghanistan concluded the Saadabad Pact, named after the Shah's palace near Tehran where the document was signed. This obliged the four states to preserve their common frontiers, not to interfere in one another's internal affairs, to commit no aggression against one another's territory, and to consult together on all matters of common interest. The pact followed a separate frontier agreement between Iran and Turkey, signed in 1932. The Saadabad agreement was primarily a means of preventing frontier disputes between the four states and, for instance, a way of ensuring that neither Iran or Iraq would give any sustenance to Kurdish rebels on Turkish territory or vice versa.[43] It was also intended to be a signal to the rest of the world that the four independent Middle Eastern states would oppose any attempts by one of the European powers to pick them off individually, as Ethiopia had been. However, as Aras pointed out to the Grand National Assembly, it contained no provisions for mutual assistance or military commitments, and had mainly psychological value.[44] Hence, it gave none of the signatories any sure protection against external aggression, quite apart from the fact that they were mostly too weak and geographically dispersed to mount an effective mutual defence.

This brought the Turkish policy-makers back to the problem of increasing their country's security in a worsening international situation.

According to one frequently repeated account, Atatürk had a conversation with the US General, Douglas MacArthur, in 1932 in which Kemal predicted that Germany would start another war between 1940 and 1946, that the United States would be drawn in and Germany would be destroyed, leaving the Soviet Union as the dominant power in Europe, and the United States and Soviet Union as the only real great powers. Unfortunately, there are no contemporary accounts of this conversation, putting the authenticity of the story in grave doubt.[45] However, it is quite clear that by the mid-1930s Atatürk and his colleagues had real anxieties about the ambitions of Italy, and later Germany, as well as the lack of effective collective security arrangements between the other European powers. Until the autumn of 1939, the Turkish government seems to have assumed that its good relations with the USSR would give it security to the north, but this still left it vulnerable to an attack from the Balkans, or in the Mediterranean by Italy. To achieve greater security, Turkey had to achieve three objectives: first, to strengthen its military position in Thrace and the Dardanelles by removing the demilitarisation restrictions contained in the Lausanne treaty, second to build up and modernise its armed forces, and third to reach an accommodation and, if possible, a defensive alliance with Britain and France while preserving the entente with Moscow. Good relations with France and Britain were also essential to achieve the first two objectives. If Germany were to start another war, then Turkey must above all prevent itself from falling into the trap of 1914.[46] As Aras explained to the British Foreign Secretary, Anthony Eden, in 1937, 'England was not merely a power, but a world power: she was ubiquitous: her interests lay everywhere'. If Britain entered the war, then Aras thought that it would defeat Germany – if not by itself, then with the help of the United States.[47] This time, Turkey had to make sure that if it could not stay out of the war, then it was at least on the winning side.

Of the three objectives, the first one turned out to be the easiest to realise. By late 1935 the British, as the principal architects of the straits regime of 1923, had come round to the realisation that the benefits of allowing the Turks to remilitarise the straits outweighed the losses. Demilitarisation reduced Turkey's capacity to defend itself against Italy, and was resented in Turkey as a restriction on the state's territorial sovereignty. On the latter score, the Turks had begun to raise the question of remilitarisation in 1932, before the threat from Italy became clear. The British also realised that, in the last resort, the Turks might decide to remilitarise by unilateral action rather than international agreement, as Germany was to do in the case of the Rhineland in March 1936. Given a

choice, the Turks preferred international agreement to an illegal remilitarisation. Accordingly, an international conference of all the Lausanne
signatories, with the exception of Italy which refused the invitation, was
convened at Montreux in Switzerland on 22 June 1936. On 20 July a new
'Convention Regarding the Regime of the Straits' was signed. The main
objections to the new arrangements came from the Soviet Union, which
was prepared to accept remilitarisation by Turkey, but which wanted to
secure free passage through the straits for Black Sea powers while closing
them to other navies. In the event, it accepted a compromise under which
Black Sea states were allowed to send warships into the Mediterranean in
peacetime, subject to some tonnage restrictions affecting 'capital ships'
which were defined as excluding aircraft carriers. Ships defined as 'light
surface vessels, minor war vessels and auxiliary vessels' (in effect, warships
of under 10,000 tons) whether of Black Sea or non-Black Sea powers, were
granted free passage in peacetime.[48] Non-Black Sea states could send warships into the Black Sea to a maximum aggregate tonnage of 30,000 tons,
or 45,000 tons if the fleet of the strongest Black Sea navy grew by 10,000
tons. In time of war, if Turkey were neutral, then warships of belligerents
would not be allowed to pass in either direction. If Turkey were at war, or
under threat of war, then it could close the straits to warships at its own dis-
cretion.[49] A clause which was not contested in principle at the time, but
which turned out to be of critical importance by the 1990s, was the provision in Article 2 of the Convention that all merchant ships, whatever
their flag or cargo, would enjoy complete freedom of navigation through
the straits in peacetime. Most importantly from the Turkish viewpoint,
Turkey regained the right to remilitarise the straits, and the previous international control commission was wound up.[50]

Between 1933 and 1937, it appears that Turkey saw its main potential
enemy as Italy, but by 1938 its principal concern became the threat from
Germany, the watershed being Hitler's takeover of Austria in March of
that year. So long as Italy was seen as the only real threat, then the Turkish
defence forces expected to deal with it on their own and with existing
resources, by concentrating on coastal defences which could prevent a
landing on the western coast of Turkey or the Aegean islands.[51] With
the emergence of the danger of a German attack from the Balkans, the
priority switched to the north-western land frontier with Bulgaria, but
Turkey's existing armed forces were inadequate to deal with this threat,
especially if offensive operations were considered. For most of the inter-
war period, the government had deliberately sacrificed guns for butter, by
concentrating its resources on developing the civilian economy, most

notably through the first five-year industrialisation plan launched in 1934. In 1938 the government increased the proportion of budget expenditure devoted to defence to around 44 per cent, from a low point of 23 per cent in 1932–33, but this still left the armed forces woefully short of modern equipment. In the same year, the total strength of the army was around 195,000 officers and men, but they were mainly armed with the weapons of the First World War. The army had very few tanks or armoured cars, and was still reliant on horses or mules for transport. As of 1937, the air force had just 131 front-line aircraft, of which only half were relatively modern, and the biggest ship in the fleet was still the cruiser *Yavuz*, formerly *Goeben* – Germany's fatal gift of 1914.[52]

By 1938, the Turks were seeking to increase their naval forces to float two new squadrons, to acquire 200–300 new front-line aircraft, and enough modern ordinance to arm ten new divisions. It was clear that it would be impossible to achieve this without foreign assistance. Accordingly, Turkey obtained an armaments credit from the British worth £6 million in May 1938, followed by a further credit worth £25 million in October 1939.[53] In the economic sphere, Britain and Germany engaged in competitive aid-giving during 1938, as Britain extended a trade credit of £10 million, matched by a loan of 150 million Reichsmarks from Germany. However, the Turks turned down a tentative offer of a neutrality treaty from Berlin and decided not to purchase any more arms from Germany, hitherto an important supplier, as from 1939. Unfortunately, little of the promised assistance from Britain and France arrived, thanks to British inability, and French reluctance, to part with it. In all this it appears that, far from Britain and France trying to push Turkey into war, the initiative came primarily from the Turkish side. In fact, Turkey acted as the suitor, with the British and French the reluctant *fiancées*.[54]

Amidst all these concerns, the death of Atatürk in November 1938 produced no perceptible change in Turkish foreign policies, as İsmet İnönü succeeded smoothly to the presidency, with Şükrü Saracoğlu succeeding Aras as his foreign minister. Like Atatürk, İnönü took a keen interest in foreign affairs, was well informed on the subject and was in close control of foreign policy throughout his period as president, which lasted until 1950. His most important objective was to secure a defensive alliance with Britain and France, without breaking Turkey's entente with the Soviet Union. Essentially, he believed that defence of the Balkans rested on co-operation with the Soviet Union, and that of the Mediterranean with the British and French. However, attempts at forging a mutual security pact with the Soviet Union, which had begun during the Montreux negotiations in June 1936, had produced no tangible result.[55] The British were also wary of the idea of an alliance. Sir Percy Loraine, as ambassador between 1934 and 1939, won credit for Britain's *rapprochement* with Turkey thanks to a personal friendship with Atatürk, but he supported the policy of negotiating with Hitler and Mussolini rather than fighting them. Atatürk was apparently unconvinced: after Italy's invasion of Ethiopia in 1935–36 he warned Loraine that if the invasion were legalised, Mussolini would go on to further adventures.[56] British and French policy remained essentially unchanged at the end of March 1939 when Aras, now the Turkish ambassador in London, proposed a non-aggression treaty between Poland, Romania, the Soviet Union and Turkey, in which all the parties would combine against any party contravening it, backed up by a British guarantee. Turkey, Yugoslavia and Greece could also accede to the Anglo-Italian agreement of 1938 providing for a common policy in the Mediterranean. However, Poland and Romania were unwilling to co-operate against Germany, and the British turned down Aras' proposal. Hitler's occupation of Czechoslovakia on 15 March and the Italian invasion of Albania on 7 April then caused a delayed reaction in London, as the prime minister, Neville Chamberlain, belatedly realised that Germany and Italy would have to be resisted, if necessary by war. On 12 April the British hastily offered Turkey the treaty of mutual assistance they had turned down less that two weeks earlier, and gave guarantees of their security to Greece and Romania on the following day. After negotiations, a joint Anglo-Turkish declaration was issued on 12 May. This announced that 'pending a definite long-term agreement of a reciprocal character' and 'in the event of an act of aggression leading to war in the Mediterranean area' the two sides would give each other 'all aid and assistance in their power'.[57]

The Anglo-Turkish declaration left the Turkish government with two urgent diplomatic tasks: first, to develop it into a definite alliance including France, and second to integrate it with their commitments to and expectations from the Soviet Union. The main obstacle to building France into the prospective alliance was a continuing dispute between the Turks and French over the province of Alexandretta (Hatay) which was attached to French-ruled Syria up to 1939. As in the case of Mosul, there was no available solution to this which would have been fair to all sides on ethnic grounds. In the mid-1930s, the province's population of 220,000 included no less than five different linguistic groups, belonging to 16 different religious denominations, of which Muslim Turks accounted for about 38–39 per cent, followed by Alawi and Ismaili Arabs (28 per cent) Sunni

Arabs (10 per cent) and other groups, mainly Arab and Armenian Christians accounting for the remaining 23–24 per cent.[58] As part of the Franklin–Bouillon pact, Turkey had accepted the attachment of the province to Syria in 1921, subject to its administrative autonomy and the protection of the cultural rights of the Turkish community. This arrangement was confirmed by the Lausanne treaty. Both the Ankara government and the local inhabitants seem to have been quite satisfied with this until 1936. However, in September of that year the French government and Syrian nationalists initialled a treaty which would, if implemented, have given Syria independence by 1939,[59] causing the Turks to launch a vociferous campaign for incorporation of the province into Turkey. To put it crudely, it appears that the Turks had trusted the French to rule the province fairly, but did not trust a prospective Arab–Syrian government. In 1938 local assembly elections produced a narrow majority in favour of retaining the status quo, but these results were ignored by the French authorities, who in July allowed Turkish troops to enter the province for joint patrols with the French. New elections were then held producing a pro-Turkish majority, and in September the local assembly declared a sovereign 'Republic of Hatay'. This paved the way for its incorporation into Turkey, and last minute disagreements between Turkey and France prevented an accord on this just before the Anglo-Turkish declaration was signed. The problems were then overcome. On 23 June 1939 France and Turkey agreed to the legal cession of Alexandretta, and issued a joint declaration identical to that between Britain and Turkey of 12 May, removing the obstacle to French participation in the prospective Anglo-Turkish alliance. The transfer was contrary to France's undertakings to the League of Nations, since Article 4 of the mandate under which it ruled Syria stipulated that it could not cede Syrian territory to any 'foreign Power', and the League never gave its formal consent to the cession. While the result was important to France in the context of its broader international objectives, it also created a lasting source of bitterness between Turkey and the independent Syrian state after the Second World War.[60]

During the following months, the British, French and Turkish governments engaged in intense negotiations over the political, military and economic terms of a proposed tripartite treaty. According to one account, the Turks initially tried to develop the pact into an offensive engagement against Italy, rather than a purely defensive one, and proposed that Britain and France should declare war on Italy first and invade Italian territory with Turkish military help. These proposals alarmed the British and French, and the eventual treaty had a purely defensive character.[61] Meanwhile the German–Turkish relationship was naturally tense. The Anglo-Turkish declaration of May 1939 had come as a surprise to the Germans, and Franz von Papen, the German ambassador in Ankara since April 1939, tried unsuccessfully to prevent its development into a formal alliance. Von Papen came to Ankara with a considerable though far from creditable reputation, since he had served in Turkey as an army officer during the First World War, had helped Hitler come to power during his period as Chancellor in 1932 and, as German ambassador in Vienna, had then paved the way for the Nazi takeover of Austria in 1938. His British opposite number was Sir Hughe Knatchbull-Hugessen, who had succeeded Loraine as British ambassador in February 1939. Von Papen's long-term goal was to convert the German–Italian axis into a triangular one, with Turkey as its third point, but to do this he first had to detach Turkey from the prospective Anglo-French alliance. His project failed at the first hurdle, since he could not overcome Turkish suspicions of Italy, which had naturally been sharpened by Mussolini's invasion of Albania. Although von Papen had apparently persuaded Berlin to soften its reaction to the Anglo-Turkish declaration, he protested strongly to Saracoğlu after the eventual signature of the tripartite treaty, on Ribbentrop's instructions. Similarly, in Berlin, Ribbentrop warned the Turkish ambassador Hüsrev Gerede that Turkey might suffer the same fate as Poland if it challenged Germany.[62]

In spite of the Turks' differences with the British and French, and objections from Germany, agreement in principal was reached on a draft treaty between Turkey, Britain and France on 1 September 1939. This assured Turkey of Anglo-French assistance if it were attacked by any European power, in return for Turkish assistance to the other two parties if they were involved in a war in the Mediterranean resulting from an act of aggression by any European power (read Italy) or if Britain and France found themselves at war as a result of their guarantees to Greece and Romania. Signature of the final treaty was then delayed until the Turks could reach a comparable agreement with the Soviet Union. Discussions on this between Ankara and Moscow had in fact been proceeding for some time. During April–May 1939 the two sides had talks on a possible Black Sea security pact, but these failed due to the reluctance of Bulgaria and Romania to enter such an arrangement, and the lack of enthusiasm shown by the British. The dialogue was re-launched by the Soviet government at the beginning of August, but the situation was then transformed by the signature of the Nazi–Soviet non-aggression pact on 23 August, which caused a sharp and hostile reaction in Turkey. The pact had a profound effect on the Turkish position, since the Turks had previously expected that the Soviet Union could be brought into a defensive alliance against Germany. Hitler also expected that his pact with Stalin would frighten the Turks into cancelling the Anglo-Turkish and Franco-Turkish declarations, and now put pressure on Moscow to reject a Turkish–Soviet pact, or at least to ensure that if such a pact were signed, then Turkey be detached from the Western powers.[63]

On 25 September 1939 – just over three weeks after Germany invaded Poland and thus started the Second World War – Foreign Minister Saracoğlu arrived in Moscow, but found it impossible to bridge the gap between Turkey's new friendship with the West and its previous one with the Soviets. Under German pressure, Stalin and Molotov insisted on a series of modifications to the proposed Turkish–British–French treaty, culminating in the demand for the exclusion of Turkish aid to the Balkans in the case of German aggression, and the closure of the straits, both of which Saracoğlu rejected. On 17 October, İnönü telephoned the British and French ambassadors in Ankara to tell them that the talks in Moscow had broken down, and that the tripartite treaty should be concluded immediately.[64] The final document, which was signed on 19 October, was on the lines agreed to before the failure in Moscow. Under Article 1 of the treaty, Britain and France pledged to give 'all aid and assistance' to Turkey if it were attacked by another European power. A reciprocal obligation was assumed by Turkey 'in the event of an act of aggression by a European Power leading to a war in the Mediterranean area in which France and the United Kingdom are involved', or if France and Britain were involved in war as a result of their guarantees to Greece and Romania (Articles 2 and 3). Although the Turks had failed to reach a security agreement with the Soviet Union, they were still anxious to avoid war with the Soviets. Accordingly, they secured a protocol to the effect that none of their obligations under the treaty would compel them to enter into a war against the Soviet Union. An additional secret agreement provided for credit of £25 million to Turkey to buy war materials, and an additional loan of £15 million in gold, repayable in Turkish commodities. Turkey was not obliged to fulfil its obligations under the treaty until all the war materials currently on order, as well as new orders to be covered by the gold loan, had been delivered. The attached Military Convention also provided that if Italy joined the war there would be a joint attack on the Italians in the Dodecanese, as soon as local command of the air and sea could be achieved, for which air bases would be constructed in Turkey. The Turks would also hold Bulgaria in check if it entered the war. Allied troops would be allowed to travel through Turkish territory, and Turkey would co-operate in the construction of whatever infrastructure was required. On all these points, the Turks had driven a hard bargain, but at this stage they seem to have been quite prepared to carry out their obligations under the treaty, should the circumstances it envisaged arise. The Turkish press, which normally reflected official thinking, blamed Germany (and, indirectly, the Nazi–Soviet pact) for the outbreak of the war but still speculated that Italy and the Soviet Union might stay out of it. Turkish diplomacy had failed to realise its optimum programme, but at the time Turkey still seemed to be strongly placed, at least on paper and with existing military assumptions.[65]

TURKISH DIPLOMACY, 1919–39: SOME SUMMARY ASSESSMENTS

Turkey's foreign policy between the two world wars can clearly be divided into two phases, with the treaty of Lausanne of 1923 marking the dividing line. During the first phase, the gradual territorial attrition of the late Ottoman empire reached its ultimate stage, as the victorious powers prepared to partition even the Turkish and Kurdish-inhabited heartland of the old empire. In the last resort, the survival of the Turkish state depended on effective military resistance and political leadership, of which the Turkish people provided the first, and Atatürk and his colleagues the second. Without this, diplomacy would have been pointless. With it, diplomacy still helped to win the eventual victory. Essentially, Turkish foreign policy-makers, like their Ottoman predecessors, exploited the balance of power and the divisions among their opponents, besides a measure of good luck. The main difference from Ottoman days was that the new Turkish state was far more internally homogeneous than the empire had been, and that its rulers set themselves limited and achievable goals. France and Italy were reluctant to back up their territorial claims with concerted or sustained military action, and were effectively detached from the hostile coalition by 1921. The United States, which might have provided protection to an independent Armenia or Kurdistan on Turkish soil, virtually dropped out of international politics after the end of 1920. For their part, the Greeks over-reached themselves, deluded by misperceptions of their own strength, and the durability and effectiveness of British support. Hence, they refused to negotiate effectively until it was too late. Both domestically and internationally, Lloyd George had gone out on a limb in giving full support to the Greeks, especially after the turning point in the

Greek–Turkish war marked by the battle of Sakarya in August 1921. His successors in government, most of whom had never fully supported his pro-Greek policy anyway, were prepared to accept the *fait accompli*, given that Britain and France were still left as the dominant powers in the Middle East, with its rich resources and strategic value. The last outcome also had the fortunate effect for Turkey of virtually removing the Middle East from its list of foreign policy concerns until 1941.

The Soviet position was also crucial in this new balance of power, even though German power had been temporarily destroyed, and the Habsburg empire removed. By the beginning of 1921, the Soviet Union was ravaged by years of war, and internationally isolated. Nonetheless, contrary to Western hopes and expectations, the Soviet government had established control over most of the old Tsarist empire. The Soviet Union was still there as a force to be reckoned with, even if the Western powers were reluctant to recognise it. The result was that the Turks could reverse the position of most of the nineteenth century, in which Russia had been the main potential enemy. The 1920s and 1930s were the first prolonged period in which they had an entente rather than confrontation with Russia since the treaty of Hünkâr İskelesi of 1833. It also depended on a change of policy by the Soviets, when they decided to jettison the idea of sponsoring a communist revolution in Turkey early in 1921. Equally, the fact that they were anti-communist did not prevent the Turkish leaders from building up a useful business relationship with the Soviet Union. The Kemalist regime was also pro-Western, in the sense that it was committed to re-establishing Turkey as a Western-style, secular state, but this was no reason for constructing an international alliance with the Western powers, unless national security required it. As usual, ideology was much less important than power politics in the formation of foreign policy.

After 1923, and until the mid-1930s, foreign relations took a back seat, as internal reconstruction and reform became the Turkish government's main priority, and the international situation did not seem threatening. For Turkish diplomacy, the main items on the agenda were problems left over from the Lausanne conference. Territorially, the Mosul settlement of 1926 was seen as a loss for the Turks, but the attachment of Mosul to Turkey would probably have brought Ankara more problems than advantages. If Turkey had won sovereignty over Mosul, then it would have had to co-exist with a far bigger Kurdish population, inhabiting a remote and mountainous country. Maintaining Turkish rule over Mosul would have been quite inconsistent with Turkish ethnic nationalism. Moreover, since the Iraqis regarded Mosul as a legitimate part of their territory, it would have created constant frictions with the independent state of Iraq. These problems would almost certainly have outweighed the value of controlling the Kirkuk oilfields. The most important benefit of the agreement at the time was that it paved the way towards a better relationship with Britain. The Turkish decision not to go to war over Mosul also demonstrated Turkey's realistic recognition of its own limitations.

The *rapprochement* with Greece was slower in coming, but when it came it was quite dramatic and effective. So far as one can judge, the Greek–Turkish treaty of 1930 derived mainly from an independent decision to bury the hatchet by both countries, rather than as a direct result of their relations with the rest of the world. Nonetheless, it contributed to a better relationship between Turkey and the Western powers, symbolised by Turkey's accession to the League of Nations in 1932. The shift was rendered more important with the emergence of the apparent Italian threat in 1933. This faced Turkey with essentially the same range of options as those confronting Ottoman policy-makers in the nineteenth century. Turkey could either stay out of alliances, relying on the balance of power to maintain security, or it could actively seek an alliance with one the main European powers, or a coalition of them. For a time, the Turks sought to delay the decision, by constructing a security pact with the Balkan states which, they unrealistically hoped, might be joined by Britain, France and the Soviet Union. In principle, the resulting Balkan pact of 1934 was a worthy project, but it eventually failed, partly because of its technical weaknesses, and partly because none of the Balkan states except Greece was ultimately prepared to stand up to the Axis.

Meanwhile, the restoration of Germany's international strength and ambitions had produced a far more serious threat, which was clearly recognised by the Turks by 1938, if not before. Atatürk scorned Mussolini, and according to one account he heartily disliked Hitler, but the Turks had a healthy appreciation of Germany's military and economic power and realised that they needed security arrangements with the other European powers to meet it.[66] At no time during the 1930s did Turkey seriously consider a security pact with rather than against Germany, its former ally of the great war: in fact both Atatürk and İnönü strongly criticised the alliance of 1914–18 which, they argued, had subordinated Turkish to German interests.[67] The alternative was an alliance with Britain and France which, the Turks hoped, could be combined with an effective security pact with the Soviet Union. The forging of such an alliance was delayed until the last months before the Second World War, partly because of the dispute with France over Alexandretta, but more importantly because Britain rejected the idea until after the German invasion of Czechoslovakia in March 1939. The resultant alliance between Britain, France and Turkey appeared to be favourable to Turkey, though it was severely weakened by the Nazi–Soviet pact, and hence the non-adherence of the Soviet Union. In this respect, Turkish diplomacy had failed, defeated by the cynical tactics of the dictators. The need to expand and modernise Turkey's armed forces had also been unmet by 1939. With these exceptions, Turkish diplomacy seemed to have played a successful game, from what must have seemed a hopeless start.

NOTES

1. Strictly speaking, Mustafa Kemal did not become 'Kemal Atatürk' until 1934, when the adoption of surnames became compulsory in Turkey. When referring to events before 1934, other personalities are referred to by their first names, with their later surnames in brackets.
2. For the text of the treaty of Sèvres and the attached agreement between Britain, France and Italy, see J.C. Hurewitz, ed., *Diplomacy in the Near and Middle East: A Documentary Record, 1914–1956* (Princeton, NJ, Van Nostrand, 1956), Vol. 2, pp. 81–9. For a full description of these and subsequent events from the Greek side, see Michael Llewellyn Smith, *Ionian Vision: Greece in Asia Minor, 1919–1922* (2nd edn, London, Hurst, 1998).
3. That is, the secret treaty of London of April 1915 and the St Jean de Maurienne agreement of April 1917: for texts, see Hurewitz, ed., *Diplomacy*, Vol. 2, pp. 11–12, 23–5. Technically, the St Jean de Maurienne agreement had lapsed after 1917, since it had never been ratified by Russia, but Italy was reluctant to abandon its claims under the London agreement. For details of the negotiations between the entente powers over the future of Turkey between 1918 and 1920, see Harry N. Howard, *The Partition of Turkey: A Diplomatic History, 1913–1923* (New York, NY, Fertig, 1966), pp. 217–41.
4. Quotation from Atatürk's 'Great Speech' (*Büyük Nutukin*, effectively, his memoirs). *Speech Delivered by Ghazi Mustapha Kemal, President of the Turkish Republic, October 1927* (Leipzig, K.F. Koehler, 1929), p. 58.
5. Roderic H. Davison, 'Turkish Diplomacy from Mudros to Lausanne', in Gordon A. Craig and Felix Gilbert, eds, *The Diplomats, 1919–1939* (New York, NY, Atheneum, 1974), Vol. 1, p. 179.
6. From Article 1 of the National Pact. Turkish text in A. Suat Bilge *et al.*, *Olaylarla Türk Dış Politikası* (Ankara University, Political Science Faculty, 1969), pp. 13–14: English translation in Hurewitz, ed., *Diplomacy*, Vol. 2, pp. 74–75. Other provisions of the National Pact made it clear that Istanbul would be included in the national territory, but accepted the idea of a plebiscite in western Thrace (Articles 4 and 5) and effectively demanded the abolition of the capitulations (Article 6: see above p. 14). The capitulations had been officially abolished by the Young Turk government in October 1914, but this had not been accepted by the entente governments.
7. Bülent Gökay, *A Clash of Empires: Turkey between Russian Bolshevism and British Imperialism, 1918–1923* (London, I.B. Tauris, 1997), pp. 77–8.

8. A note added to the declaration stated that 'as soon as the Sultan–Caliph is delivered from all pressure and coercion he will take his place within the frame of the legislative principles which will be determined by the Assembly': text in Atatürk's 'Great Speech' (see note 4 above), p. 380. For a valuable summary of these events, see Erik J. Zürcher, *Turkey, A Modern History* (London, I.B. Tauris, 1993), pp. 142–58.

9. Kemal Girgin, *Osmanlı ve Cumhuriyet Dönemleri Hariciye Tarihimiz (Teşkilat ve Protokol)* (Ankara, Türk Tarih Kurumu, 1992), pp. 118–23.

10. M.S. Anderson, *The Eastern Question, 1774–1923: A Study in International Relations* (London, Macmillan, 1966), p. 368.

11. Marian Kent, 'British Policy, International Diplomacy and the Turkish Revolution', *International Journal of Turkish Studies*, Vol. 3 (1985–86), pp. 33–8.

12. Gökay, *Clash of Empires*, pp. 52–60.

13. Quoted in Jacob M. Landau, *Pan-Turkism: From Irredentism to Cooperation* (London, Hurst, 1995), p. 74.

14. This territory had been ceded by the Ottoman empire to Russia under the treaty of Berlin of 1878, but evacuated by Russia under the Brest–Litovsk treaty between the Bolsheviks and the central powers of March 1918. The Turks, in turn, had evacuated it eight months later under the terms of the Mudros armistice, and it had since been occupied by Armenia.

15. Salahi Ransdan Sonyel, *Turkish Diplomacy, 1913–1923: Mustafa Kemal and the Turkish National Movement* (London and Beverly Hills, CA, Sage, 1975), pp. 48–65; Gökay, *Clash of Empires*, pp. 85–112; Bülent Gökay, 'Turkish Settlement and the Caucasus, 1918–20', in Sylvia Kedourie, ed., *Turkey; Identity, Democracy, Politics* (London and Portland, OR, Cass, 1996), pp. 45–76, reprinted from *Middle Eastern Studies*, Vol. 32 (1996), pp. 45–76, For the text of the Turkish–Soviet treaty of 1921, see Hurewitz, ed., *Diplomacy*, Vol. 2, pp. 95–7. Among other things, under Article 3, the treaty provided that the enclave of Nakhichevan 'shall form an autonomous territory under the protection of Azerbaijan, on condition that the latter cannot transfer this protectorate to any third state' (read, Armenia). For further information on early communist movements in Turkey, see George S. Harris, *The Origins of Communism in Turkey* (Stanford, CA, Hoover Institution, 1967), and for a detailed study of Turkish–Soviet relations between 1919 and 1921, see A. Suat Bilge, *Güç Komşuluk: Türkiye–Sovyetler Birliği İlişkileri, 1920–1964* (Ankara, Türkiye İş Bankası Kültür Yayınları, 1992), pp. 26–78.

16. On the first point, see Gökay, *Clash of Empires*, pp. 109–11. For details of the war materiel sent by the Bolsheviks to the nationalists, see Stefanos Yerasimos, *Türk–Sovyet İlişkileri, Ekim Devrimden 'Milli Mücadele'ye* (Istanbul, Gözlem Yayınları, 1979), pp. 631–6.

17. Gökay, *Clash of Empires*, p. 86.

18. Ibid., pp. 123–7; Sonyel, *Turkish Diplomacy*, pp. 96–107, 135–9 and Davison, 'Turkish Diplomacy', pp. 188–90, 192–3. For the full text of the 'Franklin–Bouillon Pact', see Hurewitz, ed., *Diplomacy*, Vol. 2, pp. 98–100.

19. Sonyel, *Turkish Diplomacy*, pp. 161–73; Davison, 'Turkish Diplomacy', pp. 196–7; Osman Okyar, 'Turco-British Relations in the Inter-War Period: Fethi Okyar's Missions to London', in William Hale and Ali İkhsan Bağış, eds, *Four Centuries of Turco-British Relations* (Walkington, Eothen Press, 1984), pp. 71–4.

20. Sonyel, *Turkish Diplomacy*, pp. 173–82; Davison, 'Turkish Diplomacy', pp. 198–9; Gökay, *Clash of Empires*, pp. 136–46.

21. Quoted in A.L. Macfie, *The Straits Question, 1908–36* (Thessaloniki, Institute for Balkan Studies, 1993) p. 181.

22. For the details, see, for example, Howard, *Partition*, pp. 281–5. Italy had originally been granted 'temporary' possession of the Dodecanese after the Turkish–Italian war of 1912: see above p. 42, note 33. For the full text of the treaty of Lausanne, see *Treaty of Peace with Turkey and other Instruments signed at Lausanne on July 24, 1923* (London, HMSO, 1923: Cmd 1929). Hurewitz, ed., *Diplomacy*, Vol. 2, pp. 119–27, gives a condensed version.

23. On the first point, any one non-Black Sea state could send into the Black Sea naval forces not greater than those of the most powerful Black Sea fleet at the time of passage. The new rules were laid down in a 'Convention on the Regime of the Straits', attached to the treaty of Lausanne. For details, see Hurewitz, ed., *Diplomacy*, Vol. 2, pp. 124–7; Harry N. Howard, *Turkey, the Straits and US Policy* (Baltimore, MD, and London, Johns Hopkins University Press, 1974), pp. 113–26 and 303–13; A.L. Macfie, 'The Straits Question: The Conference of Lausanne (November 1922–July 1923)', *Middle Eastern Studies*, Vol. 15 (1979), pp. 211–38, and Macfie, *Straits Question*, pp. 181–211.

24. Quoted in David McDowall, *A Modern History of the Kurds* (London, I.B. Tauris, 1996), p. 190.

25. The British-controlled Turkish Petroleum Company (TPC), in which the Deutsche Bank originally had a 22.5 per cent share and Calouste Gulbenkian his famous 5 per cent, had obtained a concession covering the Mosul province from the Ottoman government just before the outbreak of the First World War. The Deutsche Bank's share was transferred to French interests after the war. The British government naturally supported the TPC's claim. On the other side, the Ankara government granted a concession for, among other things, the oil rights in Mosul to a US consortium headed by Admiral Colby M. Chester, Commander Arthur Chester and Colonel Clayton Kennedy (the 'Chester concession') in April 1923. However, as Peter J. Beck concludes, 'even without oil, the British government would have been reluctant to make concessions on Mosul', and the same is almost certainly true of the Turks, see Peter J. Beck, '"A Tedious and Perilous Controversy": Britain and the Settlement of the Mosul Dispute, 1918–1926', *Middle Eastern Studies*, Vol. 17 (1981), p. 258. On the Chester concession, see Selim İlkin, 'The Chester Railway Project', in Türkiye İş Bankası, *International Symposium on Ataturk (17–22 May 1981) and Papers and Discussions* (Ankara, Türkiye İş Bankası Kültür Yayınları, 1984), pp. 769–817.

26. See Doğu Perincek, ed., *Mustafa Kemal Eskişehir-İzmit Konuşmaları* (Istanbul, Kaynak Yayınları, 1993), pp. 94–97.

27. Beck, 'Mosul Dispute', pp. 256–61; Howard, *Partition*, pp. 297–301 and Sonyel, *Turkish Diplomacy*, pp. 195–6, 223–5.

28. See above, p. 73, note 6, and p. 14.

29. *Treaty of Peace … Protocol relating to Certain Concessions Granted in the Ottoman Empire*, p. 203: *Commercial Convention*, p. 157. On the economic effects of the tariff limitation, see William Hale, 'The Traditional and Modern in the Economy of Kemalist Turkey', in J. M. Landau, ed., *Ataturk and the Modernization of Turkey* (Boulder, CO, Westview Press, 1984), pp. 153–70.

30. Z.Y. Hershlag, *Turkey, an Economy in Transition* (The Hague, van Keulen, 1958), p. 21.

31. The population figures cited here are taken from Zürcher, *Modern History*, pp. 171–2. Other sources cite far higher figures for the total of Greek refugees and deportees: for

instance, Llewellyn Smith, *Ionian Vision*, p. 319, cites a figure of 1.5 million for the number of refugees who came to Greece during and after the war of 1920–22.

32. These events are well described and analysed in a large body of literature: see, in particular, Erik J. Zürcher, *The Unionist Factor: The Role of the Committee of Union and Progress in the Turkish National Movement* (Leiden, Brill, 1984) and *Political Opposition in the Early Turkish Republic: The Progressive Republican Party 1924–1925* (Leiden, Brill, 1991). On the Sheikh Saiyid rebellion, see McDowall, *Modern History*, pp. 194–8. On the 1930 experiment, see Walter F. Weiker, *Political Tutelage and Democracy in Turkey: The Free Party and its Aftermath* (Leiden, Brill, 1973).

33. This was subsequently commuted as a single cash payment of £500,000 sterling.

34. Stephen F. Evans, *The Slow Rapprochement: Britain and Turkey in the Age of Kemal Ataturk, 1919–38* (Walkington, Eothen Press, 1982), pp. 80–97: Beck, 'Mosul Dispute', pp. 261–73: McDowall, *Modern History*, pp. 143–6: Bilge *et al.*, *Olaylarla*, pp. 75–82: Aptülahat Akşin, *Ataturk'ün Dış Politika İlkeleri ve Diplomasisi* (Ankara, Türk Tarih Kurumu, 1991), pp. 126–31.

35. Bilge *et al.*, *Olaylarla*, pp. 67–75.

36. Bilge, *Güç Komşuluk*, p. 112.

37. Quoted in Brock Milman, 'Turkish Foreign and Strategic Policy, 1934–42', *Middle Eastern Studies*, Vol. 31 (1995), p. 491.

38. Ibid., p. 487; Bilge *et al.*, *Olaylarla*, pp. 102–6.

39. Bilge *et al.*, *Olaylarla*, pp. 87–90, 119.

40. Quoted in Milman, 'Turkish Policy', p. 489. See also Mustafa Türkeş, 'The Balkan Pact and its Immediate Implications for the Balkan States, 1930–34', *Middle Eastern Studies*, Vol. 30 (1994), pp. 122–30.

41. Türkeş, 'Balkan Pact', pp. 131–41: Bilge *et al.*, *Olaylarla*, pp. 106–14: Milman, 'Turkish Policy', p. 491. Turkish–Soviet relations were another complicating factor, since the Soviet government wished to prevent Turkey from supporting Romania in a possible clash with the Soviet Union over its frontier in Bessarabia. A clause was therefore added to the effect that the guarantees only applied to the frontiers of the Balkan states with one another, and that 'under no circumstances would Turkey consider itself obliged to participate in any activity directed against the USSR', quoted in Türkeş, 'Balkan Pact', p. 137.

42. Bilge *et al.*, *Olaylarla*, p. 120: Milman, 'Turkish Policy', pp. 485–6.

43. During the Kurdish rebellion centred on Mount Ararat in 1929–30, rebel forces had moved into Turkey from Iranian territory, but conflict with Iran on this point had been removed by the subsequent Turkish–Iranian frontier agreement. See McDowall, *Modern History*, pp. 204–6.

44. Bilge *et al.*, *Olaylarla*, pp. 114–17 and Akşin, *Ataturk'ün*, pp. 198–9.

45. The story first appeared 19 years later in an unsigned article in the magazine, *Caucasus*, entitled 'Atatürk – MacArthur Astounding Political Prophets' (No. 1, 1951, pp. 1–4). It is repeated in Milman, 'Turkish Policy', p. 505 footnote 27, Akşin, *Ataturk'ün*, pp. 163–5, and (unattributed) in Altemur Kılıç, *Turkey and the World*, (Washington, DC, Public Affairs Press, 1959), p. 59. However, if it took place in the form described then one would expect to find some record of it in contemporary or near-contemporary accounts, and no such record can be found. The author is very grateful to Dr Andrew Mango for advice and information on this point.

46. Conversation between Atatürk and Loraine of May 1936, quoted in Milman, 'Turkish

Policy', p. 488.

47. Quoted in ibid., p. 490, from British Foreign Office records.
48. Montreux Convention, Articles 10, 11, 14 and Annex II B. For the full text of the Convention, with Annexes, see Turkish Straits Voluntary Watch Group, *Turkish Straits: New Problems, New Solutions* (Istanbul, Isis, for Foundation for Middle East and Balkan Studies, 1995), pp. 10–24. For details on the Montreux negotiations, see Howard, *Straits*, pp. 130–60; Macfie, *Straits Question*, pp. 213–27 and Evans, *Slow Rapprochement*, pp. 100–1. The technical definitions given in the Convention are now largely obsolete, creating new problems: see below, pp. 189–90, note 92, and Barry Buzan, 'The Status and Future of the Montreux Convention', *Survival*, Vol. 18 (1976), pp. 242–7.
49. Montreux Convention, Articles 18–21.
50. Ibid., Article 24.
51. Milman, 'Turkish Policy', p. 492.
52. Selim Deringil, *Turkish Foreign Policy during the Second World War: An 'Active' Neutrality* (Cambridge, Cambridge University Press, 1989), pp. 12–27, 31–40. See also Hershlag, *Turkey*, pp. 113–14, and William Hale, *The Political and Economic Development of Modern Turkey* (London, Croom Helm, 1981), pp. 55–9.
53. The latter loan was agreed as part of the alliance between the three countries in October 1939, see p. 69.
54. Milman, 'Turkish Policy', pp. 493–7; Deringil, *Turkish Foreign Policy*, pp. 35–8 and Türkayya Ataöv, *Turkish Foreign Policy, 1939–1945* (Ankara University, Political Science Faculty, 1965), p. 9.
55. Bilge, *Güç Komşuluk*, pp. 120–8.
56. Gordon Waterfield, *Professional Diplomat: Sir Percy Loraine of Kirkharle Bt., 1880–1961* (London, Murray, 1973), p. 221.
57. Frank Marzari, 'Western–Soviet Rivalry in Turkey, 1939 – I', *Middle Eastern Studies*, Vol. 7 (1971), pp. 67–9, 72. Quotations from ibid., p. 72.
58. Figures from Robert B. Satloff, 'Prelude to Conflict: Communal Interdependence in the Sanjak of Alexandretta 1920–1936', *Middle Eastern Studies*, Vol. 22 (1986), p. 154, and Avedis K. Sanjian, 'The Sanjak of Alexandretta (Hatay): Its Impact on Turkish–Syrian Relations (1939–1956)', *Middle East Journal*, Vol. 10 (1956), p. 380.
59. In fact, it remained a dead letter, since it was not ratified by the French National Assembly.
60. Satloff, 'Prelude', pp. 173–6: Sanjian, 'Sanjak', pp. 380–1 and Marzari, 'Western–Soviet Rivalry – I', pp. 71–2. For a Turkish account, see Bilge *et al.*, *Olaylarla*, pp. 137–44.
61. Frank G. Weber, *The Evasive Neutral: Germany, Britain and the Quest for a Turkish Alliance in the Second World War* (Columbia, MO, and London, University of Missouri Press, 1979), pp. 40–4.
62. Ibid., pp. 29–33, 36, 45; Franz von Papen, trans. Brian Connell, *Memoirs* (London, André Deutsch, 1952), pp. 446–9: Sir Hughe Knatchbull-Hugessen, *Diplomat in Peace and War* (London, John Murray, 1949), p. 149 and Ataöv, *Turkish Foreign Policy*, p. 65.
63. Marzari, 'Western–Soviet Rivalry – I', pp. 69–70, 73–7, and 'Western–Soviet Rivalry … II', *Middle Eastern Studies*, Vol. 7 (1971), pp. 201–8. Deringil, *Turkish Foreign Policy*, pp. 75–84, and Weber, *Evasive Neutral*, p. 39.
64. Marzari, 'Western–Soviet Rivalry … II', pp. 209–15; Deringil, *Turkish Foreign Policy*, pp. 85–8 and Ataöv, *Turkish Foreign Policy*, pp. 54–8. See also Bilge, *Güç Komşuluk*, pp.

134–48. Stalin also demanded that, under the expected tripartite alliance, Turkey would only be obliged to consult with Britain and France if they were obliged to carry out their guarantees to Greece and Romania, rather than actively assist them. The Turks persuaded the British and French to accept this alteration, but the negotiations broke down over the other Soviet demands. The original Turkish commitment regarding Greece and Romania was then put back into the tripartite treaty.

65. Hurewitz, ed., *Diplomacy*, Vol. 2, pp. 227–8; Marzari, 'Western–Soviet Rivalry … II', p. 215; Milman, 'Turkish Policy', pp. 496–97, and Deringil, *Turkish Foreign Policy*, pp. 88–91, 189–92.

66. See Milman, 'Turkish Policy', pp. 486–88. Milman's account of Atatürk's attitude towards Hitler is based on that of Lord Kinross, *Ataturk, the Rebirth of a Nation* (London, Weidenfeld & Nicolson, 1964), p. 322, but unfortunately Kinross does not give a source for his information. Atatürk's contempt for Mussolini, however, is well attested.

67. Deringil, *Turkish Foreign Policy*, pp. 59–64.

3

Turkey and the Second World War, 1939–45

Because it had some importance in the history of the Second World War as a whole, Turkish diplomacy between 1939 and 1945 has received a good deal of scholarly attention – more so, for instance, than in the case of either the immediately preceding or succeeding periods. At first glance, it seems fairly straightforward and consistent. Although its government had signed a tripartite alliance with Britain and France in October 1939, Turkey remained a *de facto* neutral power throughout the war, resisting strong pressure from both the Allies and Germany to join the war on their side. The careful balancing act is held up as an example of how a relatively small and militarily backward country could follow an independent path at a time of global struggle, and 'a striking example of a small state which was no helpless pawn in international politics'.[1] This policy could be seen as a natural outcome of Turkey's experiences since 1914, and the country's relative power and international position. All Turkey's leaders during the Second World War had first-hand experience of the previous one, and were naturally anxious to avoid repeating such experiences. Saving the country from the death and destruction of war was their overriding objective. Turkey's armed forces were too ill equipped to hold off a counterattack by either Germany or the Soviet Union effectively. Its political leaders were above all anxious to protect the security which they had won in 1923. Assuming it was not invaded by one of the belligerents, Turkey had practically nothing to gain and everything to lose by joining the war.

This view has a good deal to recommend it, but it does not seem plausible as an explanation of Turkish policy throughout the war years.[2] If, for instance, İnönü and his colleagues had been determined to stay out of the war from the moment they signed the alliance with Britain and France in 1939, then one would have to conclude that they blatantly intended not to carry out their commitments under it, or that they thought that the circumstances under which they were supposed to do so would never arise.

However, this would assume a degree of duplicity or naiveté on their part which is inconsistent with their overall policy performance. In discussions with foreign governments, they could certainly exaggerate some points, or obscure others, as prudence dictated, but they did not generally give commitments which they knew at the time they could not keep, and their perceptions were usually realistic. Like other political leaders in most situations, they decided policy on the basis of the existing situation, their previous experiences, and their expectations at the time. All these factors, as well as the policies of the main belligerents, altered quite dramatically at different stages of the war, and Turkish policies were altered accordingly. Hence, Turkey's wartime diplomacy can be seen as subject to significant shifts, adapted to the circumstances of a series of fairly distinct phases, and to changes within these phases.

On the policy-making side, İnönü kept a tight control over decision-making throughout the period. The watchword of his approach was caution. He put great emphasis on gaining time, at which he was an expert, and avoided bold initiatives, adapting his policies to the circumstances of the moment. He was assisted by a trusted team of advisers, but the final decision rested with the president. Within the policy-making establishment, there were some individuals who apparently took a pro-Axis or distinctly pro-Allied position, but İnönü held them in check. Nor was the military command able to take an independent line. The Chief of the General Staff, Marshal Fevzi Çakmak, had been in post since 1922, and had been appointed mainly because he was seen as a loyal supporter of Atatürk who could secure the political attachment of the army to the regime. During the war, he was much criticised for his conservative outlook on professional military matters. He had an uneasy relationship with İnönü, since he had been a rival candidate for the presidency when Atatürk died. However, he does not seem to have played an effective role in policy making, and was eventually dismissed by İnönü in January 1944. Even before then, it appears that İnönü was usually able to bypass Çakmak by settling questions with his Assistant Chief of Staff, General Asım Gündüz, so that Çakmak's influence over İnönü was minimal.[3] Throughout the war, İnönü continued his close personal interest in foreign affairs, which was evidently more direct than his control over domestic politics. His principal foreign policy advisers were all experienced colleagues, notably Şükrü Saracoğlu, who served as foreign minister from 1939 until he took over as prime minister in 1942, and Numan Menemencioğlu, the secretary-general at the foreign ministry since 1933, who became foreign minister in 1942 and is regarded as the main source of ideas in Turkish foreign policy until his enforced resignation in June 1944. İnönü had some other important advisers, but the Turkish parliament played little part in foreign policy-making, although it could reflect shifts in public opinion. Such important decisions as it discussed were normally confined to the party caucus (or 'Parliamentary Group') of the ruling Republican People's Party (CHP), which held its meetings *in camera*.[4]

SHIFTING FORTUNES AND POLICIES, OCTOBER 1939–JUNE 1941

At the time it signed the tripartite alliance with Britain and France in October 1939, it appears that the Turkish government fully expected to carry out its commitments, and that it would join the war on the Allied side if the Axis powers invaded the Balkans, or Italy started a war in the Mediterranean, as the treaty provided. It was also expected that Turkey would be able to defend its own territory against likely invaders. Since 1934, the Turkish army had redeployed more than half its forces, with the bulk of its equipment and all its modern weapons, to eastern Thrace. A system of fixed fortifications was constructed, known as the 'Çakmak line', with which visiting British officers were impressed. Hence the initial assumption seems to have been that the Turks could hold off an invasion from the Balkans, although it was recognised that they had little ability to advance beyond their own frontier. These expectations also rested on the assumption that Britain and France would make good their promises of arms deliveries to Turkey. More broadly, it appears that İnönü shared the Anglo-French belief that the war on the western front would be a long one, that it would be fought on the Maginot line, and that the Allies would ultimately win, as in 1914–18. Apart from this, it was far from certain that Italy would join the war, or that Greece or Romania would be invaded by the Axis, so the circumstances for activating the alliance might not arise.[5]

Within the first ten months of the war, both the Turks and the British had begun to revise some of their assumptions. On 29 May 1940 Çakmak reported to the ministry of defence the difficulties which the army would face in defending Thrace, especially due to the lack of motor transport. The failure of the Allies to deliver the promised armaments, together with Turkish appreciation of Hitler's lightning victory over Poland in September 1939 contributed to a more pessimistic assessment of their military position by the Turks. Meanwhile, it appears that the British had started to become worried that Turkey might not activate the alliance. In March 1940 the French proposed a plan for bombing the Soviet oil fields at Baku, so as to weaken Russia and prevent the large exports of oil which the Soviet Union was supplying to Germany. To do this, the attacking aircraft would need to overfly Turkey. According to one account (which was later disputed) René Massigli, the French ambassador in Ankara, was given to understand from Saracoğlu that Turkey would turn a blind eye to this infringement of its airspace. However, the British were lukewarm towards the idea, since they believed that the Turks might not be cooperative, or at least, that it would be best not to test them on this. Aggression by the Allies against the Soviet Union might give the Turks an excuse to stay out of the war, and Turkey's role as the bastion of the British position in the Middle East made it essential to retain Turkish support. The plan was thus dropped, mainly because of fears of the Turkish reaction. Later, Saracoğlu even denied the existence of a British–French–Turkish plan to attack Baku.[6]

Although the Turkish government's attitude towards the Baku plan remains somewhat uncertain, it is quite clear that the collapse of France in June 1940 dramatically reversed its expectations about the likely course of the war, and Turkey's own role in it. Turkey's possible participation in the war had depended on the assumption that the French fleet would be available to oppose Italy in the Mediterranean, if need be, and that the German army would be fully occupied in fighting a long war on the western front. İnönü and his government were incensed with the French for having pressed Turkey to join the fight against the Axis after they had known that their own defeat by Germany was inevitable, and there were calls in Turkey for an agreement with Germany in the face of a mutual danger from the Soviet Union. Turkish reactions to the dramatic alteration of the balance of power in the Mediterranean were also critical in the British decision to try to destroy the French Mediterranean fleet in July 1940, to prevent it falling into German hands.[7]

The results of this new situation became quite clear after Italy entered the war on 10 June 1940, and thus created the situation foreseen in Article 2 of the Tripartite treaty, which would oblige Turkey to join the war on the Allied side. The problem was made still more acute on 7 October when German troops began to enter Romania, and then on 28 October, when Italy invaded Greece from Albania, both of which events should have required Turkish belligerence under Article 3. The Turkish response to the Italian declaration of war was to back out of these requirements. A declaration of non-belligerence issued by the government on 26 June cited the protocol to the treaty which absolved Turkey from joining the war if this would involve it in armed conflict with the Soviet Union (see p. 69).

The Turks also argued that, since their alliance had been with both Britain and France, the fact that France was now dropping out of the war relieved them of their obligations. For the British, the first excuse was not convincing, since there was no proof that if Turkey joined the war against Italy, then it would be attacked by the Soviet Union, and they pressed Turkey to fulfil its treaty commitments.[8] Clearly, the real reason for Turkey's failure to act was the expectation that, with France knocked out of the ring, Britain would be unable to give any effective support, and that Turkey would be left to fight Italy and Germany virtually on its own. The fear that Stalin would then take advantage of the situation, at Turkey's expense, was a further reason for caution. Meanwhile the success of Germany's *Blitzkrieg* tactics caused a radical revision of defence plans on the Turkish side. By March 1941 the expected line of defence, in the event of an invasion from the Balkans, had been moved back to western Anatolia, prospectively abandoning Istanbul to the enemy.[9] Obviously, İnönü's government had to avoid this if it could. Henceforward, estimates of Turkey's powers of resistance varied, but it was generally recognised that the primitive state of its internal communications, which were an obstacle to a successful invasion, also restricted the Turkish army's ability to defend its country. The Turks might be brave soldiers, but their outdated equipment and lack of modern training, plus the extreme weakness of the air force, would have put them at a severe disadvantage in a war with either Germany or Russia. Above all, Istanbul and İzmir were virtually defenceless against a determined air attack.[10] After the summer of 1940, these considerations naturally informed all Turkish reactions to potential threats, or attempts to bring Turkey into the war on either side.

Although the events of 1940 forced the Turks to reconsider their position, this did not lead to a rapid *rapprochement* with Germany. Initially, Germany's aim was to secure the neutrality of Turkey – to ensure, at least, that it did not play an active role on the British side – and to try to prevent Italy from provoking the Turks into activating the alliance with Britain. After the dramatic German victories in the summer of 1940, von Papen urged Berlin that Germany should go further, by trying to convert Turkey into a pro-German neutral so as to facilitate a German attack on the British in the Middle East. This could be achieved with the participation of Russia, which could be offered concessions at the straits. Hints were meanwhile dropped to the Turks that Germany would oppose such concessions if Turkey made some concrete demonstrations of sympathy for Germany, including the dismissal of Saracoğlu, who was seen as strongly anti-German. Predictably, this demand was categorically dismissed by İnönü.[11]

Meanwhile, trade relations formed the main business of Turkish–German diplomacy. During the 1930s, Germany had manipulated a system of clearing agreements and its non-convertible currency to gain a dominating position in Turkey's foreign trade, accounting for 51 per cent of its imports and 31 per cent of its exports, but this had no effect on Turkish policy. After the signature of the alliance treaty with Britain and France, the Turks cut back their trade with Germany sharply, so that in 1940 these percentages were reduced to 12 per cent and 9 per cent respectively.[12] In June 1940, disagreements over trade agreements with Britain led Turkey to secure a new commercial agreement with Germany. However, its duration was limited to only one year, the volume of trade was still limited, and it did not include chromite, which was Turkey's most strategically vital potential export (see pp. 91–2). As a result, Turkish–German trade in 1941 remained at almost exactly the same level as in 1940.[13]

The reaction of the British to the Turkish decision not to join the war was also ambiguous. Officially, Knatchbull-Hugessen protested against Turkish reluctance until after the Italian attack on Greece. Nonetheless, Foreign Secretary Lord Halifax told the House of Lords on 11 July 1941 that the British government 'fully appreciated the circumstances which led to this decision of the Turkish Government' not to join the war.[14] Privately, a British military report estimated that if Turkey joined the war, and was attacked by Germany, then Hitler's armies could conquer the country in 16 weeks.[15] In effect, a belligerent Turkey would be more of a liability than an asset for Britain. The British came to realise that even if they could not officially accept the Turkish decision, there was little they could do about it, since they feared that further pressure on the Turks might push them towards Germany. By the end of January 1941, according to his own later account, Churchill had decided that it 'was obviously impossible to consider the treaty we had made with her [Turkey] as binding upon her in the altered circumstances'.[16] By February–March 1941, the Italian invaders had been pushed back by the Greeks, and the British were attempting to counter the impending German invasion of the Balkans by sending troops to Greece and reviving the Balkan pact. By this stage, however, they had realised that it would be pointless to try to get Turkey to join the war unless their overall military position improved dramatically, and hence they desisted from doing so.[17]

Throughout this period – indeed, throughout the war – a crucial concern for Turkey was the policy of the Soviet Union, and its relations with the belligerents. The Nazi–Soviet pact, and Russian demands to Saracoğlu during his visit to Moscow in 1939, had completely reversed the

Turks' previous expectations of cooperation with the Soviets. The Soviet Union was not only geographically close to Turkey, but the Moscow discussions of 1939 had also made it clear that it was, at the very least, likely to make demands of access to the straits which the Turks could not accept. In July 1940 Stalin accepted British mediation for an improvement in relations with Turkey, but insisted that this should be based on the participation of the Black Sea powers (presumably dominated by Russia) in the defence of the straits. This was unacceptable to the Turks, so the proposal came to nothing.[18] Moreover, Turkey's relations with the Soviet Union were inevitably overshadowed by those of Stalin with Hitler. So long as the Nazi–Soviet pact lasted there was the danger that Germany might offer the straits to Stalin, as part of the price for his neutrality or even active intervention in the war on the Axis side. Negotiations between the Germans and Soviets in November 1940 showed that these fears were well founded. Following the conclusion of the Three Power Pact for mutual aid between Germany, Italy and Japan on 27 September 1940, Molotov began to explore the possibility of Soviet collaboration with the Pact in conversations with Hitler and Ribbentrop in Berlin on 12–13 November. He emphasised that the Soviet Union regarded control of the straits as essential to its security, and claimed that he could reach an agreement with Turkey on this. The Germans responded by presenting him with a draft agreement on 26 November, which, among other things, proposed a joint commitment to detach Turkey from its alliance with Britain, 'to recognise the extent of Turkey's possessions', and to secure a revision of the Montreux Convention giving the Soviet Union free naval access through the straits. However, Molotov regarded this as insufficient, and demanded the establishment of Soviet military and naval bases at the straits. If Turkey agreed to join a projected four-power pact (that is, Germany, Italy, Japan and the Soviet Union) then the other powers would guarantee its independence and territory. If not, then 'the required military and diplomatic measures' would be taken. Bulgaria would also have to be induced to sign a mutual assistance pact with the Soviet Union, since, Molotov claimed, it was 'situated inside the security zone of the Black Sea boundaries of the Soviet Union'.[19]

These demands were too much for Hitler. Evidently, he did not want to hand over control over the straits and Bulgaria to Stalin, which would have ruled out a possible German attack on the British in the Middle East and encircled Germany from the south. Accordingly, the negotiations broke off with no positive result. Twenty-two days later, on 18 December, Hitler issued the fatal orders to begin preparations for his invasion of the

Soviet Union ('Barbarossa'). Whether or not they knew of the German–Soviet negotiations at the time, the Turks certainly learned of them four · months later, on 18 March 1941, when Hitler, anxious to show the Turks that he was on their side, told the Turkish ambassador in Berlin that he had flatly refused the Soviet demand for bases at the straits. On 25 March the Soviet government declared that it would remain neutral, in the event of a war between Turkey and the Axis, and this declaration was reciprocated by the Turks. Nonetheless, İnönü and his colleagues had been left in little doubt about Stalin's long-term ambitions.[20]

During 1940–41 events in the Middle East further embroiled Britain and Germany with Turkey. Following the fall of France, a pro-Vichy administration had installed itself in Syria, and during the summer of 1940 the British considered schemes for intervening in the country to prevent it coming under direct German or Italian control. Turkey, it was suggested, could be offered territory in Syria, including Aleppo, as an inducement for cooperating in this. However, the idea was dropped, as the Turks showed no interest in it, and the British feared the likely reactions in other Arab states to any Turkish intervention in Syria. On the Turkish side, there was probably a natural reluctance to provoke Germany. However, the Turks also appear to have been reluctant to add Syria to their national territory, which would in any case have been contrary to the principles of the National Pact of 1920. In March 1941 the Turkish government went to some lengths to emphasise publicly that it did not have any territorial ambitions in Syria. When Saracoğlu met Anthony Eden in Cyprus on 18 March he was reported by the British to have told the foreign secretary that Turkey did not covet territory in Syria as 'the Syrians were awkward customers and modern Turkey did not wish to include non-homogeneous peoples within her frontiers'.[21]

In April 1941 attention switched to Iraq, as the government was overthrown by a pro-Axis junta, which installed Rashid Ali al-Gaylani, a prominent Iraqi nationalist politician, as prime minister. Rashid Ali then restricted British reinforcements of their troops, and Iraqi forces besieged the British base at Habbaniya, some 25 miles west of Baghdad.[22] Although Rashid Ali had received hints of Axis aid, the Germans had not planned his takeover, and were ill-prepared to assist him. Hitler had no clear plans to try to eject the British from the Middle East at this stage, and was anyway heavily engaged in the Balkans and in his preparations for 'Barbarossa'. As a result, the Iraqi rebels acted too soon, and Hitler too late. On 3 May, Hitler agreed to send German warplanes to Iraq, and these played some role in the fighting against the British. The quickest way for the Germans to send arms to Iraq was to draw on the Vichy stocks in Syria, and on 5 May they obtained the approval of the Vichy government in France to this plan. An obstacle to it was the fact that the only railway from Syria to Iraq passed through Turkish territory, and the operation thus depended on Turkish permission. According to one source, the Turks had serious designs in Iraq – where the province of Mosul had only been reluctantly conceded in 1926 – which they hoped to achieve in collaboration with either Britain or Germany.[23] However, if they did have such ambitions, they evidently decided not to push them home. It appears that four trains loaded with small arms completed the trip from Syria to Iraq in the second half of May, but the remainder of the planned consignment failed to get through (in fact, the arms which were sent made no difference to the military outcome in Iraq).[24] At the same time, the Turkish government was also engaged in fruitless attempts at mediation between Rashid Ali and the British. In negotiations with the Germans during June, Turkey refused German demands for an agreement allowing the despatch of an unlimited quantity of German arms to Iraq and a defined number of German troops across Turkish territory. From the German viewpoint, the proposal was anyway too late, since the British had meanwhile moved forces into Iraq and overthrown Rashid Ali by 30 May. Meanwhile, the British were preparing to invade Syria, and on 2 June they again suggested to the Turks that they should occupy Aleppo as part of this campaign. The proposal was again turned down by the Turks, though Turkey did concentrate forces on the Syrian border. With the idea of collaboration with Turkey now dropped, a mixed force of British, Indian, Australian, Arab and Free French forces invaded Syria on 8 June, as the last German units were withdrawn. The Allied forces completed the overthrow of the local Vichy administration in Syria on 14 July. Turkey had thus been able to get out of the crisis without any serious involvement on either side.[25]

In the spring of 1941, German advances in the Balkans were Turkey's main focus of concern. When Eden visited Ankara at the end of February, with a German attack on Greece looming, the Turks told him they were convinced that their turn would come next, and that they were worried that the Soviet Union might also attack them if they were involved in war with Germany. Soon afterwards, during April and May, the British position in the Balkans collapsed, as Hitler conquered Yugoslavia and Greece. Additionally, German forces were now in full occupation of Romania and Bulgaria. Given that German troops were now only about 60 kilometres beyond its north-western frontier, Turkey was bound to try to reach some understanding with Berlin. Hitler was similarly inclined, since he wished to stabilise his southern flank in preparation for 'Barbarossa'. The expulsion of Britain from the Middle East, involving an invasion of Turkey or at least its political subordination, could wait until after Russia had been defeated. Accordingly, on 4 March 1941, Hitler wrote a personal letter to İnönü assuring him that the German occupation of Bulgaria was in no way directed against Turkey, but purely against the British in Greece, and that he had ordered his forces in Bulgaria not to go within 60 kilometres of the frontier with Turkey.[26] At a meeting with Mussolini in Salzburg on 29 April, Hitler claimed that 'Turkey was moving slowly but surely over to the Axis', that it would never be an enemy of the Axis, and would at worst remain neutral: the Turks would also like to have Russia 'as far removed as possible from their territories'.[27]

How Turkish–German relations developed immediately after this is unclear, since there are two quite contradictory accounts. According to the first account, based on German records, Saracoğlu and von Papen discussed a full-scale alliance between Turkey and Germany during May 1941. Von Papen reported that on 17 May Saracoğlu told him that Turkey would be willing to abandon the alliance with Britain in return for large arms deliveries from Germany and recognition that Iraq was within Turkey's sphere of influence. This account relates that von Papen then prepared a draft treaty, which Saracoğlu had helped to prepare, which was cabled to Berlin on 23 May. This offered Turkey the cession of some Bulgarian territory near Edirne, two or three of the Greek Aegean islands and 'the advancement of Turkish interests in the southern and eastern neighbouring zones' (presumably, in Syria and Iraq) as part of a Turkish–German alliance which would give Germany transit rights across Turkey.[28] The second account, also based on German records, suggests that the initiative for a treaty to allow Germany transit rights came not from von Papen but from Ribbentrop, who suggested on 18 May that Turkey could be offered frontier rectifications near Edirne and possibly 'one or other island in the Aegean Sea'. If Turkey resisted this offer then Ribbentrop suggested that the Turks should be told that Germany was in a position to 'blot out the Turkish state within a few weeks'. The second account goes on to relate that von Papen opposed this plan, by arguing that the idea of getting Turkey to grant transit rights to Germany was just a vain dream, and that territorial offers would not have any effect on Turkish policy. It does not suggest that Saracoğlu ever agreed to a draft treaty. The only thing that can be said for certain is that the Turks rapidly abandoned the alliance project, or that they had never adopted it anyway.[29]

Accordingly, the Germans had to be content with a simple mutual non-aggression pact with Turkey. In the Turkish–German Treaty of Friend-ship and Non-Aggression, signed on 18 June 1941, which was to be valid for ten years, the two governments agreed to respect each other's terri-torial integrity and to 'abstain from all action aimed directly or indirectly against one another'. However, the preamble to the treaty stated that these commitments were 'subject to the already existing arrangements of each party' – an obvious reference to the treaty with the British of 1939, as Saracoğlu pointed out to the Turkish parliament.[30] In his memoirs, Knatchbull-Hugessen relates that the Turks kept the British informed of their negotiations with the Germans, and that he decided that it would be counter-productive to oppose the non-aggression pact. However, it appears that at the time he criticised it strongly, as did the US govern-ment.[31] The signature of the treaty marked Turkey's furthest move towards a full, rather than merely *de facto* neutrality. Of course, the Turks could be criticised for cutting a deal with the Germans when they were supposed to be allied to the British, but they probably had no safe alterna-tive, given their strategic situation at the time. The most serious criticism of the treaty was that, in the long run, it might be of no value. After all, Hitler had broken virtually every important international agreement he had ever made, and he would have been perfectly capable of ignoring this one if and when he had been able and willing to do so. The point was made only four days later, on 22 June, when German forces finally invaded the Soviet Union.

WALKING THE TIGHTROPE: JUNE 1941–DECEMBER 1942

The beginning of 'Barbarossa' naturally caused a heartfelt sigh of relief in Ankara, since it was now unlikely that Hitler would have the forces to spare for an invasion of Turkey and the Middle East in the near future. Unsurprisingly, Turkey immediately proclaimed its neutrality in the conflict. However, the longer-term outlook was still dangerous. If the Soviet Union won this new war outright, then it would probably be left as the dominant power in eastern Europe, and able to dictate its own terms at the straits. On the other hand, if Russia collapsed and then capitulated, as it had in 1917, then Hitler might well fall on Turkey as his next victim. Obviously the best outcome for Turkey would be that Germany and the Allies would reach a negotiated settlement which would leave neither Germany nor the Soviet Union in a dominant position in eastern Europe, or that they would fight one another to a standstill. As the Italian ambassador in Ankara de Peppo put it: 'The Turkish ideal is that the last German soldier should fall upon the last Russian corpse.'[32] However, the Turks had no way of ensuring this ideal result. The best İnönü could do was to follow his own cautious instincts by playing for time, avoiding commitments, and exploiting whatever opportunities arose to strengthen Turkey's position.

The fear that Germany would attack Turkey if the Soviet Union were defeated was not baseless. The German archives show that in June 1941, before Operation 'Barbarossa' had begun, German military planners had confidently expected to defeat Russia in three months. Following this, during the late autumn and winter of 1941–42, Germany would attack Egypt from the west, and mass large forces in Bulgaria. Turkey would be forced to submit, preparatory to the launch of a German attack on the Suez canal through Turkey, Syria and Palestine, combined with an invasion of Iran from the Caucasus. In conversations with his dinner guests in September 1941, Hitler maintained that Turkey would join the Axis after the defeat of Russia, and that the Turkish ambassador in Berlin, Hüsrev Gerede, whom he claimed was in favour of cooperation with Germany, might be made Turkish foreign minister. However, the planned operation did not depend on these predictions. German planners assumed that the Middle Eastern campaign could be finished in 85 days if Turkey cooperated, or 145 days if it did not. Either way, the plan could be completed by the spring of 1942.[33] Even if they did not have the details of these plans, the Turks reasonably expected that Hitler had something of the kind in store. As early as July 1941 Fevzi Çakmak (who, paradoxically, was thought by both the Germans and the British to favour the German side) told the British Air Attaché in Ankara that Turkey hoped that the Germans would exhaust themselves in Russia, since '[W]e realise that if Germany has a quick success in Russia we will be the next sheep for slaughter'.[34] In January 1942, after the Germans had been halted before Moscow, İnönü told Knatchbull-Hugessen that he still expected an imminent invasion by Germany from Thrace, and had reinforced the Turkish positions there. Thereafter, the Turks continued to fear a sudden and probably catastrophic Luftwaffe assault on Istanbul, like that on Belgrade or Warsaw, against which they had virtually no effective protection.[35]

An important question in Turkey's relations with Germany during 1941–42 is whether Turkey hoped to gain territory in Transcaucasia and possibly other Turkic areas of the Soviet Union, in collaboration with Germany, assuming the Soviets were defeated. Certainly, von Papen promoted the proposal, as a means of bringing Turkey over to the Axis side, and it had some support in Berlin. Although Atatürk had strictly abjured pan-Turkism, it had continued as a fringe movement in Turkey during the 1930s. A so-called committee of experts on the 'Turanian' question was established in July 1941, consisting of convinced pan-Turkists, including Nuri Pasha, a brother of the Young Turk leader Enver Pasha, and now a businessman in Turkey, and Professor Zeki Velidi Toğan, a well-known pan-Turkish historian. In August 1941 Nuri visited Berlin as what von Papen described as a fully accredited representative of the Turkish government, though Turkish sources deny this. At this stage, the Turkish government had evidently decide to test the temperature on this issue, through semi-official channels. In Berlin, Nuri urged the establishment of a pan-Turanian state stretching as far as the Chinese province of Xinjiang. However, both the Germans and the Turks then abandoned this fantasy. Those Germans who favoured the idea also claimed Fevzi Çakmak as one of its supporters, but the furthest Çakmak was apparently prepared to go was to tell the Germans in May 1942 that he was willing to allow Turkish civilians to go to Germany to prepare for the establishment of separate states in the Turkic areas captured from the Soviet Union. On the other hand, Hüsrev Gerede, who had supported the idea at first, bluntly turned down the proposal that Turkey should take over Turkic areas of the Soviet Union, when Hitler suggested it to him in August 1941. It was obviously dropped completely, once it was clear that Germany was not going to crush the Soviet Union anyway.[36]

Trade was also a significant thermometer of Turkish–German relations. Here, a vital issue for both the Germans and British was the supply of chromite, which is an essential ingredient in steel-making. Germany had no domestic supplies, but Turkey had accounted for about 16 per cent of world production in 1939. The problem for the Turks was that they were allied to a country which had little economic use for their products, given that Britain had alternative sources of supply of both chromite and the agricultural crops exported by Turkey. On the other hand, the Allies could have done severe damage to Germany's war effort if they could have denied the Germans access to Turkish chromite. In October 1939 the Turks had proposed to the British that they should sell them 200,000 tons of chromite per year for the next two years. This offer was later increased to 20 years. Since this was greater than Turkey's total pre-war production, it would have pre-empted Germany from the market for the duration of the war. However, in negotiations with the British, Numan Menemencioğlu also insisted that Britain should buy agreed quantities of Turkey's other exports, on the grounds that Germany, Turkey's previous customer, would refuse to take these products if chromite were not also on offer. The British turned this deal down, and only promised to buy 50,000 tons of chromite per year in 1941 and 1942, with an option on that mined in 1943. In their 1940 trade agreement with Germany, the Turks had with-held chromite, but the failure to reach an exclusive long-term agreement with the British left them free to reverse this later. In October 1941 a new arrangement was reached with Germany, known as the 'Clodius agree-ment', after its chief German negotiator, Karl Clodius. Under this, Germany was to receive a maximum of 90,000 tons of chromite in 1943 (that is, after the contract with the British expired) and 45,000 tons in 1944. The Clodius agreement also provided for the sale by Germany of substantial amounts of military and other essential equipment to Turkey. In the summer of 1942 Turkey received a loan of 100 million Reichsmarks for the purchase of arms from Germany – supplies which Britain could not match at the time. As a result, Turkey's trade with Germany recovered, to account for 28 per cent of Turkey's total imports and 25 per cent of its total exports in 1942. The signature of the Clodius agreement partly derived from the British failure to accept the proposed exclusive deal with Turkey, but it is likely that it also reflected İnönü's desire not to provoke Germany by withholding supplies of chromite, given his country's perilous situation. The arms loan from Germany was also a further means of building up Turkey's defences – possibly against Germany itself.[37]

One other action by the Turkish government did some harm to Turkey's relations with the Allies in the longer term, as well as the inter-national reputation of İnönü's government, though the British did not publicly raise it at the time.[38] In November 1942, the government intro-duced a Property Tax (*Varlık Vergisi*) which was supposed to be applied on a one-off basis to wealthy farmers, businessmen and corporations. In theory, it was expected to have the perfectly reasonable aim of mopping up part of the windfall profits accumulated by speculators in wartime con-ditions. In practice, it was used by the local committees who fixed the tax assessments as a means of killing off commercial competition from members of the non-Muslim minorities who had remained in Istanbul after the Lausanne settlement (see pp. 55–6). As a result, non-Muslims were assessed far more severely than Muslims. Of the total collected, 53 per cent was paid by non-Muslims, compared with 36.5 per cent paid by Muslims and 10.5 per cent by foreign citizens resident in Turkey. Those who failed to pay were shipped off to a labour camp in Aşkale, in eastern Anatolia which, for a middle-class Istanbuli, was the Turkish equivalent of Siberia. Collection of the tax was slowed down in 1943, and terminated in

1944, but by this time many innocent citizens had been ruined. Its relationship to Turkey's foreign policy at the time may have only been indirect but, as Faik Ökte, a senior civil servant responsible for administering the tax in Istanbul later admitted, 'The infamous tax was also the result of racist concepts which were still influential in war-torn Europe'.[39] In the long run, it seriously damaged Turkey's international moral standing.[40]

Obviously, the beginning of 'Barbarossa' also affected Turkey's relations with both Moscow and London, since Britain and the Soviet Union were now fighting on the same side. Their first concern was to try to allay Turkish suspicions about Soviet ambitions at the straits. Accordingly, on 28 July 1941, Stalin had told İnönü that he had no interest in revising the Montreux convention. On 10 August, the British and Soviet governments issued a joint declaration, stating their fidelity to the Montreux rules, that they had 'no aggressive intentions or claims whatever regarding the straits' and that they were 'prepared scrupulously' to observe Turkey's territorial integrity. If Turkey were attacked by a 'European Power' (read Germany) then they would both come to its aid.[41] However, it does not appear that the Turks were reassured by these statements. Their suspicions were naturally strengthened by the Anglo-Soviet invasion and occupation of neighbouring Iran in August 1941. As the Turkish press pointed out, if the British and Russians had been prepared to invade a neutral country merely because it stood in their way, then they might be prepared to do the same to Turkey.[42] Following the death of Prime Minister Refik Saydam on 8 July 1942, Saracoğlu succeeded him, with Menemencioğlu becoming foreign minister shortly afterwards. After his appointment, Saracoğlu promptly announced that Turkey was 'equally loyal and friendly towards all opposing States'.[43] Nonetheless, in reality, it had serious suspicions of all of them. On 8 August von Papen reported a conversation with Saracoğlu in which Saracoğlu stated that he hoped for the collapse of the Soviet Union, allowing Germany and Turkey to sign a separate peace agreement, and to sponsor the non-Slavic minorities in Soviet territory as enemies of Slavism. Saracoğlu had a further interview with von Papen on 29 August, in which he repeated his hope for the destruction of the Soviet Union, but added that Turkey would have to preserve its neutrality.[44]

On the British side, the Turks' misgivings were recognised, and it appears that both the British and Soviet governments realised that the best they could do would be to try to keep Turkey as a neutral buffer at this stage. At a meeting with Eden in December 1941, Stalin suggested that after the war Turkey should be given the Dodecanese, certain territory in Bulgaria and possibly in northern Syria, but Eden replied that Britain could not commit itself to any post-war redrawing of frontiers.[45] As Knatchbull-Hugessen states it in his memoirs, the British government adhered to this policy of accepting Turkey's *de facto* neutrality until the end of 1942. However, behind the scenes, and by August 1942, Churchill was trying to persuade his two allies (which now included the United States) that their next priority must be to try to knock Italy out of the war, and bring Turkey in.[46] The second proposal, combined with the overall change in the tide of the war during the winter of 1942–43, was to prove the greatest problem for Turkish diplomacy from then until 1945.

ALLIED ASCENDANCY: NOVEMBER 1942–MAY 1945

To fix the exact date when the tide turned in the Second World War is not easy. Clearly, the full entry of the United States into the war following the Japanese attack on Pearl Harbour in December 1941 was probably the decisive event which determined that, in the long run, the Axis would lose the war. However, this had little immediate effect on the war in the Soviet Union and north Africa, Turkey's immediate environment. Turkey's position was not effectively changed until the winter of 1942–43 – first, by the German defeat at el-Alamein in October–November 1942 and the consequent Allied landings in Algeria and Morocco, which ended the Axis threat to the Middle East, and second, the German surrender at Stalingrad in February 1943, which made it virtually certain that Hitler's campaign in the Soviet Union would ultimately fail. In an ideal world, Turkish states-men would have best preferred a situation in which Germany accepted a peace deal with the Western Allies before Stalin completed his conquest of eastern Europe, which would have left some German power in the region to balance that of Russia. However, this hope ran counter to realities. On the one side, Hitler insisted on fighting the war to the bitter end, and attempts to overthrow or murder him were unsuccessful. On the other side, for the Allies the war was one of good against evil, and not just a conflict of national interests. Victory could only be won if the third Reich was completely destroyed. The policy of demanding the unconditional surrender of Germany, announced at the Casablanca conference in January 1943, combined with Hitler's fanaticism, precluded the possibility of a negotiated peace between Germany and the Western Allies. The Turks had to deal with the world as it was – in particular, with the Allies' campaign to bring Turkey into the war. On this score, Turkish policy was determined, first by the fear that if Turkey joined the war on the Allied side with inadequate preparation or support it would still be very vulnerable to

a retaliatory attack by Germany. Equally, Stalin might use Turkish entry
into the war as an excuse for Soviet entry into Turkey. On the other hand,
if Turkey bluntly rejected the Allies' proposals then it would be left
dangerously isolated, and in a very weak position to resist Soviet ambitions
at the straits and elsewhere in the post-war world. The fear that Britain
and the United States might offer control of the straits to Russia, as the
price for keeping it in the war – as the British had done in 1915 – was constantly at the back of Turkish minds. Hence, İnönü and his colleagues had
to play for time, to try to keep the Allies reasonably satisfied with Turkish
intentions, but to avoid committing their country to war unless this was
part of a concerted and coordinated military offensive by the Western
Allies in south-eastern Europe. Since the latter never materialised, Turkey
stayed on the sidelines, running the risk of the second of the two dangers it
faced.

The initiative for bringing Turkey into the war came principally from
Winston Churchill, and was first outlined to the US ambassador in
London, John G. Winant, and to Anthony Eden on 9 November 1942. It
depended on bringing military supplies into Turkey via Syria and elsewhere, and originally assumed that Turkey would invade the Balkans in
the spring of 1943, so as to strike at Germany's southern flank. The main
obstacles to pressing this project home were the reluctance of the Turks to
get dragged into the war, objections from both the British Foreign Office,
including Eden, who doubted its political practicality, and from military
commanders, especially on the US side, who questioned its strategic
viability.[47] Nonetheless, at the Casablanca meeting of Roosevelt and
Churchill it was agreed that Britain should take the lead in trying to bring
Turkey into the war on the Allied side. Apart from their opposition to the
policy of demanding the unconditional surrender of Germany, the Turks
were also perturbed by the idea that the Casablanca decisions meant that
they were being put into some sort of British zone of influence.[48] However,
İnönü agreed to talk directly to Churchill at a hastily arranged meeting
held in a train parked near Adana on 30–31 January 1943. İnönü's main
objective was to avoid committing Turkey to war against the Axis, and in
turn to obtain the maximum amount of military supplies for Turkey and to
warn Churchill about Stalin's likely post-war intentions. On the latter
score, the Turkish leaders were worried that pushing Turkey into a war
with Germany was intended to soften Turkey up for an invasion by Russia,
and they were not persuaded by Churchill's reassurances on this issue.
When Churchill suggested that air bases should be prepared in Turkey for
the Royal Air Force (RAF), the Turks responded that even if German

power was now not what it had been, Germany was still capable of reacting by overrunning the straits, and reducing Istanbul and Turkey's few industrial installations to rubble. Hence, it was eventually agreed that Britain would not ask for any immediate commitments from Turkey, though consideration should be given to allowing the RAF to use Turkish airfields to attack the Romanian oilfields, the Dodecanese and Crete, and to the possibility of Turkish intervention in the Balkans if there were anarchy in the region. If it became belligerent, Turkey's territory would be fully guaranteed by Britain after the war (by implication, against the Soviet Union). The only clear and immediate commitment on both sides was that Turkey should receive an increased flow of arms and infrastructural support.[49]

Following the Adana meeting, military staff meetings between the British and Turkish sides began in February 1943. The British produced plans for building up Turkish facilities to receive British air and later ground detachments, but the Turks dragged their feet at every turn, so as to delay the open deployment of British forces on their soil, citing endless problems of transportation and logistics. Turkish policy, evidently, was to postpone the date at which they might be required to enter the war indefinitely. However, Churchill did not abandon his strategy. Instead, the overthrow of Mussolini's government on 25 July 1943, and the subsequent surrender of Italy on 8 September encouraged him to induce the Turks to get off the fence. The collapse of Italy immediately raised a question mark over the future of the Dodecanese. The British proposed to answer it by sending an amphibious force to occupy the islands, but when they launched an attempt to capture the Dodecanese in September–October 1943, the Turkish role was limited to transporting food and equipment to the British in small ships, and subsequently evacuating those British troops who escaped capture to the mainland. As it was, the Dodecanese operation was a disaster for the British, as the Germans had swiftly reconquered the islands by mid-November. It was also a serious setback for Churchill's diplomacy, since it showed that Germany still had the upper hand militarily in the eastern Mediterranean, and was in a strong position to retaliate against Turkey if it joined the Allies in the war.[50]

While the struggle for the Dodecanese was going on, the British continued with their diplomatic offensive on Turkey. At this stage, the idea of bringing Turkey into the war was still supported by the Soviet Union. At meetings between Eden, Molotov and the US secretary of state, Cordell Hull, in Moscow between 19 October and 1 November 1943, the Soviet foreign minister proposed that Turkey should be told peremptorily to join the Allies. At this stage, the Soviets still wanted Turkish participation in the war, which they estimated would draw off 15 German divisions from the Russian front. Roosevelt later agreed that the Turks should be asked to allow the establishment of Allied air bases on their soil, and to enter the war by the end of 1943, provided that no Allied forces were committed to the areas which were needed for the planned Allied invasion of France (operation 'Overlord'). Eden put these proposals to Menemencioğlu at a meeting in Cairo on 5–8 November, although he assured the Turkish foreign minister that 'there was no intention to press the Turks to go into the war on an all-out basis'.[51] Menemencioğlu, however, was unpersuaded, making it clear that nothing short of a definite Anglo-American commitment to invade the Balkans would make it feasible for Turkey to join the war. The mere establishment of Allied air bases in Turkey would be tantamount to a declaration of war against Germany, without providing Turkey with a sufficient role, and at a time when it was unprepared. When Menemencioğlu queried post-war Soviet intentions, Eden threatened that the Allies might not support Turkey against the Soviet Union if it failed to meet British wishes. The talks thus ended on a bitter and unproductive note. The furthest the Turks were willing to go was contained in a message of 22 November stating that Turkey was prepared to enter the war 'in principle', but only if it received adequate protection against a German attack.[52]

In spite of these evident problems, the Allied campaign to bring in Turkey as an active partner continued until early 1944. When the question was discussed at the Tehran conference between Churchill, Roosevelt and Stalin of 28 November–1 December 1943, Stalin began to shift his ground, opposing any diversion of forces to Turkey if this would mean the postponement of 'Overlord', and evidently regarding the question of Turkish entry as unimportant. Nevertheless, the conference concluded that it was 'most desirable' for Turkey to enter the war by the end of the year, and fixed 14 February 1944 as the date by which it should become an active participant.[53] These proposals were put to İnönü at a second conference in Cairo with Roosevelt and Churchill on 4–6 December 1943. Before leaving for Cairo, İnönü had received the authority from his government and the party group to enter the war if need be, and had agreed to attend only on condition that there was a free discussion on Turkey's position, and not just on the basis of decisions already reached at Tehran.[54] He and his colleagues were still perturbed by possible Soviet intentions, and mistakenly believed that it was the Soviets, rather than the British, who were trying to push them into the war, with Britain and the

United States as their unwitting tools. They noticed that Soviet representatives were conspicuous by their absence at the discussions in Cairo and
were again warned by Churchill that if they failed to join the Allies they
might not be supported against the Soviet Union after the war. However,
they decided not to harp on their suspicions of the Soviet Union. Instead,
İnönü continued to stress Turkey's military inadequacy, and the shortfall
in supplies from the British (which the British in turn denied). Turkey's
participation in the war, İnönü argued, would depend on the organisation
of a joint Allied offensive in the Balkans. As he put it: 'What would suit
Turkey best would be that she should fight side by side with British and
American contingents in her own part of the world.' However, this idea
ran up against the rock of opposition by US military chiefs to any substantial diversion of resources from 'Overlord'. They considered that if
Turkey came into the war, this would 'burn up our logistics right down the
line', as General Marshall maintained. Even if he did not know the details
of US military misgivings on this score, İnönü realised that Roosevelt was
sceptical about the idea of bringing Turkey in, and exploited this difference
between Britain and the United States to delay action. As he later claimed,
Roosevelt 'completely understood my reluctance to bring Turkey into the
war'.[55] As a result, the conference closed on an inconclusive note, with the
Turks only committing themselves to accepting a military mission to
discuss the preparation of the proposed air bases, and reserving the right to
decide by 15 February 1944 whether they would allow the Allies to use
them.[56]

Not unexpectedly, the new military staff talks provided for by the Cairo
decisions soon ran into the sand. Von Papen, who was well informed about
the conference proceedings through the activities of the German agent
'Cicero', Knatchbull-Hugessen's valet, made it clear to the Turks that
accepting Allied aircraft on Turkish soil would mean immediate war with
Germany, and was assured by Menemencioğlu on 18 December that
Turkey would remain neutral. Meanwhile, on 12 December, the Turkish
government duly informed the Allies that Turkey would exercise its option
not to receive Allied air detachments by the target date of 15 February.[57] A
military mission arrived in Ankara, but left on 4 February 1944 after
making no progress, and the British decided to stop their programme of
re-equipping Turkey. By the middle of the year, the Soviet government
had indicated that it had lost interest in bringing Turkey into the war, and
opposed the use of British or US forces in the area, which would have
blocked Stalin's post-war plans for a general Soviet takeover in south-
eastern Europe.[58] The British also appear to have come round to the view

that there was no point in pressing for immediate Turkish entry into the war by July 1944. By October 1944, when Churchill and Stalin held their famous Moscow meeting delineating spheres of influence in eastern Europe and giving the Soviet Union dominant shares in Bulgaria and Romania, the idea of an Allied intervention involving Turkey in south-eastern Europe which would block the Soviet Union had evidently been pushed off the agenda. Churchill decided not to pressure Turkey to join the Allies, as this would merely have provoked the Soviet Union without any military benefit: by this stage Soviet troops were in occupation of Bulgaria anyway.[59]

While these developments certainly weakened Allied pressure on the Turks, it did not mean that they could now cut themselves out of Allied diplomacy on the war. Their recognition that the Allied victory was now just a matter of time was manifested by several internal adjustments. The first of these was the enforced retirement of Marshal Fevzi Çakmak in January 1944. At 68, the Marshal was by now well over the normal age of retirement, and he would have needed a special dispensation from the president to continue in his command. His conservative views on professional military matters were an additional reason for retiring him. Almost certainly however, his pro-German reputation played a part in the decision, which was seen as an attempt by İnönü to improve his relations with the Allies. Other decisions which evidently had the same intention were the withdrawal of the scandalous Property Tax in March 1944 and the trials of those involved in pan-Turkist activities which began two months later.[60] In May 1944 Menemencioğlu also attempted to move matters forward with the Soviet government, by proposing a Turkish–Soviet treaty guaranteeing the independence of the Balkan states after the war. The Soviet response was that this could only be considered if Turkey entered the war without delay – a condition which they must have known was unacceptable to the Turks. Menemencioğlu concluded that the Soviet Union wanted Turkey to participate in the war, but only if it were 'assisted' by Soviet troops who would then stay on in Turkey after the war was ended.[61] Subsequently, İnönü's attempt to placate the Western Allies, and especially the British, went further when Menemencioğlu himself was forced to resign as foreign minister on 15 June 1944, to be succeeded as foreign minister by Hasan Saka the following September. The immediate cause of Menemencioğlu's departure was a complaint by the British that he had allowed the passage of six armed German ships to pass through the Bosporus, in defiance of the Montreux convention (the Turkish counter-claim was that they were 'auxiliaries', whose passage in wartime was allowed under the convention). However, the underlying reason was the conviction of the British Foreign Office, and especially Eden, that Menemencioğlu was pro-German. Whether he really was is disputed, and it would probably be fairer to say that the policies he had followed had throughout been endorsed by İnönü, but that the president now wanted to be seen to be making a change of course, to placate the Allies.[62]

The most contentious issues in relations between Turkey and the Allies during the spring and summer of 1944 was caused by Allied pressure on Turkey to break commercial and diplomatic relations with Germany. During the first two months of 1944, the Turks had actually increased chromite shipments to Germany, causing sharp protests from the United States and Britain, who even considered imposing an economic blockade on Turkey. This idea was abandoned, since, among other things, it would make Turkey even more dependent on the Axis. In the event, diplomatic pressure proved enough. On 20 April, Menemencioğlu announced that chromite exports to Germany would cease immediately. He took this further on 26 May by agreeing that Turkey would reduce its shipments to Germany of other strategic materials by 50 per cent and would give preferential treatment to orders from Allied sources. The process was rounded off on 2 August when Turkey formally broke off diplomatic relations with Germany, forcing von Papen to return to Berlin to face an uncertain future.[63]

While straightforward on the surface, the process of breaking Turkish links with Germany was accompanied by serious discussion that, even at this late stage, Turkey might join the war and play an active part in the future of the Balkans. This partly derived from wishful thinking by Menemencioğlu, to the effect that it might be possible to arrange a negotiated peace between Germany and the Allies which would prevent the Soviet Union from taking over eastern Europe. In a dinner speech on 28 February 1944 he proposed the formation of a Balkan federation, under Turkish leadership, which would mediate between Germany and 'Pan-Slavic Europe'. The idea evidently had no support in either camp, and fell by the wayside. However, an alternative plan for Turkish intervention in the Balkans was aired in July 1944, as Soviet forces were poised to occupy Romania and Bulgaria. The Soviet Union had offered to declare war on Bulgaria if Turkey did, and the US ambassador in Ankara, Laurence Steinhardt, was convinced that Turkey would enter the war in the near future if it received additional war materiel as well as Soviet assurances regarding Bulgaria. Nothing came of the project, however – presumably because the Allies could not meet Turkish conditions. In the event, Soviet forces occupied Bulgaria in September 1944, causing a brief panic in Turkey that it might face a combined threat from Soviet and Bulgarian expansionism, which the Western Allies might not oppose. Later, however, the Turks were reassured by British attempts to establish a stable government in Greece, and recognised their common interests with Greece and Britain. Hence, they withdrew their claims to the Dodecanese in November 1944.[64]

During the final phase of the war, between February and May 1945, the focus of Turkish attention switched away from the question of participation in the war towards Turkey's position in the post-war political order and the long-feared ambitions of Stalin at the straits. In the course of the Moscow conference of October 1944, Stalin claimed that the Montreux convention was 'unsuitable', and a 'spearhead' aimed at Russia: he could not accept a situation in which Turkey might 'grip Russian trade by the throat', he maintained.[65] Against the advice of Eden and the Foreign Office, Churchill responded that Britain would have no objection to allowing free passage for Soviet warships through the straits, and that the convention was now 'inadmissible' and 'obsolete'. Stalin did not make it clear exactly what he was demanding at the straits and, in Roosevelt's absence, no decision was taken.[66] The question came back onto the agenda at the last wartime meeting of the 'Big Three' held at Yalta on 4–11 February 1945, as Stalin again raised his complaints about the Montreux convention. Churchill again accepted the principle of revision, though he and Eden added that Turkey should be given assurances that its independence and integrity would be guaranteed (an idea which was then dropped). The conference thus ended with the conclusion that the Allies would discuss the issue further, though with no specific Soviet proposals at this stage. The Soviet side did, however, agree that it would not make any approaches to Turkey without consulting its Allies, and that it would take no action likely to damage Turkey's independence and integrity. The Soviet Union's next step came on 19 March when Molotov told the Turkish ambassador in Moscow, Selim Sarper, that unspecified changes were needed to the Turkish–Soviet treaty of 1925, which was due for renewal in November 1945, eliciting the response that Turkey wished to continue a friendly relationship with the Soviet Union, and would consider proposals made by the Soviet side. In fact, the Turks were naturally perturbed by what might be in store. Their anxieties were reinforced by a Soviet proposal made at the end of March that the future of the straits should be discussed purely at the bilateral level between Turkey and the Soviet Union, suggesting clearly that Stalin wished to detach the Turks from possible Western support.

Meanwhile, on 19 March, the Soviet government formally denounced the 1925 treaty.[67] İnönü's government were thus faced with the likelihood that Stalin would make serious demands at the straits, without knowing exactly what these would be. Meanwhile another decision taken at Yalta, to the effect that membership of the proposed United Nations would be restricted to those states which had joined the war on the Allied side before the end of February 1945 induced Turkey to take the formal step of declaring war on Germany and Japan on 23 February. Even though they were probably quite uncertain of their future in the post-war world, the Turks were clearly anxious to play a part in its international institutions.

TURKEY'S NEUTRALITY, 1939–45: TACTICS, STRATEGIES AND IMPLICATIONS

After the war, İnönü and his supporters were naturally anxious to stress the success of their wartime policies, both to their fellow-countrymen and to the Western Allies. Turkey had come through the test without having fired a shot in anger, and with no loss of territory or lives. By careful diplomacy, İnönü's government had saved the country from the horrors of war which had engulfed most of the rest of Europe, and had protected Turkey's independence and territorial integrity. Turkish and Western observers stressed that, whatever the policies the Allies had adopted during the war, Turkish neutrality had been in the best interests of both sides. Belligerence by Turkey on the Allied side would probably have meant invasion and occupation by Germany – as in the cases of Greece and Yugoslavia – which would merely have been an additional burden for the Allies, and might well have resulted in eventual Soviet occupation.[68] In spite of the non-aggression pact with Germany of 1941, Turkey's basic sympathies had been with the Allies all along, it was argued.[69] This claim may not be accepted, but it is hard to deny that İnönü and his government had effectively protected Turkey's own national interests. Without doubt, Turkey's most important national interest was to avoid the destruction of war, without sacrificing its independence or any of the territory it had won in 1923. In this respect İnönü and his colleagues were entirely successful. They showed skill in bargaining with both sides, and were relatively immune to propaganda or internal political penetration from either. On the principle that countries do not have permanent friends, but only permanent interests, Turkish diplomacy had done a remarkably effective job.[70] Like those of other neutral states, the Turkish economy undoubtedly suffered from wartime shortages. These were exacerbated by the government's poor economic and financial management,[71] quite apart from the scandal of the Property Tax. However, these economic problems were as nothing compared with those which would have been produced by invasion, the probable result of joining the war on either side.

To achieve these aims İnönü and his colleagues successfully exploited Turkey's strategic position, adopting the classic method of playing one power off against another. Turkey's military weakness was a severe handicap in facing up to prospective invasions by either Germany or the Soviet Union, since it made it very hard to protect the straits against an enemy with a modern air force and mechanised ground forces. However, İnönü turned this weakness into a diplomatic asset by stressing Turkey's military unpreparedness to the Allies, and thus heading off pressure for joining the war as well as gaining military supplies. He was also able to benefit from differences between Britain and the United States on the desirability of bringing Turkey into the war. The main cause of friction between Turkey and the Allies derived from the fact that whereas they had only one identifiable enemy, Turkey faced threats from both the Axis and the Soviet Union. For the Turks, Stalin was as menacing as Hitler. However, the Turkish government was able to turn this to its advantage by, for instance, using the German threat as a reason for not joining the war on the Allied side, and that from the Soviet Union for not carrying out its commitments under the 1939 tripartite treaty in 1940. Similarly, the danger of an attack from the Soviet Union was used as a means of deflecting German calls for assistance in 1941. This diplomacy was aided by a substantial helping of good luck. In 1940, Hitler's failure to reach an agreement with Stalin on a carve-up of the Near East between them was obviously a life-saver for Turkey. The fact that Hitler also attached more importance to invading the Soviet Union than attacking the Middle East saved Turkey from a German invasion in 1941. Since Hitler's armies became bogged down and were eventually defeated in the Soviet Union, he was unable to carry through his second plan for knocking the British out of the Middle East, which would have required both the defeat of the Soviet Union and the invasion or political subordination of Turkey. At the end of the war, the fact that it was the British and not the Soviets who occupied Greece when the Germans withdrew in 1944 saved Turkey from being surrounded by a hostile power on three sides. None of these outcomes could have been determined by Turkey, but they undoubtedly helped it to survive as an independent state.

To say that Turkey was neutral during the war also disguises important shifts in its policies between 1939 and 1945, which were largely caused by changing Turkish perceptions of which side would win the war. 'Neutrality' is a loose term and can cover the position of strict and *de jure* neutrality adopted by, say Switzerland, and the *de facto* neutrality espoused by Turkey. Between October 1939 and June 1940 Turkey was not only an ally of Britain and France by treaty, but apparently fully expected to be able to carry out its alliance commitments. By the spring of 1941, with the signature of the non-aggression pact with Germany, it had moved to a more fully neutral position, virtually equidistant between the two camps, referred to by Menemencioğlu as 'active neutrality'. In 1943, it shifted back towards the Allies, while remaining non-belligerent. During 1943–44, Turkish leaders repeatedly told the Allies that they would be willing to join the war, but only as part of a major Allied offensive in the Balkans. Cynics will argue that this was a bluff – that the Turks knew that the United States opposed any serious diversion of resources from 'Overlord', and that the proposal was just a polite way of opposing British pressure to join the war. However, Turkish anxiety to prevent Stalin taking over south-eastern Europe was undoubtedly genuine, and if Britain and the United States had been willing to commit substantial forces for an invasion of the Balkans in 1943–44, it seems quite possible that Turkey would have done so too.[72] In that case, Turkey would have become a fully fledged member of the alliance partnership, abandoning even *de facto* neutrality.

While Turkish diplomacy may have been successful in keeping Turkey out of the war, it can also be argued that it ended with one significant failure, since it left the Soviet Union in a dominant position in south-eastern Europe. Throughout the war, Turkish policy-makers, Menemencioğlu in particular, had attached cardinal importance to the idea of maintaining the balance of power between the Soviet Union and its western neighbours, especially Germany, by avoiding the total destruction of German power. This had been one of the main aims of Turkish diplomacy since the nineteenth century, but during 1939–45 it proved to be quite unattainable, thanks to the Allied commitment to secure the unconditional surrender of the enemy, and Hitler's determination to fight on to the end. In an age of total war, both sides, Axis and Allied, fought for total victory. Abstract principles like the balance of power could not be used for the mobilisation of total populations, or in the defence of either democratic or totalitarian ideologies. Hitler was being fought because his regime was evil, and not just because Germany had upset the balance of power. Hence the principle of not eliminating essential national actors, which was part of the balance-of-power system, went out of the window. In staying out of the war, the Turks had to take the risk that the classic mechanisms of power politics would re-assert themselves afterwards, and that the Western powers would forget wartime alliances so as to prevent Stalin from taking over the straits, or from turning Turkey into a Soviet satellite. Apparently, in 1944 Menemencioğlu believed that this risk was worth taking, that even if Turkey stayed out of the war the Western powers would still support it against Russia in a post-war confrontation.[73] His prediction turned out to be right, but at the time the war ended there was no proof that it would, and Turkey still faced a severe challenge to its hard-won security.

NOTES

1. Annette Baker Fox, *The Power of Small States: Diplomacy in World War II* (Chicago, IL, University of Chicago Press, 1959), p. vii.
2. For a summary of these arguments, see Brock Milman, 'Turkish Foreign and Strategic Policy 1934–42', *Middle Eastern Studies*, Vol. 31 (1995), pp. 483–4.
3. Edward Weisband, *Turkish Foreign Policy, 1943–1945: Small State Diplomacy and Great Power Politics* (Princeton, NJ, Princeton University Press, 1973), p. 249. For other information on Çakmak's position before and during the war, see William Hale, *Turkish Politics and the Military* (London, Routledge, 1994), pp. 70, 78–9, 82–3.
4. Weisband, *Turkish Foreign Policy*, pp. 33–71 and Selim Deringil, *Turkish Foreign Policy during the Second World War: An 'Active' Neutrality* (Cambridge, Cambridge University Press, 1989), pp. 41–57.
5. Milman, 'Turkish Policy', pp. 498–501; Selim Deringil, 'The Preservation of Turkey's Neutrality During the Second World War: 1940', *Middle Eastern Studies*, Vol. 18 (1982), p. 34; Deringil, *Turkish Foreign Policy*, p. 97 and Sir Hughe Knatchbull-Hugessen, *Diplomat in Peace and War* (London, Murray, 1949), p. 148.
6. Deringil, *Turkish Foreign Policy*, pp. 39, 93–95, and 'Preservation', pp. 31–2; Türkkaya Ataöv, *Turkish Foreign Policy, 1939–1945*, (Ankara University, Political Science Faculty, 1965), pp. 76–8. Ataöv writes that 'Turkey would energetically oppose an attack on Baku if it involved the use of Turkish territory', p. 77.
7. Deringil, *Turkish Foreign Policy*, pp. 97–102, and 'Preservation', pp. 34–8.
8. Frank G. Weber, *The Evasive Neutral: Germany, Britain and the Quest for a Turkish Alliance in the Second World War* (Columbia, MO, and London, University of Missouri Press, 1979), pp. 49–51 and Deringil, *Turkish Foreign Policy*, pp. 104–105.
9. Deringil, *Turkish Foreign Policy*, p. 40.
10. Fox, *Small States*, pp. 11–12. Fox implies that this was recognised throughout the war, but it does not appear to have been true of Turkish and Allied expectations between 1939 and the summer of 1940.
11. A.L. Macfie, 'The Turkish Straits in the Second World War, 1939–45', *Middle Eastern Studies*, Vol. 25 (1989), pp. 240–1 and Ataöv, *Turkish Foreign Policy*, pp. 78–79.
12. See William Hale, 'Anglo-Turkish Trade since 1923: Experiences and Problems', in William Hale and Ali İhsan Bağış, eds, *Four Centuries of Turco–British Relations* (Walkington, Eothen Press, 1984), pp. 112–13. Data are taken from the Turkish official Statistical Yearbooks (*İstatistik Yıllığı*) for the years in question.
13. Ibid., p. 113 and Ataöv, *Turkish Foreign Policy*, p. 71.

14. Quoted in Knatchbull-Hugessen, *Diplomat*, p. 167.
15. Deringil, *Turkish Foreign Policy*, p. 108.
16. Quoted in Ataöv, *Turkish Foreign Policy*, p. 87.
17. Deringil, *Turkish Foreign Policy*, pp. 102–15, and 'Preservation', pp. 38–48, and Knatchbull-Hugessen, *Diplomat*, pp. 161–2, 166–7.
18. Necmeddin Sadak, 'Turkey Faces the Soviets', *Foreign Affairs*, Vol 27 (1949), p. 453.
19. Texts in J.C. Hurewitz, ed., *Diplomacy in the Near and Middle East: A Documentary Record, 1914–1956* (Princeton, NJ, Van Nostrand, 1956), Vol. 2, pp. 226–30.
20. Macfie, 'Turkish Straits', pp. 241–2 and Bruce R. Kunihom, *The Origins of the Cold War in the Near East* (Princeton, NJ, Princeton University Press, 2nd edn, 1994), p. 25. See also Franz von Papen, trans. Brian Connell, *Memoirs* (London, André Deutsch, 1952), pp. 465–8.
21. Y. Olmert, 'Britain, Turkey and the Levant Question during the Second World War', *Middle Eastern Studies*, Vol. 23 (1987), pp. 438–43. Quotation from ibid., p. 443.
22. Weber's account, drawing on British records, suggests that the British could have prevented hostile action by Rashid Ali if they had chosen to do so, and that the British Ambassador in Iraq, Sir Kinahan Cornwallis, supported by Churchill, provoked the conflict with him in order to topple him. See Weber, *Evasive Neutral*, pp. 86–9.
23. In April 1942, a year after the crisis, Knatchbull-Hugessen wrote a private letter to Sir Orme Sargent, the deputy under-secretary of state in the Foreign Office, stating (in Weber's words) that 'the Turks would have much preferred to participate in the violent repression of Rashid Ali's regime and then to have remained on patrol in Iraq, as either Britain or Germany's ally, to keep the situation there quiet' (ibid., pp. 89–90). Knatchbull-Hugessen does not mention any of this in his memoirs.
24. Lukasz Hirszowicz, *The Third Reich and the Arab East* (London, Routledge & Kegan Paul, 1966), pp. 159–64. According to British reports, Saracoğlu refused permission for the transit of arms from Syria to Iraq (Deringil, *Turkish Foreign Policy*, p. 124) but the German reports, cited by Hirszowicz, contradict this. Deringil also admits that 'the Turks ended up allowing some war material to reach Iraq from the Axis in mid-May', though they stalled with the Germans for long enough to allow the British to regain control. Ibid., p. 125.
25. Hirszowicz, *Third Reich*, pp. 170, 181–4 and Olmert, 'Levant Question', pp. 444–7. On 3 June, Saracoğlu told von Papen that Turkey was considering occupying the Baghdad railway up to Aleppo for strategic reasons (Deringil, *Turkish Foreign Policy*, p. 125) but the Turks evidently then abandoned the proposal.
26. A. Suat Bilge *et al.*, *Olaylarla Türk Dış Politikası (1919–1965)* (Ankara University, Political Science Faculty, 1969), p. 166.
27. Quoted in Ataöv, *Turkish Foreign Policy*, pp. 102–3.
28. Weber, *Evasive Neutral*, pp. 93–5.
29. Deringil, *Turkish Foreign Policy*, p. 121 (quotations from German documents). In his memoirs, von Papen refers to these negotiations only vaguely, saying that he had been trying to 'convert Turkish–German relations from their attitude of non-belligerence into a condition of true neutrality and friendship'. See Von Papen, *Memoirs*, p. 478.
30. Deringil, *Turkish Foreign Policy*, pp. 121–2; Bilge *et al.*, *Olaylarla* pp. 168–70 and Ataöv, *Turkish Foreign Policy*, pp. 92–4. For the text of the treaty, see Hurewitz, ed., *Diplomacy*, Vol. 2, p. 231, from where the quotations are taken.
31. Knatchbull-Hugessen, *Diplomat*, pp. 169–70 and Weber, *Evasive Neutral*, p. 102. Von

Papen confirms that the Turks kept the British informed about their negotiations with Germany (*Memoirs*, p. 478) though whether these included the discussion of a full alliance is unclear.

32. Quoted in Deringil, *Turkish Foreign Policy*, p. 135.

33. Hirszowicz, *Third Reich*, pp. 197–201 and Robin Denniston, *Churchill's Secret War: Diplomatic Decrypts, the Foreign Office and Turkey, 1942–44* (Stroud, Sutton Publishing/ New York, NY, St Martin's Press, 1997), p. 59.

34. Quoted in Deringil, *Turkish Foreign Policy*, p. 124.

35. Denniston, *Secret War*, pp. 53, 66.

36. Deringil, *Turkish Foreign Policy*, pp. 130–32; Ataöv, *Turkish Foreign Policy*, pp. 96–7; Weber, *Evasive Neutral*, pp. 111–17, 123–6: Charles Warren Hostler, *Turkism and the Soviets* (London, Allen & Unwin, 1957), p. 175. For further background on pan-Turkism in Turkey at this time, see Jacob M. Landau, *Pan-Turkism: From Irredentism to Cooperation* (London, Hurst, 1995), pp. 90–7, 110–35.

37. Weisband, *Turkish Foreign Policy*, pp. 101–15: Deringil, *Turkish Foreign Policy*, pp. 129, 135–36 and Fox, *Small States*, pp. 20, 29. Figures for Turkey's foreign trade are calculated from the Turkish Statistical Yearbook for 1942; see Hale, 'Anglo-Turkish Trade', p. 113. In fact, the British purchased 151,000 tons of chromite in 1941, or three times as much as they had contracted for, under a pre-emptive purchasing programme. On the other hand, Turkish deliveries of chromite to Germany in 1943 were only about half the amount provided for in the Clodius agreement. Weisband, *Turkish Foreign Policy*, pp. 105–107.

38. It was, however, publicised in a series of articles by C.L. Sulzberger in the *New York Times* in September 1943; see David Brown, 'Foreword', in Faik Ökte, trans. Geoffrey Cox, *The Tragedy of the Capital Tax* (London, Croom Helm, 1987), p. xiii.

39. Brown, 'Foreword', in Ökte, *Tragedy of the Capital Tax*, p. 14.

40. For further details see ibid. See also Edward C. Clark, 'The Turkish Varlık Vergisi Reconsidered', *Middle Eastern Studies*, Vol. 8 (1972), pp. 205–16, and Weisband, *Turkish Foreign Policy*, pp. 231–6. The percentages cited here are drawn from Clark, 'Varlık Vergisi', p. 209.

41. Denniston, *Secret War*, p. 48. Quotations from Ataöv, *Turkish Foreign Policy*, p. 98, quoting British and Turkish sources. See also Sadak, 'Turkey', p. 458.

42. Deringil, *Turkish Foreign Policy*, pp. 127–8.

43. Quoted in Knatchbull-Hugessen, *Diplomat*, p. 181.

44. Deringil, *Turkish Foreign Policy*, pp. 131–2 and Harry N. Howard, *Turkey, the Straits and US Policy*, (Baltimore, MD, and London, Johns Hopkins University Press, 1974), p. 169.

45. Howard, *Straits*, p. 165.

46. Knatchbull-Hugessen, *Diplomat*, p. 180 and Denniston, *Secret War*, p. 76.

47. Howard, *Straits*, pp. 170–1: Deringil, *Turkish Foreign Policy*, p. 142–3. On disputes between Churchill and Eden over this, see also Denniston, *Secret War*, pp. 7, 10, 76–7.

48. Weisband, *Turkish Foreign Policy*, pp. 119–32.

49. Ibid., pp. 133–9 and Ataöv, *Turkish Foreign Policy*, pp. 106–9.

50. Deringil, *Turkish Foreign Policy*, pp. 150–1; Weisband, *Turkish Foreign Policy*, pp. 163–6 and Denniston, *Secret War*, pp. 111–23. Weber relates that Turkey refused to join in the operation with its own forces because the British refused to transfer sovereignty over the islands to Turkey, but this is not confirmed by the other sources cited. See Weber,

Evasive Neutral, pp. 181–3.
51. Quoted in Weisband, *Turkish Foreign Policy*, p. 179.
52. Ibid., pp. 176–85; Howard, *Straits*, pp. 178–82 and Kuniholm, *Origins*, pp. 34–9.
53. Howard, *Straits*, pp. 182–8 and Kuniholm, *Origins*, pp. 39–40.
54. Knatchbull-Hugessen, *Diplomat*, p. 197.
55. Quotations from Weisband, *Turkish Foreign Policy*, p. 208, Howard, *Straits*, p. 188, Weisband, *Turkish Foreign Policy*, p. 214.
56. Weisband, *Turkish Foreign Policy*, pp. 201–15: Howard, *Straits*, pp. 188–94: Deringil, *Turkish Foreign Policy*, pp. 159–63: Kuniholm, *Origins*, pp. 44–9.
57. Deringil, *Turkish Foreign Policy*, pp. 163–64. The Cicero affair is almost certainly the best-known incident in Knatchbull-Hugessen's career, and von Papen relates that he valued the information produced by 'Cicero' highly (*Memoirs*, pp. 507–18) though it does not seem to have had much significant effect on Turkish foreign policy at the time. For more information, see Denniston, *Secret War*, pp. 128–40, which also provides a guide to the voluminous literature on 'Cicero'.
58. Howard, *Straits*, pp. 199, 204; Weisband, *Turkish Foreign Policy*, pp. 271–2; Kuniholm, *Origins*, p. 41 and Macfie, 'Turkish Straits', p. 245.
59. Howard, *Straits*, p. 205; Weisband, *Turkish Foreign Policy*, pp. 290–2 and Deringil, *Turkish Foreign Policy*, p. 176. For further information on the October 1944 agreement, see Kuniholm, *Origins*, pp. 109–116.
60. Weisband, *Turkish Foreign Policy*, pp. 236–7, 249–50. On the last point, see also Landau, *Pan-Turkism*, pp. 117–18.
61. Weisband, *Turkish Foreign Policy*, pp. 228–9; Howard, *Straits*, p. 199 and Kuniholm, *Origins*, pp. 52–3.
62. Deringil, *Turkish Foreign Policy*, pp. 55–7, 170–72 and Weisband, *Turkish Foreign Policy*, pp. 261–8.
63. Howard, *Straits*, pp. 197–98 and Weisband, *Turkish Foreign Policy*, pp. 257–9, 268–73. Turkey broke diplomatic relations with Japan in November 1944.
64. Weber, *Evasive Neutral*, p. 202: Howard, *Straits*, p. 203; Weisband, *Turkish Foreign Policy*, pp. 277–84 and Kuniholm, *Origins*, pp. 62–4, 217–18.
65. Quoted in Macfie, 'Turkish Straits', p. 245.
66. Deringil, *Turkish Foreign Policy*, p. 176: Ataöv, *Turkish Foreign Policy*, p. 124 and Kuniholm, *Origins*, pp. 111–12.
67. Howard, *Straits*, pp. 212–17: Kuniholm, *Origins*, pp. 219–20 and A.L. Macfie, 'The Straits Question at the Potsdam Conference: The British Position', *Middle Eastern Studies*, Vol. 23 (1987), pp. 75–6.
68. This argument is strongly advanced by Sadak, 'Turkey', p. 459.
69. See, e.g., Knatchbull-Hugessen, *Diplomat*, pp. 203–204 and Ataöv, *Turkish Foreign Policy*, pp. 130–4.
70. See, e.g., Fox, *Small States*, pp. 41–42; Deringil, *Turkish Foreign Policy*, pp. 184–5 and Kuniholm, *Origins*, pp. 68–9.
71. The author has dealt with this topic more fully elsewhere: see William Hale, *The Political and Economic Development of Modern Turkey*, (London, Croom Helm, 1981), pp. 70–1, 74–8.
72. See Weisband, *Turkish Foreign Policy*, p. 325.
73. Deringil, *Turkish Foreign Policy*, p. 166.

4

Turkey and the Cold War: The Engagement Phase, 1945–63

On 18 July 1945, just as the Second World War was ending and the Cold War beginning, the veteran Turkish journalist Ahmet Emin Yalman suggested in his newspaper, *Vatan*, that for Turkey 'The old eastern question has risen from its grave'.[1] His verdict was quite justified to the extent that, as in the period up to 1917, Turkey's territorial integrity and its future as an independent state was gravely threatened by a resurgent Russia, and that Turkey urgently needed to find allies to fend it off. On the other hand, there were significant differences between Turkey's situation during the Cold War, and that of the Ottoman empire before 1914. In the first place, the 'old eastern question' had largely been about the future of the Balkans, but these had been lost to the Turkish state in 1912–13, and later Turkish governments never tried to re-establish their old role in the region. Internal ethnic conflict, as a leading issue in the Turks' foreign relations, did not re-emerge until the late 1980s, when the Kurdish problem became a critical factor in Turkey's relationship with the Western powers and its Middle Eastern neighbours. Meanwhile, Christian–Muslim conflict in the Balkans was stilled until the disintegration of Yugoslavia in 1991.

For the Turks, the most important feature of the post-war world, was its bipolarity, and the fact that the United States and Soviet Union were the only two players who really mattered. Hence, Turkey was unable to play one European power off against another, in a fluid and usually temporary pattern of alliances and rivalries, as the Ottoman government had been able to before 1914. In effect, the range of Turkey's options was far more limited than it had been during the early period. It could not opt out of the Cold War, relying on a balance of power between the two Cold War blocs to maintain its security, like most of its Arab neighbours and other Asian and African states, without running the serious risk of Soviet aggression or political domination. Nor did it have sufficient economic, technical and military resources to protect itself, if it chose neutrality. On this account, it was virtually bound to seek a place in the Western alliance. The nuclearisation of the potential contest, and its consequent risks, were also crucial for an exposed ally like Turkey. The Turks were to receive a sharp lesson in the realities of this danger in 1962, although catastrophe was fortunately avoided. The effects of the perception that the Cold War was also an ideological struggle are harder to assess. In spite of the Turkish government's repeated claims of adherence to democratic values, it is likely that this factor was less important in motivating Turkey's attachment to the Western alliance than traditional territorial and security interests. Essentially, Turkey was forced into the Western camp in the Cold War because it was directly threatened by the Soviet Union, rather than through an *a priori* commitment to liberal democracy (indeed, the causal chain may well have been the other way round). On the other hand, the nature of the ideological divide did have an important effect on Turkey's foreign policy options, in that the Western alliance paid reasonable respect to the independence of small or medium-sized states, whereas Soviet communism did not. This factor reinforced the effect of immediate security considerations and the historical suspicion of Russia.

The effect of its Cold War alignment on Turkey's domestic political evolution between the mid-1940s and the early 1960s is more difficult to assess, since this was very far from being an externally dependent variable. On the other hand, changes in the domestic political structure had some impact on foreign relations. At the end of 1945, İsmet İnönü took the bold step of dismantling the single-party structure, and allowing the formation of an effective opposition party. This materialised as the Democrat Party, founded by two dissidents from the Republican People's Party (CHP), Adnan Menderes and Celal Bayar. In Turkey's first free and fair elections since the foundation of the republic, held in 1950, the Democrats were swept to power, with Menderes as prime minister and Bayar as president. At first glance, İnönü's decision might be seen as a result of clear foreign policy interests: if Turkey was to gain admission to the Western alliance, then it had to make itself respectably democratic. On the other hand, it is virtually impossible to prove that it was this simple logic which determined İnönü's choice. Apart from external challenges, there were powerful domestic considerations pushing him in the same direction. After years of heavy-handed rule by the CHP, there was widespread discontent, reinforced by wartime economic privations. İnönü was sensitive and flexible enough to realise that he could not hold down the lid on the kettle indefinitely, without risking a destructive explosion. Moreover, there is no clear proof that the Western powers demanded democratisation in Turkey as a condition of their support.[2] İnönü was willing to admit in private that foreign-policy considerations had affected his decision, but this seems to have been based on the general perception that the defeat of the Axis heralded the end of dictatorship worldwide, and the victory of democracy, rather than as part of a straightforward bid to win Western support in the Cold War.[3]

In the event, the Democrats' victory produced few important changes in foreign policy. If anything, Menderes and his colleagues were even more committed to the West than İnönü had been, since they shared his strategic perceptions, and reinforced this by an attachment (at least in theory) to American-style economic liberalisation. In foreign policy, they were, however, weakened by sharply declining domestic popularity and economic failures in the late 1950s. This briefly inclined them to look for some new alternatives, but without any significant effect. The Democrats were overthrown by a military coup on 27 May 1960, which pushed foreign policy into the background, but confirmed Turkey's commitment to the West. It was not until the mid-1960s that domestic political turbulence began to have serious effects on external orientations.[4]

THE CONSTRUCTION OF THE WESTERN ALLIANCE, 1945–52

At the end of the Second World War, the Turks had been left with the knowledge that Stalin was likely to push for a revision of the Montreux convention in Russia's favour, and possibly other concessions, without knowing the exact nature of his demands. Nor could they be confident that the Western powers would oppose him on this issue. It soon became clear that Stalin's project was remarkably similar to that which he had unsuccessfully proposed to Hitler in November 1940 (see pp. 85–6). In March 1945 the Soviet government officially denounced the Treaty of Friendship with Turkey which it had signed in 1925. Three months later, on 7 June 1945, Molotov told Selim Sarper, the Turkish ambassador in Moscow, that in return for renewing the treaty the Soviet Union would demand a new straits convention, negotiated solely between Turkey and the Soviet Union. This would provide for the free passage of Soviet warships through the straits and their closure to non-Black Sea states, the establishment of

Soviet bases at the straits, and the retrocession to Russia of the eastern
provinces of Kars and Ardahan which had been returned to Turkey in
1921 (see pp. 50–1).[5] Of these proposals, the Soviet plan for the establishment of Soviet bases seemed easily the most dangerous, since it threatened
the establishment of a military presence which could have been used to
secure Soviet control over the whole of Turkey. This expectation was
reinforced when Molotov hinted that the kind of treaty relationship the
Soviet Union wanted with Turkey would be similar to those it was establishing with Poland and the other satellite states. Sarper's reply was that
Turkey could not consider allowing Soviet bases at the straits, or the renegotiation of the 1921 Turkish–Soviet treaty (in other words, the retrocession of Kars and Ardahan). Any revision of the Montreux convention
would have to be a matter for international negotiation and agreement. At
a meeting in the presidential mansion in Ankara in the spring of 1945,
İnönü expressed the view that there was no immediate danger of a Soviet
invasion of Turkey, as the Soviet Union's losses in the war, and its other
commitments in eastern Europe, were too severe. However, in October,
the Turks had second thoughts about this assumption, owing to a build-up
of Soviet troops in Bulgaria, and temporarily halted demobilisation of their
own forces.[6] Throughout, there was a real fear on the Turkish side that the
Soviet Union wanted not only to gain control of the straits, but also to
convert Turkey into a satellite, as it was currently doing in the eastern
European countries. Contemporary Soviet attempts to take over Iranian
Azerbaijan, and possibly the whole of Iran, reinforced this perception, and
combined with the Soviet reinforcements in Bulgaria to create a serious
war of nerves between Turkey and the Soviet Union.[7]

After the delivery of these Soviet demands the British, who saw them as
a threat to their position in the Middle East, assured the Turks of their
support and encouraged them to stand firm. However, at this stage the
United States was very reluctant to take on distant commitments, such as
ensuring the security of the Turkish straits.[8] Hence, Western opposition to
Stalin on this issue did not become explicit at the first post-war meeting of
the 'Big Three', held at Potsdam 17 July–2 August 1945. When Stalin
repeated the proposals Molotov had earlier put to Sarper, the British
pointed out that they went well beyond what they had suggested at Yalta.
President Truman then made an unexpected intervention, proposing that
the straits and all other international waterways should be put under international control – a project which, if carried out, would have returned
Turkey to the position it had held between 1923 and 1936 under the
Lausanne convention (see p. 54). Although Stalin had failed to get British

or US support for the establishment of Soviet bases at the straits, the conference ended on an inconclusive note, with the proposal that the three governments, plus Turkey, would conduct separate discussions.[9] In fact, nothing came of this.

We cannot know for certain whether Stalin was actually intending to invade Turkey in 1945–46: quite probably, his preference was to isolate Turkey diplomatically, and then force its rulers to accept a treaty which would give the Soviet Union control of the straits, and then of the government as a whole. As Necmeddin Sadak, later the Turkish foreign minister, claimed in an article published in 1949, 'after the occupation of the Dardanelles, the Soviet Union would demand a Communist Government at Ankara and would impose one on Turkey'.[10] Essentially, the Turks had to assure themselves of a countervailing force if they were to oppose Stalin successfully. Diplomatic opposition would have been pointless if it had lacked the threat of a military response. Legally, the treaty with the British of 1939 was still valid, and was Turkey's only existing alliance. However, it was doubtful whether post-war Britain had the power or resources to support Turkey against the Soviet Union effectively, and the British did not wish to draw attention to it, although the Turks were happy to drop the provision that it should not involve them in war with the Soviet Union (see p. 69).[11] Hence, Turkey had to try to secure US assistance. Essentially, what İnönü's government had to do was, first, to make sure that the United States and the other Western powers would not support Soviet demands, second to obtain Western financial support which would make it possible to maintain the mobilisation of the Turkish armed forces (which was undertaken in response to the Russian offensive) and, third, if possible to construct an effective alliance with the West based on security guarantees, to ensure long-term protection against possible Soviet aggression.

On 2 November 1945, the United States presented a note to the Turkish government proposing an international conference to discuss the revision of the Montreux convention, at which the United States would support the principle of free passage for the warships of Black Sea powers, and limited access for the fleets of non-Black Sea states (which was what, in effect, the existing convention provided for). The fact that this response excluded the proposal for the establishment of Soviet bases was the most important point from the Turkish viewpoint.[12] This secured İnönü's first objective, but left him uncertain as to whether the West would be ready to give Turkey sufficient material support to make its diplomatic stand effective. On this point, a crucial change was that by the beginning of 1946

President Truman had been converted by Soviet actions in Iran and else-
where to adopt a much tougher approach than he had demonstrated at
Potsdam. As he wrote in a letter (which he never actually mailed) to US
Secretary of State James F. Byrnes on 3 January 1946:

> There isn't a doubt in my mind that Russia intends an invasion of Turkey
> and the seizure of the Black Sea straits to the Mediterranean. Unless Russia
> is faced with an iron fist and strong language another war is in the making.
> Only one language do they understand – 'how many divisions have you?' ...
> I'm tired of babying the Soviets.[13]

Truman's forecast of likely Soviet actions appeared to be born out in
March 1946 as the Soviet Union reinforced its substantial military
presence in Iranian Azerbaijan, thus threatening both Iran and eastern
Turkey, as well as strengthening its forces in Bulgaria which could have
been used against either Turkey or Greece. An important boost to Turkish
morale came on 6 April 1946, when the battleship *USS Missouri* paid a visit
to Istanbul, to wide public acclaim. Originally, the *USS Missouri* visit had
been arranged to bring home the body of the former Turkish ambassador
in Washington, Mehmet Ertegün, who had died in November 1944, but it
was generally accepted as an important symbol of US support for Greece
and Turkey against the Soviet Union.[14] However, it was still unclear what
concrete form this support would take. Meanwhile, the diplomatic tussle
over the straits continued. On 7 August 1946 the Soviet Union delivered
its long-delayed response to the US note of the previous November. This
merely repeated previous Soviet demands, though without reference to
Kars and Ardahan. It proposed that the regime of the straits should come
under the competence of Turkey and the Black Sea powers alone, and that
Turkey and the Soviet Union should organise 'joint means of defence of
the straits'. In response, the United States reiterated its position of
November 1945, adding that an attack on the straits would be 'a threat to
international security', and a matter for action by the UN Security
Council.[15] On 24 September 1946 the Soviets suggested to the Turks that
they should hold bilateral talks, preparatory to the revision of the
Montreux convention, but were again turned down. Subsequently, on 26
October, the Soviet government informed the British that it considered
that a conference to consider a new straits regime would be 'premature',
suggesting that it realised that attempts to persuade either Turkey or the
Western powers to accept Stalin's demands would be fruitless.[16]

In the event, this turned out to be the end of official diplomatic
exchanges on the issue, but neither the Turks nor the Western powers

could have known this at the time, and the propaganda war between Turkey and Soviet Union continued for many years to come. Since the Soviet claims had not been officially withdrawn, Stalin could have reopened the campaign whenever he wanted to. Hence, Turkey still had to find effective means of securing its defence. Meanwhile, Britain was in dire economic straits. On 21 February 1947 Clement Attlee's government announced that it would no longer be able to carry the burden of economic support to Greece and Turkey. Elsewhere, President Truman's resolve was strengthened by the fact that the Western powers had successfully faced down Stalin over Iran in 1946, allowing the Shah's government to resume rule over Iranian Azerbaijan at the end of the year. However, Greece was still ravaged by the destruction of war, with its government facing the prospect of defeat by communist insurgents backed by Albania, Yugoslavia and Bulgaria. By this stage British and US leaders had been convinced for over a year that the defence of Greece and Turkey was essential for the protection of Western interests in the eastern Mediterranean and the Middle East. However, this point was not widely appreciated in the United States, where the newly elected and Republican-dominated Congress was determined to reduce government spending. Truman decided to face the challenge by presenting the Congress and public with the grim facts, and applying for their assistance. The 'Truman Doctrine' took the form of a speech to both houses of Congress delivered on 12 March 1947, in which the President asked for approval of a US$400 million aid programme to Greece and Turkey, to last until the end of June 1948. The programme was passed by large majorities in both houses during the next two months.

The launch of the 'Truman Doctrine' marked a turning point in the history of the Cold War, as well as Turkey's search for post-war security. The internal political and economic situation was far more precarious in Greece than in Turkey, and Truman laid the main emphasis on this in his address to Congress: (accordingly, US$300 million was to be allocated to Greece, and US$100 million to Turkey).[17] However, İnönü's government was also in serious need of foreign support to continue the military expenditure needed to deter Stalin, so economic assistance was an important advantage. More importantly, Turkey's inclusion in Truman's programme was a clear signal to the Soviet Union that the United States was prepared to make a material rather than a purely symbolic contribution to the defence of Turkey. As Necmeddin Sadak explains: 'The Truman Doctrine was a great comfort to the Turkish people, for it made them feel that they were no longer isolated.'[18] Since it bolstered the Greek government against the communist insurgents, it also helped to prevent Turkey's encirclement by satellite states on three sides.

During 1948, as an additional support, Turkey began to receive Marshall Aid, and thus became a member of the OEEC (Organisation for European Economic Co-operation; later OECD, Organisation for Economic Co-operation and Development). Between then and 1950 it received around US$183 million in economic aid, under the European Recovery Programme, and around US$200 million in military aid. Although the Turks predictably complained that this aid was insufficient, and that they had been admitted to the Marshall Aid scheme only after some delay, its availability was another advantage of their developing relationship with the United States.[19] Meanwhile, with the Berlin blockade, the Cold War assumed definite shape in Europe, and its institutional structures began to emerge.

In March 1948 Britain, France and the Benelux countries signed the Brussels Treaty, providing for economic collaboration and mutual self-defence, with strong support from President Truman. Subsequently, in November 1948, Turkey formally submitted an unsuccessful application for inclusion in any future Atlantic Pact. The Turks welcomed the fact that the Western powers were now taking joint action against the Soviet threat, but were disturbed by its prospective confinement to western Europe, since their exclusion might send a signal to Stalin that the Western powers were not prepared to protect Turkey. Among various alternatives, they promoted the idea that Turkey might take the lead in forming a pro-Western alliance in the Middle East, as a means of restoring British faith in Turkey as an ally, or that a Mediterranean Pact could be established, similar to the Atlantic Pact, to include Britain, France, Greece and Turkey, and with US support. However, increasing expectations that Italy would be included in the Atlantic security system severely weakened the utility of a second structure. As the Turks argued, one could not cut the Mediterranean in two. There was also some discussion of a bilateral defence agreement with the United States, but this was blocked by the fact that Congress limited US defence spending to US$15 billion in 1948–49, and then to the same amount in 1949–50. Although the Joint Chiefs of Staff emphasised US strategic interests in Greece and Turkey, US Secretary of State George Marshall opposed spreading limited resources over too wide an area.[20] Hence, the only viable alternative for Turkey, as the Turks saw it, was to seek full membership of the Atlantic alliance. Apart from the far greater degree of security which this would bring, it would also signal Turkey's acceptance as a member of the Western comity of nations – an aim going right back to the Treaty of Paris of 1856. For İsmet İnönü, an important aim was that, in his words, Turkey should be accepted as a 'respected member of the civilised world'.[21] A symbol of this commitment was Turkey's application for admission to the Council of Europe, which was accepted in August 1949. This attachment later turned out to have important implications for Turkey's adherence (or, rather, non-adherence) to human rights and other democratic norms, but at the time it was welcomed by Turkey as a sign of its acceptance as a European nation.[22]

The North Atlantic Treaty, signed on 4 April 1949, formalised the new alliance, but gravely disappointed the Turks, mainly because Italy had been included, but Turkey and Greece rather pointedly left out. As Necmeddin Sadak, now the Turkish foreign minister, put it to US Assistant Secretary of State Dean Acheson, the Turks were still pre-occupied with the unanswered question: 'Will the United States fight if the Russians attack Turkey?'[23] Membership of NATO was seen by the Turks as the only means of getting a positive answer to this question, but it was held up for three years by some complex obstacles. The most important of these was that the Truman administration initially tended to see Turkey as part of the Middle East rather than Europe, and assumed that US interests in the region were minimal compared with those of Britain. Given budgetary constraints between 1948 and 1950, the US army still preferred to concentrate its resources on western Europe. The British, meanwhile, were primarily concerned with trying to prop up their own crumbling power in the Middle East, and advanced the idea that, rather than join NATO, Turkey should take part in a British-led Middle Eastern defence system. The Turks were willing to consider such arrangements, but only on condition that admission to NATO was part of the deal. Accordingly, Turkey submitted its first unsuccessful application for membership of the alliance in May 1950.

The global situation was then radically changed by the outbreak of the Korean war in the following month, as a result of which the US defence budget for 1950–51 was sharply increased to US$50 billion. This relieved the administration of the need to define Turkey's strategic location. Either way, the funds were now there to incorporate the Turks and Greeks into NATO. The events in Korea also demonstrated that the threat to Western security was a global one, and not confined to western Europe, bringing in the two countries (Turkey and Greece) as actors in a potential world war which might include the Middle East. A month after the start of the Korean war, the new Democrat Party government led by Adnan

Menderes announced the despatch of a Turkish brigade of 4,500 men to join the UN forces, as a clear sign of its commitment to the Western camp.[24] Undoubtedly, Menderes and his colleagues were mainly concerned to exploit this apt opportunity to prove Turkey's value and loyalty to the West, and thus gain admission to the Atlantic alliance, thus succeeding in a quest where the previous government had failed. Only one week after the decision to send Turkish troops to Korea, they put forward a formal request to join the alliance.[25]

Initially, the reaction of the US military chiefs was cautious. In September 1950 they were willing only to offer Greece and Turkey associate membership of NATO, with full membership as an eventual goal. Not surprisingly, the Turks turned down this prospect of second-class citizenship in the alliance. At the same time, the NATO Council of Ministers rejected a second application by Turkey for membership, saying that Turkey and Greece should merely be asked to participate in planning for the defence of the Mediterranean.[26] Shortly afterwards, however, a crucial change in US strategic thinking was effected by Dwight Eisenhower, as Supreme Allied Commander in Europe (SACEUR). As Eisenhower explained in a message to Truman in January 1951, he saw Europe as shaped like a bottleneck, with the Soviet Union representing the wide part, central Europe the neck, and Spain the end. If the Soviet Union tried to move forward into the central bottleneck, then the Western powers should attempt to hold it there, but also hit the wide part of the bottle hard from both flanks, using air and sea power. Turkey and Yugoslavia were essential to this strategy, as the main anti-Soviet countries on the southern flank. In the regional security context, Turkey would be vital to help repel a Bulgarian attack on Greece, but could not be expected to do so unless it were given a firm security commitment by the Western powers.[27] Elsewhere, the engagement of Chinese troops in Korea in November 1950 suggested that the Soviet Union might strike anywhere – for instance, by launching an attack through one of its satellites on either Greece or Yugoslavia, following Tito's break with Stalin. At the end of a conference of US Chiefs of Mission in Istanbul and discussions with President Celal Bayar in February 1951, George McGhee, then US Assistant Secretary of State for the Near East, South Asia and Africa, urged the US State Department that the United States should give renewed attention to the admission of Greece and Turkey to NATO. US Secretary of State Dean Acheson was converted to this view in late March 1951. Various alternatives, such as a series of bilateral pacts between the United States and Turkey and Greece, or some other multilateral arrangements between the

United States, Turkey, Britain and Greece, were considered less straight-forward or effective.[28]

Fortunately for the Turks, Truman was convinced by these arguments, and in May 1951 decided to press for the admission of Greece and Turkey as full members of NATO. This left the the United States with the task of winning over the other NATO allies. Of these, British objections were the most troublesome, since Britain attempted to make Turkish admission to NATO dependent on Turkish agreement to put Turkish troops under British command in the event of war, as part of the plan for a Middle East Command which it was unsuccessfully trying to negotiate with Egypt.[29] The Scandinavian member countries, Norway and Denmark, also resisted the plan to admit Greece and Turkey, since they were worried that this might drag them into a war in the Middle East, in which they had no interests. However, on 18 July 1951 the new British Foreign Secretary, Herbert Morrison, publicly announced a change of policy by Britain, and supported the admission of Greece and Turkey to NATO. In response, Menderes' Foreign Minister, Fuat Köprülü, told the Turkish parliament on 20 July that if Turkey were admitted to NATO, then it would take on an unspecified defence role in the Middle East. At the meeting of the NATO Council of Ministers held in Ottawa in September 1951, the United States was able to overcome objections from the other allies, and the Council eventually approved the plan unanimously. In particular, the British proposal that Turkey should be admitted to NATO only if it agreed to be part of the proposed Middle East Command as a prior condition was overruled by the United States, although the Turks did agree to discuss the proposal after their admission. Arguments then followed as to how the new members could be fitted into the NATO structure, as a result of which it was decided that their ground forces would come under NATO's Southern Command. The Turks clung resolutely and success-fully to this proposal, since, as Ekavi Athanassopoulou puts it, 'Ankara's wish for Turkey to be considered European and not Middle Eastern was all-pervasive in the minds of the Turkish cabinet members'.[30] The United States supported the Turks on this issue, and again carried the day over the British. On this basis the extension of the alliance was officially approved at a meeting of the North Atlantic Council in Lisbon in February 1952. After six years, Turkish post-war policy had finally realised its paramount objective.[31]

In retrospect, the process of transition to full membership of the Western alliance could be seen as Turkey's most important foreign policy change since the 1920s. On the Turkish side, the reasons for it are not hard to identify: the problem for the Turkish government was not to convince itself or its own people that they needed an alliance with the West, but to convince the Western powers that they needed Turkey. The end of the war had brought about a dramatic change in Turkey's strategic environment, which made the continuation of neutrality, or uninvolved dependence on the balance of power to maintain Turkey's security, a defunct option. Soviet power was now resurgent, extending to the Bulgarian frontier in the west and Transcaucasia in the east. The possibility of a communist takeover in Greece also continued until the end of the Greek civil war in 1949. In eastern and central Europe, Germany and Austria had been eliminated as balancing powers. The Soviet threat was a clear and blunt one, which obliged Turkey to seek a Western alliance. As Nikita Khrushchev later put it, Beria and Stalin 'succeeded in frightening the Turks right into the open arms of the Americans'.[32] Under previous conditions, Turkey would have been wary of accepting an alliance – including, as it did, the establishment of NATO air and naval bases on Turkish soil – for fear that this would convert it into a satellite of its allies. Such criticisms were later to surface during the 1960s, but were virtually absent at the time. Had the Western alliance been led by Britain and France, the old imperialist powers, Turkey would probably have been chary of joining it, but the leadership of the United States, which was seen as being genuinely committed to protecting the independence of small states, convincingly overcame such objections.

On the Western side, the reality of the Soviet threat, and Turkey's vital strategic situation, plus the solidity of the Turkish response, defeated suspicions about Turkey's commitment or reliability. For the Western powers, Turkey was an 'unsinkable aircraft carrier'.[33] As an internal Foreign Office memorandum concluded in April 1948, 'there will be no neutrality for Turkey in any next war, and ... the Turks recognise that they cannot play their old game'.[34] Like his Tsarist predecessors, Stalin was not only threatening Turkey, but also Western security in the Mediterranean and Middle East, so there was a strong confluence of Western and Turkish interests. It may be argued that Stalin did not have inherently aggressive intentions against Turkey, but was merely seeking to strengthen the security of his own country. However, as the Turks and their allies saw it, absolute security for the Soviet Union meant absolute insecurity for its neighbours.[35] At the same time, Turkish views about the shape of the alliance were much closer to those of the United States than those of Britain. Hence, Turkey was able to exploit the United States' dominant role among the Western powers to its advantage. Domestically,

Kemalist nationalism still had an almost exclusive hold over public opinion, and pro-Soviet sympathies were virtually non-existent. A fellow-travelling Turkish Socialist Workers' and Peasants' Party was re-established in 1946, but, like the Turkish Communist Party originally set up in 1920, it was banned within a few months, and had no internal underground support structure.[36] Hence, Turkey's attachment to the Western alliance was far more straightforward than in the cases of, say, Greece or Iran, where Soviet power was trying to expand through internal penetration rather than threats of external aggression. In spite of the transition to multi-party politics in 1945–46, and the victory of the Democrats in the 1950 elections, there was virtually no disagreement about the main lines of foreign policy, which survived the transformation in domestic politics virtually unscathed. The only point of conflict was Turkey's participation in the Korean War – the first occasion on which Turkish troops had been sent abroad since the foundation of the republic. The decision was criticised by the CHP, now in opposition, on the grounds that parliament had not been consulted. It appears, however, that this derived from Menderes' tactics of presenting the move as a *fait accompli*, rather than opposition to the decision as such by İnönü. Participation in the Korean war was widely supported by the Turkish press, and apparently by public opinion generally.[37] In the existing climate, foreign policy was almost lifted out of Turkish internal political debates for over a decade.

ALLIANCE ENGAGEMENT AND REGIONAL CONFLICTS, 1952–62

During the 1950s and early 1960s, Turkey's commitment to and engagement with the Western alliance was at its height. Admittedly, Soviet policies softened after the death of Stalin in 1953, but this had little effect on Turkish attitudes, since the Democrat Party government simply refused to believe that the supposed change of heart was genuine.[38] Nikita Khrushchev and his successors sought to replace confrontation with the West in the European theatre to Soviet support for what was now known as the 'Third World', where it was hoped that a pro-Soviet 'correlation of forces' would steadily undermine Western power and influence. This merely changed the nature of the Turkish perception of the Soviet threat, rather than removing it, since the Turks saw themselves as part of the First World rather than the Third. They were now perturbed not just by the Soviet military presence on their north-western and north-eastern borders (which was still there), but also by growing Soviet political penetration to their south, in the Middle East. Shifting patterns in the Balkans, especially Yugoslavia, were also a source of concern. Although relations with Western governments were not always entirely harmonious, Turkey had no other foreign-policy interests which clearly conflicted with those of the main Western powers, so the alliance seems to have been perceived as firm on both sides.

In May 1953, shortly after Stalin's death, the Soviet government publicly declared that it had withdrawn its claims to Kars and Ardahan, and that it did not have 'any kind of territorial claims on Turkey' (although it was not clear that it was dropping all its demands for a reform of the straits regime). Menderes' government accepted this 'with satisfaction', but made no further move to pick up the olive branch.[39] When the original term of the Montreux convention expired in November 1956, it was considered to have been automatically renewed, since none of the signatories had officially applied for its abrogation or amendment. Early in 1958, when Turkey was in serious economic difficulties, a delegation was sent to Moscow to sound out the Soviets on obtaining economic aid, but nothing came of this, and Turkey was later bailed out by an IMF rescue package.[40] There was another sign of a thaw in the Turkish attitude early in 1960, when it was announced that Menderes and Khrushchev would exchange official visits, but Menderes' government was overthrown by a *coup d'état* on 27 May 1960, before this could be accomplished. On 28 June 1960 Khrushchev wrote to General Cemal Gürsel, the head of the then military junta, proposing that Turkey should opt for neutrality, and suggesting that the two sides should hold talks on points which they had in common. This marked a change in Soviet policy, which was now demanding the neutralisation (sometimes referred to as the 'Finlandisation') of Turkey rather than its effective conversion into a satellite. However, Gürsel failed to respond, apparently because he wished to convince the Western powers that the change of regime in Turkey did not herald any weakening of its commitment to the West.[41] Both the military government and the civilian administration under İsmet İnönü, which took over in November 1961, later turned down a US$500 million aid programme from the Soviet Union, fearing that Moscow would demand political concessions in return. İnönü was also quick to allay suspicions that he might have a more neutralist policy than his military predecessors.[42]

Meanwhile, Turkish integration with Western defence structures, and the Western military presence in Turkey, developed apace during the 1950s. Three-quarters of Turkey's land forces were reserved for NATO purposes, under the Commander-in-Chief of Allied Forces, Southern

Europe (CINCSOUTH), who was based in Naples, while the air force and navy were assigned to SACEUR. Under a series of bilateral and secret agreements, important US-cum-NATO facilities were constructed in Turkey, including, most notably, an air base at İncirlik, near Adana, with other bases at Karamürsel, Çiğli and Diyarbakır, and radar stations at Karamürsel, Sinop, Samsun, Trabzon, Belbaşı and Diyarbakır. Naval facilities and storage centres were established at İskenderun (Alexandretta) and Yumurtalık. The US Air Force stationed strike aircraft armed with tactical nuclear weapons on Turkish soil, under an agreement reached in 1957, and by the late 1960s there were about 24,000 US military personnel on Turkish territory. US aid, equipment and training were also instrumental in modernising the armed forces and in propping up the Turkish economy. Total delivered US military assistance to Turkey between 1948 and 1964 came to US$2,271 million, plus US$328 million in deliveries of surplus equipment. Meanwhile, Western economic aid to Turkey between 1950 and 1962 totalled around US$1,380 million, of which the vast majority came from the USA. To put these figures into context, Turkey's annual average exports during the 1950s came to around US$320 million, and its annual imports to around US$400 million. Turkey would almost certainly have found it impossible to maintain a fairly high rate of economic growth during the 1950s (as it did), and greatly strengthen its defences at the same time, without this assistance.[43]

For the Turks, and especially for those who opposed Menderes, a worrying question was whether the US engagement with Turkey might include a US commitment to protect its government if it were threatened by internal opposition, in accordance with the 'Eisenhower Doctrine' proclaimed in 1957. The signature of a wide-ranging security agreement with the United States in the spring of 1959 which, among other things, stated that the United States would come to the aid of the Turkish government in the case of 'direct or indirect aggression' heightened these anxieties. Immediately after the *coup* which overthrew Menderes in May 1960, those responsible were worried that the deposed premier might have had some sort of secret agreement with the United States to restore him to power in such an eventuality, and were heartily relieved when the Western powers, as well as the Soviet Union, rapidly recognised their new regime.[44] However, it was only at the end of the 1950s that such fears began to re-emerge: for the most part, later commentators were able to look back on the decade as a 'golden era' in relations between Turkey and the NATO powers.[45]

During the 1950s, Turkey was also engaged in two unsuccessful projects to extend Western defence structures to the Balkans and the Middle East. The first of these invited comparison with the Balkan pact of 1934, but it was more limited in scope, being restricted from the start to Turkey, Greece and Yugoslavia, and was constructed in a situation in which the potential enemy, the Soviet Union, was already in control of most of the region. However, as in the previous case, Italian participation was effectively excluded, thanks to Italy's dispute with Yugoslavia over Trieste. On the other hand, the Turkish–Greek entente established in 1930 continued during the post-war years, thanks to both countries' alignment against the perceived Soviet threat, and their joint campaign to gain admission to NATO. In 1947, as part of the peace treaty with Italy, Turkey agreed to the transfer of the Dodecanese to Greece (a move which it had accepted in principle in 1944) and it was agreed that the demilitarisation applied in the other Greek Aegean islands under the Lausanne treaty would equally be applied in the case of the Dodecanese. Given that the big majority of the population of the islands was Greek, Turkey was in no position to oppose the transfer, even if it had wanted to.[46] Yugoslavia, however, occupied a more problematic position since, following Tito's break with Stalin in 1948, the United States had become perturbed by the possibility of a Soviet invasion of the country. With US encouragement, Turkey and Greece began discussions with the Yugoslav government, which resulted in the signature of an Agreement on Friendship and Cooperation signed on 28 February 1953. This was, however, limited in scope, and merely obliged the signatories to consult with one another on matters of common interest, and to engage in military discussions.

The Balkan alignment did not become an alliance until 9 August 1954 when a Balkan Defence Pact was signed in Bled, Yugoslavia, between the three countries. The pact declared that an attack on any of the signatories would be counted as an attack on all of them, and that they would immediately take all measures, including the use of armed force, for their common defence. If it had been carried through, the pact would have had the effect of bringing Yugoslavia under the NATO umbrella, without making it a full member of the alliance. However, it became a dead letter almost as soon as it was signed. In 1955 Khrushchev made his peace with Tito, and thus removed the pact's main *raison d'être*. Tito later became one of the leaders of the Non-Aligned Movement, whose earliest origins were supposedly marked by the Bandung conference of April 1955. At the same time, the Cyprus problem began to occupy a dominant position on the Greek foreign policy agenda, making it more difficult to follow a cooperative policy with Turkey. Hence, the second Balkan pact fell by the wayside even more quickly than had the first.[47]

Turkey's other main foreign policy concern at the time was the Middle East, and was originally derived from British and US policies. During the early 1950s the British wished to reduce their direct military presence in the region, signalled by the agreement with Egypt of October 1954 under which British troops were withdrawn from the Suez Canal zone. As a replacement Britain wished to build up a Middle Eastern alliance system which would buttress the Western and especially the British position. On the US, John Foster Dulles, secretary of state in the Eisenhower administration from the beginning of 1953, aimed to construct a defensive chain to contain the Soviet Union along its southern borders. British and US plans did not entirely coincide, since the British favoured incorporation of the core Arab countries, among whom British influence had traditionally been stronger, while the United States put the main emphasis on the 'northern tier' of states which bordered the Soviet Union – that is, primarily Turkey and Iran. Either way, Turkey was seen as an essential participant in the project, since it was judged to be the strongest regional state militarily, and was clearly committed to the West through NATO. For their part, the Turks had publicly announced in 1951 that they would take on a defence role in the Middle East if they were admitted to NATO. Apart from this commitment, they were also unlikely to oppose a project which enhanced Turkey's apparent value to the West, and thus increased the chances of overall Western support for Turkey. It appears, in fact, that at the outset Menderes had no clear-cut policy towards the Middle East, but wished to participate in Western defence structures as fully as possible, and to achieve economic and military aid additional to Turkey's entitlement as a member of NATO.[48]

During 1952–53 discussions took place on the possible formation of a 'Middle East Defence Organisation' (MEDO) but these came to nothing, since, among other things, the Arab states regarded the idea of cooperation with Turkey with grave suspicion. Apart from individual points of conflict, such as Syrian hostility over the annexation of Alexandretta by Turkey in 1939, Arab opinion tended to have a suspicious attitude towards the Turks as the former masters of the Arab lands, and resented Turkish support for Western policies on Palestine. Although Turkey had voted with the Arab states against the UN resolution partitioning Palestine in November 1947, it had recognised the state of Israel in 1949 and the two countries exchanged ambassadors at the end of that year. Subsequently, the Israelis were anxious to develop the relationship as a way of breaking out of their diplomatic isolation in the Middle East, and because they thought it would give them a window to the Arab–Muslim world. Economic relations between Turkrey and Israel also grew apace during the early 1950s.[49] However, once the Egyptians had signed an agreement with the British in 1954, the Menderes government became far more hopeful of negotiating an alliance with the main Arab states, especially Egypt.[50] Meanwhile, in 1954 Iraq signed a military assistance agreement with the USA, and on 24 February 1955 concluded the Baghdad Pact with Turkey 'for their mutual security and their defence', though how this was to be achieved was left for later detailed arrangements. Turkey played a major role in bringing Iraq into this arrangement, which Menderes evidently saw as an important way of increasing Turkey's security along its southern borders, and of enhancing Turkey's value to the West as an ally. He also managed to overcome Iraqi suspicions that the pact might be a cover for Turkish territorial ambitions in Mosul.[51] Britain joined the Baghdad Pact on 4 April, since the British knew that their existing security agreement with Iraq, which provided for two British air bases on Iraqi soil, was due to expire in 1957: hence, they needed this new agreement to help maintain their influence in the country.[52] Pakistan acceded to the Pact in September 1955, and Iran the following month. The five members met in Baghdad in November 1955, and set up a Council of Ministers and special committees for military planning, economic planning and counter-subversion. The United States never officially became a signatory, since the State Department still wished to preserve whatever chance there was of working with non-member Arab countries, such as Egypt and Saudi Arabia, and did not want to provoke Israel. Nonetheless, it was clear from the start that Washington was the principle paymaster and promoter of the project.[53]

The launch of the Baghdad Pact provoked a storm of protest in the rest of the Arab world, especially Egypt, where the Iraqi government of Nuri al-Saiyid was berated for having joined the Western camp, and having betrayed the Arabs in their common alignment against Zionism. Turkish attempts to persuade or pressure Syria and the Lebanon were quite unavailing, and in Jordan King Hussein nearly lost his throne in an upsurge of protest against possible Jordanian adherence to the pact. In 1956, the Suez war virtually ended British and French power in the region, alienated the USA, and left the pro-Western Middle Eastern states in a severely exposed position. As a result, the four regional members of the pact, pointedly excluding Britain, held a meeting in Tehran in November 1956 at which they strongly criticised the Anglo-French invasion of the canal zone, and called for the withdrawal of Israeli forces from all Egyptian territory. According to contemporary reports, Menderes was instrumental in persuading the other Pact members not to eject Britain from the organisation.[54] The final blow to the Baghdad Pact, in its original shape, came in July 1958, when a revolutionary *coup d'état* in Iraq overthrew Nuri and the pro-Western Hashemite regime. Although a meeting of the other Baghdad Pact states in London shortly afterwards declared that 'the need which called the Pact into being is greater than ever',[55] it was clear that it could not survive in its original form. The headquarters and secretariat of the alliance were moved from Baghdad to Ankara in October 1958, and Iraq formally withdrew in March 1959.[56]

In August 1959 the remains of the Baghdad Pact were reconstructed as a purely northern tier alliance of Britain, Turkey, Iran and Pakistan, with the United States continuing its observer status, known as the Central Treaty Organisation (CENTO). Like the Baghdad Pact, CENTO suffered from serious structural weaknesses, since it had no centralised military command structure comparable to that of NATO, and amounted to little more than a pledge of mutual assistance in the event of aggression against one of the members (implicitly, by the Soviet Union). Probably, the main value of CENTO in the eyes of its Middle Eastern members was that it gave them institutional mechanisms for obtaining arms and financial aid from the United States. As in the case of the Saadabad pact of 1937, the geographical dispersion and disparity of its members robbed it of much effective force as a defence organisation. Since three-quarters of Turkey's ground forces were allocated to NATO, it would have had little to spare to counter a Soviet attack on Iran, whose own forces were weak. Pakistan's adherence made little difference, since its main concern was to win US military aid and diplomatic support against India, and it had little interest in or capacity for military involvement in the Middle East.[57] However, none of the members had any serious disputes with one another, so the organisation officially survived until the Iranian Revolution gave it the final death blow in 1979. Meanwhile, in 1964 the three member states – Turkey, Iran and Pakistan – had also attempted to give their relationship a stronger economic dimension by setting up an organisation for Regional Cooperation and Development (RCD). Here again, however, the effects were limited as the three countries had few economic synergies: essentially the linkage was a purely political one, with not much military or economic depth.[58]

While the story of the Baghdad Pact is well known in outline, there is some doubt about what Turkey's attitude towards it was, or how seriously the Turks took the idea of regional collaboration. At the outset, it seems that the government was quite cynical about the idea of cooperation with the Middle Eastern nations. In March 1953 Dulles visited Ankara for discussions on the proposed Middle East Defence Organisation (MEDO). According to George McGhee, now the US ambassador in Ankara, Dulles was told by President Celal Bayar that he 'pledged to go forward with the efforts to build MEDO, if that were the policy of Turkey's allies, despite the belief that it would be a wasted effort'. Other evidence suggests that, at this stage, the Turks did not rate the value or practicality of a Middle East defence pact highly.[59] On the other hand, it appears that Turkey later took the lead in forming the pact with Iraq in 1955, and that the Turks were energetic, if quite unsuccessful, in trying to sell the project to Syria, Lebanon and Jordan. Menderes had apparently hoped for a more positive response from the Arab countries, and fatally under-estimated their antipathy to the West.[60] In fact, the US and British govern-ments were quite perturbed by Turkey's tough and threatening approach to the Syrians and Jordanians – which included, for instance, warning Syria that if it went ahead with the evolving security pact with Egypt then Turkey might break diplomatic relations with Damascus, or telling the Jordanian government that if it failed to join the Baghdad Pact, and Jordan were then at war with Israel, then it might find the Turks fighting on the opposite side.[61] After the Suez fiasco, the United States tried to fill the apparent power vacuum in the Middle East when Eisenhower launched his version of numerous presidential 'doctrines' in January 1957, pledging US support and the readiness to use US forces to protect any Middle Eastern state 'requesting such aid against overt armed aggres-sion from any nation controlled by international communism'. The 'Eisenhower doctrine' was used to justify US support to King Hussein in his clash with internal pan-Arabist opponents in April 1957 and to land US marines during Beirut in Lebanon's incipient civil war in July 1958.[62]

By this stage, it appears that Adnan Menderes had a more Dullesian-than-Dulles phobia about the dangers of communist penetration in the Middle East, and that his Western allies had to restrain him from taking a more aggressive stance in the region. During August and September 1957 a widespread belief in Washington and Ankara that Syria was in grave danger of a takeover by local communists was met by Soviet complaints that the West was plotting to encourage its local allies to attack the country. Soviet arms deliveries to Egypt and Syria after the Suez war also alarmed both the United States and Turkey. At the height of the crisis Turkey massed troops on its southern border and, according to a contemporary British Foreign Office report 'seems to have considered "going it alone" over Syria', although this would obviously have justified and strengthened the Soviet position.[63] In response, Khrushchev had threatened that if the crisis resulted in war, Turkey would not last 'even a single day'. Although the US State Department emphasised that if Turkey were attacked, the United States would carry out its defence commitments to the Turks 'with all its power', it appears that Britain and the United States were gravely perturbed by Turkey's apparently aggressive attitude to Syria, and feared that it might provoke a Soviet attack on Turkey which could lead to a full-scale conflict between the two superpowers. Unexpectedly, the crisis ended with a change of course by the unpredictable Khrushchev.[64] On 29 October 1958 the Soviet leader attended a reception at the Turkish embassy in Moscow to celebrate the anniversary of the foundation of the Turkish republic, where he declared that 'there was no threat to the Middle East at all and that the whole affair had been misunderstood'.[65] Khrushchev's apparent decision to switch to something like a peace offensive with Turkey failed to pay any immediate dividends in his relations with the Menderes government, but it did at least defuse the crisis, and Turkey withdrew its troops.

In 1958, Turkey supported the US intervention in Lebanon, allowing the use of the İncirlik air base in support, although the operation was quite clearly outside its NATO remit. Immediately after the Iraqi revolution of July 1958, it also appears that Menderes strongly urged military intervention by Turkey to restore the previous pro-Western regime, though whether he was overruled by his own generals on grounds of military impracticality, or by US pressure, is unclear.[66] In the aftermath of the revolution, the Israeli prime minister, David Ben-Gurion, paid an unannounced visit to Turkey in August 1958, and Turkey and Israel agreed to a secret 'Periphery Pact' designed to link Israel, Turkey, Iran and Ethiopia. Apparently, this would have provided for Israeli technical and military assistance to Turkey, though whether it would also have involved Turkish military support for Israel in the event of another Arab–Israeli war is unclear. Apparently the alliance – if such it was – came to nothing, and was certainly dropped after Menderes was overthrown in 1960.[67] What seems certain is that Menderes had been an enthusiastic supporter of the Baghdad Pact project, and was gravely upset by its failure. In fact, it is even suggested that he feared he might meet the same fate as Iraq's King Faisal II and the Iraqi prime minister, Nuri al-Saiyid, who were murdered by the revolutionaries.[68] Overall, the idea that Turkey engaged in the Middle East purely as the servant of Western interests, rather than on its own initiative, appears hard to sustain.

During the second half of the 1950s Turkey also became involved in another regional conflict which was to become one of its main foreign policy preoccupations in subsequent decades. Following the recognition of British rule in Cyprus in 1878 (see p. 29) Britain had formally annexed the island in 1914, and this annexation was recognised by Turkey under the treaty of Lausanne in 1923. During the Lausanne negotiations, İsmet İnönü neglected to bring up the Cyprus question, for fear that this would make the British more intransigent over the abolition of the capitulations. While it would not be true to say that Turkey was entirely unconcerned about events in Cyprus between then and the 1950s, it does appear that both the Turkish government and the Turkish Cypriots, numbering about 20 per cent of the population, were broadly prepared to accept British rule, since this was seen as the best available alternative to *enosis*, or union with Greece, and an assurance of reasonably fair treatment of the Turkish community. Similarly, successive Greek governments refused to support the movement for *enosis*, out of a desire not to alienate the British.[69] Concern for the future of Cyprus only began after the pro-*enosis* movement began to gain momentum among the Greeks, both in Greece and in Cyprus, in the mid-1950s.

The dispute came into the international arena in September 1954, when Greece submitted its case unsuccessfully to the United Nations (UN). In 1955, as the underground Greek terrorist organisation EOKA began its campaign of violence on the island, the British called a conference in London with representatives of the Greek and Turkish governments. A plan providing for a measure of self-government under continued British sovereignty, with separate representation for the Greek and Turkish Cypriots was discussed, without agreement. In negotiations with the Iraqi prime minister, Nuri al-Saiyid, over the proposed Baghdad Pact in January 1955, Menderes expressed a clear preference for the continuation of British rule in Cyprus.[70] However, at the London conference, the Turkish foreign minister, Fatin Rüştü Zorlu, took the line that if British sovereignty were to end, then the whole island should revert to Turkey. Later, in 1956, the Turkish government shifted its position to pushing for partition, under which separate Greek and Turkish halves of the island would be transferred to Greek and Turkish sovereignty respectively. Apparently, this idea had originally been suggested by the British.[71] In general, the British encouraged Turkish resistance to *enosis*. As the prime minister, Sir Anthony Eden, later wrote, 'I regarded our alliance with

Turkey as the first consideration in our policy in that part of the world'.[72] It also appears that Menderes built up Turkish protests as a means of distracting attention from his domestic failures. A shameful example of this occurred during the London conference of 1955 when demonstrations in Istanbul, which were apparently orchestrated by the government, got out of hand. A riotous mob looted or destroyed Greek (and some non-Greek) property in the city, persuading many Istanbuli Greeks to leave for Greece.[73] However, it would be quite wrong to argue that Turkish resistance to *enosis* was just artificial, or purely concocted by either the British or Menderes. Within Turkey, there was a good deal of real concern for the future of the Turkish Cypriots – probably more than on other foreign policy issues – and genuine resentment that the pro-*enosis* case virtually ignored their existence.[74] Apart from considerations of national honour and prestige, it was also argued that *enosis* would fundamentally change the strategic balance between Greece and Turkey in the Mediterranean, allowing Greece to surround Turkey on two sides. On these grounds, some Turks suggested that Turkey would have opposed *enosis* even if here had been no ethnic Turks on the island.[75]

Between 1956 and 1958 a series of plans for local self-government in Cyprus were put forward by the British government, but all foundered on the rock of Greek opposition, since the British would not yet concede the principle of sovereignty. Meanwhile, a full-scale revolt was mounted by EOKA, as Archbishop Makarios, the political as well as religious leader of the Greek Cypriots, was first interned by the British in the Seychelles in March 1956, and then released in April 1957. By 1958 the struggle was assuming the shape of a Greek–Turkish civil war, rather than just a fight between the Greeks and the British. The turning point came at the beginning of 1959, when the British recognised that they did not need to retain sovereignty over the whole of Cyprus to meet their aim of maintaining a strategic military base in the eastern Mediterranean. Initially, the Menderes government favoured the establishment of a federal state on the island, but then realised that the Greeks would reject this as a disguised form of partition. Equally, the Greek government conceded that *enosis* would be firmly opposed by both the British and the Turks. Hence, the Greek and Turkish governments came round to accepting the principle of an independent Cyprus, with a power-sharing constitution, as an alternative to either *enosis* or partition. An agreement along these lines was hammered out at a meeting between Menderes and Constantine Karamanlis, the Greek prime minister, in Zürich on 5–10 February 1959. It was accepted by the British government, the political leader of the

Turkish Cypriots, Dr Fazıl Küçük, and, much more reluctantly, by Archbishop Makarios, at a conference in London later that month.[76] At the time, Menderes described the London and Zürich agreements as neither a victory nor a defeat for Turkey, but as 'a compromise which was not against Turkey's national interests and which respected the other party's rights and interests'.[77]

The Cypriot constitution, based on the Zürich and London agreements, was issued in April 1960, and paved the way for the proclamation of the independent Republic of Cyprus in August of that year. It provided that the president of the republic would be a Greek Cypriot, and the vice-president a Turkish Cypriot, both elected by their respective communities, and assisted by a cabinet in which there were to be seven Greek and three Turkish ministers. The president and vice-president would have 'separately or jointly' the right of veto in matters affecting foreign affairs, defence and security. The legislature, comprising 50 members, would be divided between Greek and Turkish representatives in a 70 per cent–30 per cent ratio with simple majority voting, except that laws relating to municipalities or the imposition of taxes would require separate majorities of both Greek and Turkish members. The civil service was to be divided on the basis of the same ratio, and there were to be separate Communal Chambers governing religious affairs, education, culture and personal status cases, as well as separate municipalities in Greek and Turkish areas. The constitution was accompanied by a Treaty of Establishment between Cyprus and Britain, providing for two base areas under British sovereignty in the south of the island, at Dhekelia and Akrotiri. A second treaty between Greece, Turkey and Cyprus provided for the stationing of 950 Greek and 650 Turkish troops on the island.

Under a Treaty of Guarantee which was signed as part of the 1960 package between Cyprus, Britain, Greece and Turkey, the four states undertook to 'prohibit, so far as concerns them, any activity aimed at promoting, directly or indirectly, either union of Cyprus with any other State or partition of the Island', and guaranteed the independence of Cyprus and 'the state of affairs established by the Basic Articles of its constitution' (Article 2). Equally, under Article 1 of the treaty, the Cyprus government promised 'not to participate, in whole or in part, in any political or economic union with any State whatsoever'. Finally, and most crucially, Article 4 of the treaty provided that if its provisions were violated the three governments would consult with one another, but that '[I]n so far as common or concerted action may not be possible each of the three guaranteeing Powers reserves the right to take action with the sole aim of reestablishing the state of affairs created by the present Treaty'.[78] For the Turkish side these provisions, while extremely complicated, seemed quite acceptable, since they gave it a guarantee against *enosis*, and protection of the Turkish Cypriot community. On these grounds, Menderes' government could feel satisfied with the settlement even though it remained to be seen whether the Greek and Turkish Cypriots, or the two mainland governments, would be ready or able to make it work.

TURKEY AND THE MISSILE CRISIS, 1961–63

During 1960–61 the political attention of most Turks and their Western allies was almost entirely turned to domestic affairs, as the military first overthrew Adnan Menderes' government in May 1960, and then set about trying to reconstruct Turkish politics, at the cost of serious conflict within their ranks. Civilian government was eventually restored after general elections in October 1961, when an unstable coalition under İsmet İnönü was established.[79] Meanwhile, foreign policy failed to attract much more than passing attention. The Cyprus situation seemed to have stabilised, following the settlement of 1960. As already noted (p. 122), the military regime dropped Menderes' brief and inconclusive reconciliation with the Soviet Union, turning down Soviet advances and confirming Turkey's loyalty to NATO and CENTO. Behind the scenes, however, decisions were being taken which were to project Turkey into a major international crisis in 1962.

In October 1959 the Menderes government had agreed with the Eisenhower administration that 15 Jupiter intermediate-range ballistic missiles, armed with nuclear warheads, would be installed on Turkish territory. These were not the first nuclear weapons to appear in Turkey, since US aircraft armed with tactical nuclear weapons had been operating from Turkey for some time, but they significantly enhanced Turkey's potential role in a nuclear war. Although some members of the Turkish foreign ministry opposed the installation of the Jupiters, on the grounds that they might provoke an attack by the Soviet Union, they were overruled by the government and senior military commanders. The latter believed that the Jupiters would enhance Turkey's military strength, as a symbol of the alliance's readiness to use atomic weapons against any Soviet attack on Turkey. They were encouraged in this belief by the United States military, since General Lauris Norstad, as SACEUR, stressed their military value in conversations with the Turks. The missiles were installed at a base near İzmir in the autumn of 1961, although they did not become operational until the spring of 1962. They were owned by Turkey, but the US retained custody of the warheads, and they could only be used with joint permission of the US and Turkish governments. Together with two similar squadrons of Jupiters deployed in Italy, they were targeted on 45 of the 129 Soviet medium- and intermediate-range missiles aimed at Europe.[80]

As early as 1959 the planned deployment of Jupiters in Turkey had been the subject of complaints by Khrushchev to US vice-president Richard Nixon, and the Soviet leader repeated these protests publicly in May 1962. It is even suggested that he may have decided to install Soviet missiles in Cuba in retaliation for the Turkish Jupiters, or with a view to exchanging their removal for that of the Jupiters from Turkey.[81] Meanwhile, both the Eisenhower and Kennedy administrations had realised that the Jupiters would soon be outdated by the Polaris submarine-launched system, and that they were both inaccurate and increasingly vulnerable to a Soviet first strike.[82] In April 1961 President John Kennedy asked for the deployment of the Turkish missiles to be reviewed. In the following month US Secretary of State, Dean Rusk, raised the issue with Selim Sarper, now the foreign minister in the military government. According to Rusk's later account, Sarper refused to withdraw the Jupiters since 'their parliament'[83] had only just approved the expenditures for installing them and that 'it would be very embarrassing to go right back to them and say that they would be taken out. And then he said it would be very bad for the morale of Turkey as a member of NATO if they were taken out before a Polaris submarine were in the Mediterranean to take their place'.[84] As Robert Komer, later the US ambassador to Turkey, wrote in a memo soon after the crisis: '[Robert] McNamara [secretary of state for defence] knows the JUPITERS are of no military value. But the Turks, Italians and others don't – and that's the whole point.'[85] George McGhee, who was then chairman of the US Policy Planning Council, told the president in June 1961 that if the Jupiters were removed this would be seen as a sign of weakness, especially after Khrushchev's diplomatic offensive at the Vienna summit earlier that month, and also pointed to General Norstad's earlier discussions with Sarper recommending the missiles. During the spring and summer of 1962 Rusk twice raised the question in talks with the Turks, but without result, while Kennedy was told by the State Department that it would be unwise to go on pressing the point.[86]

It was after these fruitless discussions that the Cuban missile crisis erupted in October 1962, just as the Jupiters were being handed over to the Turkish authorities. The beginning of the end of the crisis came on the evening of 26 October, when Khrushchev wrote to Kennedy saying that he would withdraw the Soviet missiles from Cuba if the United States lifted its blockade on the island and agreed not to attack Cuba. However, in a second letter, delivered on the following morning, he made the withdrawal of the missiles from Cuba contingent on US withdrawal of the Jupiters from Turkey (the 'Turkey-for-Cuba trade').[87] The idea of such an exchange was discussed in Washington, but rejected since it could have provoked further demands from Khrushchev, and because the Turks would much resent the implication that 'their interests were being traded off in order to appease an enemy', as the US ambassador in Ankara, Raymond Hare, explained.[88] Kennedy's tactic was to reply only to Khrushchev's first letter, accepting the withdrawal of the Soviet missiles without a trade, and ignore the second letter. On the following day (28 October) Khrushchev agreed to this, and the crisis was settled.[89]

On this basis, it appeared that the Soviet missiles were withdrawn from Cuba without the United States having to make any concessions on the Turkish Jupiters. This was the line that was steadfastly held to by both the Kennedy administration and the İnönü government. The last of the Jupiters were removed from Turkey on 24 April 1963, following an announcement by the new Turkish foreign minister, Feridun Cemal Erkin, that they would be replaced by Polaris submarines.[90] However, in his memoirs, which were published after his death in 1968, President Kennedy's brother, US Attorney-General Robert Kennedy revealed that, on the president's instructions, he had met Anatoli Dobrynin, the Soviet ambassador in Washington, on the evening of 27 October (that is, before Khrushchev's letter agreeing to the withdrawal of the Soviet missiles from Cuba had been received). He had told the ambassador that if the Soviet Union agreed to withdraw its missiles, 'it was our judgement that, within a short time after the crisis was over, these [Jupiter] missiles would be gone'.[91] Later, it appeared that he had actually made a more specific commitment to Dobrynin, and that the US government would have been prepared to make it public if Khrushchev had not backed down first.[92]

The immediate effect of the crisis on Turkish thinking is hard to assess, since it seems that it was not until many years later that the Turks learnt definitely that, in spite of official denials, the Kennedy administration had actually given Khrushchev more than a hint of a Turkey-for-Cuba trade, and had been quite prepared to cut a deal vitally affecting Turkey's interests without consulting its government. Since it was not public knowledge at the time, the incident failed to provoke public comment to this effect, and was anyway overshadowed by a far more bitter and open dispute between Turkey and the United States over Cyprus which erupted in 1964. Moreover, since the Kennedy administration had tried to withdraw the Jupiters from Turkey before October 1962, the eventual solution could be seen as part of a policy to which it had been committed to for some time, irrespective of the missiles in Cuba. Nonetheless, a clear conclusion suggested itself to Turkish policy-makers – that the Jupiters had been more of a danger than an advantage to Turkey. At the height of the crisis, the Soviet ambassador in Ankara had warned members of the Turkish government that a nuclear war was on their doorstep. In the event of a nuclear exchange between East and West the Jupiters would almost certainly have been a Soviet nuclear target, making İzmir the Hiroshima of a potential Third World War.[93] Clearly, in its dealings with both the United States and the Soviet Union, Turkey needed to be more cautious than it had been in 1959–62.

More directly, the withdrawal of the Jupiters also removed an obvious obstacle to the development of better Turkish–Soviet relations. After 1963, there were still some US-supplied nuclear weapons in Turkey, but these were short-range weapons, as supplied to other NATO armies. They were again subject to a 'dual-key' control system, and could reasonably be seen by the Soviets as being defensive rather than aggressive.[94] In the late spring of 1963, after the withdrawal of the Jupiters, a high-ranking Turkish parliamentary delegation visited the Soviet Union for the first time since 1932. Economic contacts between Turkey and the Soviet Union had increased, and in October the Turkish newspaper, *Cumhuriyet*, published an article by Khrushchev claiming that there were now 'no serious reasons that could prevent the establishment of good neighbour relations between our two countries'.[95] This did not mean that the Soviet Union was satisfied by Turkey's position after 1963, since it was still pressing for Turkish nonalignment, but it was at least less perturbed than it had been while the Jupiters were installed on Turkish soil.

Another, and more speculative, conclusion would be that, assuming that some officials in Ankara may soon have suspected that there had been a Turkey-for-Cuba trade (even though they had no definite information to that effect), they could reasonably have concluded that, in a time of crisis, the United States might be willing to sacrifice Turkish interests for the sake of protecting its own,[96] and that exclusive reliance on US support was risky. As George E. Gruen concluded in 1980, 'the seeds were sown for a lingering suspicion in Ankara that Washington might be tempted by superpower considerations to bargain away Turkey's security interests'.[97] This was to reinforce trends towards the adoption of more flexible policies towards the superpowers, which became apparent in the second half of the 1960s.

TURKISH FOREIGN POLICY, 1945—63:
A BALANCE SHEET

Turkey's decision to join the Western camp in the Cold War was virtually inevitable. Neutrality was not seen as a viable option for Turkey in the circumstances of the time, and the only serious obstacles to be overcome were not misgivings on the Turkish side, but initial reluctance to accept Turkey as a full member of the alliance on the part of Western governments. Since the United States took some time to assess the geographical scope and intensity of the Cold War, while the British sought to use Turkey as part of a fruitless effort to preserve some of their previous role in the Middle East, Turkey's admission to the alliance was slow in coming, but nonetheless full when it did come. Initially, the focus of conflict was the old issue of the Turkish straits, but this contest was already beginning to change its shape. In 1945–46 the question of Soviet naval access to the Mediterranean, and Western access to the Black Sea, was still strongly contested, but the most problematic part of the Soviet project was the demand for bases at the straits. This was a new item on the agenda, which was a more fundamental threat to Turkey's independence and integrity. During the 1950s and afterwards, rights of naval passage through the straits became less crucial, as the development of air power, nuclear weapons and inter-continental missiles ended the supremacy of conventional naval forces as strategic or diplomatic weapons.[98] Nevertheless, the fear that the Soviet Union might try to take over Turkey as a means of controlling the straits was still the most important single reason for Turkey's attachment to NATO. Although successive Turkish governments were fiercely anti-communist, Turkey's commitment to the West derived from traditional considerations of territorial control and international power, not ideology. The perceived threat from communism may have heightened its worries, but did not create them originally.

Engagement in the alliance posed three potential risks for Turkey: first that the Western powers, primarily the United States, might reduce Turkey to a satellite; second, that the alliance might drag Turkey into a global and possibly nuclear war originating in a conflict in which Turkey's national interests were only peripherally involved; and third, that Turkey might in turn have national interests which conflicted with those of the alliance as a whole. On the first score, there is no convincing evidence that

the United States controlled Turkey's domestic political system or intervened effectively in domestic politics to protect its own interests – indeed, it
did not need to do so, since internal opposition to the alliance was
extremely weak. The fact that NATO was a multilateral alliance, including all the main western European states, also helped to diffuse the US role
within it. Even at the point of crisis in 1960, when Menderes was overthrown, foreign policy was not an issue in the internal upheaval, and it
appears that the US government did not even predict the *coup*, far less
arrange it.[99] Nor did it make any moves to restore Menderes after the
event. On the second score, the Turks themselves were evidently prepared
to take risks in this regard – as, for instance, they did in 1950, when
Turkish troops were sent to Korea, or in 1959, when they accepted the
installation of the Jupiter missiles. On the other hand, the risk of involvement in a global nuclear war was only narrowly avoided at the time of the
Cuban missile crisis in 1962, whose origins had little to do with Turkey's
immediate interests, so the implicit dangers of the alliance were obvious, if
fortunately unrealised. On the third score, the Cyprus conflict did pose the
risk of a clash with NATO – or at least with Greece – over an issue with
which Turkey was closely concerned. As yet, however, it had not involved
the danger of a conflict with the Western powers, since the British were
generally fairly supportive of the Turkish position, and the United States
was not yet involved.

Two main criticisms can be made of Turkish diplomacy at the time.
The first is that Turkey was insufficiently sensitive to the shift in Soviet
policy which followed the death of Stalin, and should have made more
effort to defuse its confrontation with the Soviet Union after Khrushchev
came to power. However, it is uncertain how much Turkey could have
gained from such a shift, and likely that it could have lost important advantages. Even if Turkey could have gained from closer economic relations
with the Soviet Union, it might have lost heavily if Western aid had been
reduced as a result. Even if the Soviet security threat were reduced, the
balance of military power would have been so heavily in favour of the
Soviet Union, if Turkey had been neutral, that the risk of political subordination if not outright invasion would still have been serious. A second
and more convincing criticism is that Turkey's policy in the Middle East
was misconceived, and counter-productive. Certainly, Menderes' promotion of the Baghdad Pact was based on a fundamental misperception of
the interests and policies of the main Arab states, which had no desire to
line up in a Cold War conflict in which they felt quite uninvolved, and
repudiated an alliance with the United States, which was seen as the main

patron of Israel. Menderes' aggressive attitude to Syria in 1957 almost certainly promoted the Soviet cause rather than obstructed it, and his threatened intervention in Iraq in 1958 could have produced a serious crisis in relations with both the Soviet Union and the Arab states. A change of policy towards the region was thus predictable in the succeeding period.

NOTES

1. Quoted in Bruce R. Kuniholm, *The Origins of the Cold War in the Near East* (Princeton, NJ, Princeton University Press, 2nd edn, 1994), p. 255.

2. For instance, the survey of British and US diplomatic archives for the post-war period by Ekavi Athanassopoulou does not reveal any such suggestion, although she refers to the possible link. Ekavi Athanassopoulou, *Turkey – Anglo-American Security Interests, 1945– 1952: The First Enlargement of NATO* (London, Cass, 1999), p. 73. On the other hand, it would probably have been difficult for the Western powers to persuade their own public opinion and legislatures to support Turkey if Turkey's domestic political structures had been patently undemocratic – particularly in the case of the US Congress. Since this was not the case, the argument has to remain speculative. It is noticeable, however, that in an article written in 1954 for a US audience, George McGhee, the US ambassador in Turkey between 1951 and 1953, emphasised that Turkey had now become 'a democracy in practice as well as form', and that under Menderes it was committed to 'giving maximum encouragement to free enterprise and foreign investment'. George C. McGhee, 'Turkey Joins the West', *Foreign Affairs*, Vol. 32 (1954), pp. 626–9.

3. See Dankwart A. Rustow, 'Transitions to Democracy: Turkey's Experience in Historical and Comparative Perspective', in Metin Heper and Ahmet Evin, eds, *State, Democracy and the Military: Turkey in the 1980s* (Berlin, de Gruyter, 1988), p. 245 n. 10 and George S. Harris, *Troubled Alliance: Turkish-American Problems in Historical Perspective, 1945–1971* (Washington, American Enterprise Institute for Public Policy Research and Hoover Institution, 1972), p. 39.

4. For fuller accounts of Turkey's domestic politics during this period, see in particular Kemal H. Karpat, *Turkey's Politics: The Transition to a Multi-Party System* (Princeton, NJ, Princeton University Press, 1959); Feroz Ahmad, *The Turkish Experiment in Democracy, 1950–1975* (London, Hurst, for Royal Institute of International Affairs, 1977), pp. 11–176 and Erik J. Zürcher, *Turkey, A Modern History* (London and New York, NY, I.B. Tauris, 1993), pp. 215–52.

5. The return of Kars may have been demanded because of its strategic importance as a fortress. However, in his memoirs Nikita Khrushchev later suggested that the secret police chief, Lavrentii Beria, put the idea to Stalin, as a fellow-Georgian, on the grounds that the territory demanded had been part of Georgia (in fact, Kars had been part of Armenia between 1918 and 1920). Ironically, Stalin had himself negotiated the present frontier between Turkey and the then Soviet state in 1921, and presumably felt that he had given away too much. Officially, the Soviet fiction was that the territories were being demanded by the Soviet Republics of Armenia and Georgia, rather than the Soviet Union as such. See Bruce R. Kuniholm, 'Turkey and the West Since World War II', in Vojtech Mastny and R. Craig Nation, eds, *Turkey Between East and West: New*

Challenges for a Rising Regional Power (Boulder, CO, Westview, 1996), p. 45.

6. Athanassopoulou, *Turkey*, pp. 44–5.

7. Kuniholm, *Origins*, pp. 255–9: Harry N. Howard, *Turkey, the Straits and US Policy*, (Baltimore, MD, and London, Johns Hopkins University Press, 1974), pp. 216–19.

8. Athanassopoulou, *Turkey*, p. 43.

9. A.L. Macfie, 'The Straits Question at the Potsdam Conference: The British Position', *Middle Eastern Studies*, Vol. 23 (1987), pp. 77–9.

10. Necmeddin Sadak, 'Turkey Faces the Soviets', *Foreign Affairs*, Vol. 27 (1949), p. 460.

11. Athanassopoulou, *Turkey*, pp. 46, 53.

12. For text, see Howard, *Turkey, the Straits*, pp. 326–7. Other minor amendments to the convention proposed by the United States were the replacement of references to the League of Nations with 'United Nations', and the elimination of Japan as a signatory, both of which were accepted by the Turks. Under Article 29 of the convention, proposals for amendment could be submitted at the end of each five-year period following its entry into force: 9 November 1946 would have been one such date.

13. Quoted in Kuniholm, *Origins*, p. 297, and Howard, *Turkey, the Straits* p. 239. For a broader debate about the issues involved, see Melvyn Leffler, 'The American Conception of National Security and the Beginnings of the Cold War', *American Historical Review*, Vol. 89 (1984), pp. 346–81, and Bruce Kuniholm's 'Reply' in the same volume, pp. 385–90.

14. Kuniholm, *Origins*, pp. 317–19, 335–7, 356–7.

15. Quoted in Howard, *Turkey, the Straits*, pp. 243, 246.

16. Kuniholm, *Origins*, pp. 372–3.

17. Ibid., pp. 410–17. For the text of the 'Truman Doctrine', see ibid., pp. 458–63.

18. Sadak, 'Turkey', p. 461.

19. Figures from William Hale, *The Political and Economic Development of Modern Turkey* (London, Croom Helm, 1981), pp. 74–5. See also Athanassopoulou, *Turkey*, pp. 70–5.

20. Athanassopoulou, *Turkey*, pp. 105, 109–14, 116, 130 and Ekavi Athanassopoulou, 'Western Defence Developments and Turkey's Search for Security in 1948', in Sylvia Kedourie, ed., *Turkey: Identity, Democracy, Politics* (London, Cass, 1996), pp. 78–9, 86, 89–93, 99–102: reprinted from *Middle Eastern Studies*, Vol. 32 (1996), pp. 77–108.

21. Quoted in Athanassopoulou, *Turkey*, p. 130.

22. A. Suat Bilge *et al.*, *Olaylarla Türk Dış Politikası* (Ankara University, Political Science Faculty, 1969), pp. 242–3.

23. Quoted in George McGhee, *The US–Turkish–NATO Middle East Connection* (London, Macmillan, 1990), p. 60.

24. Ibid., pp. 54–5, 77–8 and Kuniholm, 'Turkey and the West', pp. 46–8.

25. Athanassopoulou, *Turkey*, pp. 163–5.

26. McGhee, *US–Turkish*, pp. 72–74 and Bilge, *et al.*, *Olaylarla*, pp. 244–5.

27. Kuniholm, 'Turkey and the West' pp. 48–9.

28. McGhee, *US–Turkish*, pp. 78–85 and Athanassopoulou, *Turkey*, pp. 196–97, 200–1.

29. On the 'Middle East Command' proposal, see John C. Campbell, *Defense of the Middle East:: Problems of American Policy* (New York, NY, Praeger, 1960), pp. 40–48. The Egyptians regarded possible Turkish involvement in this as crude support for a British attempt to maintain their military presence in Egypt. Paradoxically, in the spring of 1951 they had also hoped to bring Turkey into a neutralist pact of Middle Eastern states – an apt illustration of the misperceptions on both sides. Michael M. Bishku,

'Turkey and its Middle Eastern Neighbours since 1945', *Journal of South Asian and Middle Eastern Studies,* Vol. 15 (1992), p. 57.

30. Athanassopoulou, *Turkey,* p. 220

31. Ibid., pp. 218–20, 227–8; McGhee, *US–Turkish,* pp. 87–88 and Bilge *et al., Olaylarla,* pp. 247–52.

32. Quoted in Kuniholm, 'Turkey and the West', p. 45.

33. Harris, *Troubled Alliance,* p. 56.

34. Quoted in Athanassopoulou, 'Turkey's Search', p. 85.

35. Philip A. Petersen, 'Turkey in Soviet Military Strategy', *Foreign Policy* (Ankara, Foreign Policy Institute), Vol, 13 (1986), p. 75.

36. See Aclan Sayılgan, *Solun 94 Yılı, 1871–1965* (Ankara Mars Matbaası, 1968), p. 260.

37. Ahmad, *Turkish Experiment,* p. 391 and Hüseyin Bağcı, *Demokrat Parti Dönemi Dış Politikası* (Ankara, İmge Kitabevi, 1990), pp. 24–8. On other issues, İnönü's Republican People's Party (RPP) fully supported Turkey's accession to NATO in 1952, and (less enthusiastically) the Baghdad Pact of 1954. See McGhee, *US–Turkish,* p. 92 and 'Turkey', p. 617 and Bilge *et al., Olaylarla,* p. 279. Later, however, the RPP criticised Turkey's attachment to the Eisenhower Doctrine of 1957, Turkey's support of US intervention in the Lebanon in 1958, and the cooperation agreement with the United States of March 1959, see Harris, *Troubled Alliance,* pp. 66–9 and Bağcı, *Demokrat Parti,* p. 97. İnönü also criticised the Zürich and London agreements on Cyprus of 1959, see Suha Bölükbaşı, *Turkish–American Relations and Cyprus* (Lanham, MD, University Press of America, for White Burkett Miller Center of Public Affairs, University of Virginia, 1988), pp. 35–36. However, this had virtually no effect on government policy at the time.

38. Bağcı, *Demokrat Parti,* p. 77.

39. Quoted in Ferenc A. Vali, *Bridge Across the Bosporus: The Foreign Policy of Turkey* (Baltimore, MD, and London, Johns Hopkins Press, 1971), pp. 174–5. See also Alvin Z. Rubinstein, *Soviet Policy Toward Turkey, Iran and Afghanistan: The Dynamics of Influence* (New York, NY, Praeger, 1982), pp. 14–15. Officially, the claim to Kars and Ardahan was supposed to have been dropped by the Soviet republics of Georgia and Armenia: see note 5.

40. Hale, *Political and Economic,* pp. 106–7.

41. Duygu Bazoğlu Sezer, 'Turkey's Security Policies', in Jonathan Alford, ed., *Greece and Turkey: Adversity in Alliance* (London, Gower, for International Institute of Strategic Studies, 1984), pp. 56–7; Kemal H. Karpat, 'Turkish–Soviet Relations', in Kemal H. Karpat *et al., Turkey's Foreign Policy in Transition* (Leiden, Brill, 1975), pp. 86–7 and Rubinstein, *Soviet Policy,* p. 17.

42. Bölükbaşı, *Turkish–American Relations,* pp. 48–9 and A.H. Ulman and R.H. Dekmejian, 'Changing Patterns in Turkish Foreign Policy', *Orbis,* Vol. 11 (1967), pp. 774–5.

43. Sezer, 'Turkey's Security', pp. 64–5; Kuniholm, 'Turkey and the West', pp. 50–1 and Hale, *Political and Economic,* pp. 104–5, 108–10, 230. See also Baran Tuncer, 'External Financing of the Turkish Economy and its Foreign Policy Implications', in Kemal H. Karpat *et al., Turkey's Foreign Policy in Transition* (Leiden, Brill, 1975), pp. 218–21. Figures for total US aid cited here exclude PL480 wheat deliveries. The annual average growth of GNP at constant prices ran at 6.4 per cent between 1950 and 1960, although there was a marked slowdown in the late 1950s.

44. See Ulman and Dekmejian, 'Changing Patterns' p. 773, and William Hale, *Turkish*

Politics and the Military (London, Routledge, 1994), p. 120.

45. Bruce R. Kuniholm, 'Turkey and NATO: Past, Present and Future', *Orbis*, Vol. 27 (1983), p. 424.

46. Vali, *Bridge*, p. 227, and Andrew Wilson, *The Aegean Dispute* (London, International Institute for Strategic Studies, Adelphi Papers No.155. 1980), p. 3.

47. Bilge *et al.*, *Olaylarla*, pp. 255–68, and Vali, *Bridge*, pp. 199–201. In fact, Yugoslavia was not represented at Bandung, although Tito certainly became one of the prime supporters of non-alignment. As Fred Halliday points out, the Bandung conference was one of Afro-Asian rather than non-aligned states, and the Non-Aligned Movement as such was not established until the Brioni conference of 1961. See Fred Halliday, 'The Middle East, the Great Powers and the Cold War', in Yezid Sayigh and Avi Shlaim, eds, *The Cold War and the Middle East* (Oxford, Clarendon Press, 1997), p. 18. As an indicator of this, Turkey's then foreign minister, Fatin Rüştü Zorlu, attended the Bandung conference, but used it as a platform to attack the idea of neutrality in the Cold War. Later Zorlu told the Turkish parliament that he had attended on Western insistence, presumably so that the pro-Western viewpoint would at least be repre- sented, see Bilge *et al.*, *Olaylarla*, pp. 291–4. Zorlu also boasted that he had 'knocked Nehru down' at Bandung, in his attacks on the Indian premier's advocacy of non- alignment, quoted in Bishku, 'Turkey', p. 63.

48. Bağcı, *Demokrat Parti*, pp. 43–4.

49. Amikam Nachmani, *Israel, Turkey and Greece: Uneasy Relations in the Eastern Mediterranean* (London, Cass, 1987), pp. 5–12, 44–5, 61–3; McGhee, *US–Turkish*, pp. 124–60, 186– 207; Baruch Gilead, 'Turkish–Egyptian Relations 1952–1957', *Middle Eastern Affairs*, Vol. 10 (1959), p. 357and Ara Sanjian, 'The Formulation of the Baghdad Pact', *Middle Eastern Studies*, Vol. 33 (1997), pp. 229–31. In 1946, when Turkey recognised Syria's independence, it also agreed not to insist on Syrian recognition of the Turkish annexa- tion of Alexandretta (Hatay), in return for Syrian assent not to present formal demands for its return to Syria. Subsequently, Syrian–Turkish relations on this issue varied with the ups and downs of Syrian internal politics, but by the mid-1950s Syrian pressure had re-emerged, exacerbated by Turkey's role in the Baghdad Pact and Syrian oppo- sition to it. See Avedis K. Sanjian 'The Sanjak of Alexandretta (Hatay): Its Impact on Turkish–Syrian Relations (1939–1956)', *Middle East Journal*, Vol. 10 (1956), pp. 383–92. On Turkish–Israeli relations at this time, see Bishku, 'Turkey', pp. 59–61.

50. See G.E.K., 'The Turco–Egyptian Flirtation of Autumn 1954', *The World Today*, Vol. 12 (1956), pp. 450–3, and Gilead, 'Turkish–Egyptian', pp. 359–60.

51. Ayşegül Sever, 'The Compliant Ally? Turkey and the West in the Middle East, 1954–58', *Middle Eastern Studies*, Vol. 34 (1998), p. 75 and Sanjian, 'Formulation', pp. 242–5. For the text of the Baghdad Pact, see *Middle East Journal*, Vol. 5 (1955), pp. 177–8; for earlier drafts, see Sanjian, 'Formulation', pp. 248–57.

52. Under a bilateral Anglo-Iraqi treaty signed at the same time as the British accession to the Baghdad Pact, the Iraqis were eventually to take over the two air bases, but the British were to help maintain them, and supply and train the Iraqi air force. The RAF also retained landing and overflight rights in Iraq, see Campbell, *Defense*, pp. 57–8, and Sanjian, 'Formulation', pp. 237, 259.

53. Campbell, *Defense*, pp. 49–54, 57–62 and Bilge *et al.*, *Olaylarla*, pp. 273–88.

54. Bilge *et al.*, *Olaylarla*, p. 303 and Bağcı, *Demokrat Parti*, pp. 80–1. Turkey also withdrew its ambassador from Tel Aviv (though without severing diplomatic relations), 'until the

Palestine question is solved in a just and lasting manner in accordance with United Nations resolutions' (quoted in Bishku, 'Turkey', p. 61). Technically, mutual representation remained at the level of chargé d'affaires (with one interruption in 1980) until the end of 1991, when Turkey decided to restore relations at ambassadorial level, but it never officially broke off diplomatic relations with Israel.

55. Quoted in Vali, *Bridge,* p. 285.
56. Perhaps unexpectedly, Turkish–Iraqi relations were restored quite quickly after this, and a Turkish delegation attended celebrations in Baghdad marking the first anniversary of the coup in July 1959. Probably, the main reason for this was that Iraq's new ruler, Abdul Karim Qassem, refused to join the then United Arab Republic of Egypt and Syria, and expressed sympathy towards Turkey. By this stage, the Turks had evidently decided that the Baghdad Pact was truly dead, and that they would have to make the best of a bad job. Iraq's rivalry with Syria, and Turkish hostility towards Damascus, probably played an additional part in the reconciliation. See ibid., p. 301.
57. According to Israeli sources, the Turks had been unenthusiastic about including Pakistan in the original Baghdad Pact alliance, due to the geographical distance between the two countries, and because they did not want to antagonise India. However, they had been persuaded to accept it as a member under US pressure. Nachmani, *Israel, Turkey and Greece,* p. 72 (citing Israeli diplomatic reports).
58. Campbell, *Defense,* pp. 191–2, 242–3 and William Hale and Julian Bharier, 'CENTO, R.C.D. and the Northern Tier: a Political and Economic Appraisal', *Middle Eastern Studies* Vol. 8 (1972), p. 218.
59. McGhee, *US–Turkish,* pp. 149–56: the quotation is from ibid., p. 156. See also Sanjian, 'Formulation', pp. 229–31.
60. See Bishku, 'Turkey', p. 58.
61. Sever, 'Compliant Ally?' pp. 76–80.
62. See, e.g., Campbell, *Defense,* pp. 121–4, 127–31, 140–5: the quotation is from ibid., p. 122. See also Bağcı, *Demokrat Parti,* pp. 83–5.
63. Quoted in Philip Robins, *Turkey and the Middle East* (London, Frances Pinter, for Royal Institute of International Affairs, 1991), p. 26.
64. George E. Gruen, 'Ambivalence in the Alliance: US Interests in the Middle East and the Evolution of Turkish Foreign Policy', *Orbis,* Vol. 24 (1980), p. 372 and Sever, 'Compliant Ally?', pp. 81–3. As Sever suggests (p. 86), Menderes may have blown up the contest with Syria to distract the Turkish public from economic complaints, in view of the upcoming general elections held on 27 October 1957, but there is no documentary evidence of this. Bağcı, however, repeats this suggestion, arguing that once Menderes had won the elections, he rapidly wound the crisis down. Bağcı, *Demokrat Parti,* p. 95.
65. Quoted in Sever, 'Compliant Ally?' p. 83.
66. See ibid., pp. 83–4; Bağcı, *Demokrat Parti,* p. 97, and Robins, *Turkey and the Middle East,* p. 27. On the last point, George S. Harris supports the first argument, and Richard D. Robinson the second: see Harris, *Troubled Alliance,* pp. 65–6, and Richard D. Robinson, *The First Turkish Republic* (Cambridge, MA, Harvard University Press, 1963), p. 187. Following the revolution in Iraq, US and British military planners had themselves prepared contingency measures for a joint military intervention in Iraq. This project was supported by Duncan Sandys, Britain's hawkish minister of defence, but was turned down by the United States and the British Foreign Office, on the grounds that it was

not feasible militarily, plus the expectation that the new Iraqi ruler, Abdul Karim Qassem, would act as a counterpoint to Nasser in the Middle East. See Stephen Blackwell, 'A Desert Squall: Anglo-American Planning for Military Intervention in Iraq, July 1958–August 1959', *Middle Eastern Studies*, Vol. 35 (1999), pp. 3–4.

67. According to Nachmani, 'Israel would enjoy the support of the Turkish "giant" and of its army', in return for 'scientific cooperation in highly sensitive spheres', Israeli technical and economic assistance, and the export of Israeli military equipment to Turkey. See Nachmani, *Israel, Greece and Turkey*, p. 75. See also Robins, *Turkey and the Middle East*, p. 77.

68. Bağcı, *Demokrat Parti*, p. 97.

69. Suha Bölükbaşı, 'The Johnson Letter Revisited', *Middle Eastern Studies*, Vol. 29 (1993), pp. 507–08. This situation can perhaps be seen as similar to that in Alexandretta between 1921 and 1936, see p. 67.

70. Sanjian, 'Formulation', p. 243.

71. Tozun Bahceli, *Greek–Turkish Relations since 1955* (Boulder, CO, Westview, 1990), pp. 36–40.

72. Quoted in Robert Stephens, *Cyprus, a Place of Arms: Power Politics and Ethnic Conflict in the Eastern Mediterranean* (London, Pall Mall, 1966), p. 138, from Eden's memoirs, Sir Anthony Eden, *Full Circle* (London, Cassell, 1960), p. 414.

73. Menderes unconvincingly claimed that the riots were the work of 'communist' provocateurs, and some restitutions were made. The government's responsibility was, however, made clear when Menderes and his colleagues were placed on trial following the coup of 27 May 1960. See Walter F. Weiker, *The Turkish Revolution, 1960–1961* (Washington, DC, Brookings Institution, 1963), pp. 33–5.

74. For instance, in its submission to the United Nations of 1954, the Greek government did not even mention the existence of a Turkish community on the island. Vali, *Bridge*, p. 237.

75. Ibid., pp. 236–45: Stephens, *Cyprus*, pp. 139–50; Stanley Kyriakides, *Cyprus: Constitutionalism and Crisis Government* (Philadelphia, PA, University of Philadelphia Press, 1968), pp. 37–42 and Suat Bilge, 'The Cyprus Conflict and Turkey', in Karpat *et. al.*, *Turkey's Foreign Policy*, pp. 137–43.

76. Stephens, *Cyprus*, pp. 157–60, 163–7; Kyriakides, *Cyprus*, pp. 48–52 and Bahceli, *Greek–Turkish*, pp. 44–6.

77. Quoted in Bölükbaşı, *Turkish–American Relations*, p. 36.

78. For the text of the constitution, and the accompanying Treaty of Establishment and the Treaty of Guarantee, see *Cyprus* (London, HMSO, Cmnd. 1093, 1960), from where these quotations are taken (pp. 86–7). For a more detailed discussion of the constitution, see Kyriakides, *Cyprus*, pp. 55–71.

79. For details, see Weiker, *Turkish Revolution, passim*; Ahmad, *The Turkish Experiment*, pp. 147–76 and Hale, *Turkish Politics*, pp. 119–49.

80. Kuniholm, 'Turkey and the West', pp. 51–2, and personal communication from İsmail Soysal.

81. However, the latter point is disputed by Donald L. Hafner, 'Bureaucratic Politics and "Those Frigging Missiles": JFK, Cuba, and US Missiles in Turkey', *Orbis*, Vol. 21 (1977), p. 330. Hafner argues that the eventual offer by Khrushchev for such an exchange was merely 'a hasty, uncoordinated gesture designed to salvage some gain from a bad situation'.

82. Kuniholm, 'Turkey and the West', pp. 51–2; Barton J. Bernstein, 'The Cuban Missile Crisis: Trading the Jupiters in Turkey?', *Political Science Quarterly*, Vol. 95 (1980), pp. 99–100, and 'Reconsidering the Missile Crisis: Dealing with the Problem of the American Jupiters in Turkey', in James A. Nathan, ed., *The Cuban Missile Crisis Revisited* (New York, NY, St Martin's Press, 1992), pp. 58–9, 65–6.

83. Presumably a reference to the unelected Constituent Assembly, which had been set up by the military regime in January 1961.

84. Dean Rusk, interviewed in James G. Blight and David A. Welch, *On the Brink: Americans and Soviets Reexamine the Cuban Missile Crisis* (New York, NY, Noonday Press, 1989), p. 173.

85. Quoted in Kuniholm, 'Turkey and the West', p. 53.

86. Ibid., p. 52: Robert F. Kennedy, *Thirteen Days: A Memoir of the Cuban Missile Crisis* (New York, NY, Norton, 1961), pp. 72–3, and Bernstein, 'Reconsidering', pp. 62–3. See also McGhee, *US–Turkish*, p. 166, and Hafner, 'Bureaucratic Politics', pp. 309–11.

87. Kennedy, *Thirteen Days*, pp. 64–8, 71–2, 160–4.

88. Quoted in Bernstein, 'Reconsidering', p. 76.

89. Kennedy, *Thirteen Days,* pp. 80–2.

90. Bernstein, 'Reconsidering', pp. 98–9; James A. Nathan, 'The Heyday of the New Strategy', in Nathan, ed., *Cuban Missile Crisis,* p. 23, and Bilge *et al.*, *Olaylarla*, p. 352.

91. Kennedy, *Thirteen Days*, pp. 86–7.

92. Bernstein, 'Reconsidering', p. 96, and Blight and Welch, *On the Brink*, pp. 83–4.

93. Vali, *Bridge,* p. 129, and Nazih Uslu, 'Turkey's Relationship with the United States, 1960–1975' (unpublished PhD thesis, University of Durham, England, 1994), pp. 184–5.

94. Press conference given by Süleyman Demirel in February 1970: reprinted in Harris, *Troubled Alliance*, p. 236.

95. Quoted in Rubinstein, *Soviet Policy*, p. 19.

96. In 1970 İsmet İnönü complained openly that this had been done in 1962, in spite of his earlier denials. This leaves open the question as to whether he or others may have been more suspicious than he had admitted at the time. Ibid., p. 93, n. 10.

97. Gruen, 'Ambivalence', p. 369. Interestingly, Gruen reaches this conclusion without reference to Robert Kennedy's secret offer to Dobrynin.

98. An apt illustration of this was the lack of Turkish or Western opposition to the passage of the Soviet aircraft carrier *Kiev* through the straits in 1976, see below, p. 189–90, n. 92.

99. Weiker, *Turkish Revolution,* pp. 13, n. 17, 160.

5

Turkey and the Cold War: Global Shifts and Regional Conflicts, 1964–90

The apparent relaxation of relations between the superpowers after 1962 was bound to have significant effects on the position of a front line state like Turkey. In this new environment, Turkey's perceptions of an imminent military threat from the Soviet Union declined, perhaps belatedly, as the focus of East–West conflict shifted away from Europe towards Africa, east Asia and the Middle East – a process which had begun in the mid-1950s. By the mid-1960s, there was a growing realisation that, even if there were a war in Europe, Turkey was not likely to be a primary Soviet target, especially if there were no nuclear missiles sited on its territory.[1] In effect, Turkey now had more room for manoeuvre than it had during the earlier phase of the Cold War. In particular, it could take the risk of improving its relations with the Soviet Union and the non-aligned nations without endangering its national security.

Some differences also arose between Turkey and its allies over strategic planning during the 1960s, as NATO began to adopt the strategy of 'flexible response', as an alternative to massive nuclear retaliation to an attack by the Warsaw Pact. This contained worrying aspects for the Turks, since it suggested that NATO might be willing to sacrifice Turkish territory so as to gain time in a super-power conflict, and was only accepted by Turkey, along with other members of the alliance, in 1967. Similarly, Turkey declined to cooperate in the proposal for a 'Multilateral Force' (that is, submarines equipped with Polaris missiles and crews of mixed nationalities).[2] These changed perceptions coincided with and were reinforced by the emergence of the Cyprus dispute as a major and at times dominant element in Turkey's foreign policy. This brought out serious conflicts of interest between Turkey and the United States: in fact, between 1964 and 1980 relations between the two countries were more tense than at any other time in the post-war period. Difficulties in the relationship with Washington naturally strengthened the trend towards a less monocentric foreign policy on the Turkish side.

Turkish diplomacy was also affected by changes in domestic politics between 1960 and 1980. Until 1960, Turkey had been governed successively by İsmet İnönü's Republican People's Party (CHP) and the Democrat Party of Adnan Menderes. There had been sharp conflicts between the two parties – almost entirely on domestic issues – but both had, in their time, enjoyed large and firm parliamentary majorities which provided a relatively stable background for policy making. This situation had not substantially altered during the military regime of 1960–61. However, when it left office, the military endowed Turkey with a new and more liberal constitution, combined with an electoral system based on proportional representation, which vastly increased the range of views represented in parliament. Ideological positions which had previously been virtually absent from public political discourse, notably socialism and Islamism with their concomitant foreign policy commitments, were now openly aired, even if they were far from gaining majority support. Greater plurality in the party structure also had important effects on the stability and effectiveness of government. In September 1960 the Democrat Party was dissolved by the military regime. Just one year later Menderes and two of his former ministers (including the foreign minister Fatın Rüştü Zorlu) were hanged. However, this did not prevent the formation of a virtual successor, in the shape of the Justice Party (JP). Neither the CHP nor the JP, as the two main parties, won an overall majority in general elections held in September 1961, forcing İnönü to soldier on at the head of three shaky coalitions until February 1965, when a temporary government took over in preparation for the October 1965 elections. These were convincingly won by the JP, now led by Süleyman Demirel, which gave Turkey what proved to be a rare interval of stable single-party government lasting until March 1971. At that point, the army intervened again, and oversaw a semi-military regime, nominally under civilian 'supraparty' government, until 1973.

With the return to elected civilian politics in October 1973, hopes that a stable and effective administration could be formed were dashed, as no party won an overall majority in either of the two general elections held in 1973 and 1977. As a result, Turkey had no less than seven successive governments in as many years – first an unlikely coalition between the CHP, now led by Bülent Ecevit, and the pro-Islamist National Salvation

Party (MSP) between January and November 1974; then a short-lived non-party caretaker government, followed by a right-wing coalition under Demirel known as the 'Nationalist Front' between March 1975 and June 1977. A minority government under Ecevit then lasted for less than two weeks, before being succeeded by a second 'Nationalist Front' under Demirel, which stayed in office until January 1978. With the help of defectors from the JP, Ecevit then returned to the premiership, but his third government collapsed in October 1979, giving way again to Demirel, who this time headed a minority JP government. Meanwhile, between 1977 and 1980, Turkey seemed to be heading towards a total political and economic collapse, thanks to weak and unstable government and a rising tide of political terrorism from violent extremists of both right and left, combined with soaring inflation and huge deficits in the balance of payments. This led almost inevitably to a third military takeover, which overthrew Demirel's government in September 1980. The main effects of these turmoils were domestic, but they also had important consequences for Turkey's foreign relations. After 1973, the overriding preoccupation of governments was to hold onto power, or prevent their rivals from gaining it. While they might try to promote changed external policies, they had little opportunity to develop new strategies effectively, or do more than react to immediate crises. Their hold on power was tenuous, and policies had to be bargained for with fractious and demanding coalition partners. As a result, Turkish foreign policy became a prisoner of chronic domestic instability and economic crisis, making effective planning very hard to achieve or implement.[3]

PARTIAL DISENGAGEMENT: TURKEY, THE SUPERPOWERS AND CYPRUS, 1964–80

While changes in the global environment, and the missile crisis of 1962, certainly had some effect in promoting changes in Turkish policy during the 1960s, Cyprus turned out to be the crucial determining issue, since it awakened popular emotions which few other questions could have done. In 1959, after the signing of the Zürich agreements, İsmet İnönü had prophetically remarked: 'As long as both communitities are not convinced that *enosis* is not possible in the long run, we will have a difficult time to ensure that other articles of the constitution are implemented.'[4] Unfortunately, this expectation proved well founded. The constitutional settlement achieved in 1960 proved impossible to operate, since the Greek Cypriots, most of whom had apparently not abandoned the dream of *enosis*,[5] were little inclined to respect the rights which the Turkish Cypriots had been given under the constitution. Equally, the Turkish Cypriots were determined to exercise them to the full, even to the point of constitutional breakdown. In effect, power-sharing demanded a degree of collaboration and consensus from both sides which was sorely lacking. In November 1963 President Makarios put forward 'thirteen points' of constitutional amendment which, if accepted, would have removed most of the special rights of the Turkish Cypriots. This caused the effective withdrawal of the Turkish Cypriots from the government, and serious intercommunal fighting in which the Turks were the main sufferers. In the course of these and subsequent clashes, about one-third of them were driven from their homes and became refugees in their own country, pushed back into a series of enclaves.[6]

As the crisis deepened during 1964, İnönü apparently decided on a policy of brinkmanship designed to induce the United States to broker a peaceful settlement. On 31 January the British proposed that a NATO force should be sent to the island on a three-months' peacekeeping mission, during which the Turks would promise not to intervene. Reversing its previous stand, the United States agreed to contribute troops to this operation, but the idea was flatly rejected by Makarios. As an alternative, the UN Security Council resolved on 4 March to create a UN peacekeeping force, but this was not organised in time to prevent further clashes.[7] At the beginning of June 1964, İnönü's government was seriously considering landing forces on the island, exercising its rights under Article 4 of the 1960 Treaty of Guarantee: in fact, on 2 June the government decided to launch a military intervention (quite how it planned to do this is not clear).[8] However, on 4 June İnönü received a blunt letter from US President Lyndon Johnson warning him that the other members of NATO 'have not had a chance to consider whether they have an obligation to protect Turkey against the Soviet Union if Turkey takes a step which results in Soviet intervention', and that Turkey could not use US-supplied weapons for an invasion of Cyprus. Given that the Soviet government had been strongly supportive of Makarios, this was not an empty threat.[9] During a visit to Washington on 22–23 June, İnönü was apparently persuaded that the United States would now take matters more firmly into its own hands, and both he and the Greek premier George Papandreou agreed to the appointment of the former US Secretary of State Dean Acheson as President Johnson's mediator.[10] It is impossible to know whether Turkey would have invaded Cyprus in 1964 if Johnson had not taken this action, and possible that it would not, since İnönü's approach was essentially cautious. Apart from the possibility of a Soviet reaction, the Turkish army would have had difficulty in carrying out the operation, owing to its lack of landing-craft.[11] In August 1964 units of the Greek Cypriot National Guard, which had been illegally established two months earlier under the leadership of General George Grivas, threatened to wipe out the Turkish Cypriot enclave near Kokkina. In response, the Turkish Cypriots organised their own militia, but Turkey limited itself to air strikes against Greek Cypriot positions. Subsequently, something like peace was re-established on the island, but it was one which left the Turks at a grave disadvantage.

The most important effects of the 'Johnson letter' were felt in Turkish–US relations. Most Turks felt, quite simply, that US intervention had shown that the United States favoured the Greeks, since it had prevented Turkey from exercising its assumed military superiority, which was the only way of overcoming the Turks' numerical inferiority on the island. Cyprus was not the only source of Turkish–US frictions, since these were exacerbated by other problems such as the legal immunity of US military personnel in Turkey,[12] but it was easily the most important one. Anti-US protests were voiced most vociferously by the Turkish Workers' Party (commonly known by its Turkish acronym, TİP), Turkey's first legal Marxist party, which openly called for Turkey's withdrawal from NATO and the severance of all political links with the United States. TİP contested the general elections of 1965 and 1969, although it won no more than a tiny fraction of the vote,[13] and failed to secure a place in government. Nonetheless, the party's strident anti-US stance awakened wide sympathies, mainly because it managed to canalise strong nationalist sentiments along with its Marxist rhetoric. The reaction forced Prime Minister Demirel to at least be seen as protecting Turkish as against US interests. In July 1969, after years of negotiation, a Defence and Economic Cooperation Agreement was signed between Turkey and the United States, in which the Turkish side sought to ensure that all joint defence activities were conducted within the limits of NATO commitments, and that all joint defence installations were the property of the Turkish republic. On this basis, there were some retrenchments of American freedom of action and a cutback of US personnel in Turkey.[14]

Turkish disenchantment with the United States also led to a *rapprochement* with the Soviet Union which had been on offer from the Soviet side for some time, but hitherto rejected by the Turks. The perceived reduction in the Soviet threat to Turkey, combined with the realisation that Soviet support for the Greek Cypriots seriously weakened Turkey's position on the Cyprus question, reinforced this important change of policy. On 8 August 1964, following the Turkish air strikes in Cyprus, the Soviet news agency, Tass, had warned that if Cyprus were invaded 'the Soviet Union will help the Republic of Cyprus to defend her freedom and independence … and is prepared to begin negotiations on this matter immediately'.[15] Turkey had an obvious interest in reducing this threat, as the possibility of a conflict with the Soviet Union over Cyprus made it more vulnerable to US pressure. Since the Soviet government had long sought some sort of accommodation with Turkey, the Soviet–Turkish détente developed quickly. A delegation from the Supreme Soviet, headed by Politburo member Nikolai Podgorny, visited Turkey in January 1965, initiating a series of official visits by the leaders of the two countries. The most visible product of the new relationship was in the economic field. In March 1967, Turkey accepted a US$200 million credit from the Soviet Union for seven industrial projects. This was followed by two further credits of US$288 million and US$700 million, in 1972 and 1975 respectively. By the end of the 1970s Turkey was reported to have received more Soviet economic assistance than any other Third World country.[16] In 1972 Turkey and the Soviet Union signed a Declaration on the Principles of Good Neighbourly Relations, although this did not amount to much in practical terms. More immediately important for Turkey was a significant shift in the Soviet position on Cyprus, as the Soviet government evidently decided that it would be more profitable to try to accommodate the Turks than give unconditional support to the Greeks. After 1964, and especially after the *coup d'état* in Athens of April 1967 which brought a fanatically right-wing military government to power in Greece, Turkey and the Soviet Union were united in strong opposition to *enosis* and 'the observance of the legitimate rights and interests of both communities in Cyprus'.[17] In particular, the Soviet Union sought to prevent a Greek takeover of Cyprus, which would have opened the way for the establishment of US bases on the island. This did not mean that Turkish policy on Cyprus had full Soviet support, but at least the Turks had secured an end to active hostility from Moscow.

During 1966–68 these changes led, for the first time, to a serious and open debate in Turkey about whether the country should remain in NATO. On the left, Professor A. Halûk Ülman, later a foreign policy adviser to Bülent Ecevit, argued the case for neutrality by claiming that membership of NATO required Turkey to maintain an oversized army, thus diverting resources away from civilian development projects, which would be a better defence against communism. Were there to be a conventional war in another theatre, the alliance would drag Turkey into it, even if it arose for reasons remote to Turkey's national interests. Were the war to be nuclear, then Turkey would become the victim of instant devastation. If Turkey were neutral, but was nonetheless attacked by the Soviet Union, then the United States would assist it anyway since it could not allow the Soviet Union to dominate the Middle East. The contrary argument was put by other commentators such as the retired Admiral Sezai Orkunt, and İhsan Sabri Çağlayangil, Demirel's Foreign Minister. Çağlayangil took the most strongly pro-NATO line, arguing that membership of the alliance did not place unacceptable burdens on Turkey, and that if it were neutral it would have to divert more rather than less resources to defence. Orkunt supported this point, adding that if Turkey quit NATO it would face serious shortages of military spare parts, almost all of which were US supplied. Moreover, withdrawal from the alliance would seriously weaken Turkey in its conflict with Greece over Cyprus, since the United States might well increase military aid to Greece at Turkey's expense. At the same time, Turkey continued to be heavily reliant on Western, and especially US, economic assistance, to close the gap in its external accounts, meet interest payments on its growing foreign debt, and finance vital investments. After 1964 these were channeled through an aid consortium of the OECD, in which the United States took the lead, followed by what was then West Germany. During 1960–64 such transfers were running at an average of around US$243 million per year, rising to an average of US$284 million per year during 1965–69, equivalent to over half of Turkey's foreign exchange earnings from trade and other sources. In spite of the growth in aid from the Soviet Union, Turkey's foreign policy options remained somewhat restricted by its reliance on borrowing from the West. The balance of the arguments thus came down in favour of remaining in NATO, while avoiding commitments to support the United States in the Middle East and other theatres, which might push Turkey into the position of a US satellite.[18]

These conclusions were reinforced by Turkish reactions to Soviet policies in other regions during the late 1960s. While Soviet spokesmen might profess friendship for Turkey, actions like the Soviet invasion of Czechoslovakia in 1968, and the contemporary Soviet naval build-up in the eastern Mediterranean, inevitably weakened the case for neutrality. As İsmet İnönü, then the leader of the opposition, publicly concluded, 'We have examined the NATO agreement and announced our stand. The recent Czech events have shown how correct this stand was'. Foreign Minister Çağlayangil underlined this point, warning that global détente had been 'gravely impaired' by events in Czechoslovakia.[19] As a result, a strong balance of opinion supported the idea that Turkey should stay in NATO, but avoid becoming stridently pro-US, and protect its own national interests within the alliance.

Turkish–US relations were also affected – this time more favourably – by a renewed crisis over Cyprus in 1967. Although Demirel had criticised İnönü's alleged lack of assertiveness in 1964, he in fact continued a cautious policy, by beginning direct negotiations with Greece. These continued after the Greek colonels' coup, and resulted in meetings between the Greek and Turkish prime ministers at the border towns of Keşan and Alexandroupolis (Dedcağaç) on 9–10 September 1967. During the talks, Demirel agreed to the union of Cyprus with Greece in return for the granting of a Turkish sovereign base area (similar to those enjoyed by the British), but this condition was turned down by the Greeks.[20] Just over two months later, on 15 November, Cyprus again exploded when the Greek Cypriot National Guard attacked the two Turkish Cypriot villages of Kophinou and Aghios Theodhoros. After threatened air strikes from Turkey, the Greek Cypriots withdrew from the two villages the following day. However, on 17 November Demirel decided to stiffen his response by demanding from the Greek government that it withdraw the 12,000 troops it had infiltrated into the island, well above the limits allowed by the 1960 settlement (see p. 132), and disband the National Guard. On the same day, parliament gave the government authority to send Turkish troops abroad – implicitly, to Cyprus.[21] Meanwhile preparations were made for a sea-borne invasion of Cyprus, though whether Turkey could or would have successfully accomplished this is open to some doubt, thanks to equipment shortages on the Turkish side, and the presence of the US Sixth Fleet, which might have intercepted it.[22] Greece rejected the Turkish demands on 22 November, but on the following day the former US Secretary for Defence, Cyrus Vance, flew into Ankara as a personal emissary of the US President. Lyndon Johnson had evidently decided not to repeat the mistake of issuing a blunt veto to the Turks, but to try mediation. After some stalling, on 30 November the Greek mainland government changed its tune by agreeing to withdraw its troops from Cyprus, disband the National Guard and recall Grivas. This did not mark a complete victory for the Turks, since Makarios later refused to dismantle the National Guard. However, Vance had persuaded the Greek mainland government to accept the most important Turkish demands, and thus helped to restore the standing of the United States in the eyes of Turkish opinion. The change in the Soviet attitude was also notable, since the

Soviet Union strongly opposed the junta in Athens, and refused to criticise the expected Turkish invasion.[23]

During the following years, the main focus of concern in Turkey switched back to domestic problems, as the Demirel government was forced to resign by a military pronunciamento on 12 March 1971. For the next 30 months, Turkey was governed by a series of weak but supposedly 'supra-party' governments which in fact followed the off-stage directions of the military chiefs. All the available evidence suggests that military intervention was an entirely home-grown event, and that the US government or its agencies played no part in bringing it about, though the Nixon administration was certainly quite supportive of the semi-military regime once it was established.[24] During 1971–73 the main bone of contention in Turkey's foreign relations was a dispute with the United States over the cultivation of the opium poppy, which was an important source of income for some Turkish farmers, especially in the province of Afyonkarahısar (the name means 'opium-black-castle'). The crop had been grown quite legally in Turkey for many years, since it is an important ingredient in legal pain-killing drugs. However, the Nixon administration was extremely concerned by the growth of heroin addiction in the United States, and sought to ban opium cultivation in Turkey, to prevent diversion into the illegal market. In June 1971 the semi-military government under Nihat Erim yielded to US pressure, by agreeing to implement a complete ban on production, to begin in the autumn of 1972. This move stirred up a wave of popular opposition, on the grounds that Turkey had sacrificed an important source of legitimate income, merely to please the United States. Eventually, in July 1974, the succeeding civilian government under Bülent Ecevit revoked the ban, but implemented measures to prevent diversion into the illegal market by enforcing what was known as the 'poppy straw process' of harvesting. These measures were accepted in Washington: in fact the Ford administration encouraged the government in taking these measures, and the dispute was thus laid to rest.[25] Unfortunately, the Turkish (and Kurdish) criminal underworld still plays a role in the international heroin trade, but mainly because Turkey is an important transit route for drug-trafficking, rather than an original source of production.

Turkey returned to elected civilian government in 1974 with two new actors on the political stage. In May 1972 Bülent Ecevit unexpectedly captured the leadership of the CHP from the veteran İsmet İnönü, and then attempted to turn the party into a social democratic party on the western European model, while retaining the commitment to Kemalist secularism and espousing the idea of a more independent foreign policy within NATO. Meanwhile, Turkey's first successful Islamist party emerged, in the shape of the National Salvation Party (MSP) led by Necmettin Erbakan. The MSP had stridently anti-Western views on cultural questions, but little in the way of a developed foreign policy, apart from a strongly nationalist outlook. A coalition government of these two unlikely bed-fellows was formed in January 1974. Five months later, it faced the most severe foreign policy test encountered by any Turkish government since the late 1940s, when the Greek military junta sought to oust Makarios and effectively establish the union of Greece with Cyprus. In 1968 inter-communal negotiations on a new constitution had begun between Glafcos Clerides, representing the Greek Cypriots, and Rauf Denktash on the Turkish Cypriot side, but these broke down in 1973 as Makarios would not accept a settlement definitely ruling out *enosis*.[26] In November 1973 Colonel Demetrios Ioannides, who was fanatically hostile to Makarios and committed to achieving *enosis*, replaced Colonel George Papadopoulos as the strongman of the Athens junta. Three months later, following the death of Grivas, the reconstructed junta took over full control of the Greek Cypriot National Guard and EOKA-B, the extremist successor to the EOKA terrorist organisation of the 1950s. This produced a sharp reaction from Makarios on 6 July 1974, when he made public a letter he had sent to the Greek president, General Gizikis, demanding the immediate withdrawal of the 650 mainland Greek officers in the National Guard.[27] The Athens junta responded on 15 July, when Makarios was deposed by the National Guard and EOKA-B, to be replaced by Nikos Sampson. Sampson was the worst possible choice from every viewpoint, since he had virtually no support in Cyprus, and was notorious for his killings in EOKA's campaign against the British in the 1950s, and his hatred of the Turks.

As co-guarantors of Cyprus' independence, the British were against military action, since there were thousands of British tourists and residents on the island who would have been vulnerable to retaliation by the Greeks, and the maintenance of the British bases was heavily dependent on co-operation from the Greek Cypriots. The British did, however, act to save Makarios, who was transported to London via the British base at Akrotiri. In Washington, US President Nixon was embroiled in the final stages of the Watergate scandal, while his Secretary of State, Henry Kissinger, was preoccupied with Middle East peacemaking, following the Arab–Israeli war of October 1973. Hence the United States failed to take sufficiently strong action to defuse the crisis until it was too late. This left Turkey as the sole regional power likely to take a strong stand.

The Cypriot *coup* of 15 July caught Ecevit's government by surprise. It had few well-developed plans for what it sought to achieve in Cyprus, though it was committed to some sort of federal solution,[28] and opposed the return of Makarios, given his attitude in the inter-communal negotiations. In the conditions of the time, geographical federation would have been difficult to apply in Cyprus, since the Turkish Cypriots did not inhabit a single stretch of territory, but were scattered in pockets around the island, complicating the military problem of protecting them. On the other hand, Turkey now had sufficient landing-craft and other equipment to carry out a successful invasion of Cyprus, provided it was not physically opposed by Britain or the United States. The expectation that this would not happen was a crucial factor in convincing the Turks that they could go ahead with the invasion if it were necessary. The Ecevit government also realised that it might provoke a war with Greece, but calculated that it could take this risk.[29] Turkey would base its action on Article 4 of the 1960 Treaty of Guarantee, although this allowed it to intervene only after consulting with the other guarantor powers, and with the sole aim of re-establishing the state of affairs set up by the treaty – that is, the independence and territorial integrity of Cyprus.[30]

On 16 July, the day after the Sampson *coup*, Ecevit held a meeting with his military commanders in the National Security Council, at which it was decided to carry out preparations for a landing, to be launched on 20 July. According to the military planning, the operation would be completed in two stages. In the first stage, Turkish forces would secure a bridgehead in the northern part of the island, after which negotiations would begin for a new constitutional settlement. If the Greeks refused this, then a second advance would be ordered, to gain sufficient territory where the Turkish Cypriots could be settled for their security. Prior to the launch of the first operation, Turkey would first consult with the British and try to secure a diplomatic solution, though Ecevit was not hopeful that this could be achieved. The idea of a military intervention was strongly supported by Erbakan, though the former prime minister, Nihat Erim, was cautious. In private, Demirel attacked the proposal, on the grounds that it could provoke a war with Greece. He argued that even if Turkey did occupy Cyprus or part of it, world opinion might restore Makarios to power, and the Turks would be left no better off. However, his party's parliamentary group was later to give full support to military intervention.[31]

On 17 July Ecevit flew to London for emergency meetings with the British government. However, as he had expected, he was unable to persuade them to take joint action, by allowing Turkish forces to operate from British bases on Cyprus. Meanwhile, Nixon's Under-Secretary of State, Joseph Sisco, also arrived in London to attempt mediation, but had virtually no effective diplomatic ammunition to persuade the two sides. Accordingly neither Sisco, Kissinger or the British could persuade Ecevit to call off the invasion, which was launched in the early morning of 20 July. Britain and the United States did not act effectively to prevent it, and the Soviet government made it clear that it was prepared to accept a limited Turkish intervention provided the independence of Cyprus were preserved. More broadly, the fact that the Greek junta had put itself clearly in the wrong increased general acceptance of the Turkish action. By the time a cease-fire was brought about on 22 July through Resolution 353 of the UN Security Council, Turkish forces held a small triangle of territory in the north of the island. This still left about 50,000–60,000 Turkish Cypriots, or about half the Turkish Cypriot population, outside Turkish protection. It evidently fell short of what the Turkish military had planned to achieve during the first two days, since Turkish troops continued local advances after the cease-fire had been declared. Turkish Cypriot areas outside the northern triangle were still surrounded by the National Guard, and apparently in grave danger. Immediately after the Turkish landings on 20 July the Greek government decided in principle to declare war on Turkey, and on the following day Ioannides, now a brigadier-general, demanded that the army should attack the Turks directly across the river Maritsa in Thrace. The Greek armed forces were quite unprepared for such an operation, and the military regime fell apart. On 23 July Constantine Karamanlis was recalled from exile to head a civilian government in Athens. Simultaneously, Sampson fell from power in Cyprus, and Glafcos Clerides was made head of a provisional Greek Cypriot government on 24 July.[32]

Peace talks between Britain, Turkey and the new Greek government opened in Geneva on 25 July. By 29 July they had reached a deadlock, but at that point Kissinger persuaded Ecevit that acceptance of UN Resolution 353 did not mean that Turkey would have to withdraw its forces immediately, and the parties signed a joint declaration on the following day. This represented a considerable success for the Turks since, while it confirmed the joint acceptance of a military standstill and the establishment of buffer zones between the two sides, it linked the withdrawal of Turkish forces to the achievement of 'a just and lasting solution acceptable to all parties concerned' and noted 'the existence in practice ... of two autonomous administrations' on the island – an implicit recognition that the former unitary republic could not be restored.[33]

The British, Greek and Turkish delegations, which were later joined by Clerides and Denktash, reassembled in Geneva on 9 August, supposedly to work out the basis of a new constitutional settlement. The need to secure the end of the threat to the Turkish Cypriots outside the triangle was also an important objective for the Turks. However, by the time the second Geneva conference began, the two sides had dug themselves into irreconcilable positions. On the Turkish side, Erbakan favoured the idea of outright partition of Cyprus, and was persuaded by Ecevit to accept the principle of an independent Cypriot state only on the basis of a geographical federation of the two communities. On the Greek side, Makarios, who was still in exile, opposed any constitutional negotiations with Turkey, and George Mavros, the Greek foreign minister and representative at Geneva, would only accept negotiations on the basis of the 1960 constitution.

On 10 August the second Geneva conference got down to business when Denktash put forward proposals for a bizonal federation, with a Turkish state in the north of the island. Under American pressure, the Ankara government agreed two days later to what was known as the 'cantonal' plan, under which the Turkish Cypriots would be given six separate cantons, around existing settlements, within a federal structure, as an alternative. Some sort of federal solution was evidently favoured by both Kissinger and James Callaghan, the British foreign secretary. When the Turkish foreign minister, Turan Güneş, put the bizonal and cantonal plans to him on 13 August, Clerides asked for a 48-hour recess to consider the proposals. This was refused by Güneş, and the next day Turkish forces began a second advance, which effectively sectioned off the northern part of the island, from Kokkina in the west to Famagusta in the east. Neither Britain or the United States took any effective action to halt the second Turkish advance. When Clerides requested the Soviet observer at the Geneva conference, Viktor Menin, for a limited Russian military presence in Cyprus, he was asked whether this had been cleared with the United States, suggesting that there may have been a US–Soviet understanding that neither superpower would intervene unilaterally.[34] Although Turkey and the Turkish Cypriots were still committed in principle to maintaining an independent federal Cypriot state, the island was in practice partitioned (as some Turks argued it had been since 1963–64) with the Turks controlling about 36 per cent of its territory. About 150,000 Greek Cypriots were forced to flee as refugees to the south, while 120,000 Turkish Cypriots regrouped in the north, completing the physical division.

After the second Turkish advance, Ecevit apparently expected that the

Greek side would soon come back to the negotiating table,[35] but the Greeks solidly refused to return to Geneva. Turkey had a clear military superiority in Cyprus, but could not convert this into political influence, so as to gain a Cyprus settlement in accordance with its own objectives. Ecevit had enjoyed broad international support at the time of the first landings, but sacrificed it by embarking on the second offensive so precipitately. He also had difficulties in converting Erbakan to the idea of negotiations, and this was one of the main factors leading to his resignation on 7 November 1974. In February 1975 Rauf Denktash proclaimed the 'Turkish Federated State of Cyprus' in the north, presumably as a preliminary to the negotiation of a federal constitution, but this move was unrecognised by any state except Turkey. On 28 April 1975 inter-communal negotiations began in Vienna under UN auspices. These failed to make any real progress until 12 February 1977, when Makarios and Denktash, meeting in Nicosia, agreed to four important guidelines on which future negotiations would proceed. For Makarios, this included the important concession that 'We are seeking an independent, non-aligned, bi-communal Federal Republic.' The two sides also agreed to discuss what were called the 'three freedoms' – that is freedom of movement between the two parts of the island, freedom of settlement, and the right to own property in either part – 'taking into consideration the fundamental basis of a bi-communal federal system'.[36] However, this potentially important turning point failed to produce any positive results. Makarios died on 3 August 1977, to be succeeded by Spyros Kyprianou as Greek Cypriot president, but the two sides could not agree on the respective powers of the central government and constituent states, or the geographical division between the two. Hence the intercommunal negotiations dragged on, seemingly endlessly and fruitlessly, as Cyprus was overtaken on the list of Turkey's concerns by far more pressing domestic problems.[37]

While the Cyprus dispute ground on during the 1970s, relations between Greece and Turkey became further embittered by a series of bilateral conflicts. Of these, the most acute related to offshore mineral rights in the Aegean. As a signatory to the Geneva Convention on the Continental Shelf of 1958, which grants coastal states rights to sea-bed resources at a depth of less than 200 metres contiguous to their coasts, Greece claimed exclusive offshore mineral rights to about two-thirds of the Aegean, since Greek islands extend to within a few miles of the coast of Turkey. Exploration licences to search for oil were granted by Greece in 1970, and a small commercial find was made near the northern island of Thasos in 1974. The Greek claim was disputed by Turkey, which suggested the division of resources by a median line down the middle of the Aegean, or joint exploration and production by the two countries. Conflict erupted in May 1974 when the Turks sent a survey ship into areas claimed by Greece, but was then overtaken by events in Cyprus of later that year. After a second incident in July–August 1976, Greece made unsuccessful appeals on this issue to the UN Security Council and the International Court of Justice in The Hague. The dispute then subsided, although there was no settlement, as Greece argued that it should be submitted for adjudication by the Court, while Turkey preferred bilateral negotiations, with outstanding issues to be decided by the Court. On the Turkish side, the conflict assumed importance not for economic reasons (the oil resources of the Aegean are thought to be very limited) but out of the fear that claims to sea-bed resources might some day be converted into claims to sovereignty over the adjacent sea and air space.[38]

Similar fears were critical in a simultaneous dispute in which Greece claimed the right to extend its territorial waters from the present six miles to the internationally recognised norm of 12 nautical miles. Given the large number of Greek islands, this would give Greece control of about 64 per cent of the Aegean, compared with about 10 per cent for Turkey. Under international law, Greece would be obliged to allow innocent passage to both merchant shipping and warships of any nation through its territorial waters. Nonetheless, the Turks still concluded that they would be vulnerable to total enclosure by Greece, and announced that a declaration by Greece of a 12-mile limit would be treated as a *casus belli*. The Greeks also fortified their Aegean islands, in spite of the demilitarisation required by the Lausanne treaty, while in 1975 Turkey reconstructed its Fourth Army as an 'Army of the Aegean', which was pointedly excluded from Turkey's commitment to NATO. Other disputes centred over the rights of the Turkish–Muslim minority in Thrace and the greatly depleted Greek community in Istanbul, as well as flight-control rights in the Aegean. None of these conflicts are or were insoluble (indeed, the flight control dispute was settled in 1980) but they further embittered historical rivalries between the two nations, and added to the problems created by Cyprus.[39]

The Cyprus crisis of 1974 also had important effects on Turkey's relations with the United States. Until this time, ethnic politics in Washington had not played a decisive role in the relationship, [40] but in September 1975 a powerful pro-Greek lobby in the US Congress secured the passage of a resolution banning military sales and aid to Turkey until the president could show that substantial progress had been registered towards a settlement of the Cyprus problem. The fact that there were an estimated 1.25 million Greek–Americans at the time, compared with only 54,000 Turkish–Americans,[41] gave the Greeks a clear advantage on this issue. The ban was opposed by President Ford and Secretary of State Henry Kissinger, but it nonetheless came into effect on 5 February 1975. In response, Demirel's government suspended the Defence Cooperation Agreement of 1969, and in July ended all operations at all US facilities in Turkey, other than those deemed to have a purely NATO function. This had a serious effect in curtailing the United States' ability to monitor Soviet troop movements, and missile and underground nuclear tests in the southern region of the Soviet Union, which depended on the use of radar and other facilities on Turkish soil. In fact, the signs are that the embargo had at least as damaging an effect on US military capabilities as on those of Turkey. In October 1975, under strong pressure from the Ford administration, Congress agreed to a partial lifting of the embargo, by limiting it to supplies covered by grants and deferred credit sales. Turkey was in any case able to circumvent US restrictions by buying supplies from other NATO countries, such as Italy and Germany. Certainly, the Turkish armed forces were seriously short of modern equipment by the late 1970s, but this was probably as much an effect of the government's critical financial straits, and a desperate shortage of foreign exchange, as the direct result of the arms embargo. In the event, the embargo was completely lifted by Congress in August 1978, allowing the re-opening of major US facilities in the following October.[42]

In view of the sharp public reaction in Turkey to Johnson's letter of 1964, it is perhaps surprising that the arms embargo of 1975–78 had comparatively little political effect. There were no massive demonstrations against the United States, such as one might have expected, and Turkish comment was relatively restrained. After he took over the premiership at the beginning of 1978, Bülent Ecevit began to suggest that Turkey might pull out of NATO if the embargo were not lifted, causing consternation in Washington.[43] However, there were no moves to withdraw Turkey from NATO's military structures, as Greece and France had done. The fact that the catharsis in US–Turkish relations had already been passed in the 1960s may have played a part in this, but the knowledge that opinions in Washington were divided also moderated Turkish reactions. Not only did the Ford administration clearly oppose the embargo, but Jimmy Carter, the successful candidate in the 1976 presidential elections, also changed his position on this issue. During the election campaign, he had indulged in some pro-Greek rhetoric, but after his inauguration, he rapidly reversed his stance, in line with military and diplomatic opinion, and supported the total and unconditional lifting of the embargo in 1978. Nor is there any evidence that the arms embargo had any effect in softening Turkish policies on Cyprus, though it may have moderated anti-US feelings in Greece.[44]

In the late 1970s, the difficulties in Turkey's relationship with the United States, together with the perceived decline in the Soviet threat and Turkey's economic problems, persuaded Bülent Ecevit to adopt what he called 'a new national security concept and new defence and foreign policies'. Ecevit argued that Turkey was shouldering an unfairly large burden within NATO and was over-dependent on the United States. Accordingly, it should slim down its forces, develop its own defence industries and 'establish an atmosphere of mutual confidence in our relations with the neighbouring countries'.[45] Ecevit appeared to adopt a more 'Third Worldist' stance than his predecessors. In July 1978, Ecevit's foreign minister attended the non-aligned ministers meeting in Belgrade, and it was suggested that Ecevit sought an independent role for Turkey in NATO similar to that of Romania in the Warsaw Pact at the time. In June 1978 his government signed what was called a Political Document on the Principles of Good Neighbourly and Friendly Cooperation with the Soviet Union, but this went much less far than the fully fledged non-aggression pact which the Soviet government had been working for. During his visit to Moscow for the conclusion of the agreement, Ecevit announced that his government would be reducing its cooperation with the United States and NATO, on the grounds that the Soviet Union no longer constituted a threat to Turkish security. However, this fell well short of closing down the US bases on Turkish soil, or a withdrawal from NATO, as the Soviets had hoped.[46] As Ecevit explained it, his 'new concept of national defence … should be compatible without continued membership of NATO. … In spite of everything we do not intend to leave NATO'.[47] In practice, it was hard to see what Ecevit's policies amounted to in practical terms, besides a less committedly pro-US attitude. The only tangible example of this was his extreme reluctance to allow the United States to use Turkish bases for flights by U-2 reconnaissance aircraft to monitor the expected Strategic Arms Limitation Treaty (SALT II) between the superpowers.[48] Apart from the fact that Ecevit never stayed in office for long enough to put any effective new strategies into operation, and was too beset by domestic problems, the more conservative administrations led by Demirel had also backed the idea of a more 'diversified' foreign policy and had, for instance, reacted sharply to the arms embargo. Hence, it has to be concluded that Turkey's disengagement from the Western alliance during the 1970s was, at best, very partial, hesitant and uncertain.

RE-ENGAGEMENT AND THE DECONSTRUCTION
OF THE COLD WAR, 1980–89

During the first half of the 1980s, Turkish foreign policy – particularly in relation to the superpowers – entered a phase of re-engagement in the Western alliance, in the sense that the previous tension in Turkish–US relations abated markedly, talk of altering Turkey's position within NATO subsided, and some of the old suspicion and hostility returned to Turkish–Soviet relations. As in the case of the previous phase, this realignment had both international and domestic political causes. At the end of the 1970s, global developments heightened tensions between the superpowers, and re-established the importance of Turkey's role in the Western alliance, as well as the Turks' attachment to the West. The Iranian Revolution of February 1979 meant that Turkey was now the West's only ally in the northern tier, and its value as a listening post and barrier to any potential Soviet advance into the Middle East was reinforced. US anxieties about the future security of the region were further enhanced by the Soviet invasion of Afghanistan in December 1979. For US policy-makers like Zbigniew Brzezinski, Jimmy Carter's national security adviser, the area to the east of Turkey was seen as an 'arc of crisis', with the possibility of a Soviet invasion or internal takeover of Iran envisaged as a distinct possibility. In retrospect, such scenarios may seem exaggerated, but they were genuinely believed in at the time, and informed Western policy accordingly. Although it is improbable that Turkey's leaders believed that the Soviet Union was on the point of invading Turkey, the Soviet invasion of Afghanistan severely weakened the case for detachment from NATO in domestic political debates, by demonstrating what could happen to a relatively weak nation on the borders of the Soviet Union which opted for neutrality.[49] Even when the assumed threat to the Middle East abated during the 1980s, the perception on both sides that the Soviet Union was still a threat continued with the inauguration of Ronald Reagan as president in 1981. This was enhanced by the apparent immobilism on the part of the ailing gerontocracy of Leonid Brezhnev and his successors, who still ruled in the Kremlin.

Changes in Turkey's domestic politics occurred slightly later than those in the global environment, but were no less influential in the redirection of foreign policy. On 12 September 1980, the descent into political anarchy and economic collapse was abruptly halted by Turkey's third coup since 1960, when the four force commanders of the Turkish armed forces, headed by the Chief of the General Staff, General Kenan Evren, overthrew Demirel's government, and rapidly suppressed the terrorist organisations of both the ultra-left and ultra-right which had almost brought the country to its knees during the previous two years. Islamist, extreme nationalist and leftist organisations were banned, and all pre-*coup* parties dissolved. In November 1982 a new constitution, somewhat more restrictive than its predecessor, was introduced and Evren was declared president for the next seven years. While the military regime also succeeded in putting the economy back on the rails, its attempt to construct a civilian political system according to its own blueprint was far less successful. In the elections held in November 1983 the party favoured by the military and led by a retired general, Turgut Sunalp, was roundly defeated by Turgut Özal's Motherland Party, as the standard-bearer of the centre right. After their suppression by the military, leftist forces failed to revive in the 1980s, and were bitterly divided by personal and other rivalries.

Meanwhile Özal, who won a second electoral victory in 1987, continued as prime minister until taking over from Evren as president in 1989. He provided Turkey with a period of stable single-party government which it had lacked since the late 1960s, as well as the possibility of constructing and carrying through a consistent foreign policy and decisive leadership. Constitutionally, Bülent Ecevit and Süleyman Demirel were banned from politics by the military regime until 1992, but this did not prevent them from setting up their own parties under proxy leaders (in Ecevit's case, his wife Rahşan) known as the Democratic Left Party and True Path Party, respectively. The two former leaders successfully campaigned for a removal of the bans in 1987. However, neither they nor a new centre-left party, the Social Democratic Populist Party,[50] led by İsmet İnönü's son, Erdal İnönü, succeeded in breaking Özal's grip on power until 1991. Similarly, Necmettin Erbakan effectively revived his former National Salvation Party as the Welfare Party under a proxy leader in 1983. Having been prevented by the generals from competing in the 1983 elections, Erbakan's party failed to win any seats in 1987. At this stage, Erbakan seemed to have been left in the wilderness, with part of his electoral base captured by the Motherland Party, which made a distinct bid for the support of moderate Islamic voters.[51]

The most distinctive feature of Özal's programme was a commitment to economic liberalisation, mirroring that of Ronald Reagan and Margaret Thatcher. This was notably successful in restoring economic growth and Turkey's external balances, and created important ideological bonds with the contemporary Western leaders. Like them, Özal believed that 'the second half of the seventies witnessed the failure, not only of the communist system, but also ... of the post-war model of society based on Keynesian economics and the welfare state'. In visionary mood, he hoped to see Turkey as a member of the European Community, in which '[H]er ethnocentricity will have come to an end; her conception of history, her foreign policy and her outlook on life will effectively have become secular. She will enjoy a truly global and humanist perspective, in which the pejorative distinction between Christians and others will have disappeared.'[52] Although this vision was far from realised, it can be seen as part of a process by which some of the tensions and mutual suspicions between Turkey and the West which had emerged during the 1960s and 1970s, were being broken down.

The clearest sign of the new relationship with the United States was the signature of a new Defence and Economic Cooperation Agreement (DECA) in March 1980, for which the lifting of the arms embargo had obviously cleared the way. Under the new DECA, the US retained the use of 12 of its most vital bases in Turkey, including İncirlik and essential intelligence gathering stations, while 13 other facilities reverted to exclusive Turkish use. The Carter administration also promised increased military and economic aid to Turkey, although this fell short of the Turks' ambitious military shopping list.[53] In subsequent years, annual US military assistance to Turkey peaked at US$715 million in 1984, falling to US$526 million in 1988, as the Cold War gradually scaled down. Nonetheless, Turkey was still the third largest recipient of US military assistance, after Israel and Egypt. In 1986 the reduction of conventional forces in western Europe allowed the United States and other NATO members to transfer surplus military material to Turkey, along with Greece and Portugal. The DECA of 1980 also provided for the expansion of Turkey's own defence industries through the transfer of technology and equipment. The most prominent part of this programme was the establishment of a factory to produce the F-16 fighter, in collaboration with the US company, General Dynamics, which produced its first aircraft in 1987, although there were many other similar projects.[54] For successive Turkish and US administrations, the most serious hurdle to the expansion of this relationship was strong pressure in Congress, from both pro-Greek and pro-Armenian lobbies, to limit US aid to Turkey, and to maintain a 10:7 ratio in aid to Turkey and Greece (that is, to allow US$10 in aid to Turkey for every US$7 in aid to Greece). After the expiry of the 1980 DECA in 1985, Turkey pushed hard for stronger guarantees on aid deliveries, and signed a new DECA only after US Secretary of State George Shultz agreed that the administration would vigorously press Congress on this issue. In 1987,

Congress nevertheless cut the proposed aid package to Turkey for 1988 from US$914 million to around US$570 million. This was accompanied by a determined but unsuccessful campaign by a group of pro-Armenian congressmen to have 24 April declared an official day of mourning for the 1.5 million Armenians who they claimed had been killed by the Turks in 1915. In response, President Evren called off a long-planned trip to Washington, and the government began to restrict US use of the İncirlik base. Although a Side Letter to the DECA remained unratified by the Turkish parliament, both sides agreed to operate it. Eventually, the agreement was renewed for another four years in 1988, since, it spite of the decline in the Soviet threat, Turkey still needed military, and some economic assistance, from the United States.[55]

Not surprisingly, the strengthening of ties between Turkey and the United States in the early 1980s was accompanied by growing tension in relations between Ankara and Moscow. The Soviet military intervention in Afghanistan was strongly criticised by the Turks: although Turkey did not directly assist the Afghan *mujahiddin,* several thousand Afghan refugees of 'Turkic' (in fact, Kirghiz) extraction were given shelter in Turkey. The signature of the DECA in 1980 was a further setback for Soviet policy, and led to sharp attacks on the Turkish government in the Soviet press.[56] On the Turkish side, suspicions were increased by a Soviet military build-up in the Caucasus in the early 1980s, and the Soviet rearming of Syria after the Israeli invasion of Lebanon in 1982.[57] Soviet aid to Turkey virtually dried up at the same time. The frosty relationship with the Soviet Union continued until 1985, when Mikhail Gorbachev succeeded Konstantin Chernenko as Secretary-General of the Soviet Communist Party. Essentially, Gorbachev's policies centred on economic reconstruction and greater openness in the internal organisation of the Soviet Union, combined with a greater emphasis on cooperation rather than conflict with the West, which eventually led to the end of the Cold War by 1989–90.

Soviet policies towards Turkey during the Brezhnev era had been based on the 'national capitalism' school of thought within Soviet strategy. This had assumed that the large number of developing countries which were not of socialist orientation could nonetheless be brought round to pro-Soviet positions through the exploitation of contradictions between them and the advanced capitalist states. Under Gorbachev, this policy was seen to have failed. In spite of the conflicts between Turkey and the United States, and the impressive volume of Soviet aid to Turkey, it had paid almost no political dividends. Turkey was still a firm member of NATO, and there were still numerous US bases on Turkish soil. Problems in the

US–Turkish relationship were the result of pressure by ethnic lobbies in Congress, not Soviet policy. Hence, the argument for 'economic inter-dependence' advanced under Gorbachev proposed that all states were part of a single global economic system, in which it was in the interests of all to cooperate.[58] During the second half of the 1980s, Turkey was able to develop better relations with both the Soviet Union and the Western powers simultaneously, for the first time since the 1930s.

The main effects of this transformation were seen in the economic field. Between 1987 and 1990, the bilateral trade volume between Turkey and the Soviet Union almost quadrupled, from US$476 million to US$1.8 billion. The most important element in this was the supply of Russian natural gas to Turkey, through a pipeline via Bulgaria constructed in 1987. This resulted from an agreement reached in September 1984, shortly before Gorbachev came to power. Turkish contractors also began to win important construction contracts in the Soviet Union. Meanwhile, the dramatic improvement in Turkey's external accounts under Özal meant that Turkey now became a provider of credits to the Soviet Union, rather than the other way round. In 1989 the Turkish Eximbank extended two credit lines of US$150 million each to the Soviet Union for the purchase of Turkish consumer goods, with further and larger credits granted in 1991.[59]

While these momentous changes in global politics had significant effects on Turkey's relations with the superpowers, its local difficulties with Greece over the Aegean and Cyprus continued virtually unchanged. In Cyprus, the intercommunal negotiations dragged on until 1983 without result. In November of that year – just before the end of the military regime in Turkey – the Turkish Cypriots laid claim to national sovereignty, by proclaiming the 'Turkish Republic of Northern Cyprus' (TRNC), with Rauf Denktash as president, but their state was refused international recognition by any government except that of Turkey. Since the Greek Cypriots now refused face-to-face discussions, the UN Secretary-General, Javier Perez de Cuellar, pressed ahead with 'proximity talks' between the two sides. In 1984 these came close to producing a new agreement, when Denktash accepted a constitutional package establishing a federal republic with a Greek Cypriot president and Turkish Cypriot vice-president, a division of powers within federal institutions, and fairly substantial residual powers to the constituent states. The area controlled by the Turks would be reduced to around 29 per cent of the island. Perez de Cuellar had expected that Greek Cypriot President Kyprianou would accept this package at a summit meeting in New York in January 1985, but in the event he turned it down. No effective progress was made later, in spite of the succession of Kyprianou by George Vassiliou as Greek Cypriot president in 1988.[60]

In bilateral relations with Greece, a significant hurdle was overcome when the military regime agreed to Greece's readmission to the military structures of NATO in 1980. However, the bilateral Aegean disputes between Greece and Turkey continued. The simmering tension between the two countries came back onto the boil in March 1987 when the Canadian-controlled oil company which had made the Thasos find announced that it would drill in an area outside Greek territorial waters, claimed by Turkey. This prompted the Turks to send their own survey ship, *Sismik I*, into the Aegean. Greek warships were reportedly prepared for action in response. The crisis was then defused when Turgut Özal announced that the *Sismik I* would not sail into disputed waters unless the Greeks moved in to drill new wells. Confidential talks then began between the two sides, leading to a direct meeting between Özal and the Greek premier, Andreas Papandreou, at an economic conference in the Swiss resort of Davos in January 1988. This resulted in an agreement to avoid mutual antagonisms, or a repetition of the 1987 crisis. Regular contacts between diplomats, the military, the press and businessmen would be encouraged to this end. Unfortunately, the so-called 'spirit of Davos' did not last, and failed to resolve any of the substantive questions at issue between the two countries. By the end of the 1980s, Greek–Turkish relations had returned to their depressingly familiar situation of mutually suspicious stand-off.[61]

Elsewhere in the Balkans, the closing years of the Cold War had one erratic – and for those involved, tragic – effect. In the late 1980s the regime of Theodore Zhivkov, Bulgaria's last long-standing communist ruler, apparently sought to prop up its faltering domestic popularity by launching a campaign against the country's Turkish community. In spite of emigrations to what became Turkey during the Balkan wars and afterwards, the Turkish minority in Bulgaria during the 1980s still numbered about 900,000, or about 10 per cent of the total population of the country.[62] Under a treaty signed between Turkey and Bulgaria in 1925, the Turkish minority's rights and status were protected. Turkish governments took the view that, as Bulgarian citizens, the Bulgarian Turks had the right to fair treatment, but Turkey should respect Bulgaria's territorial integrity. Politically, Turkey needed to maintain good relations with Bulgaria if it could. Nonetheless, about 150,000 Bulgarian Turks were expelled to Turkey during 1950–51, apparently in revenge for Turkey's participation in the Korean war on the UN side. During the 1970s, another 116,000 emigrated to Turkey, under an agreement allowing for the reunion of divided families. Beginning in 1984, the Bulgarian authorities launched a campaign of forced assimilation and oppression, in which the Bulgarian Turks were obliged to adopt Bulgarian names or prevented from performing religious ceremonies. Many thousands were arrested and imprisoned, or uprooted from their homes after being forced into internal exile. Turkey protested, and gained support from such bodies as the UN and the Organisation of the Islamic Conference (OIC), but to no effect. In 1989 the Zhivkov regime apparently panicked at the rise of organised protests among the Turks, by deciding to expel them *en masse*. During June–August 1989 about 312,000 people fled to Turkey, carrying what possessions they could. Large protest meetings were held in Istanbul, at which Turgut Özal issued empty threats of marching on Sofia. However, the scale of the exodus was such that on 21 August the government decided to re-impose visa requirements which it had lifted in June, effectively stopping the flow of refugees. Fortunately, the crisis was ended in November 1989, when Zhivkov was overthrown, and conditions for the Turkish minority were rapidly improved.[63]

TURKEY AND THE MIDDLE EAST, 1964–89

While Turkey's relations with the superpowers were profoundly affected by global changes between the 1960s and 1980s, its relationship with its Middle Eastern neighbours followed a largely independent though fluid course, and was relatively unaffected by domestic political pressures. The shift in Turkish foreign policy in the mid-1960s was marked by a determined attempt to rebuild bridges with the Arab world. The most immediate reason for this was the aim of winning the Arab states away from their previous support for Makarios and, more broadly, to try to convince them that Turkey had abandoned the obviously futile approaches of the Baghdad Pact. The pact was now severely criticised in Turkey for its alienation of Arab nationalism, and for allegedly subordinating Turkey's national interests to those of the Western alliance.[64] By the mid-1970s, an important economic incentive had been added to this agenda. The oil price rises of 1973–74, followed by the further rises of 1980–81, combined with Turkey's growing consumption of imported oil, vastly increased its dependence on the Middle Eastern oil-exporting countries. Turkish exports to the Middle East were slow to develop in response, but when they did so during the 1980s the results were impressive. Turkey's imports from the region rose from a trifling US$64 million in 1970 to US$2.8 billion in 1985, and its exports from US$54 million to around US$3 billion during the same period. For Turkish construction companies, who had a cumulative total of US$15.5 billion worth of contracts by 1985, the region also became an important market, which attracted a total of around 200,000 emigrant Turkish workers between 1970 and 1985.[65] All these interests entailed constructing better links with all the main Middle Eastern countries. Essentially, Turkish policy towards the region tried to uncouple its regional policy from its alliance with the Western powers as far as possible, and to build up bilateral rather than multi-lateral linkages with the main states in the region. Above all, Turkish policy sought to avoid taking sides in regional disputes, either between states or within them.

As part of this approach, Turkey began to be a good deal more cautious in supporting the United States in the Middle East than it had been during the 1950s. The guideline for Turkish policy-makers was that they could not commit themselves to anything which could not at least be presented as part of their functions within NATO, and thus as an unavoidable alliance commitment, or as having an entirely humanitarian purpose. In the 1967 Arab–Israeli war Turkey remained strictly neutral, and refused the United States the use of its bases for refuelling or supply. The Demirel government supported UN Resolution 242 calling for Israeli withdrawal to its pre-war frontiers, although it refused to join the Arab states in condemning Israel as the 'aggressor'. While Turkey allowed the United States to use Turkish bases to evacuate civilians from Jordan in 1970 and from Iran in 1979, during the Yom Kippur war of October 1973 it specifically forbade the US Air Force to use the İncirlik base for anything other than routine NATO missions. Turkey also refused to cooperate with the abortive mission to rescue US hostages from Tehran in 1980. During the early 1980s, it also appears that it fought shy of providing bases for the proposed US Rapid Deployment Force in the Middle East. The furthest it was willing to go in this direction was shown in 1982, when the military regime accepted what was called a 'co-locator operating bases agreement' providing for the modernisation of ten existing airfields in eastern Turkey, and the construction of two new ones. However, it was stipulated that these were to be used strictly in accordance with NATO defence plans.[66]

Turkey's attempts to adopt an even-handed policy in the Middle East were most in evidence in its policies towards the Arab–Israeli struggle, and during the Iran–Iraq war of 1980–88. On the first score, during the 1970s it began to adopt a more pro-Palestinian tilt. Its recognition of the

Palestine Liberation Organisation (PLO) in 1976, and the opening of a PLO office in Ankara in 1979, were the most overt signs of this. However, the shift was slow and hesitant, mainly because Turkey was suspicious of collaboration between the Palestinians and leftist-cum-Kurdish terrorist movements in Turkey. Hence, Turkey was careful to limit its support to the PLO, rather than to the more radical Palestinian factions such as those headed by George Habash and Naif Hawatmeh, which were apparently supported by Greece and Syria.[67] Another problematic factor in Turkey's relationship with the Arab states was its standing in the OIC. Here, the obstacle did not derive from Turkey's continuing recognition of Israel or its links with the United States, but from its own secularist constitution, and the determination of most of the political élite to preserve it. In 1969, when Demirel's foreign minister, İhsan Sabri Çağlayangil, attended the OIC summit of Muslim Heads of State in Rabat, the move triggered sharp criticism from the pro-secularist establishment in Turkey. In response, the government followed a generally low-key approach, arguing that the OIC was not 'religious', and emphasising the importance of its economic links with Arab countries. Although Turkey played a full part in the OIC, it never became a *de jure* member, since its parliament never ratified the charter of the organisation.[68]

This limited reorientation towards the Islamic world may have been seen as part of the rise of political Islam in Turkey. However, although Necmettin Erbakan took his place in governments headed by both Ecevit and Demirel he does not seem to have had much influence on foreign policy, and his call for a rupture of Turkey's links with NATO and other Western organisations went unheeded. In the Middle East, Turkey refused to break off relations with Israel, even though these were kept at a low level to avoid exciting Arab susceptibilities. Like many other countries, Turkey was strongly critical of the Israeli annexation of east Jerusalem in 1980, and there was some sympathy among liberal as well as Islamist opinion for the Palestinian *intifada* (uprising) which began in December 1987. On the other hand, there was important if quiet cooperation between the Turkish and Israeli security forces, notably in 1982 during the Israeli invasion of Lebanon, when Israeli forces captured a number of Turkish terrorists and handed both them and information on Turkish and Armenian terrorist groups to the Turkish authorities. After 1986, Turkish–Israeli relations started to improve markedly, as the Turks began to realise the importance of winning the support of the pro-Israeli lobby in Washington as a means of overcoming their problems with the US Congress. Apparently under pressure from Washington, Turkey upgraded its relations with Israel in

1986 by sending a senior diplomat, Ekrem Güvendiren, to head its legation in Tel Aviv.[69] This accommodation was facilitated by the beginnings of the Arab–Israeli peace process, marked by the PLO's acceptance of Israel's existence and the principle of a 'two-state solution' in Palestine in 1988. Just as the contemporaneous deconstruction of the Cold War made it possible for Turkey to develop good relations with both the West and the Soviet Union, so the changes in Middle Eastern politics made it easier to maintain friendships with both the Arabs and the Israelis.[70]

Turkish policies towards Iran and Iraq, two of its immediate neighbours, depended on walking another tightrope, especially during the 1980–88 war between the two countries. With Iraq, the task was not too difficult, since Ankara and Baghdad had no serious mutual disputes. Their common interests were reinforced by the emergence of powerful Kurdish separatist movements in both countries during the 1980s. With the beginnings of the revolt within Turkey by militants of the PKK (Kurdistan Workers' Party (*Partiya Karkeren Kurdistan*)) in 1984, Özal's government was worried by the contemporary power vacuum in Iraqi Kurdistan. In October 1984 it concluded an agreement with Baghdad under which Turkish forces could carry out 'hot pursuits' into Iraqi territory against the PKK, obviating the need to secure separate permission from Iraq on each occasion.[71] Potentially, relations with Iran could have been far more difficult to handle. So long as the Shah ruled, Turkish–Iranian relations were reasonably cooperative, and institutionalised through CENTO and its sister organisation, the RCD (see p. 127). Nonetheless, in the mid-1970s, the Turks were somewhat perturbed by the Shah's exaggerated ambitions of turning Iran into the dominant power in the Middle East. In 1979, much more dramatically, the Iranian Revolution turned Iran into a militantly Islamist and anti-Western state, in direct opposition to Turkey's alignments, both domestic and international. Recognising realities, Turkey was careful not to take an openly anti-Iranian attitude after the revolution, since it was anxious not to isolate Iran and thus possibly push it into the Soviet sphere of influence. Thus, when the United States imposed a trade embargo on Iran in November 1980, following the taking of US embassy hostages in Tehran, Turkey refused to follow suit. Hence, Turkey and Iran continued a correct if often frosty relationship.[72] The RCD organisation was dissolved along with CENTO in 1979, but was later revived in 1985 as the Economic Cooperation Organisation, or ECO, with the initial membership of Iran, Turkey and Pakistan, and its headquarters in Tehran.

By the end of 1980, the outbreak of the Iran–Iraq war had turned

Iranian attentions elsewhere, and made both Iran and Iraq heavily dependent on Turkey economically, both as a source of supply of non-military
imports, and as a transit route to the outside world. For Turkey, the main
cost of the war was that it gave the Iraqi Kurds a chance to relaunch their
campaign for an independent Kurdish state, with Iranian help, and provided the PKK with bases in Iraq for attacks on Turkish territory.
However, this was outweighed by economic and broad strategic gains. In
particular, their dependence on Turkey as a transit route and a source of
imports gave the Iranians a solid reason for not alienating the Turks.[73] For
Iraq, the oil export pipeline from Kirkuk to the Turkish port of
Yumurtalik, near İskenderun, originally built in 1977, was a vital lifeline,
and it was expanded to a total capacity of 1.5 million barrels per day by
1987. Hence, Turkey reaped economic benefits from the war, as its
exports to the two countries grew from US$220 million in 1981 to just over
US$2 billion in 1985, at which point they accounted for over a quarter of
Turkey's total exports. In this case, sitting on the fence turned out to be
profitable, as well as the most politically prudent policy, although exports
to the two countries decreased during 1986–88, as they apparently began
to run short of funds.[74] Turkey was also lucky in that neither Iran or Iraq
was able to win a clear-cut victory. For instance, when Iran captured the
Iraqi Kurdish town of Halabjah in March 1988, there were fears in
Ankara that it might move on to seize Kirkuk, allowing the Kurds to establish an autonomous state in Iraq, and cutting off the Kirkuk–Yumurtalik
pipeline. In the event, Iraqi forces recaptured Halabjah in June 1988,
having earlier subjected the town to a barbaric poison-gas attack in which
around 5,000 civilians died. As a result of the Iraqi counter-offensive,
around 60,000 Kurdish refugees entered Turkey. After initial reluctance,
they were settled in four separate camps in south-eastern Anatolia. Hence,
when Iran accepted a UN-brokered cease-fire in July 1988, the end of the
war caused relief in Ankara.[75]

This is not to suggest that Turkey's relations with all the Arab states
developed positively during the 1980s. As usual, the relationship with
Syria proved to be the most difficult to handle, as new disputes were added
to Syria's long-standing grievance over the Turkish annexation of
Alexandretta in 1939. While the Iraqi regime cooperated with Turkey
against the Kurdish resistance, Syria actively supported it, by giving
shelter to Abdullah Öcalan, the leader of the PKK, as well as providing
logistical and training support to his organisation in Syrian-occupied
Lebanon. The conflict intensified, as Turkey launched its ambitious
Southeast Anatolia Project to use the waters of the Euphrates and Tigris

for electricity generation and irrigation, threatening the supply of water to Syria and Iraq, for whom this was a vital resource. In 1987, as Turkey was beginning construction of the giant Atatürk dam on the Euphrates, Özal visited Damascus and secured an agreement with Syrian President Hafiz al-Assad under which Turkey would continue to supply a minimum average flow into Syria of 500 cusecs (cubic metres per second) in return for a Syrian commitment that neither country would support violent resistance groups operating in the territory of the other. On paper, this was a highly satisfactory conclusion for Turkey, but Syria later insisted that the figure of 500 cusecs was acceptable only while the dam was being filled, and that an average flow of 600–700 cusecs would be demanded once it was completed. Nor did Syria halt its support for the PKK, in spite of constant denials. Meanwhile, Özal promoted an ambitious plan, christened the 'peace pipeline', to supply water from the Ceyhan and Seyhan rivers in Turkey (which are hydrologically separate from the Euphrates) to Syria, Jordan and western Saudi Arabia, and via a second 'Gulf Pipeline' to eastern Saudi Arabia and the smaller Arab Gulf states. This project has never got off the drawing board, since the political problems of supply across so many states and the huge cost apparently make it impractical, though it showed the strength and direction of Özal's ambitions to make Turkey a major economic and political player in the region. Instead, water has become a source of conflict rather than cooperation between Turkey and its southern neighbours, complicating other disputes and historical resentments.[76]

TURKEY AND EUROPE, 1959–90

One of the effects of Turkey's membership of the Western alliance was that its bilateral relations with the Western states became far less critical than they had been previously. Britain has a special role as a co-guarantor of the Cyprus settlement of 1960, while West Germany re-emerged as its biggest trading partner, enjoying a high prestige with the Turkish public at the time, as well as being a source of financial and military assistance.[77] However, political relations with the western European nations were important to Turkey mainly because they were partners of the United States, rather than as independent political actors in their own right, as they had been before 1945. The relationship began to change shape with the launch of the European Economic Community (EEC), originally consisting of Germany, France, Italy and the three Benelux countries, in 1957. In June 1959 Greece submitted an application for membership of the

EEC, followed by Turkey in the following month. The result was that Greece became an associate member of the Community in July 1961, to be followed again by Turkey, which signed an Association Agreement with Brussels on 12 September 1963. On the Turkish side, the reasons for the application were political rather than economic. International recognition as a member of the Western community of nations had been an objective of Turkish leaders since the days of the *Tanzimat*, and was seen as a logical extension of Turkey's membership of NATO and other Western organisations. The need to avoid being outflanked by Greece was also an important motive, and almost certainly hastened the Turkish decision. The economic objective of gaining easier market access to the EEC, which already accounted for about 35 per cent of Turkey's exports, added to the incentive. On the Community side, there were some doubts, mainly in France, as to whether Turkey could be counted as a 'European' nation, but these were overcome by the recognition of Turkey's strategic role in the Cold War, the need to be even-handed between Greece and Turkey, and the general desire to emphasise that the EEC was an expanding association, open to new members and cultures.[78]

While Turkey's main motivations for signing the Association Agreement of 1963 were political, the content of the Agreement was almost entirely economic. It outlined a process by which Turkey was to achieve a customs union with the Community, to be followed by possible full membership, to take place in three stages. During a preliminary stage, which was to last from 1964 to 1973, the EEC would extend preferential trading conditions to Turkey, plus some direct financial aid. This would be followed by a transition stage, during which both sides would eliminate tariff and other barriers to trade, so as to establish a customs union. Once the application of the Agreement had advanced far enough for Turkey to carry out the obligations of Community membership, then under Article 28 the parties would 'examine the possibility of the accession of Turkey to the Community'.[79] In this way, the existing member states did not commit themselves to accepting Turkey as a full member of the Community, as some Turkish commentators tried to argue, but they did at least agree to consider the question at some future date, provided Turkey could meet the conditions of membership.[80] Politically, the most important gain for Turkey was the symbolic recognition by Walter Hallstein, the president of the European Commission at the time, that 'Turkey is part of Europe'.[81]

The Association Agreement was accepted by Turkey in 1963 with little internal debate or dissent. However, this situation did not repeat itself in November 1970, when the two sides signed an Additional Protocol. This laid down the rules for application of the transition stage, scheduled to last from 1973 until 1980 at the earliest, or 1995 at the latest. Initially, the Community regarded Turkey's desire to proceed rapidly to the second stage as rather premature, since there had been little preparation, but it was again persuaded by the political arguments in favour of developing the relationship. In Ankara, the Demirel government was firmly committed to the ultimate goal of full membership, and unrealistically hoped that Turkey could precede Britain, Ireland, Denmark and Norway in this. However, new forces in Turkish politics, notably the Islamists led by Necmettin Erbakan, were firmly against the move, on both ideological and protectionist grounds. Scepticism about the desirability of reducing tariff and other trade barriers was later to be shared by the CHP under Bülent Ecevit, and the more *étatist* school of thought within the state bureaucracy, notably in the State Planning Organisation. Nonetheless, following the military intervention of March 1971, the Protocol was ratified by the Turkish parliament in July of that year.[82]

By the late 1970s opposition to the arrangement became more vociferous, as the gradual removal of trade barriers was impeded. The Demirel administration complained that Turkey was not being given sufficient access to the Community's agricultural market, and at the beginning of 1978 the Community began to impose restrictions on the import of cotton yarns and textiles, Turkey's main industrial exports.[83] Meanwhile, following the restoration of democratic government in Greece in 1974, the Karamanlis administration applied for full membership of the Community, and eventually achieved this in 1981. Later, it was argued that by not submitting an application at the same time as Greece, Turkey had missed the boat with the Community, which might have accepted both proposals together (or possibly, have turned down both).[84] The position of Turkish migrant workers in the Community also became a critical issue, since by 1976 their number had reached around 600,000, plus about one million dependants, with annual remittances to Turkey running at an estimated US$1 billion. Under Article 36 of the Additional Protocol, the two sides were due to begin the process of allowing free movement of workers between Turkey and the Community in 1976. When the target date arrived, the EEC merely agreed to improve the freedom of movement of Turkish workers already in the Community, and to give the Turks priority if its manpower needs could not be met by other Community members, effectively making this commitment a dead letter.[85] In October 1978, beset by mounting political as well as economic problems, Ecevit's government froze Turkey's obligations under the Protocol. Progress was not resumed until after Demirel returned to power in October 1979, but was then halted once more by the military takeover of September 1980.

The earlier military interventions of 1960 and 1971 had provoked little or no reaction from the main European states, but that of 1980 was different. The European public was now more conscious of a need to protect democratic norms in allied states. The European Parliament, which was more concerned with issues of ideological principle than were national governments or bureaucrats, now exercised more authority within Community structures. The European reaction also left Turkey's military rulers in a dilemma. On the one hand, they were firmly committed to a modernist, Western identity for Turkey, and were thus concerned to defend and promote links with the Western powers. On the other hand, their authoritarian streak was at odds with western Europe's commitment to democratic standards, and its desire to see that Turkey adhered to them. In this way, Turkey's domestic regime, rather than just its foreign policies, became of prime importance in its relations with western Europe. On the surface, the United States was less vociferous than western Europe on the need to respect human rights and secure a rapid return to democratic government, but nevertheless kept up some behind-the-scenes diplomatic pressure on Ankara in this direction. In effect both sides had to walk a tightrope. On their side, the Western powers needed to keep the issue of democratisation on the agenda, without pushing the Turkish government so far on this issue that it became totally alienated and uncooperative. On the other side, Turkey's military rulers needed to show sufficient concern for Western susceptibilities, without openly admitting that their policies were being partly dictated by their Western allies (which would have undermined their domestic standing) or restricting their freedom of manoeuvre domestically to an unacceptable degree. Fortunately both sides managed to walk the tightrope with a fair degree of success.[86]

The first reaction to the 1980 *coup* came from the Council of Europe, a separate body which Turkey had joined in 1949. Membership of the Council had mainly symbolic significance, since it lacked any economic or military clout, but the symbolism was nevertheless important to the Turkish élite, as a mark of Turkey's European credentials. The Turkish delegation was withdrawn from the Council's Parliamentary Assembly shortly after the *coup*, and not restored until some months after civilian rule had been re-established, though Turkey's membership of the Council was not formally suspended. More materially, in May 1981 the Turkey–EC Association Council agreed on a draft package of economic aid to Turkey, known as the Fourth Financial Protocol. In the following month the value of this was increased to 600 million ECU but, under pressure from the European Parliament, the release of this was made conditional on effective moves to restore democracy. In November 1981, following the military regime's ban on all existing political parties, the European Commission hardened its position by deciding that, in these conditions, it would not resume any discussions on the release of the funds. Owing to Greek objections, the package has remained frozen ever since. Whether the withdrawal of aid by itself made a substantial difference to the military government's policies is hard to say with certainty – and the previous case of the US arms embargo would suggest that it did not. However, its symbolic significance was considerable, and probably played an unacknowledged role in encouraging the regime to return to democracy under acceptable conditions. At the same time, the Western powers were able to promote their objectives without provoking an acrimonious or open break with Turkey.[87]

Although many western European observers had initial doubts about the democratic credentials of the restored civilian regime, Turgut Özal's accession to power in 1983 changed the picture dramatically, since he was committed in principle to liberalising Turkey's international trade, regardless of the effects on relations with the Community. In fact, in 1987 Özal told the Turkish parliament that 'the aim of the economic liberalisation programme and our reforms was to facilitate our integration into the European Community as a full member'.[88] This may have been something of a misrepresentation, since Özal would almost certainly have sought to liberalise the Turkish economy anyway, but his reforms certainly assisted the process of economic integration with the Community. In spite of Özal's personal attachment to Islam and occasional appeals to the moderate Islamist vote in domestic politics, he was convinced that this should not be a barrier to Turkey's eventual accession.[89] Accordingly, the removal of trade barriers was resumed after 1983, and in April 1987 Özal's government submitted a formal application for full membership. Although this turned out to be premature, what was now the European Community (EC) was bound to consider it, and the Commission prepared its official Opinion on the application. After a long delay, this was issued in December 1989 and formally accepted by the Community's Council of Ministers in February 1990. In essence, the Commission's Opinion was a polite rebuff of the Turkish application. In the economic sphere, it referred to the 'substantial development gap between the Community and Turkey', which meant that Turkey would have great difficulty in shouldering its obligations under the Community's economic and social policies. In the political context, it cited Turkey's disputes with Greece, the Cyprus problem, and the fact that its human rights regime and 'respect for the identity of minorities' had 'not yet reached the level requited in a democracy'. On these grounds, it recommended that no accession negotiations should begin until after 1993 at the earliest, with no subsequent date set. In the meantime, the two sides should concentrate on the completion of the customs union, as planned in the Additional Protocol.[90] At the time the Opinion was issued, Commissioner Abel Matutes confirmed that Turkey was still eligible to become a full member of the Community in principle.[91] Nonetheless, it was clear that, not without reason, Turkey's west European partners were anxious to delay the process for as long as possible.

TURKISH DIPLOMACY, 1964–79: SOME CRITICAL ASSESSMENTS

Changes in global politics between the mid-1960s and late 1980s clearly gave Turkish diplomacy some new opportunities, but these were offset by new problems. As global conflicts softened, regional ones asserted themselves, and were to prove just as hard to handle. In its relations with the superpowers, Turkey exploited successfully, though perhaps belatedly, the possibilities of a better relationship with the Soviet Union by expanding economic opportunities and converting Moscow from a hostile to a neutral force on the Cyprus question. In effect, it exploited its ability to gain strategic rent, both economic and political, from both sides in the Cold War. However, there were fairly tight limits to détente between Turkey and its northern neighbour. Faced with the classic choice between alliance and neutrality, Turkey remained committed to the Western alliance. In the last analysis, those who favoured neutrality lost the argument, because they could not show that the potential gains outweighed the likely losses and dangers. Admittedly, perceptions of the Soviet threat had substantially altered by the 1960s. The security of the straits – the centre of attention for both the Turks and the Western powers for almost two centuries – became a less crucial question, thanks to the development of nuclear weapons and inter-continental missiles.[92] On the other hand, Turkey could not afford to break away from the Western alliance, which served as an ultimate protection against the Warsaw Pact, and a source of military and economic aid that would probably not have been available otherwise. Turkish neutrality would probably have redounded to Greece's advantage, and Soviet policies in the Middle East and eastern Europe did not inspire the Turks with confidence. Ecevit's claim to have adopted new policies did not amount to much, beyond a change of tone, and was quite rapidly abandoned in the 1980s. Hence, Turkey's membership of NATO survived both the 'Johnson letter' of 1964 and the US Congressional arms embargo of 1975–78. During the 1980s, most of the heat went out of the argument, as there were few objections to the strengthening of Turkey's links with the United States in the first half of the decade, while in the second half Özal was in the happy position of being able to continue Turkey's commitment to the alliance and improve its relationship with the Soviet Union simultaneously.

The two factors which made a successful foreign policy more difficult to execute between the mid-1960s and the 1980s were, first, the resurgence of local contests and interests which conflicted with those of the Cold War and, second, the irruption of domestic political factors and instabilities into foreign policy-making, both in Turkey and on the Western side. Until 1964, foreign policy did not figure prominently in the contest between Turkey's two main parties, since there was a broad consensus on the need for the NATO alliance, and public opinion was not much exercised by foreign policy issues. Equally, Western governments were mainly satisfied with Turkey's foreign policies, and relatively little concerned with its internal political practices. The Cyprus conflict changed this picture dramatically, since it brought out a clear clash between Turkey and the United States, and excited nationalist fervours in both Greece and Turkey which few other issues could have done. In Turkey, this effect was probably enhanced by far-reaching social and cultural changes, as an increasing number of ordinary citizens gained access to information about the outside world, through newspapers and broadcasting, and were less inclined to leave foreign policy-making to the traditional élite of diplomats, generals, and senior politicians. Balancing internal pressures with external realities became a difficult task, which was exacerbated by serious instability in internal politics, especially during the 1970s. For a time, leftist ideas had some influence on external relations, though the resurgence of politicised Islam seems to have had little direct effect on foreign policy, apart from destabilising the domestic political system. During the 1970s internal pressures also began to affect US policies towards Turkey, mainly in the form of ethnic lobbies, of which Turkish diplomacy had little experience or skill in dealing with.[93] Similarly, the weaknesses of Turkish democracy, notably in the field of human rights, began to affect western European policies, which had hitherto paid little attention to Turkish domestic politics, being primarily motivated by Turkey's international strategic importance.

In dealing with that part of its foreign policy agenda which was not directly part of the Cold War contest, Turkish policy had mixed success. In handling the Cyprus problem in 1964 and 1967, İnönü and Demirel were both cautious. The 1967 experience was more successful from the Turkish viewpoint than that of 1964, but it still left the Turkish Cypriots in a hazardous and exposed position, with the essential problem of how to reconstruct the Cypriot state no nearer solution. The shocked public reaction in Turkey to the 'Johnson letter' of 1964 was evidently based on the misapprehension that since Turkey was strategically more important to NATO than Greece, and was a faithful member of the Western alliance, the United States would support Turkey against the Greeks. The opposite expectation, that the United States could not afford to be anything other than neutral in a dispute between two NATO allies, should have been apparent from the start, but it was hard for the Turks to swallow. The crisis of 1974 was different, in that Turkey appeared to have a clearer mandate for intervention, under the 1960 Treaty of Guarantee. If Turkey had not invaded, then Cyprus would probably have been united with Greece, the Turkish Cypriots massacred or expelled, and the Greek Colonels' regime consolidated. Most of the blame for the crisis could clearly be laid at the door of the Greek junta, though both Makarios and the British and US governments failed to acquit themselves well – the last two through their failure to take sufficiently strong action against the junta at an early stage. On the Turkish side, Ecevit took a gamble that Greece would not attack Turkey in response (or that, if it did, Turkey could repel it) which turned out to be justified. On the other hand, by launching the second stage of the invasion so precipitately, without allowing Clerides the 48-hour recess he had asked for, Ecevit lost the moral advantage he had held at the time of the original Turkish landings. In the end he was no nearer to getting the Greeks to accept a workable federal settlement, since his expectation that the shock of the second invasion would force them to come back to the conference table in a chastened mood proved misplaced. Its policy during the Cyprus crisis of 1974 was probably the furthest Turkey ever went to striking out on its own, independently of NATO, but the outcome suggested that it had little ability to dictate its own political terms in the ensuing situation. The struggle then proliferated into a series of bilateral Greek–Turkish disputes, for which Greece shared as much of the blame as Turkey. Ecevit and his successors could not resolve them, even though Özal's peace talks with Andreas Papandreou of 1988 prevented a head-on military collision.

The development of Turkey's relationship with western Europe followed a separate course, which was at least to some degree independent of the Cold War. In launching the initiative, the Turks almost certainly underestimated the difficulties involved, but felt that they had little alternative. Membership of the new Europe was seen as a logical part of the Kemalist heritage, and abandoning the effort would have given Greece an easy advantage. On the other hand, Turkey's economic problems, and Ecevit's neutralist and *étatist* leanings, created difficulties which almost led to breakdown in the late 1970s. Whether Turkey actually missed an important opportunity in 1974–75, when it failed to follow Greece in applying for full membership of the Community, can be endlessly debated, but the argument is ultimately unprovable. In eventually submitting Turkey's application in 1987, Özal may also have overestimated his chances of securing a successful outcome, but by the time it came the Community's reply was widely expected, and Turkey received the best response it could reasonably have expected.

The Middle East was probably the most successful theatre for Turkish foreign policy at the time – the precise opposite of the experiences of the 1950s. Turkey's Middle Eastern relations were usually easier to handle, since they aroused fewer domestic political passions than conflicts with Greece, or relations with the United States. Even though they showed formal respect for the institutions of Islam, most Turkish Muslims, then as now, had little sense of identity with the Arab world, and were disinclined to support its causes. So far as one can judge, this sentiment was reciprocated. The Arabs felt little brotherhood towards the Turks and were, for instance, not disposed to support them over Cyprus. Hence, the Turkish government's hopes that a more friendly approach towards the Arabs would induce them to swap sides, by abandoning their support for the Greek Cypriots in the UN and other bodies, was misplaced. On the other hand, the Turks were able to overcome some of the old suspicions that they were no more than the United States' gendarme in the Middle East, and to develop profitable commercial relations accordingly. During the Iran–Iraq war, they were able to turn an external conflict to their advantage by making both sides dependent on Turkish good will. Through careful diplomacy, relations with Israel were continued, even if this aroused Arab suspicions. The relationship with Syria was more problematic, and became complicated by Kurdish separatism in Turkey, and Syria's role in it, as well as the conflict over the Euphrates. As in the case of the Cyprus, this created problems which were to last long after the end of the Cold War.

NOTES

1. This is suggested by Alvin J. Rubinstein, *Soviet Policy Toward Turkey, Iran and Afghanistan: The Dynamics of Influence* (New York, NY, Praeger, 1982), p. 25.
2. Ferenc A. Vali, *Bridge across the Bosporus: The Foreign Policy of Turkey* (Baltimore, MD, and London, Johns Hopkins University Press, 1971), pp. 120–1 and Mehmet Gönlübol, 'NATO, USA and Turkey', in Kemal H. Karpat *et al.*, *Turkey's Foreign Policy in Transition* (Leiden, Brill, 1975), pp. 43–5. Turkey's refusal to join the proposed Multilateral Force was possibly motivated by a desire not to antagonise the Soviet Union, at a time when Ankara was trying to persuade the Soviets to adopt a less pro-Greek policy on Cyprus, see below, pp. 151. On the other hand, Faruk Sönmezoğlu sees the Turkish refusal to support the Multilateral Force as a reaction to the 'Johnson letter' of 1964. See Faruk Sönmezoğlu, *ABD'nin Türkiye Politikası (1964–1980)* (Istanbul, Der Yayınevi, 1995), p. 37.
3. For fuller accounts of Turkey's domestic politics between 1961 and 1980, see Feroz Ahmad, *The Turkish Experiment in Democracy, 1950–1975* (London, Hurst, for Royal Institute of International Affairs, 1977), pp. 177–388; Erik J. Zürcher, *Turkey, a Modern History* (London and New York, NY, I.B. Tauris, 1993), pp. 253–91 and C.H. Dodd, *The Crisis of Turkish Democracy* (2nd edn, Wistow, Eothen Press, 1990), Chs 1–2.
4. Quoted in Suha Bölükbaşı, 'The Johnson Letter Revisited', *Middle Eastern Studies*, Vol. 29 (1993), p. 510.
5. As a sign of this, in 1960 Makarios himself alluded to the idea that 'the realisation of our hopes and dreams is not complete under the Zurich and London Agreements'. Quoted in Zenon Stavrinides, *The Cyprus Conflict: National Identity and Statehood* (Wakefield, Loris Stavrinides, 1976), p. 40. As late as June 1967 – after the Colonels' takeover in Athens – the Greek Cypriot House of Representatives passed a resolution calling for 'uniting the whole and undivided Cyprus with the Motherland, without any intervening stages', while the following October Makarios told a Greek Cypriot newspaper that 'the real victory will be achieved when Cyprus will be annexed to Greece without any concessions whatever'. Quoted in ibid., p. 64.
6. For details, see Robert Stephens, *Cyprus, a Place of Arms: Power Politics and Ethnic Conflict in the Eastern Mediterranean* (London, Pall Mall, 1966), pp. 168–94, and Stanley Kyriakides, *Cyprus: Constitutionalism and Crisis Government* (Philadelphia, PA, University of Philadelphia Press, 1968), pp. 72–157.
7. Bölükbaşı, 'Johnson Letter', pp. 506, 513–15.
8. Sönmezoğlu, *ABD'nin Türkiye Politikası*, p. 14.
9. For the full text of the 'Johnson letter' and İnönü's reply, see *Middle East Journal*, Vol. 20 (1966), pp. 386–93. The letter was supposed to be secret, but in fact tendentious versions of it reached the Turkish press at the time, suggesting even that the United States would have been prepared to use force to prevent Turkey from invading Cyprus. In 1965 the two governments belatedly agreed to make the full text public, but by this time most of the damage to US–Turkish relations had been done. See Parker T. Hart, *Two NATO Allies at the Threshold of War: Cyprus: A Firsthand Account of Crisis Management, 1965–1968* (Durham, NC, and London, Duke University Press, 1990), p. 15.
10. Bölükbaşı, 'Johnson Letter', p. 517.
11. Ibid., p. 521. See also Suha Bölükbaşı, *Turkish–American Relations and Cyprus* (Lanham,

MD, University Press of America for White Burkett Miller Center of Public Affairs, University of Virginia, 1988), pp. 66–8. Turkey had no landing-craft at the time, and would have had to transport troops to Cyprus in ordinary cargo vessels and small boats, running the risk of heavy casualties, and unacceptable delays. There is also some mystery about the timing of the planned operation, if there was one. Interviewed on 12 June 1963, İnönü stated that an invasion had been planned for 4 June, but that 'one day before I was warned by Washington not to use American arms for purposes not approved by America. Mr Johnson said that if the Russians took action, our NATO guarantees might not hold'. Quoted in Jacob M. Landau, *Johnson's 1964 Letter to İnönü and Greek Lobbying of the White House* (Jerusalem, Hebrew University of Jerusalem, Jerusalem Papers on Peace Problems 28, 1979), pp. 6–7. However, the 'Johnson letter' was not delivered until 5 June. Assuming that İnönü was not misquoted, or had not become badly confused over dates only one week after the event, this suggests either that he had received another warning from Johnson prior to the 'Johnson letter', or possibly that he had decided to abandon the planned invasion the day before the letter was delivered.

12. These disputes had in fact begun during the 1950s. See George S. Harris, *Troubled Alliance: Turkish–American Problems in Historical Perspective, 1945–1971* (Washington, DC, American Enterprise Institute for Public Policy Research and Hoover Institution, 1972), pp. 56–61. See also Sönmezoğlu, *ABD'nin Türkiye Politikası*, pp. 44, 50–1.

13. To be exact, 3.0 per cent in 1965 and 2.8 per cent in 1969.

14. See Harris, *Troubled Alliance*, pp. 128–47, 160–9 and Ferenc A. Vali, *Bridge*, pp. 137–46.

15. Quoted in Rubinstein, *Soviet Policy*, p. 30.

16. Bruce R. Kuniholm, 'Turkey and NATO: Past, Present and Future', *Orbis*, Vol. 27 (1983), p. 427.

17. Quoted in Rubinstein, *Soviet Policy*, p. 32. On Soviet–Turkish relations during the 1960s and early 1970s, see ibid., pp. 26–32, and A.H. Ulman and R.H. Dekmejian, 'Changing Patterns in Turkish Foreign Policy, 1959–1967', *Orbis*, Vol. 11 (1967), pp. 779–80.

18. Vali, *Bridge*, pp. 158–63 and Baran Tuncer, 'External Financing of the Turkish Economy and its Foreign Policy Implications', in Karpat, ed., *Turkey's Foreign Policy*, pp. 218–24. Tuncer appears to exaggerate the last point, but his data only run up to 1969, before the level of Soviet aid reached substantial proportions.

19. Quoted in ibid., pp. 83, 209. The impact of the Soviet occupation of Czechoslovakia in Turkey was accentuated by the fact that, following his removal from Prague, Alexander Dubcek was briefly stationed in Ankara as Czech ambassador.

20. Bölükbaşı, *Turkish–American*, pp. 132–3. These proposals were similar to those put forward by President Johnson's special envoy, Dean Acheson, in 1964–65, under which Turkey would have received a sovereign base area in the north-eastern Karpas peninsula, together with Turkish cantons in which the Turkish Cypriots would be granted local autonomy, in return for agreeing to the union of the rest of the island with Greece. This was accepted by the Turkish side assuming that the 'base area' included the whole of the Karpas peninsula, whereas the Greek side preferred to cede a far smaller base, and only for a period of 25 years. The plan was also rejected outright by Makarios. See Bölükbaşı, 'Johnson Letter', p. 519; Stephens, *Cyprus*, pp. 200–1, and Sönmezoğlu, *ABD'nin Türkiye Politikası*, p. 18. According to a later account by Nihat Erim, who was the Turkish representative at talks in Geneva in August 1964, Acheson

asked him and General Turgut Sunalp, then the Chief of the General Staff, 'can you go to the area allocated to you, and occupy it with military forces, without shedding too much blood? If you can do that, go ahead and take it. The American Sixth Fleet will not come out against you. On the contrary, it will protect you': (Sönmezoğlu, *ABD'nin Türkiye Politikası*, p. 19, quoting Erim's memoirs. See also Bölükbaşı, 'Johnson Letter', p. 519.

21. Sönmezoğlu, *ABD'nin Türkiye Politikası*, p. 23.
22. By 1967, Turkey still only had two landing-craft, six helicopters and 150 parachutes: troops would have had to be landed from conventional vessels, and their position would have been precarious. See Bölükbaşı, *Turkish–American*, p. 135.
23. Ibid., pp. 133–46; Harris, *Troubled Alliance*, pp. 122–4, and Clement H. Dodd, *The Cyprus Imbroglio* (Hemingford Grey, Eothen Press, 1998), p. 27.
24. For further details on the events of March 1971, see Ahmad, *Experiment*, pp. 288–91, and William Hale, *Turkish Politics and the Military* (London, Routledge, 1994), pp. 184–93.
25. See James W. Spain, 'The United States, Turkey and the Poppy', *Middle East Journal*, Vol. 29 (1975), pp. 295–309.
26. For details, see Polyvios G. Polyviou, *Cyprus: Conflict and Negotiation, 1960–1980* (London, Duckworth, 1980), pp. 62–126, and Dodd, *Cyprus Imbroglio*, pp. 27–9.
27. For the full text of Makarios's letter, which was written on 2 July, see Necati Ertekün, *The Cyprus Dispute and the Birth of the Turkish Republic of Northern Cyprus* (Nicosia, Rustem, 2nd edn, 1984), pp. 236–9.
28. The coalition protocol issued by the Ecevit government in January 1974 called for a federal settlement, a demand confirmed by foreign minister Turan Güneş who confirmed the government's opposition to a 'unitary state'. But it appears that the government was willing to reduce this to a 'functional federation' – in other words, a power-sharing agreement broadly similar to the 1960 constitution, but which recognised the Turkish Cypriots as a separate community. On the other hand, the Turkish Cypriot leaders, notably Rauf Denktash, preferred the idea of a geographically based federation. See Bölükbaşı, *Turkish–American*, pp. 178–79. After the Sampson *coup*, the Ecevit government also adopted this position.
29. Information from a senior member of the foreign ministry at the time. The Turkish forces now had 100 landing-craft, 15,000 parachutes and 100 helicopters. At the time of the initial landings on 20 July, 70 per cent of the landing-craft were held back from the operation, and kept in readiness for an invasion of the Greek Aegean islands, suggesting that if Greece had counter-attacked, Turkey would have occupied the islands as a later bargaining chip. Bölükbaşı, *Turkish–American*, pp. 189, 195.
30. See pp. 132–3.
31. Ibid., pp. 185–90, and Mehmet Ali Birand, *30 Hot Days*, (London, Nicosia and Istanbul, Rustem, 1985), pp. 1–11, originally published in Turkish as *30 Sıcak Gün* (Istanbul, Milliyet Yayınları, 1975).
32. Birand, *Hot Days*, pp. 6–9, 11–14, 17–25, 36–7, 41–2, 47–8; Bölükbaşı, *Turkish–American*, pp. 191–7 and Theodore A. Couloumbis, *The United States, Greece and Turkey: The Troubled Triangle* (New York, NY, Praeger, 1983), pp. 90–6.
33. For the full text of the declaration, see Ertekün, *Cyprus Dispute*, pp. 248–9. For other accounts of the first Geneva conference, see Birand, *Hot Days*, pp. 61–76, and Bölükbaşı, *Turkish–American*, pp. 200–2.

34. The incident is related by Polyviou who attended the conference as a Greek Cypriot delegate, and Bölükbaşı. See Polyviou, *Cyprus*, p. 177, and Bölükbase, Turkish–American, p. 211. Birand, who also attended as a journalist, relates that he told Güneş that 'the Soviet Union had pledged support for Greece', but does not suggest that this included military support. Birand, *Hot Days*, pp. 81–2. For detailed accounts of the second Geneva conference, from different viewpoints, see Birand, pp. 81–113, Bölükbaşı, *Turkish–American*, pp. 202–211, and Polyviou, *Cyprus,* pp. 162–85.

35. Bölükbaşı, *Turkish–American*, p. 211.

36. For full text, see Ertekün, *Cyprus Dispute*, p. 278, and Polyviou, *Cyprus,* pp. 205–6.

37. For details of the intercommunal negotiations between 1974 and 1980, see Ertekün, *Cyprus Dispute,* pp. 37–103; Polyviou, *Cyprus,* pp. 203–217, and A.J.R. Groom, 'The Process of Negotiation, 1974–1993', in C.H. Dodd, ed., *The Political, Social and Economic Development of Northern Cyprus* (Hemingford Grey, Eothen Press, 1993), pp. 16–45.

38. Andrew Wilson, *The Aegean Dispute* (London, International Institute for Strategic Studies, Adelphi Papers No. 155, 1980), pp. 4–10, 13–14, 22–3, 30 and Suha Bölükbaşı, 'The Turco-Greek Dispute: Issues, Policies and Prospects', in C.H. Dodd, ed., *Turkish Foreign Policy: New Prospects* (Wistow, Eothen Press, for Modern Turkish Studies Programme, SOAS, 1992), pp. 33–8.

39. Wilson, *Aegean Dispute*, pp. 3, 6–7, 11–12, 16–18, 23–4; Couloumbis, *Troubled Triangle*, pp. 117–30 and Bölükbaşı, 'Turco-Greek Dispute', pp. 38–49.

40. The 'Johnson letter' of 1964 may have been partly the result of Greek–American lobbying but there were almost certainly strong strategic reasons for Johnson's policy at the time – notably the fear of a strong Soviet reaction. See Landau, 'Johnson's 1964 Letter'.

41. Couloumbis, *Troubled Triangle*, p. 108.

42. Ibid., pp. 103–6: Richard C. Campany, Jr, *Turkey and the United States: The Arms Embargo Period* (New York, NY, Praeger, 1986), pp. 55–6, 63–4; Duygu Bazoğlu Sezer, 'Turkey's Security Policies', in Jonathan Alford, ed., *Greece and Turkey: Adversity in Alliance* (London, Gower, for International Institute of Strategic Studies, 1984), pp. 64–5 and Rubinstein, *Soviet Policy*, p. 47.

43. Sönmezoğlu, *ABD'nin Türkiye Politikası*, p. 112.

44. Couloumbis, *Troubled Triangle*, pp. 106–7; Campany, *Turkey*, p. 63, and Sezer, 'Security Policies', p. 67.

45. Bülent Ecevit, 'Turkey's Security Policies', in Alford, ed., *Greece and Turkey*, p. 138. This is the text of an address delivered to the International Institute of Strategic Studies in London while he was prime minister in May 1978.

46. Rubinstein, *Soviet Policy*, pp. 40–1 and Gareth Winrow, 'Gorbachev's New Political Thinking and Turkey', paper delivered to conference of British International Studies Association, University of Warwick, December 1991, p. 7.

47. Statement in Bonn, 12 May 1978: quoted in Wilson, *Aegean*, p. 25.

48. George E. Gruen, 'Ambivalence in the Alliance: US Interests in the Middle East and the Evolution of Turkish Foreign Policy', *Orbis*, Vol. 24 (1980), p. 376.

49. For an overall assessment of these changes, see Duygu Bazoğlu Sezer, 'Turkey and the Western Alliance in the 1980s', in Atila Eralp, Muharrem Tünay and Birol Yeşilada, eds, *The Political and Socioeconomic Transformation of Turkey* (Westport, CT, Praeger, 1993), pp. 218–20.

50. The party was formed in 1985, following a merger between the Social Democracy

Party, led by İnönü, and the previous People's Party.

51. For fuller accounts of Turkish politics during the 1980s, see Dodd, *Crisis*, Chs 3–5; Nicole and Hugh Pope, *Turkey Unveiled: Ataturk and After* (London, Murray, 1997) Chs 10–13; Hale, *Turkish Politics*, pp. 246–300 and Kemal H. Karpat, 'Turkish Democracy at Impasse: Party Politics and the Third Military Intervention', *International Journal of Turkish Studies*, Vol. 2 (1981). For a detailed narrative of the *coup* of 1980 and the events leading up to it, see Mehmet Ali Birand, trans. M.A. Dikerdem, *The Generals' Coup in Turkey: An Inside Story of 12 September 1980* (London, Brassey's Defence Publishers, 1987).

52. Turgut Özal, *Turkey in Europe and Europe in Turkey* (Nicosia, Rustem, 1991), pp. 300, 304.

53. Gruen, 'Ambivalence', pp. 365–6, and Rubinstein, *Soviet Policy*, p. 51.

54. George E. Gruen, 'Turkey Between the Middle East and the West', in Robert O. Freedman, ed., *The Middle East from the Iran Contra Affair to the Intifada* (New York, NY, Syracuse University Press, 1991), p. 404, and Ömer Karasapan, 'Turkey's Armaments Industries', *Middle East Report*, January–February 1987, pp. 27–31.

55. Gruen, 'Turkey', pp. 405–6, and Mahmut Bali Aykan, 'Turkish Perspectives on Turkish US Relations Concerning Persian Gulf Security in the Post-Cold War Era: 1989–1995', *Middle East Journal*, Vol. 50 (1996), p. 345. See also the author's contribution to Itamar Rabinovich, Haim Shaked and Ami Ayalon, eds, *Middle East Contemporary Survey*, Vol. 11, 1987 (Boulder, CO, Westview Press, 1909), p. 673.

56. Rubinstein, *Soviet Policy*, pp. 42–3, 48–50.

57. Ali L. Karaosmanoğlu, 'Turkey's Security and the Middle East', *Foreign Affairs*, Vol. 62 (1983), pp. 159, 173.

58. Winrow, 'Gorbachev's New Political Thinking', pp. 2–4, 8–9. Winrow's analysis follows that of David E. Albright, 'The USSR and the Third World in the 1980s', *Problems of Communism*, Vol. 38 (1989), pp. 50–70.

59. Winrow, 'Gorbachev's New Political Thinking', pp. 10–11. The timing of the gas agreement suggests that there may well have been a change in Soviet thinking under Chernenko, but the point needs investigation. For Turkey, the agreement had a primarily economic, rather than political motivation, thanks to the urgent need to reduce air pollution in Ankara, Istanbul and other cities.

60. Dodd, *Cyprus Imbroglio*, pp. 37–42.

61. For details, see the author's contribution to the 1987 edition of *Middle East Contemporary Survey*, Vol. 11, p. 672 (see note 55) and the 1988 edition Vol. 12, p. 765.

62. This figure apparently excluded the Pomaks – that is, Bulgarian-speaking Muslims.

63. Kemal Kirişci, 'Post Second World War Immigration from the Balkan Countries to Turkey', *Turkish Review of Balkan Studies* (Istanbul, annual), Vol. 2 (1994/95), pp. 176–8; *Turkey Almanac 1989* (Ankara, Turkish Daily News, 1989), pp. 406–9, and Hugh Poulton, *Top Hat, Grey Wolf and Crescent: Turkish Nationalism and the Turkish Republic* (London, Hurst, 1997), pp. 299–302.

64. Mahmut Bali Aykan, 'The Palestinian Question in Turkish Foreign Policy from the 1950s to the 1990s', *International Journal of Middle East Studies*, Vol. 25 (1993), p. 94, and Kemal H. Karpat, 'Turkish and Arab–Israeli Relations', in Karpat *et al.*, *Turkey's Foreign Policy*, pp. 122–5.

65. Philip Robins, *Turkey and the Middle East* (London, Pinter, for Royal Institute of International Affairs, 1991), pp. 100–7.

66. Kuniholm, 'Turkey and NATO', pp. 426, 438–9; Aykan, 'Palestinian Question', pp.

95, 97; Gruen, 'Ambivalence', pp. 372–3, 377, and Karaosmanoğlu, 'Turkey's Security', pp. 160, 163, 168–70.

67. M. Hakan Yavuz and Mujeeb R. Khan, 'Turkish Foreign Policy toward the Arab–Israeli Conflict: Duality and the [*sic*] Development', *Arab Studies Quarterly*, Vol. 14 (1992), pp. 80–1; Aykan, 'Palestinian Question', p. 98 and Bülent Aras, 'The Impact of the Palestinian–Israeli Peace Process in Turkish Foreign Policy', *Journal of South Asian and Middle Eastern Studies*, Vol. 20 (1997), pp. 57–9.

68. Michael M. Bishku, 'Turkey and its Middle Eastern Neighbours since 1945', *Journal of South Asian and Middle Eastern Studies*, Vol. 15 (1992), p. 65: Aykan, 'Palestinian Question', p. 99 and Karaosmanoğlu, 'Turkey's Security', p. 167. In 1976 the Demirel government announced that Turkey would become a full member of the OIC, but in fact this never came about.

69. Yavuz and Khan, 'Turkish Foreign Policy', p. 81.

70. Aras, 'Impact', pp. 60–2; Aykan, 'Palestinian Question', pp. 104–5; Gruen, 'Turkey between Middle East and West' pp. 413–15 and Robins, *Turkey and the Middle East*, pp. 79–86.

71. In fact, the first Turkish incursion into northern Iraq occurred in May 1983. See Suha Bölükbaşı, 'Turkey Copes with Revolutionary Iran', *Journal of South Asian and Middle Eastern Studies*, Vol. 13 (1989), p. 103.

72. Ibid., pp. 95–9 and John Calabrese, 'Turkey and Iran: Limits of a Stable Relationship', *British Journal of Middle Eastern Studies*, Vol. 25 (1998), pp. 77–8.

73. Bölükbaşı, 'Turkey Copes', pp. 99–101.

74. See Henri J. Barkey, 'The Silent Victor: Turkey's Role in the Gulf War', in Efraim Karsh, ed., *The Iran–Iraq War: Impact and Implications* (London, Macmillan, in association with Jafee Center for Strategic Studies, Tel Aviv University, 1989), pp. 135–9. After 1985, Turkey's exports to the two countries fell back, in line with the decline in oil prices, and the Turks had difficulty in persuading the Iraqis to pay their existing commercial debts. In the case of trade with Iran, there were also complaints by the Iranians about the way it was conducted. See ibid., pp. 139–40, and Bölükbaşı, 'Turkey Copes', pp. 100–1. See also Robins, *Turkey and the Middle East*, pp. 53–4, 58–62, 103. On the rise of the PKK and Kurdish politics during the 1980s, see David McDowall, *A Modern History of the Kurds*, (London, I.B. Tauris, 1996), pp. 418–31; Michael M. Gunter, *The Kurds in Turkey* (Boulder, CO, Westview, 1990), pp. 57–91, and Kemal Kirişci and Gareth Winrow, *The Kurdish Question and Turkey: An Example of Trans-state Ethnic Conflict* (London, Cass, 1997), pp. 126–36.

75. Bölükbaşı, 'Turkey Copes', pp. 105–6, and McDowell, *Modern History*, pp. 357–61.

76. Robins, *Turkey and the Middle East*, pp. 49–52, 87–99. On the Euphrates dispute, see also Suha Bölükbaşı, 'Turkey Challenges Iraq and Syria: The Euphrates Dispute', *Journal of South Asian and Middle Eastern Studies*, Vol. 16 (1993), pp. 9–32, and Gün Kut, 'Burning Waters: The Hydropolitics of the Euphrates and Tigris', *New Perspectives on Turkey*, Fall 1993, pp. 1–17. For the texts of the 1987 agreements between Turkey and Syria, see H. Fahir Alaçam, 'Turkish–Syrian Relations', *Turkish Review of Middle East Studies* (Istanbul), Vol. 8 (1994/95), pp. 12–14. Distribution of the waters of the Tigris and Euphrates also involves conflict between Turkey and Iraq, but this has dropped into the background thanks to Iraq's international isolation since the Gulf war of 1991. See below, pp. 302–3.

77. See Vali, *Bridge*, pp. 107, 154–6.

78. Selim İlkin, 'A History of Turkey's Association with the European Community', in Ahmet Evin and Geoffrey Denton, eds, *Turkey and the European Community* (Opladen, Leske and Budrich, 1990), pp. 35–6; Roswitha Bourguignon, 'The History of the Association Agreement between Turkey and the European Community', in ibid., p. 52: Mehmet Ali Birand, 'Turkey and the European Community', *World Today*, Vol. 38 (1978), pp. 52–3, and Heinz Kramer, 'Turkey and EC's Southern Enlargement', *Aussenpolitik*, Vol. 35 (1984), pp. 101–4.

79. Association Agreement, Article 28. For the full text of the Agreement, and of the Additional Protocol of 1970, see *Official Journal of the European Communities: Information and Notices*, Vol. 16, No.C 113.

80. For instance, Seyfi Taşhan suggests that Turkey became an associate member of the EEC 'with the understanding that it would eventually become a full member'. See his 'The Case for Turkish Membership', in Evin and Denton, eds, *Turkey*, pp. 71–2. However, Bourguignon is far more guarded, confirming that 'full membership was not automatically fixed by the agreement'. See his 'Association Agreement', p. 53. See also John Redmond, *The Next Mediterranean Enlargement of the European Community: Turkey, Cyprus and Malta?* (Aldershot, Dartmouth Publishing, 1993), p. 26.

81. Quoted in Redmond, *Next Mediterranean Enlargement*, p. 23.

82. İlkin, 'Turkey's Association', pp. 40–4.

83. Bourguignon, 'Association Agreement', pp. 55–6; Kramer, 'Turkey and EC', pp. 105–7.

84. The first suggestion seems quite far-fetched, since the obstacles to Greek accession, both economic and political, were far fewer than in the case of Turkey. However, it might have been a useful diplomatic ploy for the Turks, and some Western parliamentarians hinted to them at the time that they should submit an application. See David Barchard, *Turkey and the West* (London, Routledge & Kegan Paul for the Royal Institute of International Affairs, 1985), pp. 64–5.

85. See Nusret Ekin, 'Turkish Labor in the EEC', in Werner Gumpel, ed., *Die Türkei auf dem Weg in die EG* (Munich and Vienna, R. Oldenbourg, 1979), pp. 88–94, 96, and İsmet Ergün, 'The Problem of Freedom of Movement of Turkish Workers in the European Community', in Denton and Evin, eds, *Turkey*, pp. 185–6, 189–90.

86. See İhsan D. Dağı, 'Democratic Transition in Turkey, 1980–83: The Impact of European Diplomacy', *Middle Eastern Studies*, Vol. 32 (1996), pp. 125–9, 138–9: reprinted in Sylvia Kedourie, ed., *Turkey: Identity, Democracy, Politics* (London and Portland, OR, Cass, 1996).

87. Ibid., pp. 129–32, 137–9; Barchard, *Turkey and the West*, pp. 58–9, and Bourguignon, 'Association Agreement', pp. 58–9.

88. Quoted in Meltem Müftüler, 'Turkish Economic Liberalization and European Integration', *Middle Eastern Studies*, Vol. 31 (1995), p. 85.

89. See Özal, *Turkey in Europe*, pp. 281–304.

90. For the full text of the Opinion, see Commission des Communautés Européennes, Sec (89) 2290, 'Avis de la Commission sur la demande d'adhésion de la Turquie à la Communauté' (Brussels, December 1989).

91. 'Press Conference by Mr Matutes on Membership of Turkey to the Community' (Brussels, Commission of the European Communities, December 1989: ref BIC/89/393).

92. The most striking illustration of this occurred in 1976 when the Soviet aircraft-carrying

cruiser *Kiev* steamed through the straits to the Mediterranean. On most criteria, the *Kiev* and her sister ships could be defined as aircraft-carriers, whose passage was forbidden under the Montreux convention. However, the Soviet navy classified her as an 'anti-submarine cruiser', and both the Turkish and NATO authorities accepted her passage. This partly reflected Turkey's desire not to provoke the Soviet Union where possible, and partly the fact that the *Kiev's* presence did not produce a fundamental alteration of the balance of power in the Mediterranean. The development of ship-borne missiles also rendered many of the Montreux rules quite obsolete, since they referred to tonnage and the size of ships' guns, which were virtually irrelevant in the nuclear age. See Barry Buzan, 'The Status and Future of the Montreux Convention', *Survival*, Vol. 18 (1976), pp. 242–7.

93. Kemal Kirişci, 'Turkey and the United States: Ambivalent Allies', in B. Rubin and T. Keaney, eds, *US Allies in a Changing World* (London, Cass, 2000).

6

Turkish Foreign Policy after the Cold War: Strategic Options and the Domestic Environment

The end of the Cold War, the collapse of communist rule in eastern Europe and the dissolution of the Soviet Union during 1989–91, altered Turkey's international environment as profoundly as either of the two previous transformations, of 1918–23 and 1945. The security threat from the Soviet Union, which had originally been the main cause of Turkey's attachment to the Western alliance, had effectively ended. On the face of it, this restored the situation of the 1920s, but to an even greater degree, since the Soviet state had constitutionally dissolved, Russia had contracted territorially, and a series of small successor states had emerged in the Black Sea region, central Asia and Transcaucasia. Having been previously surrounded on three sides by what was, in effect, a single state far more powerful than itself, Turkey was now surrounded by smaller neighbours which were weaker than itself both militarily and (with the arguable exception of Greece) economically.[1] If policies had been determined purely by considerations of military security, and the Western alliance had had no other functions, this should have allowed Turkey to revert to neutrality. That this did not happen was mainly due to the fact that the world of the 1990s was very different from that of the 1920s. The Western military alliance acquired new missions to replace those of meeting the Soviet challenge, in which Turkey could play an important role. Moreover, NATO was only one of a number of institutional and ideological bridges between Turkey and the West. Other non-military links, such as that with the European Union (EU),[2] and Turkey's continued commitment to political and economic liberalism, meant that there was a fairly high degree of continuity between its Cold War and post-Cold War orientations. Even though Turkey's foreign policy agenda expanded into new areas, it remained a committed member of NATO, and an aspirant for full EU membership. As in earlier periods, and as a senior official of the Turkish foreign ministry put it in 1999, Turkey needed to stay in the alliance 'not only because of NATO's important security guarantee, but also because this membership is a clear manifestation of her Western voca-tion'.[3] While the Western alliance retained its value for the Turks, Turkey also was able to re-invent its value to the Western powers.

Turkish foreign policy during the 1990s was profoundly affected by the global transformation. However, the domestic political environment also had a strong influence over the direction (or lack of it) of foreign policy. At home, Turgut Özal's hold on power was severely reduced by his party's defeat in the general elections of 1991, and ended with his death in 1993. This opened a phase of serious governmental instability, which severely limited government abilities to formulate or implement effective policies. More radical political currents – primarily, though not entirely, those of politicised Islam – also tried to challenge previously accepted positions. The rise of Kurdish separatism, and the resulting internal war against the Kurdistan Workers' Party (PKK), together with the increasingly contro-versial restriction of human rights in Turkey, had profound effects on the country's foreign relations. Finally, economic demands and ambitions came to have an increased role in foreign policy-making. Given the com-plexity and importance of Turkey's foreign relations during the decade, this chapter seeks to examine each of these themes, leaving Turkish policy towards the main countries with which it interacted to later pages.

GLOBAL CHANGES: FOREIGN POLICY OPTIONS AND DEBATES

Both in Turkey and abroad, the post-Cold War situation sparked off a quite unprecedented debate about where Turkey's international future lay, in which a wide variety of views were expressed. During 1989–90 some commentators suggested that the end of the Soviet threat had reduced Turkey's international influence, since it had now lost its role as the corner-stone of Western security in the eastern Mediterranean. More broadly, it was argued that NATO would lose its importance and be replaced by alternative security structures.[4] In this situation, Turkey might be seen as a strategic and political liability rather than an asset to the West – strategically because it had a host of complex regional security concerns (which, it was apparently assumed, were not shared by the Western powers), and politically because of its non-membership of the EU, its internal Kurdish problem, poor human rights record, and conflicts with Greece. Turkey's leaders liked to present their country to the Western powers as a bridge between Europe and the Middle East and central Asia, but there was a risk that western Europe might prefer to see it as a barrier against a hostile 'other', left outside European structures. In the absence of closer ties with western Europe, this line of argument suggested that Turks would look elsewhere for new areas of opportunity, such as those in the newly independent states of central Asia and the Black Sea, although the bilateral relationship with the United States would continue, and even strengthen.[5]

On the other side of the argument, less radical assessments argued that Turkey's links to the West had not lost their importance to either side. The end of the Cold War had not been all bad news for Turkey, and its new opportunities were complementary rather than contradictory to its links with the Western powers. This more conservative view, and its conclusions, were echoed by both official and private observers on both sides. In an interview in the Istanbul daily *Cumhuriyet*, in December 1989, Bülent Ecevit pointed out that the decline in Soviet power 'should be a cause of satisfaction rather than regret', since it had vastly reduced the risk of global war, even though new dangers had arisen.[6] These were elaborated at a NATO summit meeting in Rome held in November 1991, which accepted that the alliance did not now face 'calculated aggression', but would need to deal with instabilities outside the then NATO area in central Europe, in what was still then the Soviet Union, and in the Middle East and southern Mediterranean. They would arise from emerging ethnic conflicts, contested borders, and economic hardship, resulting in weapons proliferation, the rise of extremist ideologies and inter-state disputes.[7] Given its geographical position, Turkey's role in NATO would continue to be vital for the West in these 'out-of-area' missions. On the Turkish side, a meeting between the then foreign minister, Mesut Yılmaz, and 17 Turkish ambassadors, held in Rome in December 1989, concluded that Turkey would definitely remain in NATO, though it would try to develop closer ties with the Soviet Union and the Warsaw Pact states. To achieve membership of the EC, Turkey would need to take further steps towards democracy and improve its human rights record. Externally, its main security threats would come from the south and east, from Iraq and Syria (interestingly, this assessment was made some time before the eruption of the Gulf crisis of 1990–91).[8] Similarly, a position paper prepared by the Foreign Policy Institute in Ankara in 1993 concluded that Turkey's security rested mainly on its national power, but it still needed alliances 'with countries with whom we have identical interests and share common threat perceptions'.[9]

The idea that Turkey would be drawn away from the West by new opportunities in central Asia and elsewhere – that it might seek an 'Middle Eastern' or 'Turkic' identity rather than a 'Western' one – was also disputed by experienced observers like Paul Henze, who pointed out that the supposed new choices were 'not contradictory or competitive, they are complementary'. It was in the interests of western Europe and the United States to regard Turkey as an 'integral component' which could also 'maximise its relations with the Middle East and Central Asia', he claimed.[10] It could also be argued that for Turkey an active policy outside Europe was important partly because it increased the value of Turkish friendship for Western policy-makers in the post-Cold War environment. Hence, as Ziya Öniş suggested, Turkey 'should look simultaneously to both the East and the West' and accept the fact that 'Islam constitutes an important part of its cultural heritage'.[11] It seemed generally agreed that Turkey was important for the West, especially the United States, mainly in the Middle Eastern context – a perception primarily deriving from its role during the Gulf crisis of 1990–91 and subsequent developments in the region. Hence, the US Assistant Secretary of State Richard Holbrooke claimed that 'Turkey is replacing Germany as the cutting edge of Europe', and described Turkey as the United States' 'new European front'.[12] The idea that the Western powers would place Turkey primarily in a Middle Eastern strategic context also threatened to re-open the debate as to whether it should be classified as a 'Middle Eastern' or a 'European' country, which had delayed its original admission to NATO during 1949– 51 (see pp. 116–17, 119).[13] On the other hand, it was most unlikely that the Turkish élite would assist Western policy in the Middle East, if Turkey's 'Western' identity was not also accepted by Western governments.

Not surprisingly, Turkish politicians were sometimes inclined to exaggerate their country's new role, especially when addressing domestic audiences. As President, Turgut Özal was credited with the remark that 'the twenty-first century will belong to the Turks' (alternatively, that it 'will belong to Islam').[14] At the same time, it was argued that there was no 'peace dividend' for Turkey, since it was confronted with a series of regional and internal security threats which made it essential to continue a high defence posture. In an article published in 1996, Şükrü Elekdağ, formerly under-secretary at the Turkish Foreign Ministry and ambassador to Washington, argued that Turkey still faced the danger of a 'two and a half front war' (the two main fronts being against Greece and Syria, which might act together, and the 'half' front being the internal struggle against the PKK).[15] This suggestion was borne out by Turkish defence spending during the 1990s which, like that of Greece, continued to account for a larger share of its GNP than in the case of other NATO countries.[16] Critics could argue that this high rate of military expenditure derived partly from the influential role played by the military in internal politics, or the need to fight the PKK and confront Greece over Cyprus, both of which might have been avoided by more flexible policies. However, the fact that Turkey lived in an unstable and potentially threatening neighbourhood was hard to deny. Putting these factors together, an academic judgement by Kemal Kirişci nevertheless was that while Turkey was 'at the heart of one of the world's most volatile regions', it now had the opportunity to raise its international profile by putting new issues on the international agenda, and mobilising support for its positions by the international community.[17]

PARTY POLITICS DURING THE 1990s:
CONFLICTS AND INSTABILITY

In Turkey, as in other countries, a striking effect of the collapse of communism in Europe was the virtual collapse of the 'old left', which had started to have some impact on Turkish foreign policies during the 1960s and 1970s. In the new situation, centre-left parties abandoned much of their commitment to socialism domestically, and began to adopt foreign policies which could be accommodated to a world in which the Western powers, especially the United States, were clearly dominant. Meanwhile, the traditionally pro-Western parties of the centre-right were being challenged by radical voices from Islamist and ethnic nationalist movements. In the Turkish case, these trends had antedated the end of the Cold War since, as has been noticed earlier, the traditional left had been fatally weakened by the military takeover of 1980, and Turgut Özal's uninterrupted hold on power between 1983 and 1991. Similarly, the Islamist alternative, represented by Necmettin Erbakan's MSP, had already come into prominence during the 1970s, though it had made relatively little impact on Turkish foreign policy at the time. As a result, the global transformation could be seen as having reinforced changes which had begun several years earlier.

Whether Turkish governments could exploit the new opportunities apparently presented by the end of the Cold War, and how they would do so, also depended on whether they could depend on a stable domestic power base. This turned out to be the Achilles heel of Turkish foreign policy, since external problems were seriously exacerbated by internal weaknesses and conflicts. In the search for effective democratic government, the record of the 1990s was a generally dismal one. No single party won an overall majority in parliament in any of the three general elections, held in 1991, 1995 and 1999, and Turkey slipped back into the position of chronic governmental instability which it had experienced during the 1970s, although the story of the slide into near-anarchy and eventual military takeover of 1978–80 was fortunately not repeated. In short, Turkey suffered from a chronic lack of domestic political leadership. The old leaders who now returned to power, like Bülent Ecevit and Süleyman Demirel, lacked solid overall support, and seemed too old to fill the leadership gap. On the other hand, the new and younger party leaders thrown up by the events of the 1990s, like Tansu Çiller and Mesut Yılmaz, failed to perform as effective replacements. Radical leaders from outside the political establishment, like Necmettin Erbakan, were too controversial, since they had ideas which were either unworkable, or at least poorly worked out, and their presence exacerbated the instability of the system.

Between 1987 and 1991 Turgut Özal's apparently solid hold on domestic political support was badly eroded by his government's economic failures, in particular, its failure to control inflation, which ran at an average annual level of 66 per cent between 1988 and 1991.[18] When he had succeeded Kenan Evren as President in 1989, Özal had been constitutionally obliged to sever all official links with the Motherland Party. However, in practice, he continued to control both the party and the government from behind the scenes. In this situation, his prime minister, Yıldırım Akbulut, was little more than a proxy, and failed to impress either the party or the public as an effective leader. In a party convention held in June 1991, he was successfully challenged by his former foreign minister, Mesut Yılmaz, who now took over as official party chairman and prime minister. Unwisely, Yılmaz decided to call an early general election in October 1991, in which the Motherland Party came in a poor second, with 112 seats, well behind Süleyman Demirel's True Path Party (DYP) which won 179 seats. Erdal İnönü's Social Democratic Populist Party (SHP) won 91 seats, with 61 seats going to a temporary alliance between the Islamists of the Welfare Party, and the Nationalist Endeavour Party, formed by Alparslan Türkeş, the leader of the ultra-nationalist right as a successor to his previous Nationalist Action Party (MHP).[19] Bülent Ecevit's Democratic Left Party (DSP) also succeeded in winning a toehold in parliament, by capturing seven seats. Although there was relatively little difference in terms of policies between the Motherland and True Path parties, the fierce rivalry between Demirel and Özal prevented any collaboration between the two, and Demirel formed an unwieldy coalition with the social democrats. His government lasted until 17 April 1993, when President Özal suddenly died of a heart attack. Since Demirel decided to take over the presidency, to which he was elected by parliament on 16 May, a new prime minister and leader of the DYP had to be found. Unexpectedly, a special party convention elected Tansu Çiller, who took over the premiership on 25 June 1993.

Tansu Çiller's installation aroused high hopes, since she was thought of as a liberal, and the appointment of a woman prime minister in a Muslim country was regarded as an important milestone. Her defects were her lack of political experience and her weak grip on the levers of power within her own party. Her government was also badly shaken by one of Turkey's periodic economic crises in the spring of 1994, causing a rapid devaluation of the Turkish lira and a slump in economic growth. Loss of confidence in the government was compounded by unproven allegations of corruption against the prime minister and her husband, but was also affected by turmoils on the centre-left of the political spectrum which were beyond her control. In 1992 a group of MPs led by Deniz Baykal had left the SHP to re-establish the Republican People's Party (CHP). This re-united with the SHP in February 1995, under Baykal's leadership, as the CHP. In the following September, Baykal pulled his party out of the coalition. After an unsuccessful attempt by Mrs Çiller to form a minority government, a new DYP–CHP coalition was stitched together in November, but only on the condition, demanded by Baykal, that new elections be held on 24 December.

The serious governmental instability which had developed after 1993 was exacerbated by the results of the December 1995 elections, in which Erbakan's pro-Islamist Welfare Party became the biggest single party in the assembly, with 158 of the 550 seats. The remainder of parliament was evenly split between the DYP and the Motherland Party, with 135 and 132 seats respectively, followed by Ecevit's DSP (76 seats) and a much reduced CHP (49 seats). After months of fruitless bargaining, Mesut Yılmaz formed a coalition with Mrs Çiller on 12 March 1996, but this fell apart just one month later. Reversing her previous stand of fierce opposition to political Islamism, Tansu Çiller then formed an alliance with Necmettin Erbakan, resulting in a coalition between their two parties which took office on 26 June, with Erbakan as premier. From the start, the coalition was wracked by dissent between its two constituents, and was further weakened by the revelation of damaging links between parts of the government and the police service with organised crime, which was revealed by an automobile crash at Susurluk, in western Anatolia, on 3 November 1996.[20] Meanwhile, Erbakan's moves towards creeping Islamisation (especially in education) aroused the ire of Turkey's staunchly secularist generals, as well as much of an emerging civil society. On 18 June 1997, in the face of repeated warnings from the military-dominated National Security Council, as well as mounting public protests, Erbakan resigned, hoping to reconstruct the government under Mrs Çiller's premiership. However, back-bench defections from the DYP to a short-lived Democratic Turkey Party (DTP) robbed the coalition of its majority. Accordingly, President Demirel passed on the baton to Mesut Yılmaz, who formed a minority government, in coalition with Ecevit's DSP and the DTP, on 30 June 1997. Subsequently, in February 1998, the Welfare Party was closed down by order of the Constitutional Court for breaking articles of the constitution protecting secularism, and Necmettin Erbakan was banned from running for public office for the next five years. Nonetheless, a successor party was rapidly formed, in the shape of the Virtue Party, nominally under the leadership of Recai Kutan.[21]

Yılmaz's third government (and Turkey's ninth since 1991) managed to hold on to power for fifteen months, but was weakened from the start by its dependence on the uncertain support of the CHP. On 25 November 1998, in the wake of unproven corruption allegations against the government, Baykal withdrew this lifeline, and the government was defeated in a vote of confidence. On 30 July 1998, parliament had voted to hold early general elections in April 1999, and the hunt was now on for a caretaker government which could hold the fort until polling day. After seven weeks of uncertainty, Bülent Ecevit eventually formed a minority caretaker administration on 17 January 1999 with outside support from the Motherland Party and DYP, but could achieve little pending the elections. The results of the poll, held on 18 April 1999, were a serious set-back for Tansu Çiller, Mesut Yilmaz and Recai Kutan, whose tallies were reduced to 85, 86 and 111 seats respectively. They were also a disaster for the CHP, which failed to surmount the 10 per cent threshold, below which parties cannot win any seats in parliament. With 136 seats, Ecevit's DSP was now the biggest party in the assembly, but the surprise winner was the MHP, formerly the vehicle for Alparslan Türkeş and his brand of ultra-nationalism.[22] Following Türkeş' death in 1997, the party leadership had been captured by the sober and distinctly uncharismatic Devlet Bahçeli, who succeeded both in converting the party to a more moderate but uncertain position, and in making it the second largest party in parliament by winning 129 seats in the elections. Although many DSP members had serious suspicions about the MHP,[23] based on its role in fomenting ultra-rightist terrorism in the late 1970s, Bahçeli was determined to project a new, more responsible image for his party. Accordingly, he took his place as deputy premier in a tripartite coalition with the DSP and the Motherland Party, under Ecevit's premiership, which took office on 28 May 1999. With 350 of the 550 seats in parliament behind it, the new government had a bigger majority than any government since 1991. During its first few months, it proved far more active and effective in tackling Turkey's domestic and external problems than its predecessors, though whether its installation meant the end of continual internal upsets was still uncertain.

TURKEY'S KURDISH QUESTION AND HUMAN RIGHTS

While the instability of government seriously damaged Turkey's capacity to develop sustained foreign policy initiatives, its domestic and foreign policies were also affected by the rising challenge of Kurdish nationalism.[24] Since the Kurdish problem became a major issue in Turkey's foreign relations, an account of it needs to be given. The campaign of violence, with terrorist attacks against civilian targets as well as the military which had been started by the PKK in 1984 gathered pace during the early 1990s. Throughout this period, the PKK leader Abdullah Öcalan was an unacknowledged guest of the Syrian government, and benefited from Syrian logistic support as well as the use of training camps in the Syrian-occupied Bekaa valley in the Lebanon. The Kurdish cause also won more international publicity after Saddam Hussein's brutal repression of the Kurdish rebellion in Iraq, just after the Gulf war of 1991. On 5 April 1991, following the flight of around 500,000 mainly Kurdish refugees to the Iraqi–Turkish border, and even larger numbers to Iran, the UN Security Council passed Resolution 688. Under the Resolution an international force, initially numbering around 20,000 troops from 11 countries, established a 'safe haven' in northern Iraq, to which all the refugees were able to return by the end of May.[25]

'Operation Provide Comfort', as it was initially known, solved the immediate problem of the refugees, but exacerbated Turkey's internal Kurdish problem, since it attracted international attention to the Kurdish cause, and provided a base (or at least a power vacuum) in northern Iraq from which PKK insurgents could attack targets in Turkey. Exploiting this position, and benefiting from continued support by Syria, the PKK was able to intensify its campaign. By 1993, it almost seemed on the verge of leading a mass popular uprising on the lines of the Palestinian *intifada* – running its own 'liberated zones', extorting taxes, suppressing activities by the other political parties, and ruthlessly punishing alleged 'collaborators'.[26] In March 1993, and perhaps encouraged by rather vague and indirect contacts with President Özal via the Iraqi Kurdish leader, Jelal Talabani, [27] Öcalan declared a unilateral cease-fire. However, this failed to provoke any effective political response by the Turkish government, which was in any case preoccupied by the internal political turmoils following the death of Turgut Özal in April 1993. What may well have been a serious missed opportunity to end the fighting was in any case abruptly ended on 24 May when the PKK's local commander in Bingöl province, Şemdin Sakık, attacked a bus carrying unarmed soldiers and civilians, murdering 37 people in cold blood.[28] As a result, the war against the PKK was resumed full scale.

After 1993, the PKK's chances of achieving long-term political or military success gradually receded. By 1994–95 the Turkish army and gendarmerie were starting to regain the upper hand in south-eastern Anatolia, where the fighting was concentrated, and by 1998 they had re-established control over most of the region. International support for the idea of an independent Kurdish state simultaneously weakened, especially after the outbreak of bitter fighting in Iraq during 1994–96 between Talabani's Patriotic Union of Kurdistan (PUK) and the rival Kurdistan Democratic Party (KDP) headed by Masud Barzani. Turkey also became engaged in the struggle for power in northern Iraq, first by a renewed incursion into Iraqi territory against the PKK in 1992, and then by a far larger attack in 1995. These were followed by further operations in 1996 and afterwards, in which the Turkish forces collaborated with Barzani's *peshmerga* militia, so that by 1997 the PKK was finding it far more difficult to operate from Iraqi territory (see pp. 309–10).[29]

Meanwhile, successive Turkish governments took an uncertain but generally hawkish line against non-violent activities by Kurdish political groups in Turkey. In April 1991, under a 'Law for the Struggle against Terrorism' (No. 3713), the Motherland Party government withdrew an absurd and virtually unenforceable law, introduced by the military regime in 1983, under which any use of Kurdish 'for the expression and dissemination of thought' in Turkey had been a punishable offence. Accordingly, after 1991 publications in Kurdish became legally allowable, though Kurdish-language broadcasting was still banned. Nonetheless, under Article 8 of the same law, any publications 'aiming to damage the indivisible integrity of the Turkish Republic' remained strictly illegal, and their authors and publishers subjected to tough prison terms. After their establishment of a coalition government in November 1991, Süleyman Demirel and Erdal İnönü made a well-publicised visit to the south-east, in which Demirel proclaimed that 'Turkey must recognise the Kurdish reality'.[30] The October 1991 elections also brought to parliament a group of 22 Kurdish MPs, elected on the SHP ticket, who then joined the People's Labour Party (HEP), Turkey's first distinctly pro-Kurdish party.[31] This was closed down by order of the Constitutional Court in June 1993, but its members officially left the party shortly before this took effect, and were able to set up a successor party, known as the Democracy Party (DEP).

In March 1994, Tansu Çiller's government engineered the arrest of 13 DEP MPs by lifting their parliamentary immunity. The party was closed down and they were charged with treason. Six of them managed to flee abroad, but the remainder were imprisoned and one was murdered. A third pro-Kurdish party was then set up, as the People's Democracy Party (HADEP) under Murat Bozlak. This was allowed to compete in the 1995 and 1999 elections, as well as the local elections of 1999. It emerged as the leading party in a number of south-eastern provinces on both occasions, and in 1999 succeeded in winning the mayoralties in Diyarbakır and a number of other south-eastern towns and cities. However, it won less than 5 per cent of the national vote on both occasions, and thus failed to capture any seats in parliament. The party also suffered from a good deal of official harassment, and by 1999 both Murat Bozlak and around 100 other party members were in prison, on charges of assisting the PKK. Officially, HADEP disavowed terrorism, but many of its grass-roots supporters were also supporters of the PKK, and the party found it hard to distance itself from it.[32]

What was certainly a turning-point, and possibly the end, of the PKK's career, came during the winter of 1998–99. After a fierce Turkish diplomatic offensive against Syria, backed up with the threat of military action, Syrian President Hafiz al-Assad's government expelled Öcalan on 7 October 1998, and he left for Moscow (see p. 305). On 12 November he made a dramatic appearance in Rome airport, where he was arrested for carrying a false passport, and then tried to gain political asylum in Italy. The Italian authorities expelled their unwelcome guest on 16 January 1999, when he set off on another safari to Belarus, Russia and Greece. Öcalan eventually arrived at the Greek ambassador's residence in Nairobi, Kenya, on 2 February, carrying a Greek Cypriot diplomatic passport. On

16 February he was captured by a Turkish security team, while on his way to Nairobi airport, and brought back to Turkey, where he was placed on trial before a State Security Court on 30 May.[33] On 29 June the court sentenced him to death under Article 125 of the Turkish Penal Code, which makes it an offence to attempt to remove any part of Turkish territory from the control of the state, and he was found guilty of causing the deaths of thousands of innocent people.[34] If Öcalan were to be executed, the consititution would require parliament to pass a positive vote to that effect. In fact, no death sentences had been carried out since 1984, and prime minister Bülent Ecevit and his DSP favoured abolishing the death sentence as a matter of principle. Western European governments also made it quite clear that if Abdullah Öcalan were hanged, then Turkey would have little chance of starting accesson negotiations with the EU. After the Turkish Court of Appeal (*Yargıtay*) had upheld the sentence on 25 November 1999, the European Court of Human Rights requested Turkey for a stay of execution, to allow it to investigate the case. Ecevit's government stated that it would respect this, and it seemed likely that the execution would be postponed indefinitely, even if parliament did not abolish capital punishment altogether.[35]

The prospect of an end to the armed struggle against the PKK naturally caused profound relief in Turkey, but it left the government with the job of deciding whether, and how, it could tackle the broader political aspects of the Kurdish problem. The struggle had also been fought at enormous cost. It was officially reported in March 1999 that around 4,400 soldiers and police had been killed by the PKK since 1984, plus over 1,200 'village guards' (that is, Kurdish militiamen armed by the government) and around 5,300 civilians, mostly their fellow-Kurds, who had been murdered by the PKK in terrorist attacks.[36] Accepting the frequently-quoted total of 30,000 deaths since 1984, this suggests that around 19,000 PKK militants had been killed by the security forces. Between 500,000 and three million people had been obliged to leave their homes, in many cases because their villages had been forcibly evacuated and then burnt down by the army.[37] These evacuations had seriously alienated millions of Kurdish citizens from the Turkish state, and this effect had been exacerbated by persistent human rights abuses by the security forces. There had also been around 1,600 officially 'unsolved' murders, mostly of left-wing pro-Kurdish activists who had reportedly been killed by the shadowy Islamist-Kurdish 'Hizbullah' organisation, allegedly with the connivance of the authorities.[38]

Undoubtedly, the cost to the government had been very heavy.

Estimates for the costs of the military operations vary widely, but it was suggested that in 1994–95, when the campaign was at its height, around 250,000–300,000 troops, or almost half the total strength of the armed forces, was deployed in the south-east, and that the war was costing as much as US$7 billion annually, or about 4 per cent of Turkey's gross national product (GNP) at the time.[39] Apart from its domestic political effects, the struggle severely weakened Turkey's foreign policies, since it badly undermined the idea that Turkey could be presented as a democratic model to other Muslim countries, severely damaged its chances of developing its links with western Europe, and gave unfriendly states a ready weapon for interference.

Besides the Kurdish question, general restrictions on human rights, especially the freedom of expression, also had serious effects. During the 1990s, some improvements in Turkey's restrictive laws were admittedly enacted, and some moves were made to reduce the regular use of torture by the police. In 1991 (ironically, as part of the 'Law for the Struggle against Terrorism') Articles 142 and 143 of the Penal Code, which had previously been used to prosecute anyone convicted of supposedly Marxist activities or propaganda, were removed. In November 1992, the periods for which suspects could be held before being charged were sharply reduced, although these limits were much extended in the case of charges alleged to affect state security or where a state of emergency is in force.[40] In July 1995 Tansu Çiller's government succeeded in pushing through a package of amendments to the constitution, in connection with Turkey's campaign to gain entry into a customs union agreement with the EU (see p. 236) but these only affected such things as the rights of trades unions and other associations to form links with political parties, and did not really address the complaint that overall restrictions on the free expression of dissident views were still far too severe. Later, in October 1995, some amendments were made to Article 8 of the 'Law for the Struggle against Terrorism', and around 100 people who had been convicted under the previous version were released. However, this did not go far enough to affect the substance of the criticism that Article 8 punished people merely for the expression of views rather than actual criminal acts.[41]

These improvements – such as they were – still left Turkey's constitution and laws well short of accepted democratic standards. Under Articles 13 and 14 of the constitution enacted by the military regime in 1982, any activity deemed injurious to the territorial integrity of Turkey, or supportive of the idea of an Islamic state, is deemed unconstitutional.[42] Article 159 of the Penal Code makes any 'insult' to 'the Turkish identity, the Turkish Republic, the Grand National Assembly ... or the military or security forces' a punishable offence, while Article 312 criminalises any attempt 'to incite hatred based on class, race, religion or ... between different regions'. These restrictions are additional to those contained in Article 8 of the 'Law for the Struggle against Terrorism' of 1991.[43] In spite of some improvements in the human rights regime after 1995, by the summer of 1999 numerous writers and human rights activists were still being imprisoned for the mere expression of oppositional views, especially on the Kurdish question.[44] Examples included those of Akın Birdal, chairman of the Turkish Human Rights Association, who received a ten-month prison sentence for a speech made in 1996 calling for 'peace and understanding' with the Kurdish minority, and Oral Çalışlar, a journalist on *Cumhuriyet*, who was sentenced to 13 months' imprisonment for publishing an interview with Abdullah Öcalan six years earlier.[45] The regular use of torture by the police, and the presence of a military judge among the three judges in each of the State Security Courts, where most of these cases were tried, was also a constant source of criticism, both domestically and internationally.

On 18 June 1999, the newly installed Ecevit government succeeded in changing the constitution, so as to remove the military judges, primarily to avoid a prospective annulment of the verdict in the Öcalan trial by the European Court of Human Rights. The government also secured legislation to increase punishments for policemen found guilty of torture, and facilitate their prosecution, although the results of this were uncertain. More broadly, Bülent Ecevit declared that, as part of an amnesty law, the government was determined to release all prisoners held on 'thought crimes', though he admitted that there were constitutional obstacles to this.[46] In the event, a law passed in August 1999 provided that those who had been imprisoned for written published statements, or statements on radio or television, would be released, on condition that they did not repeat these supposed 'crimes' for the next three years. The same rule would be applied to those whose cases were pending, or in the case of future prosecutions. However, this failed to answer the criticism that undemocratic restrictions on freedom of speech should simply have been removed from the statute book. A so-called 'Repentance Law' passed at the same time, granted an amnesty to those who had been members of the PKK and turned themselves in, but did not extend the concession to those held responsible for attacks on the security forces.[47] Both abroad, and among liberal opinion in Turkey, there was clearly a growing realisation that Turkey's human rights regime needed urgent improvement, for both internal and external reasons, but achieving this had so far proved very difficult. For the Ecevit government of 1999, it appeared that opposition from hard-liners within the MHP, Ecevit's coalition partners, may have been responsible for the half-heartedness of reform.[48] However, over the longer period, it was likely that stiff opposition from well-entrenched forces in the police and military, as well as among right-wing politicians, had also acted as a severe brake on improvement.

FOREIGN POLICY-MAKING: ACTORS, PARTIES AND PUBLIC OPINION

As previous chapters have explained, the circle of foreign policy actors had only begun to broaden in Turkey during the 1960s, as new political currents and a loosening of the consensus on foreign policy had started to develop.[49] The process of foreign policy-making is one of the least well-studied aspects of Turkish foreign policy, and suggestions can often only be speculative, or illustrated by occasional examples. Nonetheless, what could be described as the group of 'state actors' apparently continued to be the dominant decision-makers during the 1990s. These included, principally, the president, prime minister, and foreign minister, plus the commanders of the armed forces (combined, since 1961, in the National Security Council) and the professional diplomats in the foreign ministry. Thanks to the weakness of successive governments, the military regained some of its role as an independent policy-maker.[50] There were also differences of approach between individuals within the state élite. In particular, during his period as president between 1989 and 1993, Turgut Özal was more visionary, and more prepared to take risks and new policy directions, than either his predecessors or successor. More broadly, he tried to convert the presidency into an independent source of policy and power. After his death, Süleyman Demirel, who had taken relatively little interest in foreign policy during his previous stints as premier, oversaw a return to a more conservative, traditionalist and institutionalised style in foreign policy.[51]

Outside the state establishment, radical alternatives suggested by Islamist or ultra-nationalist movements were certainly voiced, but they were seldom able to implement their agendas, and then only partially. Other non-state actors, such as business and ethnic groups, did however apparently begin to have some impact on policy making, and the positions taken by political parties could make a difference, when those parties were in power. So far as can be seen, policies often emerged as the result of compromises between the state and non-state actors, or between the party leaders themselves (especially since all governments after 1991 were coalitions). Where compromises were not struck, then the result could be wavering or inconsistent policies – most notably, during the period of the Erbakan–Çiller coalition of 1996–97.

In Turkey, as in other countries, surveys of public opinion on foreign policy questions need to be taken cautiously, since most people do not give a high priority to the subject, and may give random answers to avoid appearing ignorant or indifferent. A survey conducted by the Strateji-Mori polling organisation in Istanbul in 1997 found that 57 per cent of the respondents described themselves as 'not-interested' in foreign policy, with only 23 per cent 'interested': not surprisingly, those with higher education were more likely to be interested than those without. When respondents were asked to rank foreign countries by order of favourability, Japan headed the list, followed by Turkey's NATO partners. Muslim countries, notably Saudi Arabia and Iran, scored moderate-to-low ratings, with Russia and Greece at the bottom of the scale. When answers were restricted to supporters of the Welfare Party, the positions of the NATO and Muslim countries were reversed: Pakistan, Iran and Saudi Arabia came in close behind Japan, with Russia and Greece still at the bottom. Generally, the respondents strongly favoured strengthening Turkey's links with the EU.[52] These positions were generally reflected in the media, in which the main national dailies and commercial TV companies (which in many cases are owned by the same groups) strongly supported a pro-Western secularist position, while the minority of pro-Islamist newspapers and broadcasters adopted the opposite stance.[53] At the same time, the media as a whole could take stridently nationalist stands towards particular incidents – as for instance, in the crisis with Greece over the islet of Kardak (Imia) in 1996 – which made crisis management far more difficult (see p. 255).

During the 1990s, there was much discussion of whether Turkey was developing a 'civil society' similar to those of Western democracies, in which non-governmental organisations, such as business groups, trades unions and voluntary bodies, were coming to play a bigger role in the country's politics.[54] Of these, probably the most influential were business associations, notably the Turkish Industrialists and Businessmen's Association (TÜSİAD) and the Union of Chambers (TTOBB). Both these groups, like the two main labour confederations, Türk-İş and DİSK, supported pro-Western and anti-Islamist policies,[55] though the Islamist–nationalists had their own business association, MÜSİAD, and labour confederation (Hak-İş). Within Turkey, there were also emergent lobbies formed by people of particular ethnic origins. Besides the obvious case of the Kurds, these included citizens of Bulgarian, Bosnian, Chechen and Abkhazian origin, though just how influential they were at points of crisis can be disputed, particularly in Turkey's relationships with Russia, and its policies in the Balkans (see pp. 260–1, 268–9).

The political parties reflected this variety of views, though with a general preponderance on the pro-Western secularist side.[56] While most of the parties did not make foreign policy a major issue in addressing the electorate (for instance, their election manifestos in 1995 and 1999 seldom devoted more than about 5 per cent of their space to the subject) and tended to restrict themselves to vague generalities, the centre-right Motherland Party and the DYP were generally pro-Western. They supported Turkey's bid for eventual membership of the EU, while also claiming that they would develop links with the central Asian and Middle Eastern countries. The most distinctive stand was that taken by the Welfare Party. In the 1995 election campaign, the party opposed the idea of gaining full membership of the EU, which it described as a 'Christian Union' and called instead for a 'Muslim Union'. It accepted the development of commercial links with Europe, though it called for a revision of the customs union with the EU, which came into effect in 1996. However, by 1999, its successor, the Virtue Party, had dropped the references to a 'Muslim Union', and even accepted the project for Turkish membership of the EU as a 'basic goal', as well as the need to 'continue Turkey's effective role within NATO'.[57] On the centre-left, the DSP, retained something of Bülent Ecevit's 'Third Worldist' approach of the 1970s, calling for a vaguely defined 'regionally-centred foreign policy depending on national interests'.[58] It supported the principle of gaining full EU membership eventually, though it appeared to attach less immediate importance to this than the two centre-right parties, claiming that while the door to Turkey's membership appeared to be closed, 'other doors [apparently in "Eurasia"] are opening before Turkey'. It also emphasised the need to defend the rights of the Turkish Cypriots, stating even that it supported the independence of the Turkish Republic of Northern Cyprus.[59] Finally, the MHP, the newcomer to power in 1999, predictably stressed ethnic nationalist values. While it accepted the goal of eventual membership of the EU, it was also keen on the idea of developing economic, cultural and social relations with what it called the 'Turkish' republics of the former Soviet Union, calling for the establishment of a 'Ministry of the Turkish World' within the Turkish government, and a 'Common Market of the Turkish World'.[60] As in the case of other parties, it is likely that such commitments

were designed mainly for rhetorical effect, rather than for a serious exami-
nation of the practicalities involved. More generally, how these positions
worked themselves out in policy terms could be seen in successive government's policies in different theatres, which is described later.

THE GROWING ECONOMIC AGENDA

During the 1990s, as in earlier decades, Turkish governments realised that
their success or failure in delivering economic benefits, in the form of
higher incomes and employment, and better social services, was one of the
main criteria by which they would be judged by the electorate. A successful economic programme primarily required effective domestic policies.
However, economic needs also became an important factor in foreign
policy. In particular, governments needed to increase the country's exports
and service earnings, so as to avoid the frequent balance-of-payments
crises which had bedevilled the economy up to the 1980s, and secure
access to foreign capital. In foreign policy, this meant that Turkish governments had to try to prevent political conflicts with important trading
partners, and avoid isolationist policies which could have cut them off
from international financial markets or potential investors. An important
effect of the end of the Cold War was that export markets in the former
Soviet Union, which had previously been restricted by the state-controlled
economic system were now relatively open to Turkish, as to other
exporters. At the same time, the government sought to use Turkey's growing economic power, relative to that of most of its immediate neighbours,
as an instrument in foreign policy. Increasing regional economic links and
dependencies would, it was believed, help secure greater regional political
stability. This approach was advocated, in particular, by Turgut Özal
who, during his term as president between 1989 and 1993, adopted the
classic liberal concept that growing economic interdependence between
states would generate better political relations. This was reflected in his
earlier advocacy of the 'peace pipeline' project in the Middle East (see
p. 174) and later in the sponsorship of such projects as the Black Sea
Economic Cooperation Zone and greater Turkish participation in the
economic development of Transcaucasia and central Asia (see pp. 269,
294).[61]

Economic trends during the decade mirrored those which had begun
during the 1980s. GNP continued to grow, from around US$151 billion in
1990 to US$210 billion by 1998, at exchange rate parities, or an average
annual growth rate of around 4.2 per cent per year. Meanwhile, exports

rose from US$13 billion in 1990 to US$31.1 billion in 1998, and imports from US$22.6 billion to US$45.5 billion over the same period. As a result, total foreign merchandise trade, as a proportion of GNP, rose from 23.5 per cent to 36.5 per cent.[62] In effect, economic growth meant that external dependence was increasing.

Turkey's external accounts also came to include important invisible items. Thus, in 1998, Turkey earned US$7.2 billion from tourism, US$17 billion from other services such as transport and contractors services, and US$2.5 billion in interest payments on foreign financial holdings by Turkish citizens and firms, plus around US$5.7 billion in remittances from Turkish workers abroad, mainly in Germany. In return, it spent US$15.3 billion in services outflows, of which US$4.8 billion was accounted for by interest on its external debt.[63] Thanks to the 'invisibles' surplus, Turkey was generally able to pay its way internationally. The economy also moved higher up the technological ladder. By 1998 industry and construction accounted for about 28 per cent of GNP, compared with 17 per cent for agriculture and 55 per cent for services. Manufactured products accounted for 88 per cent of total exports in 1998. Heading the list of export items were textiles and clothing (29 per cent of total exports), iron and steel (8.4 per cent) and machinery and vehicles (14.1 per cent).[64]

While the Turkish economy was growing, it was also plagued by very poor management by successive governments. Thanks to a massive public sector deficit, inflation ran at an average rate of almost 79 per cent per annum between 1990 and 1998, and the exchange rate of the Turkish Lira fell from US$1.00 = TL2,609 in 1990 to US$1.00 = TL314,464 in 1998. Meanwhile, the total outstanding external debt rose from US$49.2 billion at the end of 1990 to US$102.7 billion at the end of 1998, and the debt-service ratio (that is, interest payments as a proportion of GNP) from 3.7 per cent in 1994 to 7.0 per cent in 1998.[65] In effect, Turkey had a growing economy and foreign trade, but high inflation, a very weak currency, and mounting external debts.

Obviously, the direction of Turkey's foreign trade also had important implications for its foreign policies. In 1990, the then European Community accounted for just under 46 per cent of Turkey's total foreign merchandise trade (that is, exports plus imports) and trade with other OECD countries, primarily the United States and Japan, for another 19 per cent. The Middle East accounted for 13 per cent of total trade, the Soviet Union for 5 per cent, and all other countries for the remaining 17 per cent.[66] By 1998, the most significant change had been the increased role of the countries of the former Soviet Union (officially grouped together as the Commonwealth of Independent States, or CIS) in Turkey's foreign trade, strengthening a trend which had begun in the 1980s. Part of this was accounted for by normal trade passing through regular commercial channels, but there was also an unexpected flow of what was called 'suitcase trade' – that is, purchases in Turkey by citizens of the former Soviet republics, and other eastern European countries, who took clothing, household goods and other supplies home with them. Beginning in 1996, the Turkish Central Bank began to show 'suitcase trade' (which consisted entirely of exports) as a separate item in the balance-of-payments figures, though it gave no breakdown by countries. However, assuming that 90 per cent of 'suitcase' exports went to the CIS countries, it can be assumed that in 1998 such exports were worth around US$3.3 billion, in addition to normally recorded exports to the CIS of US$2.7 billion, and imports from the CIS of US$3.7 billion. Including the 'suitcase' exports, trade with the CIS now accounted for about 12.7 per cent of Turkey's total foreign trade – a far higher proportion than during the Cold War. Meanwhile, the share of the Middle East in total trade had shrunk to 5.9 per cent. This occurred mainly as a result of lower oil prices, which reduced the cost of Turkey's imports from the region (which consist largely of crude oil) as well as the market for imports in the oil-producing countries. The imposition of economic sanctions on Iraq in 1990 further restricted Turkey's trade with the Middle East. Meanwhile, the shares of the EU and other OECD countries remained at roughly the same levels as they had been in 1990, at 49.1 per cent and 16.8 per cent respectively.[67] The situation can be summed up by saying that the 1990s saw a marked increase in Turkey's economic links with what had been the Soviet Union, and a proportionate decline in those with the Middle East. At the same time, the EU, the United States and Japan retained a dominant position in Turkey's foreign trade.

The dominance of the main Western industrial countries was repeated in Turkey's trade in services, and in financial flows, though the CIS was also gaining an increased role in some respects. From the data on tourist entries, it would appear that of the 9.7 million visitors who entered Turkey in 1997, around 62 per cent were from the OECD countries, of which 2.3 million were from Germany, and about 16 per cent from the CIS (mainly Russia).[68] However, the tourist industry is extremely sensitive to perceived political or other risks, and puts a high premium on avoiding international conflicts or internal disturbances. An example of this occurred in 1999, when tourism income was expected to fall back sharply as a result of agitation in Europe over the capture of Abdullah Öcalan. There is no exact data on the origin of other services' income, but it can safely be said that the majority of earnings from construction contracts, an important item in this category, came from the Middle East, with Russia and the rest of the CIS emerging as important markets. Emigrants' remittances came largely from Germany and other EU countries, and the legal status of Turkish workers in Germany became another item on the foreign policy agenda.

In terms of financial flows, Turkey was alomost entirely dependent on the advanced industrial nations. Direct foreign private investment in Turkey remained extremely low, given the size of the economy, running at an average of only just over US$1 billion per year during 1990–98. However, Western and Japanese investors provided nearly all of what there was: of the total foreign investment approved during the first half of 1999, 96 per cent was accounted for by the OECD countries.[69] Whether Turkey could attract more private investment depended largely on whether it could provide a more stable domestic political and economic environment, and better legal conditions,[70] but it also underlined the need to maintain good political relations with the West. By the 1990s what could be classified as foreign aid credits were relatively unimportant. Thus, of the total external debt stock, only 7.9 per cent was accounted for by loans from the World Bank, International Development Association (IDA), International Finance Corporation (IFC) or the European Investment Bank (EIB) and other EU institutions, and only a tiny fraction (0.23 per cent) by credits from the Islamic Development Bank. The remainder consisted of commercial borrowing, almost entirely from Western or Japanese banks and financial institutions.[71] Meanwhile, to reassure external financial markets, Turkey was in frequent need to negotiate stand-by and other agreements with the IMF and World Bank – most notably in 1994, following a financial crash in Turkey, and later in the autumn of 1999. Whether these attempts were successful largely depended on how well the government managed the domestic economy, and carried out necessary structural economic reforms, but the maintenance of enerally good relations with the United States and the other main industrialised nations was clearly an important background condition.

By the late 1990s, Turkey faced one further economic problem which had an important impact on its foreign policy. Because of the paucity of domestic reserves of carbon fuels, especially oil and natural gas, the country faced a large and potentially very critical energy deficit. By the late 1990s, total demand for energy was rising at over 10 per cent per year, and this increase was expected to continue well into the next century. In 1997, the last year for which full figures are available, total annual energy consumption ran at around 72 billion tons oil equivalent, of which 46 billion tons was imported. Within this, oil – 87 per cent of which was imported – accounted for 30 billion tons, and natural gas for 8.8 billion tons equivalent.[72] Hydroelectric plants, such as the giant Atatürk Dam on the Euphrates, had raised output substantially during the 1990s, but there were serious physical and environmental limits to the further development of this source. Importing crude oil did not appear to raise important political problems, since there were any number of potential suppliers, the only problem being that of price, over which Turkey had virtually no control. From the political viewpoint, natural gas was the most critical item, since it was relatively cheap and served as a pollution-free fuel for heating and power generation. As a sign of this, Turkey's consumption of natural gas rose from 1.2 billion cubic metres in 1988 to an expected 13 billion cubic metres in 1999, with forecasts of annual consumption of around 50 billion cubic metres by 2010.[73]

Some gas was being imported by special tankers in liquid form (liquefied natural gas – LNG) but it would normally have been more economical to build pipelines directly to the producing countries. As of 1999, the only such pipeline in operation was that from Russia, passing through Bulgaria, which had been inaugurated in 1987 (see p. 167) but Turkey needed both to arrange a new and more direct pipeline from Russia and to diversify its sources of supply. The most obvious potential alternative suppliers were Iran, Turkmenistan and perhaps Egypt and Iraq, but building pipelines from these countries meant settling tricky questions of securing transit rights as well as finance. (Increasing the country's dependence on Iraq or Iran raised separate political problems). Turkey also had ambitions plans of becoming an important actor in the expected central Asian oil and gas industry by serving as a transit route from the Caspian basin to world markets, notably through the construction of the long-discussed Baku–Ceyhan oil pipeline and a planned transcontinental gas pipeline from Turkmenistan (see pp. 275–7, 295–6). Even if these ambitions remained unrealised, however, Turkey still had an urgent need for new gas pipelines, simply to meet the requirements of its own economy.

NOTES

1. Obviously, this statement does not hold true if one counts Russia as a 'neighbour' of Turkey: however, the essential point about the transformation for the Turks was that it left Russia far weaker than previously.
2. Officially, the European Community became the European Union when the treaty of Maastricht went into effect in November 1993.

3. Ömür Orhun, 'The Uncertainties and Challenges Ahead: A Southern Perspective', *Perceptions* (Ankara), Vol. 4, No. 1 (1999), p. 30.

4. See Sabri Sayarı, 'Turkey, the Changing European Security Environment and the Gulf Crisis', *Middle East Journal*, Vol. 46 (1992), pp. 10–11.

5. Ian O. Lesser, 'Bridge or Barrier? Turkey and the West After the Cold War', in Graham E. Fuller *et al.*, *Turkey's New Geopolitics: From the Balkans to Western China* (Boulder, CO, Westview, 1993), pp. 102, 129. Lesser elaborates his argument in a later paper, 'Turkey's Strategic Options', *International Observer* (Rome) Vol. 34 (1999), p. 82.

6. *Cumhuriyet*, 27 December 1989.

7. Gareth M. Winrow, 'NATO and the Out-of-Area Issue: The Positions of Turkey and Italy', *Il Politico* (Pavia), Vol. 58 (1993), p. 640. For a Turkish perspective, see also Gülnur Aybet, 'NATO's New Missions', *Perceptions* (Ankara), Vol. 4, No. 1 (1999), pp. 65–78.

8. Bruce R. Kuniholm, 'Turkey and the West', *Foreign Affairs*, Vol. 70 (1991), p. 40.

9. Foreign Policy Institute, 'Turkey's Foreign Policy Objectives', *Foreign Policy* (Ankara), Vol. 17, Nos 1–2 (1993), p. 3.

10. Paul B. Henze, 'Turkey: Toward the Twenty-First Century', in Fuller and Lesser, eds, *Turkey's New Geopolitics*, p. 2.

11. Ziya Öniş, 'Turkey in the Post-Cold War Era: In Search of Identity', *Middle East Journal*, Vol. 49 (1995), pp. 48–9.

12. Quoted in Meltem Müftüler-Baç, 'Turkey's Predicament in the Post-Cold War Era', *Futures*, Vol. 28 (1996), p. 257. See also Kuniholm, 'Turkey and the West', p. 34.

13. Ekavi Athanassopoulou, 'Ankara's Foreign Policy Objectives after the End of the Cold War: Making Policy in a Changing Environment', *Orient*, Vol. 36 (1995), p. 278.

14. Quoted in ibid., p. 276.

15. Şükrü Elekdağ, 'Two and a Half War Strategy', *Perceptions*, (Ankara), Vol 1 No. 1 (1996), p. 57.

16. In the case of Greece and Turkey, for 1997, the figures were 4.5 per cent and 4.2 per cent respectively. See *The Military Balance, 1998/99* (London, Oxford University Press for International Institute of Strategic Studies, 1998), pp. 55, 67.

17. Kemal Kirişci, 'New Patterns of Turkish Foreign Policy Behaviour', in Çiğdem Balım, ed., *Turkey: Political, Social and Economic Challenges in the 1990s* (Leiden, Brill, 1995), pp. 1, 4.

18. Data from *Country Report, Turkey* (hereinafter *EIU:CRT*), 1st Qtr 1993 (London, Economist Intelligence Unit), p. 3. The following summary of Turkish domestic politics during the 1990s is based on the author's contributions to Ami Ayalon, ed., *Middle East Contemporary Survey, 1990* (Vol. 14, Boulder, CO, Westview, 1992), and to the subsequent editions for 1991, 1992, 1993 and 1994 (vols 15–18). For fuller details on the period 1995–98, see also William Hale, 'Turkey's Political Landscape: A Glance at the Past and the Future', *International Observer* (Rome), Vol. 34 (1999), esp. pp. 31–5. Nicole and Hugh Pope add valuable information on the Özal period, in Nicole and Hugh Pope, *Turkey Unveiled: Ataturk and After* (London, John Murray, 1997) Chs 11–13.

19. In 1992, Türkeş led 19 MPs out of the Welfare Party, to re-establish his Nationalist Endeavour Party: this later reverted to its original title of Nationalist Action Party.

20. For further details see Hale, 'Turkey's Political Landscape', p. 31, and Hugh Poulton, 'The Turkish State and Democracy', *International Observer* (Rome), Vol. 34 (1999), pp. 60–1.

21. This ban was partially lifted by an amendment to the Political Parties Law, passed on 12 August 1999, which appeared to allow Erbakan to run for parliament as an independent candidate, pending the expiry of the five-year exclusion. However, it remained doubtful at the time whether he would actually be able to do so. There was also strong evidence that he continued to influence the Virtue Party from behind the scenes, and that Kutan's control over the party was weak.

22. See note 19, above.

23. Notably by Mrs Rahşan Ecevit: see the interview with her in *Milliyet* (Istanbul, daily) of 15 May 1999.

24. For further details on Turkey's involvement in the Gulf crisis, and its relations with the Iraqi Kurds and Baghdad, see below, pp. 219–23, 307–11. For fuller accounts of Turkey's Kurdish problem during the 1990s see David McDowall, *A Modern History of the Kurds* (London, I.B. Tauris, 1996), Ch. 20; Robert Olson, ed., *The Kurdish Nationalist Movement in the 1990s: Its Impact on Turkey and the Middle East* (Lexington, KY, University of Kentucky, 1996); Michael M. Gunter, *The Kurds and the Future of Turkey* (New York, NY, St Martin's Press, 1997), Ch. 3; Kemal Kirişci and Gareth Winrow, *The Kurdish Question and Turkey: An Example of Trans-state Ethnic Conflict* (London, Cass, 1997), Chs 5–6; Henri J. Barkey and Graham E. Fuller, *Turkey's Kurdish Question* (Lanham, MD, Rowman and Littlefield, 1998), Chs 3–6, and 'Turkey's Kurdish Question: Critical Turning Points and Missed Opportunities', *Middle East Journal*, Vol. 51 (1997) and Philip Robins, 'The Overlord State: Turkish Policy and the Kurdish Issue', *International Affairs*, Vol. 69 (1993).

25. See p. 222. See also Kemal Kirişci, 'Turkey and the Kurdish Safe Haven in Northern Iraq', *Journal of South Asian and Middle Eastern Studies*, Vol. 19 (1996), pp. 21–3, and Mahmut Balı Aykan, 'Turkey's Policy in Northern Iraq, 1991–95', *Middle Eastern Studies*, Vol. 32 (1996), pp. 345–6.

26. Kemal Kirişci, 'The Kurdish Question and Turkish Foreign Policy', in Lenora Martin, ed., *The Future of Turkish Foreign Policy* (forthcoming).

27. See Gunter, *The Kurds and the Future of Turkey*, pp. 75–7, and William Hale, 'Turkey', in Ami Ayalon, ed., *Middle East Contemporary Survey 1993* (Vol. 17, Boulder, CO, Westview, 1995), pp. 678–9, and p. 695, note 22.

28. See Barkey and Fuller, 'Turkey's Kurdish Question', p. 70. There was some evidence at the time that Öcalan had not ordered the Bingöl attack. See Gunter, *The Kurds and the Future of Turkey*, pp. 78–80. In his trial in June 1999, Öcalan confirmed this claim, and said that he had later issued orders for Şemdin Sakık's murder (*Milliyet*, 2 June 1999). If so, then the incident suggests at the least that he had little control over his own followers on the ground. In 1998 Sakık broke away from the PKK organisation, and took refuge in northern Iraq, where he was later apprehended by Turkish forces and placed on trial. In May 1999 he and his brother, Arıf, were convicted and sentenced to death under Article 125 of the Penal Code.

29. See Robert Olson, 'The Kurdish Question and Turkey's Foreign Policy, 1991–1995: From the Gulf War to the Incursion Into Iraq', *Journal of South Asian and Middle Eastern Studies*, Vol. 19 (1995), p. 20; Barkey and Fuller, *Turkey's Kurdish Question*, Chs 2–5; Müftüler-Baç, 'Turkey's Predicament', p. 261, and Kirişci, 'Kurdish Question'.

30. Quoted in *Milliyet*, 9 December 1991.

31. HEP had originally been formed by deputies elected on the SHP ticket in 1987 who had then been expelled from the party by Erdal İnönü in 1989. For the 1991 elections,

they re-established a temporary alliance with the SHP.

32. Henri J. Barkey, 'The People's Democracy Party (HADEP): The Travails of a Legal Kurdish Party in Turkey', *Journal of Muslim Minority Affairs*, Vol. 18 (1998), pp. 129–38; Barkey and Fuller, *Turkey's Kurdish Question*, pp. 84–9, and Gunter, *The Kurds and the Future of Turkey*, p. 73.

33. For further details on Öcalan's peregrinations between October 1998 and February 1999, see *Briefing* (Ankara, weekly), 22 February 1999, pp. 20–1.

34. *Milliyet*, 30 June 1999.

35. Reuters, 30 November, 5 December 1999 and *The Independent*, 13 December 1999.

36. Report by the Turkish General Staff, issued in March 1999: see *Briefing*, 15 March 1999, p. 17.

37. Figures from the Governor's Office of the 'Emergency Region' in the south-east, issued in 1999, cited a total of 380,000 evacuations, but admitted that the real figure was much higher than this. Meanwhile, non-governmental organisations claimed there had been a total of three million 'internal refugees'. See ibid., 21 June 1999, p. 17.

38. The Turkish 'Hizbullah' had no connection with its Lebanese namesake. Some of the unsolved murders may also have been due to internecine feuding within Hizbullah. In 1998, the authorities turned against the organisation, and began a hunt for its followers. See Poulton, 'Turkish State', pp. 59 60, and Barkey and Fuller, *Turkey's Kurdish Question*, p. 73.

39. Olson, 'Kurdish Question', pp. 23–5. The International Institute for Strategic Studies in London cites a far lower figure of US$2.2 billion for 1995, or a total of US$16.5 billion since 1984. See '1998 Chart of Armed Conflict', in *The Military Balance, 1998/99* (see note 16).

40. *Turkey Confidential* , (London, monthly: now discontinued) December 1992, p. 5.

41. Poulton, 'Turkish State', pp. 56, 58 and Heinz Kramer, 'The EU-Turkey Customs Union: Economic Integration amidst Political Turmoil', *Mediterranean Politics*, Vol. 1 (1996), p. 69.

42. Article 14 also bans Marxist political activities, but the force of this was removed in 1991 by the withdrawal of Articles 141 and 141 from the Penal Code. See above, p. 203.

43. See Poulton, 'Turkish State', pp. 57–8, from where these quotations are taken.

44. In March 1999, the Turkish Human Rights Association – anything but a government source – reported that the number of unsolved murders and people imprisoned for 'crimes of thought' had risen between 1996 and 1998. However, there had been a substantial reduction in the numbers of deaths in custody and reported cases of torture. See *Briefing*, 3 May 1999, p. 12.

45. Ibid., 24 May 1999, p. 10 and 7 June 1999, p. 4.

46. *Milliyet*, 19 June, 25 June, 13 August, 30 August 1999.

47. Ibid., 29 August, 30 August 1999. The partial amnesty did not apply to those who made supposedly 'illegal' statements at public meetings and the like, rather than publish or broadcast them in the media.

48. Ecevit himself dropped broad hints that this had been the case. See ibid., 30 August 1999.

49. The following account draws on the author's article, 'Foreign Policy and Turkey's Domestic Politics', in David Shankland, ed., *The Turkish Republic at 75 Years* (Hemingford Grey, Eothen Press, 1999).

50. See Lesser, 'Turkey's Strategic Options', p. 81.
51. Sayarı, 'Turkey, the Changing', pp. 18–20.
52. Selim Oktar, 'The Turkish Foreign Policy Environment: A Public Opinion Perspective': paper presented to a Conference on 'The Domestic Context of Turkish Foreign Policy', The Washington Institute for Near East Policy, Washington, DC, July 1997, Tables 14, 19, 20, 23. This ranking compares interestingly with surveys carried out in 1965, in which the then West Germany received the highest support among foreign countries, after the United States. See Ferenc A. Vali, _Bridge across the Bosporus: The Foreign Policy of Turkey_ (Baltimore, MD, and London, Johns Hopkins University Press, 1971), pp. 107–8.
53. There are, however, some important contrasts between the positions of different pro-Islamist newspapers on foreign policy questions. See Sencer Ayata, 'Perceptions of International Relations and Turkish Foreign Policy in the Islamist Press', paper presented to a Conference on 'The Domestic Context of Turkish Foreign Policy', The Washington Institute for Near East Policy, Washington, DC, July 1997.
54. See, e.g., Binnaz Toprak, 'Civil Society in Turkey', in Augustus R. Norton, ed., _Civil Society in the Middle East_, Vol. 2 (Leiden, Brill, 1995); Nilüfer Göle, 'Towards an Autonomization of Politics and Civil Society in Turkey', in Metin Heper and Ahmet Evin, eds, _Politics in the Third Turkish Republic_ (Boulder, CO, Westview, 1994), and Jenny B. White, 'Civic Culture and Islam in Urban Turkey', in Chris Hann and Elizabeth Dunn, eds, _Civil Society: Challenging Western Models_ (London, Routledge, 1996).
55. However, until the mid-1990s, there had been differences of views within the business community, particularly on the customs union with the EU. See Mükerrem Hiç, _Turkey's Customs Union with the European Union: Economic and Political Prospects_ (Ebenhausen, Germany, Stiftung Wissenschaft und Politik, 1995), pp. 17–19.
56. This account is based on the main parties' election manifestos for the 1995 and 1999 elections. The author is very grateful to Ayşegül Keçeciler for supplying copies of the 1995 manifestos, and to Dr Ali Çarkoğlu for obtaining those for 1999.
57. Virtue Party 1999 election manifesto, pp. 17–18.
58. DSP 1995 election manifesto, pp. 94–6.
59. DSP 1999 election manifesto, p. 19.
60. MHP 1999 election manifesto, p. 6.
61. Soli Özel, 'On Not Being a Lone Wolf: Geography, Domestic Plays, and Turkish Foreign Policy in the Middle East', in Geoffrey Kemp and Janice Gross Stein, eds, _Powder Keg in the Middle East: The Struggle for Gulf Security_ (Lanham, MD, Rowman and Littlefield, 1995), pp. 167–70. For a fuller discussion of economic issues in Turkish foreign policy, see William Hale, 'Economic Issues in Turkish Foreign Policy', in Alan Makovsky and Sabri Sayarı, eds, _Changing Dynamics in Turkish Foreign Policy_ (Washington, DC, Washington Institute for Near East Policy, 2000).
62. Data for 1990 from _EIU:CRT_, 4th Qtr 1993, p. 3. For 1998 data, see _Briefing_, 22 March 1999, p. 32.
63. _EIU:CRT_, 2nd Qtr 1999, p. 34.
64. Ibid., p. 5 and _Briefing_, 8 March 1999, p. 36.
65. _EIU:CRT_, 4th Qtr 1994, p. 3, and 2nd Qtr 1999, p. 5.
66. _Statistical Yearbook of Turkey 1990_ (Ankara, State Institute of Statistics, 1991), pp. 492–3.
67. _Briefing_, 8 March 1999, p. 36, 22 March 1999, p. 32.
68. _Statistical Yearbook of Turkey 1998_ (Ankara, State Institute of Statistics, 1999), pp. 450–1.

Strictly speaking, this includes visitors other than tourists, such as students, business-men and other foreigners working in Turkey. However, this discrepancy does not seem important for present purposes. Figures for the number of entrants also ignore the fact that visitors from some countries may spend more per head than others, but there appears to be no way of investigating this precisely.

69. *Briefing*, 14 June 1999, p. 30, 19 July 1999, p. 33.
70. In August 1999, the Ecevit government took an important step forward, when the con-stitution was altered to allow for international arbitration of disputes with foreign firms involving public service contracts, and widening the scope of privatisation. This was expected to be an important requirement for the expected negotiation of a new stand-by agreement with the IMF. See ibid., 16 August 1999, pp. 10–13.
71. Ibid., 8 March 1999, p. 38.
72. *Statistical Yearbook of Turkey 1998*, pp. 325, 363. In 1998, total estimated energy con-sumption increased to 82 billion tons oil equivalent, of which 47 billion tons was imported, but a breakdown of this total by different fuels was not available. See *Briefing*, 15 February 1999, p. 25.
73. *EIU:CRT*, 1st Qtr 1997, p. 27; *Briefing*, 26 July 1999, p. 22.

7

Turkey and the West after the Cold War

During the 1970s and 1980s, with the emergence of what was to become the European Union (EU) in 1993, it became possible to distinguish Turkey's relations with the United States from those with the other Western powers. This trend continued during the 1990s. While there were important nuances distinguishing the policies of the western European countries from one another,[1] Turkey's relations with these countries were dominated by its relationship with the EU, which became distinctly uneasy. On the other hand, the overall strengthening of relations between Ankara and Washington continued during the 1990s. The importance of the relationship, especially as seen from the US side, was increased by Turkey's role in the Gulf crisis of 1990–91 and its aftermath, although the results also created new problems for Turkish governments, and some conflicts with the United States. A new entente developed between Turkey and Israel, which reinforced Turkey's alliance with the United States. However, Turkey's position in NATO also became complicated by plans for a 'new European security architecture', in which the EU countries sought to develop independent (or at least semi-independent) defence structures, and in which Turkey's prospective role was uncertain. Finally, its relationship with the EU generally became very problematic, as the EU countries began to address the question of whether they could accept Turkey as part of their enlargement process.

TURKEY AND THE UNITED STATES AFTER THE COLD WAR

In 1992, when Turkey's Defence and Economic Cooperation Agreement (DECA) with the United States came up for renewal, it was extended for only one year. Turkey then asked for a renegotiation of its terms, but in practice the agreement was renewed automatically on an annual basis.

Meanwhile, the US military presence in Turkey, with which the DECA was mainly concerned, was drastically reduced. This was part of the Unites States' global policy of reducing its military commitments world-wide, now that the Cold War was over. By the middle of 1994, eight of the twelve US military bases previously established in Turkey had been closed, or handed over to the Turkish forces. The previous tension over the presence of these bases, which had emerged in the 1960s, was correspondingly reduced, although the vital NATO airbase at İncirlik, near Adana, continued in operation, and was to be of crucial importance during the Gulf war of 1991 and its aftermath. US military aid to Turkey was also scaled down substantially – partly because of congressional opposition over human rights and other issues, but partly also because there seemed to be less need for it; it was discontinued altogether in 1999.[2]

For most of the 1990s, the alliance between Turkey and the United States seemed firm because in many policy areas the two countries had common interests and common approaches. Both supported the admission of new eastern European members to NATO, achieved in the cases of Poland, Hungary and the Czech Republic in 1999,[3] and that of the states of the former Soviet Union to the Organisation for Security and Cooperation in Europe (OSCE), NATO's Partnership for Peace programme, and the North Atlantic Cooperation Council. In the early 1990s, the United States helped to sponsor the idea that Turkey could be projected as a model of democracy and the liberal economic system in the newly independent states of central Asia, but enthusiasm for this project then seems to have dropped off markedly. Although there were some differences between Turkey and the United States in their approaches to Russia, the US government strongly supported the plan to build an 'East–West energy corridor', linking the states of the Caspian basin to world markets via Turkey, and avoiding Russian territory (see pp. 275–7).[4] Turkey also played an active role in supporting actions by the UN, and then by the United States and the rest of NATO, in Bosnia-Herzegovina, beginning in 1993–94. It appears that initially the Turkish foreign ministry may have been unenthusiastic about plans for a bombing campaign against the Serbs, following the eruption of the Kosovo crisis in 1998–99, but once the campaign began, Turkey gave it its full and active support – a policy in which the Turkish government was strongly supported by public opinion at home (see pp. 260–5).

For both sides, the Gulf crisis of 1990–91 was a critical turning-point, since it gave Turkey an important actual and potential role in US policy in the Middle East, which had been in abeyance since the collapse of the

Baghdad Pact. Hence, it seems worthwhile to give a summary of this part of the story at this point.[5] Immediately after the Iraqi invasion of Kuwait on 2 August 1990, it seemed that Turkey would try to adhere to its previous policy of remaining strictly aloof from Middle Eastern conflicts, [6] but events quickly showed that it would be quite impossible to reconcile this with the need to maintain its relationship with the United States, the UN, and the Western powers generally. Saddam Hussein's refusal to evacuate Kuwait, and the imposition of an economic embargo on Iraq by the United Nations under Security Council Resolution 661 of 6 August 1990, meant that the government was rapidly obliged to change course. Accordingly, on 8 August it was announced that Turkey would suspend all commercial dealings with Iraq, and close the oil pipeline from Kirkuk to Yumurtalık, which carried about half of Iraq's oil exports. After this, and as a war in the Gulf seemed ever more likely, the government was faced with three crucial questions: first, whether it would send troops to join the coalition forces in the Gulf; second, whether it would open a second front against Iraq along the Iraqi–Turkish border, if war broke out; third, whether it would allow the coalition powers (principally the United States) to use İncirlik for attacks on targets in northern Iraq, given that this was not strictly within the base's NATO functions.

It appears that, left to himself, Turgut Özal would have given a positive reply to all three questions.[7] Constitutionally, the president's policy-making powers were limited, but Özal enjoyed the potential advantage that the Motherland Party had a large majority in parliament, and that the prime minister, Yıldırım Akbulut, was a weak figurehead, who effectively acted as his proxy. With his regular contacts with world leaders, Özal apparently tried to act single-handedly in directing Turkish policy during the crisis. However, he had to face the fact that Turkish public opinion was distinctly unenthusiastic about the prospect of direct Turkish involvement in a war in the Gulf, in which no clear national interests seemed to be at stake.[8] This was reflected in parliament, where the opposition, consisting of Süleyman Demirel's DYP and the SHP led by Erdal İnönü, opposed Özal's activist policy. More crucially, an important segment of the Motherland Party, led by Akbulut's former foreign minister, Mesut Yılmaz, effectively supported the opposition line.[9]

The strength of the opposition was important to Özal since, under Article 92 of the constitution, parliament would have to pass a special resolution authorising the declaration of a state of war, the despatch of Turkish troops abroad, or the reception of foreign troops on Turkish soil.[10] If parliament were not in session, then the president could 'decide on the use of the Turkish Armed Forces' by himself, but only if Turkey were subjected to 'sudden armed aggression' by another state. On 12 August 1990 Akbulut asked a hastily reconvened parliament for these powers, but the strength of the opposition within his own party forced the government to add the rider that it could only exercise them if Turkey were attacked. In effect, this left the government with no more powers than the president would have had anyway during the summer recess. After parliament reconvened for its autumn session, on 5 September, Akbulut repeated the request for powers to send Turkish troops abroad or receive foreign forces in Turkey. This was accepted, although parliament refused the government permission to declare war (this was probably a pointless restriction, since most modern wars have been undeclared). However, by this stage, the opposition to direct involvement by Turkish forces in the looming Gulf war was clear enough. It was underlined by the successive resignations of first, the foreign minister Ali Bozer, on 12 October, then of the defence minister Safa Giray on 18 October, and finally of the Chief of the General Staff, General Necip Torumtay, on 3 December 1990, although it is not clear in all these cases whether the resignations were directly attributable to Özal's policy in the Gulf crisis.[11] It was only at the last minute, on 17 January 1991, as the air war in the Gulf was beginning, that parliament renewed its war powers vote to the government, and made it clear that this would include permission for the coalition air forces to use İncirlik and other bases in Turkey for attacks on Iraq.[12]

Meanwhile, Turkey had also been concerned to secure an assurance from NATO that if it were attacked by Iraq, then the other NATO powers would come to its assistance. This was confirmed, in principle, at a NATO meeting held on 12 August 1990, and on 2 January 1991 it was announced that Germany, Italy and Belgium would be sending 40 aircraft to Turkey. However, most of the aircraft which were sent were obsolete machines, suggesting that the reaction of Turkey's European allies, apart from Britain and France, was only half-hearted, thus causing Turgut Özal to launch sharp verbal attacks on the Germans in particular, as unreliable allies.[13] Whether this additional NATO presence made much practical difference is doubtful, since far more powerful US, British and French air detachments were in any case stationed at İncirlik, and would almost certainly have been used to help defend Turkey if Saddam had attacked its territory. The US also sent a detachment of Patriot missiles to İncirlik, to improve the Turks' quite inadequate anti-missile defences.

As the war against Iraq raged during January–February 1991, coalition aircraft made regular sorties from İncirlik and were of substantial value to the allies in attacking Iraqi targets in the north of the country. Prior to the outbreak of the fighting, Turkish forces along the border with Iraq had also been built up to around 120,000 men, with air support and armour, to oppose an Iraqi ground attack, although the Turkish General Staff apparently judged that this was unlikely.[14] These reinforcements pinned down about eight Iraqi divisions in the north of the country, which could otherwise have been used against the coalition forces in the south. Although Turgut Özal had apparently urged that if Iraq broke up then Turkish forces should intervene in northern Iraq so as to seize the province of Mosul with the Kirkuk oilfield, this idea was dropped, and was opposed by the Turkish generals, on political as well as military grounds.[15] Turkey thus came through the conflict without having fired a shot in anger, and having rendered positive assistance to the allied cause.

Naturally enough, Turgut Özal was not inclined to underrate this contribution, and claimed in a television broadcast on 2 March 1991 that 'our country has passed a test with flying colours and has proved to the world at large that it is a country that can be trusted'.[16] Soon afterwards, however, events took a grave turn for the worse, as Saddam Hussein brutally suppressed the rebellion by the Kurds of north-eastern Iraq, and around 500,000 destitute refugees fled to the border with Turkey, with even larger numbers fleeing across the Iraqi–Iranian frontier. Their presence faced the Turks with an unexpected dilemma. On the one hand, they could hardly deny any assistance to the refugees in their desperate plight, which was shown nightly on the world's television screens. On the other hand, they were most reluctant to allow them to settle in Turkish territory (as they had in the case of the earlier refugees of 1988) since this would have faced the Turkish authorities with the possibility of having to look after a very large number of refugees for an indefinite period, and would have severely exacerbated Turkey's domestic Kurdish problem. On 7 April, Özal proposed a way out by suggesting that the UN should take control of territory in northern Iraq, so that the refugees could return to a 'safe haven'. This idea was then adopted by the British and US governments. Under UN Security Council Resolution 688 of 5 April 1991 an international force of around 20,000 troops was stationed at Silopi, near the border with Iraq, to support the operation. Virtually all the refugees had returned to Iraq by the end of May, as part of what was called 'Operation Provide Comfort'. The Silopi ground force was withdrawn in September 1991, but thereafter Saddam's forces were kept out of the 'safe haven' by a special detachment of US, British and French aircraft based at İncirlik, which enforced a no-fly zone in Iraq north of the 36th parallel.[17]

This left Western policy quite heavily dependent on Turkish cooperation and consent, since the mandate for 'Operation Provide Comfort' (in particular, permission to use the İncirlik base for a non-NATO operation) had to be regularly renewed by the Turkish parliament, normally at six-month intervals.[18]

For Turgut Özal, the primary reason for supporting the coalition in the Gulf war was that it would re-establish Turkey's strategic importance in the eyes of the Western powers, especially the United States: its effects on Turkey's relations with the Middle East was secondary to this. Hence, he seized the opportunity to demonstrate to the Western governments that the alliance with Turkey would still be essential, even though the Soviet threat had ended. In effect, he wished to reinvent Turkey's value to the West. So far as the United States was concerned, he was largely successful, since the success of 'Operation Provide Comfort' depended on Turkish support. Turkey's possible role in opposing Islamic radicalism, sponsored by Iran, and supporting Western interests in central Asia, were additional diplomatic cards which Özal could play. However, his expectation that Turkey's contribution to the defeat of Saddam Hussein would induce the western European countries to react more favourably to Turkey's application for admission to the EU proved too optimistic. The question of Turkish accession to the EU raised a host of problems which were still unsolved, and the leaders of most of the western European states (Germany, in particular) did not seem to have put Middle Eastern security at the top of their foreign policy agendas.[19] Özal had also hoped that the war would result in the fall of Saddam Hussein, and his replacement with a democratic regime in Iraq which could work out a settlement with the Kurds, restore Baghdad's control in the north of the country, and thus prevent the PKK from using it as a base for its attacks in Turkey. In fact, after the Iraqis had been ejected from Kuwait, he had apparently urged President Bush to order an advance to Baghdad, and then tried to persuade him to support the Kurdish rebellion in Iraq, hoping that this would bring about Saddam Hussein's overthrow.[20] Here also, Özal's hopes proved unfounded. In spite of economic sanctions, which were themselves costly for Turkey, Saddam Hussein retained his grip over most of the country. There was no internal settlement with the Kurds, and Western policy effectively left a power vacuum in north-eastern Iraq, which strengthened rather than weakened the PKK.

Quite frequently, it is argued that Özal's policy during the crisis marked an important turning-point, in which Turkey abandoned its non-interventionist policies in the Middle East, in favour of acting as a regional power for the first time since the demise of the Baghdad Pact.[21] Certainly, Özal himself encouraged this idea, stating that 'my conviction is that Turkey should leave its former passive and hesitant policies and engage in an active foreign policy. The reason I made this call is because we are a powerful country in the region.'[22] In pursuit of this idea, he had apparently hoped that after the war long-term security in the Gulf could be regionalised, by means of military and economic cooperation between the Gulf states themselves, plus Turkey. Unfortunately, the regional states proved too divided or weak to assume this function, which was effectively taken on by the Western powers, principally the United States, without Turkish participation.[23]

Against this, it is suggested that in practice Turkish policies during the crisis did not really deviate from previous approaches, which essentially rested on preserving friendly relations with the Middle Eastern states while still paying due attention to Turkey's membership of the Western alliance. Nor is the idea that Turkish policy was a 'one-man show' by Özal born out by the record, since two important parts of his agenda – Turkish participation in the land force in the Gulf, and a 'second front' against Iraq – remained unrealised.[24] In fact, Turkish policy was a compromise between Özal's ambitions, and stiff domestic opposition from the public, parliament and the army. The trade embargo against Iraq, and the closure of the Kirkuk–Yumurtalık pipeline, was admittedly an important step for Turkey, which had hitherto managed to maintain economic ties with all the Middle Eastern states. Nevertheless, these actions were virtually inevitable. Turkey could not have flouted a clear resolution of the UN Security Council without doing very serious damage to its relations with both the UN and the Western powers generally. Similarly, denying the coalition forces the use of İncirlik for operations against Iraq would have fatally undermined Özal's claim that Turkey was still a valuable ally for the West in the post-Cold War era. Probably, the most important policy shift was the promotion of the 'safe haven' plan in Iraq, since this involved Turkish engagement with the Iraqi Kurds, which Ankara had previously avoided, and implied that there might be an unofficial partition of Iraq. However, it has to be seen as an *ad hoc* arrangement to deal with an unexpected emergency, rather than part of a pre-planned strategy.

Whatever assessments of Özal's diplomacy are made, it clearly had a lasting effect on relations between Turkey and the United States, since 'Operation Provide Comfort' created an important incentive for Washington to maintain good relations with the Turks, as well as new points of conflict between the two countries. The economic cost to Turkey of maintaining trade sanctions against Iraq was also a serious one, since Iraq had previously been one of Turkey's most important trading partners, and its lost trade and other earnings probably cost the Turkish economy around US$2 billion per year.[25] In 1991, this was compensated for by special payments of around US$2.2 billion, mainly from Kuwait and Saudi Arabia. This fell back to around US$900 million in 1992, and then tailed off altogether.[26] Not surprisingly, Turkey pressed for the lifting of the sanctions, provided Saddam Hussein adhered to the UN's conditions.

More critically, the question of continuing the mandate for 'Operation Provide Comfort' turned out to be a contentious one in Turkey. Although Özal had originally proposed it, Turkish suspicions about the objective of the operation came to the surface, especially after Süleyman Demirel returned to power in November 1991. Essentially, these rested on the fear that the special force might be used by the United States for other operations in the Middle East, over which Turkey had no control, or that it was part of a Western project to promote the establishment on an independent Kurdish state, with serious implications for the future of Turkey's own Kurdish problem. At worst, this developed into what has been called the 'Sèvres syndrome' – that is, the suspicion that the Western powers were bent on dismantling Turkey territorially, just as they had tried to do in the abortive treaty of Sèvres of 1920 (see p. 45–6). After he assumed the presidency following Özal's death in April 1993, Demirel himself referred to the Sèvres treaty, arguing that Turkey could never win the support of the West, however hard it tried to democratise its internal political system.[27] This complaint may have been voiced partly as an excuse not to implement the needed improvements in Turkey's human rights regime, but it also struck a sympathetic chord among nationalist opinion at home.

On the other side of the argument, the reasons for continuing 'Operation Provide Comfort' were clear enough. These rested on the fact that Turkey could not afford to provoke an open conflict with the United States over an important part of US policy in the Middle East, and that so long as the 'Operation Provide Comfort' force was based in Turkey, the Turks retained at least some leverage over how it was used. Apart from this, its withdrawal might have tempted Saddam Hussein into launching another assault on the Iraqi Kurds, causing a repetition of the refugee crisis of 1991 which had been the original reason for launching the operation. The increased protection which it would give to Turkey if Saddam Hussein were to launch a military attack against it was also obvious. On these grounds, the Turkish military chiefs, who continued to maintain close relations with their US counterparts, were strongly in favour of continuing 'Operation Provide Comfort'. The Turkish foreign ministry supported this line on the grounds that the continued instability in northern Iraq necessitated the extension of the mandate. Hence, there was a consensus among those in power that the benefits of regularly renewing the mandate outweighed the potential costs. While in opposition, both Süleyman Demirel and Erdal İnönü had opposed the operation, but once in power after 1991 they accepted it, as did both Tansu Çiller and Bülent Ecevit, during their respective premierships.[28]

'Operation Provide Comfort', and US–Turkish relations generally, were put to their severest test during the period of the Erbakan–Çiller government of 1996–97. In 1994, Necmettin Erbakan had strongly attacked the mandate for 'Operation Provide Comfort', describing it as a 'Second Sèvres', and claiming that it was a sinister Western plot to divide the Muslim countries. Once in power, however, he evidently came under pressure to reverse his stance, both from the military, and from his coalition partner and foreign minister, Tansu Çiller, on whom he relied to maintain his government's majority in parliament. Hence, in July 1996, the government agreed to renew the mandate for the operation until the end of the year. When the issue came up again in December 1996, the mandate was again renewed, although the government managed to extract some cosmetic changes, and the name of the operation was changed to 'Northern Watch' as from the beginning of 1997.[29] At the same time, other aspects of Erbakan's foreign policy – most notably, his ill-judged attempts to cultivate relations with Libya and Iran, two of United States' most prominent *bêtes noires* in the Middle East – severely irritated US opinion, and caused serious headaches for US policy-makers (see pp. 298–9). As Morton Ambramowitz, a former US ambassador in Ankara, put it in August 1996: 'How do you deal with a NATO ally led by a man who is fundamentally anti-NATO, fundamentally anti-Semitic and fundamentally pro-Islamist, even when he's largely behaving himself?'[30]

After the Erbakan–Çiller government was ousted from power in June 1997, Turkish–US relations returned to a more normal state, but essential problems remained. Of these, the position and status of what was in effect a separate Kurdish political entity in Iraq was probably the most important. In 1992, after the failure of negotiations between Saddam Hussein's government and the two main Kurdish groups in Iraq – the KDP led by Masud Barzani, and Jelal Talabani's PUK – elections were held for a regional parliament, and the two leaders agreed to share power in a 'federated state'. This prospect was strongly opposed by Turkey, which was anxious to prevent the foundation of anything which might be presented as the nucleus of an independent Kurdistan. Nevertheless, Ankara also developed a dialogue with the Iraqi Kurdish leadership, which is discussed later (pp. 307–10).

Meanwhile, US policies towards the Iraqi Kurds continued to have an important effect on Turkish–US relations. In 1994–96, as the entente between Barzani and Talabani broke down into civil war, international support for Kurdish independence waned, leaving the Turks with a less difficult task.[31] In August–September 1995, US officials succeeded in bringing representatives of the two warring Kurdish factions together for peace talks in Dublin. These failed to produce a settlement, but the outcome was not unsatisfactory for Turkey, since it was able to send observers to the talks, and have its concerns publicly noted. At the same time, the US turned a blind eye towards repeated military incursions by Turkey into northern Iraq. In August 1996, the civil war between the Iraqi Kurdish leaders and their followers was resumed, with Masud Barzani even forming a brief alliance with Saddam Hussein against his rival.[32] Eventually, the US returned to the task of trying to construct a settlement in September 1998, as part of the Clinton administration's attempt to build a united Iraqi opposition against Saddam Hussein. In talks in Washington, the two Kurdish factions accepted an agreement aiming to revive the 1992 accord, but this encountered immediate objections from Turkey. As a result, Barzani and Talabani were brought together for a second round of talks in Ankara, in which the two Kurdish leaders agreed that Turkey could continue military operations in northern Iraq against the PKK, while the Turks were given assurances that references to a 'federation' in the Washington agreement could not be construed as undermining Iraq's territorial integrity.[33]

Turkey and the United States thus seemed to have reached an accommodation on this issue, in which Washington recognised Turkey's interests, while the Turks recognised that, through their role in maintaining 'Operation Northern Watch' they could exercise some influence over US policy. This sense of Turkish–US accord on the Kurdish issue was further enhanced by the important help which the US Central Intelligence Agency (CIA) and State Department apparently gave to Turkey in the capture of Abdullah Öcalan in February 1999.[34] A few months later, in August 1999, the prompt and generous assistance given by both the US government and public to aid the victims of the İzmit earthquake disaster was widely appreciated in Turkey, suggesting that the Turkish–US relationship was not just a government-to-government one, but was bringing the two peoples together as well.[35] The sense of accord was strengthened in the last months of 1999, as the United States strongly encouraged western European leaders to admit Turkey to the EU. When President Clinton visited Turkey in November for the Istanbul summit of the OSCE, he arrived three days early, so as to allow for talks with Prime Minister Ecevit and human rights and other non-governmental organisations, besides addressing the Turkish parliament (the only foreign head of state to have done so, unless Rauf Denktash is counted as such). With his wife and daughter, President Clinton visited the earthquake survivors in their tents, showing striking informality and sympathy, which was starkly contrasted with the usually dour and aloof demeanour of most of Turkey's own politicians.[36] Thus, by the end of the decade, the Turkish–US relationship seemed to have returned to a degree of warmth and popular support which it had not known since the 1950s.

Naturally, this strengthening of Turkish–US ties did not mean that Turkey was regarded as above criticism in the United States. However, the nature of the argument seems to have changed, as traditional ethnic lobby politics were replaced by a wider concern in Congress over such issues as human rights and the Kurdish problem. At the beginning of 1990, Senator Robert Dole proposed a motion seeking to designate 24 April as 'a national day of remembrance of the Armenian genocide of 1915–23',[37] but this was defeated in the Senate, and thereafter the issue seems to have dropped into the background. However, when the aid bill to Turkey for fiscal 1995 was discussed in Congress in July 1994, a provision was added suspending 10 per cent of the total, subject to Turkey making progress on human rights and the Cyprus problem. Since President Clinton signed the bill in this form, it was clear that the administration accepted this condition. Later, congressional opposition forced Turkey to abandon plans to acquire US attack helicopters, while the delivery of warships which Turkey had paid for was held up. The fact that US military aid to Turkey ceased anyway in 1999 removed a point of discord.[38] The change in the relationship was illustrated by an incident on 24 April 1999, when President Clinton sent a message of support to the US Armenian community, mentioning such words as 'genocide'. Instead of the strong reaction which might earlier have been expected in Turkey, the foreign ministry merely responded by saying that this 'was only a message for internal consumption, and therefore not to be taken seriously'.[39] Overall, maturity and level-headedness now seemed to be the keynotes on both sides.

TURKEY, NATO AND EUROPEAN SECURITY

Alongside its bilateral links with the United States, Turkey's membership of NATO continued to be a vital part of its links with the West, since this was the most important Western institution of which it was a full member, and in which it enjoyed clear treaty rights. Occasionally, Turks voiced doubts about whether NATO would honour its security commitments to Turkey, now that the Soviet Union had ceased to exist. As an example, in 1996, Şükrü Elekdağ suggested that 'Turkey benefiting from NATO's collective defence should not be counted on any more. From now on Turkey has to fight against any threat directed to her survival and security solely by her own national means'.[40] This suggestion may well have been encouraged by the lukewarm reaction of several European NATO members to Turkey's call for defensive assistance during the Gulf war of 1991, but it does not seem to have been a universal one. For the most part, Turkish commentators continued to emphasise the importance of NATO for Turkey, and vice versa. The same point was confirmed on the NATO side: as Javier Solana, then NATO's Secretary-General, put it in 1996, 'in a world of rapid change, Turkey's partnership in the Alliance is more vital than ever'.[41]

During the 1990s, the main shadow over Turkey's position in the Western alliance arose from plans by the EU to build its own security structures which would, at least to some extent, be independent of both NATO and the United States. The danger for Turkey was that since it was not a member of the EU, it might be shut out of the new European security structures, or at least left in a 'half-in, half-out' situation, as it was within the EU itself. Unfortunately, there was little discussion of this issue in the press or parliament, and the debate was effectively confined to a small circle of professionals. However, it was of great potential importance for Turkey's relationship with the Western powers.

Under the Maastricht treaty of 1991, the EU countries undertook to develop their 'defence vocation', as 'an integral part of the development of the Union'.[42] The vehicle for this was to be the Western European Union (WEU), a body which had been virtually moribund since its foundation in 1954. The WEU's role would be to 'strengthen the European pillar of the Atlantic Alliance and to formulate a common European defence policy'.[43] Within this, France and Germany proposed the creation of a 'European Security and Defence Identity' (ESDI) to be developed outside NATO.[44] In 1962, Turkey, along with Norway and Iceland, became associate members of the WEU, since the three countries were members of NATO, but not of the EU.[45] Turkey's main complaint about this arrangement was that, although it participated in all the military activities of the WEU, and had a seat (though no veto powers) in the WEU Council, it was excluded from EU decisions which had a direct bearing on the WEU's activities.[46] As Kamran İnan, a former foreign minister who was then on the opposition benches, asked in June 1996: 'Why should Turkey contribute to the defence of Europe if there is no guarantee that the WEU would contribute to the defence of Turkey?'[47] Admittedly, critical defence issues were still settled by the NATO Council, in which Turkey fully participated, so that in practice the WEU was not much more than a talking shop. Nonetheless, the idea that they might be excluded from future defence structures under the EU aegis was profoundly disquieting for the Turks. More broadly, it is also likely that the main cause for Turkish resentment was psychological – that is to say that, as in the case of the EU, the west Europeans were treating the Turks as no more than distant relatives, allowed into the European garden, but not into the house. A simple way out of this problem, suggested by Stephen Larrabee,[48] would have been to give Turkey full membership of the WEU, but not of the EU, at least for the interim. However, the existing EU members tended to oppose this on the grounds that it would make it impossible to integrate the WEU (or its successor organisation) into the EU, which was seen as an ultimate, though not undisputed, aim.

In response to the Turkish complaints, it has been argued that in practice 'Turkey's associate membership of the WEU is no different in operational terms from full membership'.[49] Turkish officers participated fully in the military planning of the WEU, Turkish diplomats attended the bi-weekly meetings of the ambassadors of all the WEU states and associates, and its parliamentarians participated in the WEU Assembly, meeting twice a year.[50] The relationship between NATO and the WEU (and hence Turkey's position) was also a complicated one. At a NATO Council meeting in Berlin in June 1996, the alliance adopted the concept of Combined Joint Task Forces, as multi-national formations, under which forces assigned to NATO could be used for operations led jointly or entirely by the WEU. The Berlin meeting also decided that the ESDI concept would be developed within NATO, not outside it. A WEU Ministerial Declaration issued in Erfurt in November 1997, made it clear that 'Turkey would have the right to a full role of participation and decision-making in any WEU-led operation using NATO assets and capabilities' (including multi-national formations), whether or not it included these formations.[51] However, this was accompanied by a declaration by Tansu Çiller, then

Turkey's foreign minister, that Turkey might veto the use of NATO assets in such operations.[52]

In general terms, the idea that a 'European pillar' could eventually replace NATO, or operate without it, was also disputed. In 1991 Manfred Wörner, then the Secretary-General of NATO, suggested that 'we must be realistic and realise that neither the emerging European Political Union nor the WEU will have for the foreseeable future an operational defence capability able to be deployed without US/NATO assistance'.[53] This prediction turned out to be justified by experiences in the former Yugoslavia during the 1990s, as the EU members signally failed to develop an effective common foreign policy, and military interventions were conducted under the auspices of the UN or NATO, not the WEU. The point was made with particular force during the bombing campaign against the Serbs of 1999, which was conspicuously dependent on US air power. As Heinz Kramer has pointed out, most of the NATO asscts which could be made available for WEU-led operations are in fact US asscts, making the WEU's ability to act on its own very limited.[54]

Nevertheless, by the late 1990s, leaders of the EU states seemed to be determined to proceed with the development of the ESDI concept. At their meeting in St Malo in December 1998, the British and French prime ministers called on the EU 'to develop the capacity for autonomous action and the means to effect this', though they also made it clear that one objective of this was to 'enhance the vitality of NATO'.[55] They also agreed that the WEU would eventually be absorbed into the EU.[56] This challenge was taken up at the NATO conference held in Washington on 23–24 April 1999, the alliance's fiftieth anniversary. A critical question was whether, in the resultant declaration on the ESDI project, the WEU would be allowed to use NATO assets and capabilities automatically. If so, then, as the Turkish side argued, Turkey would be excluded from decisions on the use of such assets. In Washington, President Demirel claimed that this 'would be tantamount to pushing Turkey out of all European decision-making bodies and asking us to become soldiers to die for a decision that we have been allowed to make no contribution in reaching'.[57] Fortunately for the Turks, the United States came round to accepting this view. Accordingly, Article 30 of the final declaration on 'The Alliance's Strategic Concept' confirmed that decisions to allow the WEU to use NATO assets would only be made 'on a case by case basis and by consensus'.[58]

In spite of the Washington declaration, the prospect remained that the EU would try to press ahead with establishing its own defence institutions, and that the WEU would be dissolved or be absorbed into new structures

established by the EU: in fact, at the meeting of the European Council in
Cologne in June 1999, the EU leaders agreed that all the necessary
decisions to achieve this would be taken by the end of the year 2000. Later,
at the European Council meeting in Helsinki in December 1999, they
adopted a plan to set up a rapid reaction force of up to 60,000 soldiers
to conduct EU-led military operations. If this occurred, Turkey could
apparently be locked out of the new structure, unless or until it was
accepted into the EU as a full member.[59] This approach could be strongly
criticised, since Turkey's geographical situation, between the Balkans, the
Middle East and Transcaucasia, placed it at the heart of the zone where
challenges to European security were most likely to arise. As Gülnur Aybet
concludes, 'a European security architecture cannot be envisaged without
Turkey'.[60] In December 1998 the British foreign secretary, Robin Cook,
appeared to have conceded this point when he told the North Atlantic
Council that 'as we take this project forward, we do not just seek the
tolerance of colleagues who are not members of the European Union; we
want their enthusiastic support for the enterprise in which we are engaged
and also their participation wherever it is appropriate'.[61] The Turks
seemed quite entitled to reply that in that case, they should be granted
full participation in decision making within the new security structures,
irrespective of whether Turkey could or eventually would be admitted as a
full member of the EU.

While this debate over future arrangements for European security was
not the only one which affected Turkey's relationship with NATO during
the 1990s, it was certainly the most important. Among other issues, the
application of the CFE treaty limiting conventional forces in Europe,
signed in 1990, had some important effects for Turkey. One of these was
that, after the dissolution of the Soviet Union, the successor states took
over the limitations on conventional weapons which the treaty had stipulated. However, during 1993, Russia applied for a relaxation of these
limitations, on the grounds that it needed to deploy increased military
forces in the Caucasus for 'peace-keeping operations'. This proposal was
strongly opposed by Turkey, and by the rest of NATO, although there was
subsequent evidence that Armenia and Azerbaijan, as well as Russia, were
all exceeding the CFE limits. Meanwhile, Turkey was able to keep a broad
swathe of territory along its borders with Syria, Iraq and Iran outside the
zone of application of the treaty.[62] Eventually, at the OSCE summit in
Istanbul in November 1999, the CFE treaty was revised, so as to provide
for national ceilings in five categories of conventional weapons, with sub-
limits on separate flanks. However, since Russia was still violating these

ceilings in the Caucasus, through its campaign in Chechnya, the Western signatories, including Turkey, agreed not to submit the revised treaty to their national legislatures until Russia fulfilled its part of the bargain.[63]

Elsewhere, the CFE treaty had a paradoxical effect on the conventional arms holdings of Greece and Turkey, since it stipulated ceilings which in several cases were higher than their actual inventories at the time the treaty was signed. Moreover, it did not prevent qualitative improvements, providing the numerical ceilings were adhered to (for instance, the replacement of obsolete aircraft by modern machines). In a process known as 'cascading', other NATO members were able to transfer modern hardware which was disallowed by the treaty in the central European front to Greece and Turkey. As a result, Turkey received over 1,000 modern tanks and 600 armoured cars from Germany and other NATO countries, and ended up with a modernised arsenal 25 per cent bigger than when it had started the CFE process. In effect, both as a result of 'cascading', and of separate purchases of new equipment by Greece and Turkey, disarmament in central Europe had led to re-armament in the Aegean, and there seemed to be a good case for promoting a separate arms limitation treaty covering the two NATO countries.[64]

TURKEY AND THE EUROPEAN UNION

Looking at the trend in Turkey's foreign relations since the end of the Cold War and the beginning of 1999, John Roper suggests that 'everything that has happened ... has widened the gap between Western Europe and Turkey'.[65] Although the transformation of the international scene admittedly increased Turkey's regional security concerns, in which the western European countries did not always have a direct interest, it seems safer to say that Turkey's relationship with the EU actually followed a fluctuating and uncertain course during the 1990s. Between 1990 and 1995, the two sides seemed to be moving closer together, as the Turks recovered from the rebuff they had suffered from the rejection of their membership application of 1987, and work went ahead to implement the plan for a customs union, which was brought into effect at the beginning of 1996. After this, the trend went into reverse. On the one side, the EU governments decided that Turkey would not be included in the enlargement process which was expected to bring the eastern European states into the EU, and voices were raised to the effect that Turkey could never be admitted to the EU for 'cultural' (read religious or maybe racial) reasons. Bodies such as the European Parliament and the Council of Europe also raised legitimate concerns about human rights abuses in Turkey, putting Turkey's domestic political system firmly on the foreign policy agenda.

Potential economic problems arising from any Turkish accession were also a source of worry for the EU states throughout the period, though they did not always come to the forefront of European debates. To summarise, there was a widespread expectation that if Turkey became a full member, it would create a heavy drain on the EU budget, and that free movement of labour would create serious problems for the receiving countries. The first concern is based on the fact that Turkey is a substantial agricultural producer, and could make serious demands on EU funds under the present Common Agricultural Policy (CAP) as well as on its regional and social funds. On the other hand, Turkey's contributions to the budget would be relatively small, leaving it as a large net beneficiary. Various estimates of the probable size of this burden have been made, but the actual amount would obviously depend on the rules applied by the EU at the time of accession. On the second score, Germany, in particular, was perturbed by the prospect that free movement of labour would aggravate existing social tensions and economic problems in the country, and this probably accounted for much of the popular resistance to the idea in German society.

On the Turkish side, the installation of the government led by Necmettin Erbakan in 1996–97 also led to question marks over the depth of Turkey's 'European vocation', making it easier for the reluctant Europeans to shunt the Turkish ambition into a siding. During 1998, Turkish–EU relations were stuck in the doldrums, but they then seemed to be recovering after the installation of the Ecevit administration in 1999, which appeared to be ready to implement at least some of the domestic reforms which the western Europeans were demanding. For their part, the main EU members swung back to the view that they could not leave Turkey out in the cold indefinitely. More unexpectedly, the generous response of the EU countries (among many others) to the earthquake disaster of August 1999 appeared to herald a dramatic improvement in the psychological atmosphere on both sides. The change of heart in western Europe – which was strongly encouraged by the United States – eventually bore fruit in December 1999, when Turkey was finally ranked as a candidate for accession.

After their measured rebuff to Turkey's application for full membership (see pp. 178–9) the European Commission attempted to sugar the pill in June 1990 by issuing what was unofficially known as the 'Turkey package' – or the 'Matutes package' – of policy initiatives.[66] This proposed that there should be a renewed effort to achieve a customs union between Turkey and the EC, as foreseen in the original Association Agreement of 1963, enhance cooperation in the industrial and other fields, and to release the funds provided for in the Fourth Financial Protocol of 1981 (see pp. 177–8). The last step was blocked by Greece, which continued its veto on activating the Protocol, although other parts of this project were taken up. At their meeting in Lisbon in June 1992, the EC heads of state and government agreed that 'the Turkish role in the present European political situation is of the greatest importance', and called for the further development of relations with Turkey in line with the plan envisaged in the Association Agreement.[67] In November of the same year, the Association Council agreed to restart the process for implementing the customs union, and a working programme for the achievement of this was agreed to at another meeting of the Council one year later. Meanwhile, at a meeting held in Copenhagen in June 1993, the European heads of government, meeting as the European Council, confirmed the decisions of the Lisbon summit, and also agreed on a series of conditions, known as the 'Copenhagen criteria', which new member states would have to meet. These included, first, the existence of stable democratic institutions providing for the rule of law, the respect of human rights and protection of minorities; second, the existence of a functioning market economy and, third, the ability to adhere to the principles of political, economic and monetary union.[68] There was not much doubt that Turkey could meet the second of these criteria, while the last seemed too vague to act as an exact yardstick, but the first condition was clearly very problematic in the Turkish case.

So far as the free movement of goods was concerned, the construction of the customs union proved easier to achieve than would have been the case earlier, since Turkey had in any case been moving fairly steadily towards a liberalised import regime since the early 1980s, and groups within the business community who had previously been worried about their ability to compete in an open market with western European industry had been generally brought round to the opposite point of view.[69] Hence, the customs union agreement was eventually signed in Brussels at a meeting of the Association Council on 6 March 1995. This was expected to go into effect at the beginning of 1996, after further legal and tariff changes had been implemented by Turkey. Two important political conditions were attached to the agreement, however. The first was that, to overcome Greek objections, the EU agreed to start accession negotiations with the Greek Cypriot government of the Republic of Cyprus within six months after the end of the Intergovernmental Conference which was to consider revisions to the Maastricht treaty (in effect, in 1998). This raised complex problems in Turkey's relations with Greece and with Cyprus which are returned to later, and which were likely to continue for some time (see pp. 255, 258–9).

The second hurdle was that, to go into effect, the customs union agreement would have to be ratified by the European Parliament in Strasbourg. This was a more immediate problem, since successive resolutions of the parliament suggested that, even though the customs union was officially restricted to the economic field and would not oblige the EU to start accession negotiations with Turkey, Turkey's poor human rights regime, and the government's handling of the Kurdish problem, would have an important impact on the Parliament's decision. In 1994, it had strongly criticised the lifting of the parliamentary immunity of the MPs of the pro-Kurdish Democracy Party (DEP) and the closure of the party (see p. 201). More immediately, as soon as the customs union agreement was signed in March 1995, the Parliament passed a resolution condemning the Association Council for accepting it, on the grounds that it was inconsistent with Turkey's shortcomings in human rights, its policies on the Kurdish problem, and the continuing dispute over Cyprus.[70]

In the European Parliament, opposition to the customs union continued during 1995, and was if anything intensified by the Çiller government's handling of the DEP case, and the confirmation of long prison sentences on the party's former MPs in October. The constitutional changes pushed through by the government in July were judged quite insufficient, as were the minor amendments to Article 8 of the 'Law for the Struggle against Terrorism' enacted in October. Instead, the European Parliament demanded complete withdrawal of Article 8, or at least its radical revision (see pp. 200–1, 203).[71] Nonetheless, as the time drew near for a vote in the Parliament to ratify the agreement, the MEPs came under strong pressure to change their position from the EU member-state governments, which were understandably reluctant to abandon an agreement they had already signed. Pressure in favour of the customs union also came from the United States, as well as Tansu Çiller, who suggested that its implementation would act as a barrier to the further rise of Islamic radicalism in Turkey, an idea which was echoed by the French President, Jacques Chirac. Hence, on 13 December 1995 the MEPs ratified the agreement (in some cases, reluctantly) by 343 votes to 149. However, in their resolution of 13 December they also asked the European Commission to monitor the human rights situation in Turkey closely, and to report to the Parliament annually on this.[72]

In the economic sphere, the implementation of the customs union marked the most important milestone in the development of Turkey's relations with the EU and its predecessors since the signature of the Additional Protocol in 1970. As from the beginning of 1996, Turkey was obliged to abolish all import duties 'and charges having equivalent effect' on all merchandise imports from the EU, in return for a similar undertaking by Brussels, and to apply the EU's relatively low common external tariff in its trade with third countries. Although agricultural products were excluded from this provision, the two sides committed themselves to achieving free trade in this sector eventually. Turkey was also required to pass effective laws for the protection of patents and other intellectual property, and to eliminate barriers to competition within the country.[73] For the Turkish government, one of the major problems created by the customs union was the loss of revenue caused by the ending of taxes on industrial imports from the EU, and the reduction of those on imports from third countries, which was put at between US$2.6 billion and US$3 billion per year. Accordingly, the EU agreed to give Turkey ECU 375 million ($495 million) in budgetary assistance over the next five and a half years, as well as access to EU funds under its Mediterranean programme, and concessionary loans from the European Investment Bank, although the budgetary assistance was then blocked by a Greek veto.[74]

On balance, Turkey made more economic concessions under the customs union than did the EU, since it had previously had a protective trade regime, whereas the only important remaining barriers to trade which had to be lifted by the EU were quotas on the imports of textiles and garments (the removal of which was admittedly an important gain for Turkish exporters). Prior to the signature of the agreement, pessimists had predicted that the ending of trade barriers would be harmful to Turkey, since it would suck in a flood of imports, without giving Turkish industry equivalent gains in exports.[75] In 1996, these expectations seemed to be borne out, as Turkey's imports from the EU countries grew by 36 per cent over the levels of 1995, while its exports to them rose by only 3.6 per cent, leaving a deficit in merchandise trade with the EU of US$11.6 billion. In subsequent years, however, it was apparent that this had only been a temporary trend. During 1997–98, Turkish exports to the EU rose by 16.5 per cent over the 1996 volume, while imports grew by 4.3 per cent, reducing the deficit to US$10.7 billion in 1998, with a further fall in the deficit expected for 1999.[76] In practice, it appeared that changes in trade volumes between Turkey and the EU depended on the relative level of demand in the two markets, rather than on the customs union itself. There was no evidence that free trade with the EU was driving Turkish industry to the wall – instead, the Turkish economy was gaining from easier access to western Europe, and more competition in the domestic market.

In principle, the customs union should also have led to more foreign direct investment in Turkey, since overseas firms would benefit by being able to export industrial products to the EU, and import machinery and other inputs from it, duty free, while taking advantage of Turkey's lower labour costs. In practice, however, this hope remained unrealised, due to investors' uncertainties about the political situation in Turkey, and lingering bureaucratic and legal obstacles (see p. 211). In short, the Turkish economy gained rather than lost from the customs union, even if Turkey failed to make full use of all the opportunities which were available to it. Politically, also, Tansu Çiller could not have refused to go ahead with it, since to do so would have been tantamount to signalling to Brussels that Turkey had abandoned its ambitions of eventual accession to the EU. On the contrary, in December 1995 she publicly announced that 'the customs union is not enough for us, our basic goal is full membership of the European Union'.[77]

By implementing the customs union, the two sides had chalked up an important success. However, it can be argued that they had only been tackling the economic part of their agenda, which was easier to address. The political obstacles, which were harder to resolve, remained as real as ever. In fact, they acquired additional importance because the collapse of communism in eastern Europe opened the prospect of expansion of the EU to the east, and west European leaders had to ask themselves whether they wanted Turkey to be part of this process. In effect, the question of whether they should start accession negotiations with Turkey, or at least commit themselves to doing so at some point in the future, was now hard to avoid. In 1989–90, while they were still responding to the Turkish application of 1987, they had been able to shelve the question, but the hard decision could not be put off indefinitely.

During 1996–97, the outlook was also badly affected by Turkey's highly unstable domestic politics. The installation of the coalition government led by Necmettin Erbakan in June 1996 had a damaging effect on Turkey's relations with the EU, as well as those with the United States, and for much the same reasons. In the December 1995 election campaign, Erbakan's Welfare Party had strongly opposed the project to gain full membership of the EU, which it characterised as a 'Christian Union', and called instead for a 'Union of Muslim Countries', though it did accept the need to remove barriers to trade with Europe.[78] Erbakan had also suggested that Turkey might leave the customs union, or at least revise it (quite how was unclear).[79] Once in office, however, he came under strong pressure from his coalition partner, Tansu Çiller, to leave the customs union untouched, much as he had done in the case of the 'Operation Provide Comfort'. On the other hand, Turkey made no moves towards advancing the case for accession, and Welfare Party spokesmen made it clear that they were opposed to the idea in principle on 'cultural' grounds.[80] Tansu Çiller, as the foreign minister and the main architect of the customs union on the Turkish side, seemed to be caught between two fires, as Erbakan attempted to launch a pan-Islamist project which was clearly at variance with her ideas, rendering her previous claim that the customs union would stem the tide of Islamism quite hollow. In effect, the Turkish government looked like a car with two drivers, each trying to steer it in opposite directions.

Unfortunately, the sense of alienation was heightened by similar moves on the European side. In March 1997, as Erbakan's attempts to stay in power were gradually failing, the leaders of the European Christian Democrat parties, including the German Chancellor, Helmut Kohl, and the former Belgian premier, Wilfred Martens, issued a joint declaration after a meeting in Brussels, claiming that 'the European Union is a civilisation project and within this civilisation project Turkey has no place'.[81] Apart from the arrogant and prejudiced implication that Turkey was not a 'civilised' country, this declaration was bound to have the worst possible effect on Turkey, since it implied that Turkey could never become a member of the EU, however much progress it made in political reform or economic modernisation. In effect, Erbakan's argument that the EU was a 'Christian club' seemed to be confirmed. Subsequent attempts by the EU to state that this was not EU policy, and that Turkey was still eligible for membership in principle failed to have much effect. On the contrary, the impact of the Brussels declaration was strengthened in July by the launch by the Commission President, Jacques Santer, of his 'Agenda 2000' programme. This proposed that in 1998 accession negotiations should begin with east European countries in what became known as the 'fast track' – that is, Poland, Hungary, the Czech Republic, Slovenia and Estonia, with Turkey conspicuous by its absence from the list of candidates.

Worse was to come on 12–13 December 1997, at the Luxembourg meeting of the European Council, when Cyprus was added to the 'fast track' list, and a 'slower track' list was announced, including Bulgaria, Latvia, Lithuania, Romania and Slovakia, with which the EU would begin accession negotiations at some time in the future. The summit adopted a

'European Strategy for Turkey', which was invited to be included in the new European Conference bringing together all the applicant states and the existing EU members, but its omission from either list served as a deadening blow to Turkey's ambitions.[82] The European Council could also be accused of applying double standards, since it had not excluded Slovakia from the list of candidates, although the Commission had reported in July 1997 that it had not reached the required human rights criteria. It was unfortunate also, that its decision came at a time after the fall of the Erbakan government, when its successor under Mesut Yılmaz was trying to re-establish Turkey's relations with the Western powers. Hence, in a statement issued immediately after the Luxembourg meeting, the Turkish government argued that 'Turkey has not been evaluated within the same framework, the same well-intentioned approach and objective criteria as the other candidate countries', and that the Luxembourg decision was based on 'partial, prejudiced and exaggerated assessments'. It stated that the government would maintain its existing links with the EU, but that 'development of these relations is dependent on the EU's fulfilment of its obligations' – in effect, that Turkey would freeze its relations with Brussels until Turkey was clearly put on the list of enlargement candidates.[83] Following the Luxembourg summit, there were also renewed calls from some Turkish politicians for a revision of the customs union agreement, but this was generally recognised as impractical; as Kemal Kirişci succinctly puts it, 'there was among the élite a recognition that Turkey was closely bound to Europe economically and that it really did not have anywhere else to go'.[84]

During 1998, the Yılmaz government adhered to this policy of disengagement. It thus missed an opportunity to put Turkey's case, by not attending the first meeting of the European Conference in London in March 1998, or the EU's Cardiff summit in the following June. Nonetheless, the Cardiff meeting tried to pave the way for the inclusion of Turkey as one of the 12 candidate countries, and confirmed the need for a more detailed timetable if the 'Strategy for Turkey' were to be implemented.[85] This apparent shift in EU attitudes was not maintained, however. In November 1998, the Commission prepared a report which raised some hopes that Turkey might be put on the candidates list, but these were dashed when the EU leaders turned down the report at a summit in Vienna in the following month. During the latter part of 1998 the Yılmaz administration was in any case preoccupied by trying to preserve its own survival, while the caretaker government under Bülent Ecevit which held the fort between January and April 1999 was too weak to take any new initiatives in either domestic or foreign policies. Meanwhile, the temporary refuge given to Abdullah Öcalan by Italy between November 1998 and January 1999, and Germany's refusal to comply with a request from the Italians that he should be extradited to Germany, where there was an existing warrant for his arrest, caused further resentment in Turkey, on the grounds that the two countries had failed to carry out their commitments under international agreements to suppress terrorism. The affair also led to widespread anti-Italian demonstrations in Turkey, and an unofficial boycott of Italian goods, although this does not appear to have had any definite effect on trade between the two countries.[86] After Öcalan's capture in Nairobi, the failure of the EU to issue any sort of condemnation of Greece for its role in the affair (presumably because to do so would have raised uncomfortable questions about the actions of Italy and Germany)[87] did nothing to improve the atmosphere in relations between Ankara and Brussels.

Following the elections of April 1999, and the establishment of a new coalition under Bülent Ecevit, prospects of a thaw in relations with the EU began to improve. Ecevit favoured a strongly nationalist line on the Cyprus question, but he also supported the widening of human rights in Turkey for domestic reasons, irrespective of its effects on Turkey's foreign relations. His coalition partners in the Nationalist Action Party (MHP) had an ultra-nationalist tradition, but the party's leader, Devlet Bahçeli, seemed prepared to take a back seat in the determination of foreign policy, and his party did not oppose the idea of eventual accession in principle. Among the EU states, also, the defeat of the German Christian Democrats in the 1998 elections, and their replacement by a Social Democratic Party (SPD)–Green coalition under Gerhard Schroeder, substantially improved the chances of a successful dialogue between Turkey and the EU, since the new German government seemed anxious to turn over a new leaf in Germany's relations with Turkey. Hence, there were hopes that at the EU summit held under the German term presidency in Cologne on 3–4 June 1999, the European leaders might agree to a statement declaring Turkey to be a candidate for full membership. Unfortunately, the Cologne meeting failed to produce any results, since a draft declaration to this effect was vetoed by Greece and Sweden. The Greek veto was predictable, but the Swedish one was based on the claim that Turkey should produce more solid evidence of progress on human rights.[88]

In spite of the setback in Cologne, in July 1999 the German foreign minister, Joschka Fischer, visited Turkey and was reported to have told President Demirel that the Luxembourg decision had been a mistake, and that Germany would support Turkey's candidacy at the next meeting of the European Council, which was due to be held in Helsinki in December 1999.[89] As in the case of Turkey's relations with the United States, the psychological atmosphere was then dramatically changed by the earthquake disaster of 17 August, in which the swift government and public aid to Turkey by western Europe emphasised to the Turks that, in the last analysis, their only reliable friends were in the West.[90] The visible improvement in relations with Greece also contributed to this result (see p. 257). On the Turkish side, the 'Sèvres syndrome' seemed to be definitely on the wane, although whether this surge of goodwill could be converted into concrete action was still uncertain. These doubts were increased with the approach of the Helsinki summit, as the Swedish government, supported by Denmark, proposed that Turkey would have to meet tight and detailed conditions regarding human rights and its treatment of the Kurds before it could even be put on the candidates list.[91] In Greece, Prime Minister Costas Simitis also appeared to toughen his position, by suggesting that there would have to be 'concrete progress' on the Cyprus question, 'as well as an improvement in Greek–Turkish relations in all aspects', before Turkey could be declared a candidate.[92] On 3 December, the Swedish foreign minister, Anna Lindh, announced that her government had withdrawn its objections; more surprising was a vote in the European Parliament on the previous day, agreeing that Turkey could become a candidate without prior conditions.[93] However, this still left the position of Greece in some doubt.

Fortunately, when the European heads of government duly assembled in Helsinki on 10 December 1999, these uncertainties were overcome, and the main EU governments, which by this stage clearly favoured Turkey's candidature, carried the day. Turkey was thus firmly placed as a candidate for accession, along with the eastern European applicants, plus Cyprus and Malta. Important conditions were nonetheless laid down, before accession talks could begin. In particular, Turkey would need to settle its bilateral disputes with Greece, and substantial, if not complete, progress would have to be made towards a settlement of the Cyprus problem (see pp. 258–60). The EU would begin an 'enhanced dialogue' with Turkey on human rights, while Turkey would need to meet the Copenhagen criteria on this issue, and in its treatment of the Kurds. It was also clear that the EU itself would face formidable tasks of internal reform if enlargement were to be made workable, such as extending the use of qualified majority voting, and further reform of its agricultural and regional policies.[94] The conditions regarding Cyprus and relations with Greece evidently caused some misgivings on the Turkish side, and the EU had to send Javier Solana, now its representative for foreign affairs on a last-minute trip to Ankara to explain the details and overcome objections. On their side, Bülent Ecevit and his colleagues would have found it hard to meet the EU's proposals with an outright refusal, so it was not surprising that the prime minister confirmed that Turkey had accepted the invitation late on 10 December. On the following morning, Ecevit flew to Helsinki to join the assembled EU leaders. Before leaving, he admitted that 'there might be some details that we could not digest', but claimed that 'in general, the acceptance of our candidacy under equal conditions is a great success for Turkey', and went on to suggest that 'we will be ready for full membership earlier than expected'.[95] In Helsinki, he conceded that Turkey still had much ground to cover in improving its human rights regime, but said that these problems could be overcome, 'given the dynamism of the Turkish people and their attachment to democracy'.[96] His confidence may not have been universally shared, granted the persistence of hard-line views (especially on the Kurdish question) among his coalition partners in the MHP and parts of the security forces. Nevertheless, it was clear that an important new chapter had been opened in Turkey's relations with western Europe, with long-term implications for its domestic as well as foreign policies.

Compared with its relations with the EU, Turkey's links with other European institutions and individual states were generally of secondary importance during the 1990s, but they need some description. On the first score, the Council of Europe was the most significant body, since Turkey was a party to the European Convention on Human Rights, and since 1991 had accepted the compulsory jurisdiction of the European Court of Human Rights, which worked under the Council's auspices. The fact that many of Turkey's laws and practices contravened the provisions of the Convention was naturally a frequent source of criticism. By accepting the jurisdiction of the Court, Turkey allowed its own citizens to appeal to Strasbourg in cases involving infringements of human rights, provided all judicial procedures in Turkey had been exhausted. In such cases, where the Court found against it, the Turkish authorities paid due compensation to the victims. Nonetheless, Turkish practices were one of the most frequent causes of actions by the Court; for instance, of the 116 cases pending at the Court at the beginning of 1998, 16 concerned Turkey.[97] By the end of 1999, the position of the European Court on the case of Abdullah Öcalan was also of critical importance (see p. 202).

Among the individual states of western Europe, Germany deserves special attention since it was easily and consistently Turkey's biggest trading partner, accounting for around 20 per cent of its exports and 15 per cent of its imports, and is the home of around 2.2 million Turks, many of them now of the second generation.[98] Of this, around one-tenth to one-quarter are estimated to be of Kurdish origin.[99] Germany's critical role in Turkey's overall relations with the EU has been referred to already. Apart from this, the presence of a large number of Turks as well as Turkish Kurds in Germany, has become an important issue in Germany's foreign and domestic politics, since it means that the Kurdish issue has a fairly high priority for German policy-makers. In 1992, and again in 1994, German military aid to Turkey was twice interrupted, after the use of German-supplied equipment against the Turkish Kurds caused sharp reactions in the Bundestag, but this issue then dropped off the agenda, as the aid programme ended in 1995 anyway. Meanwhile, the Kurdish community in Germany was important to the PKK, as a source of financial and political support. The attitude of the German authorities towards the PKK was ambiguous. In 1993 Germany, like France, officially banned the PKK on its territory, but the authorities tended to turn a blind eye towards pro-PKK organisations, so long as they did not provoke violence in Germany. Essentially, they wished to prevent clashes between the Kurdish community and the state, or between Kurds and Turks.[100] Meanwhile the broader issue of Turkish immigration to Germany dropped off the agenda in the 1990s, as immigration had virtually ended, and the decisions of 1976 on the question of free movement seemed to have been tacitly accepted by Turkey (see p. 176).

The presence of such a large foreign community raised social and other problems in Germany, but these were largely a matter for the German authorities, and did not have much impact on Turkish–German relations at the government level.[101] However, the legal status of the immigrants became an important issue between Turkey and Germany, since German laws made it very difficult for foreign citizens who were not of German descent to acquire German citizenship, even if they had led blameless lives for many years in Germany, or even been born there.[102] The Turkish government backed calls for allowing the immigrants easier access to German citizenship, in particular by permitting dual citizenship. This demand was resisted by the Kohl government, but the SPD–Green administration was committed to changing the laws. Accordingly, it was announced in March 1999 that Germany would grant dual citizenship to children born of foreign parents in Germany, but they would have to choose between German nationality and that of their parents on reaching adulthood. Meanwhile, the minimum period of residence for adult foreigners who wished to acquire German nationality would be reduced from 15 to eight years.[103] This fell well short of the Turkish government's request for general dual citizenship, but it does not seem to have wanted to press the issue too hard.

NOTES

1. The author has examined this point elsewhere; see William Hale, 'Turkey and the EU: The Customs Union and the Future', *Boğaziçi Journal* (Istanbul), Vol. 10 (1997), pp. 244–6. For fuller surveys, see the papers in the journal *Cahiers des Études de la Mediterranée Orientale et du Monde Turco-Iranien* (Paris), Vol. 8, pp. 79–116.

2. Mahmut Bali Aykan, 'Turkish Perspectives on Turkish–US Relations Concerning Persian Gulf Security in the Post-Cold War Era: 19891995', *Middle East Journal*, Vol. 50 (1996), pp. 345–6; Kemal Kirişci, 'Turkey and the United States: Ambivalent Allies', in B. Rubin and T. Keaney, eds, *US Allies in a Changing World* (London, Cass, 2000).

3. At one point, while she was premier, Tansu Çiller threatened to veto NATO enlargement if Turkey were not included in that of the EU, but this turned out to be an empty threat.

4. Kirişci, 'Turkey and the United States'. See also Gülnur Aybet, 'NATO's New Missions', *Perceptions* (Ankara), Vol. 4, No. 1 (1999), p. 73.

5. For fuller accounts, see Philip Robins, *Turkey and the Middle East* (London, Pinter, for Royal Institute of International Affairs, 1991), pp. 69–70, and his 'Turkish Policy in the Gulf Crisis: Adventurist or Dynamic?' in C.H. Dodd, ed., *Turkish Foreign Policy: New Prospects* (Wistow, Eothen Press, for Modern Turkish Studies Programme, SOAS, 1992). See also Sabri Sayarı, 'Turkey: The Changing European Security Environment and the Gulf Crisis', *Middle East Journal*, Vol. 46 (1992), pp. 13–14, 16–20, and William Hale, 'Turkey, the Middle East and the Gulf Crisis', *International Affairs*, Vol. 68 (1992). In preparing this account, the author has drawn on his paper.

6. As a sign of this, after a meeting of the National Security Council on 3 August, it was announced that Turkey would not close the Kirkuk–Yumurtalık pipeline. See *Milliyet* (Istanbul, daily), 4 August 1990.

7. In a television interview in January 1991, Özal claimed that, after August 1990, he had wanted to send a Turkish detachment to join the coalition forces in the Gulf. See *Summary of World Broadcasts*, (London, BBC) 22 January 1991. However, in his memoirs, General Necip Torumtay, who was Chief of the General Staff until 3 December 1990, states that the government did not give any orders to that effect at the time – the idea was simply floated by the president, he claims, and the prospective gains and losses examined by the foreign ministry and the General Staff (he does not say to what effect). See Necip Torumtay, *Orgeneral Torumtay'ın Anıları* (Istanbul, Milliyet Yayınları, 1994), p. 112. On the question of opening a second front against Iraq, see below, notes 11 and 15.

8. According to a poll published by the Istanbul daily *Hürriyet* in September 1991, 61 per cent of respondents stated that they opposed Turkish involvement in the prospective Gulf war. Cited by M. Hakan Yavuz and Mujeeb R. Khan, 'Turkish Foreign Policy Toward the Arab–Israeli Conflict: Duality and the [*sic*] Development', *Arab Studies*

Quarterly, Vol. 14 (1992), pp. 84–5.

9. Yılmaz had resigned as foreign minister in February 1990, stating at the time that he had done so 'because there was no possibility left for my working comfortably' in the government. Quoted in *Milliyet*, 22 February 1990. However, there was speculation that he resented frequent interference in the work of his ministry by the president and other members of the cabinet.

10. Under Article 92, parliamentary permission would not be needed if such action were required by 'international treaties to which Turkey is a party [in effect, the North Atlantic treaty] or by the rules of international courtesy', but neither of these conditions applied in this case.

11. In Bozer's case, there was widespread speculation at the time that this was the case, although the minister merely accused 'those playing a role behind the scenes' of causing his resignation. *Milliyet*, 13 October 1990. Safa Giray's departure from the government apparently had little to do with the Gulf crisis, but mainly derived from a dispute with Akbulut over the composition of the Istanbul delegation to the Motherland Party's annual convention for 1991. In Torumtay's case, the situation appears to have been more complicated, since he stated at the time that he resigned merely 'because I see it as impossible to continue my service under the principles and perception of the state which I believe in'. Quoted in Torumtay, *Anılar*, p. 130. Nevertheless, in his memoirs, he also makes it clear that he and his fellow generals opposed proposals by Özal that Turkey should open a second front against Iraq if war broke out (ibid., pp. 115–16). See also note 15, below. For his part Özal declared on 6 December that 'some generals are not keeping in step and are acting to preserve the status quo. While we are taking brave steps forward, they are trying to put the brakes on.' Quoted in *Milliyet*, 7 December 1990.

12. *Financial Times*, 18 January 1991.

13. *Guardian*, 25 January 1991.

14. However, the General Staff did consider it 'probable' that Saddam Hussein might launch air or missile attacks against Turkey, and prepared plans for counter-attacks by the Turkish air force against Iraq in response. Torumtay, *Anılar*, p. 113.

15. Ibid., p. 116. In their account, Nicole and Hugh Pope confirm that Özal had wanted to open a second front in Iraq, basing this on information from Güneş Taner, a minister of state at the time. According to Taner's statement, the United States supported the idea, but the Turkish government decided that the United Nations would force Turkey to leave Mosul if it occupied the province, there was no money to pay for the campaign, and the General Staff 'forecast that 40,000–50,000 Turkish lives would be lost in an offensive'. Nicole and Hugh Pope, *Turkey Unveiled: Ataturk and After* (London, John Murray, 1997), p. 220. For other statements by Özal, to the effect that he wanted Turkey to occupy Mosul, see ibid., p. 226.

16. *Summary of World Broadcasts*, 4 March 1991.

17. Kemal Kirişci, 'Turkey and the Kurdish Safe Haven in Northern Iraq', *Journal of South Asian and Middle Eastern Studies*, Vol. 19 (1996), pp. 21–3, and Mahmut Balı Aykan, 'Turkey's Policy in Northern Iraq, 1991–95', *Middle Eastern Studies*, Vol. 32 (1996), pp. 345–6.

18. Initially, the name used for the relief operation in Iraq was 'Provide Comfort' with the İncirlik operation being referred to as 'Poised Hammer'. Turkish writers generally use the latter term (*Çekiç Güç*, or 'Hammer Force' in Turkish) for the whole operation,

but 'Provide Comfort' seems to have been the preferred title elsewhere, and is used through this account in preference.

19. See Sayarı, 'Turkey: Changing', p. 14.
20. Pope, *Turkey Unveiled*, p. 228 and Aykan, 'Turkey's Policy', p. 345.
21. See for example, Meltem Müftüler-Baç, 'Turkey's Predicament in the Post-Cold War Era', *Futures*, Vol. 28 (1996), p. 259.
22. In his television broadcast of 2 March 1991. *Summary of World Broadcasts*, 4 March 1991.
23. Aykan, 'Turkish Perspectives', pp. 348–9.
24. Aykan, 'Turkey's Policy', p. 344.
25. Author's estimate at the time, for the Economist Intelligence Unit. Turkish estimates were a good deal higher than this: for instance, in 1993 the government estimated the total loss since the embargo began as US$20 billion over a four-year period, or an average of US$5 billion per year. See Aykan, 'Turkey's Policy', pp. 353–4.
26. See the author's contributions to Ami Ayalon, ed., *Middle East Contemporary Survey* for 1991 (Vol. 15), p. 713, and for 1992 (Vol. 16), p. 773 (Boulder, CO, Westview, 1993, 1995).
27. Aykan, 'Turkish Perspectives', p. 357, note 57. See also Kirişci, 'Turkey and the United States', and his 'The Kurdish Question and Turkish Foreign Policy', in Lenora Martin, ed., *The Future of Turkish Foreign Policy* (forthcoming).
28. Aykan, 'Turkey's Policy', pp. 354–5. See also Michael M. Gunter, *The Kurds and the Future of Turkey* (New York, NY, St Martin's Press, 1997), pp. 98–9.
29. Philip Robins, 'Turkish Foreign Policy under Erbakan', *Survival*, Vol. 39 (1997), p. 85. Simultaneously, the French contingent was withdrawn from the force, though the British continued to support the United States in maintaining it.
30. Quoted in ibid., p. 99.
31. Robert Olson, 'The Kurdish Question and Turkey's Foreign Policy, 1991–1995: From the Gulf War to the Incursion into Iraq', *Journal of South Asian and Middle Eastern Studies*, Vol. 19 (1995), p. 2.
32. Kirişci, 'Turkey and the Kurdish Safe Haven', p. 23; Michael M. Gunter, 'The Foreign Policy of the Iraqi Kurds', *Journal of South Asian and Middle Eastern Studies*, Vol. 20 (1997), pp. 13–19 and Aykan, 'Turkey's Policy', p. 361.
33. Kirişci, 'Kurdish Question'.
34. Officially, the United States denied any direct involvement in Öcalan's capture, though it referred vaguely to diplomatic and intelligence operations in the affair. See *Briefing* (Ankara, weekly), 1 March 1999, p. 25. Although the details of the incident are still murky, it is clear that the United States had put strong pressure on Italy not to give Öcalan political asylum. After he arrived in Nairobi on 2 February 1999, the CIA immediately informed Turkish intelligence. Öcalan was captured by a Turkish security team in the early hours of 16 February, on his way from the Greek ambassador's residence to the airport, in an operation in which the Kenyan authorities apparently cooperated. Whether he left the residence of his own volition, believing that he would be granted asylum by The Netherlands, or because the Greeks expelled him under intense diplomatic pressure from the United States and Kenya, is unclear, however. See *The New York Times*, 20 February 1999 and *Milliyet*, 21 February 1999.
35. A notable exception was that of the Minister of Health, Osman Durmuş, of the MHP,

who claimed that the hospital ship sent by the US Navy was not needed. However, this and similar remarks by the minister provoked harsh criticism in the Turkish press. See *Milliyet*, 23 August 1999, which headlined the story 'An Amazing Mentality'.

36. *Briefing*, 22 November 1999, pp. 7, 28; 29 November 1999, p. 3 and *International Herald Tribune*, 22 November 1999.
37. *Briefing*, 5 March 1990, p. 3.
38. Aykan, 'Turkish Perspectives', p. 351, and Kirişci, 'Turkey and the United States'.
39. Quoted in *Briefing*, 26 April 1999, p. 5.
40. Şükrü Elekdağ, 'Two and a Half War Strategy', *Perceptions* (Ankara), Vol. 1 No. 1 (1996), p. 55.
41. Javier Solana, 'NATO in Transition', in ibid., p. 17.
42. Quoted in John Roper, 'The West and Turkey: Varying Roles, Common Interests', *International Spectator* (Rome), Vol. 34 (1999), p. 92.
43. Quoted in Anthony Hartley, 'Maastricht's Problematical Future', *World Today*, Vol. 48 (1992), p. 181.
44. Gülnür Aybet, *NATO's Developing Role in Collective Security* (Ankara, Ministry of Foreign Affairs, Center for Strategic Research, 1999), p. 46.
45. In addition, there are now five 'observers' (Austria, Denmark, Finland, Ireland and Sweden) which either originally were or have since become full members of the EU, but chose not to become full members of the WEU for political reasons, and nine 'associate partners' from eastern Europe (Bulgaria, the Czech Republic, Estonia, Hungary, Latvia, Lithuania, Poland, Romania and Slovakia) making up a total of 27 members of the 'WEU family'.
46. Heinz Kramer, 'Turkey's Place and Role in the Emerging European Security Architecture', paper given to seminar series of Modern Turkish Studies Programme, SOAS, London University, 25 April 1997, p. 16, and Gülnur Aybet, 'Turkey and European Institutions', *International Spectator* (Rome), Vol. 34 (1999), p. 109.
47. Quoted in Kemal Kirişci, 'Post Cold-War Turkish Security and the Middle East', *MERIA Journal* (published on internet), No. 2 (1997).
48. F. Stephen Larrabee, 'US and European Policy towards Turkey and the Caspian Basin', in Robert D. Blackwill and Michael Stürmer, eds, *Allies Divided: Transatlantic Policies for the Greater Middle East* (Cambridge, MA, MIT Press, 1997), p. 169.
49. Aybet, 'Turkey and European Institutions', p. 109
50. Kramer, 'Turkey's Place', p. 16.
51. Roper, 'West and Turkey', p. 92 and Aybet, *NATO's Developing Role*, p. 48.
52. Kirişci, 'Post-Cold War'.
53. Quoted in Hartley, 'Maastricht's Problematical Future', p. 181.
54. Kramer, 'Turkey's Place', p. 17.
55. Stephen J. Gommershall, 'Nato and European Defence', *Perceptions*, (Ankara), Vol. 4 No. 1 (1999), p. 78.
56. Aybet, *NATO's Developing Role*, p. 53.
57. Quoted in *Briefing*, 26 April 1999, pp. 22–3.
58. For the full text of the declaration, see Aybet, *NATO's Developing Role*, pp. 84–101. The phrase quoted appears on p. 90.
59. Ibid., pp. 53, 55 and *Sunday Times*, 12 December 1999. The author is much indebted to Dr Gülnür Aybet for advice on this and related points. Other countries in the same

position were Norway and Iceland, plus the new NATO members in eastern Europe – that is the Czech Republic, Hungary and Poland.

60. Aybet, 'Turkey and European Institutions', p. 109.

61. Quoted in Gommershall, 'Nato', p. 77.

62. Christopher Tuck, 'Greece, Turkey and Arms Control', *Defense Analysis*, Vol. 12 (1996), p. 24. See also Gülnur Aybet, 'The CFE Treaty: The Way Forward for Conventional Arms Control in Europe', *Perceptions* (Ankara), Vol. 1, No. 1, (1996), pp. 25–6, 29–31, and the author's contribution to Ami Ayalon, ed., *Middle East Contemporary Survey* for 1993 (Vol. 17), p. 686.

63. *Briefing*, 22 November 1999, p. 17. The author is again indebted to Dr Gülnur Aybet for advice on this point.

64. Tuck, 'Greece, Turkey', pp. 26–7.

65. Roper, 'West and Turkey', p. 90.

66. In preparing this summary of Turkey–EU relations between 1990 and 1996, the author has drawn on two earlier papers: see William Hale, 'Turkey: A Crucial but Problematic Applicant', in John Redmond, ed., *Prospective Europeans: New Members for the European Union* (New York and London, Harvester Wheatsheaf, 1994), and his 'Turkey and the EU'. For fuller accounts, see also the chapter on Turkey in John Redmond, *The Next Mediterranean Enlargement of the European Community. Turkey, Cyprus and Malta* (Aldershot, Dartmouth, 1993); Meltem Müftüler-Baç, *Turkey's Relations with a Changing Europe* (Manchester and New York, NY, Manchester University Press, 1997) especially Chs 5–6, and Heinz Kramer, 'Turkey and the European Union: A Multi-Dimensional Relationship with Hazy Perspectives', in V. Mastny and R. Craig Nation, eds, *Turkey between East and West: New Challenges for a Rising Regional Power* (Boulder, CO, Westview, 1996).

67. Quoted in Müftüler-Baç, *Turkey's Relations*, p. 95.

68. Ibid., pp. 95–6; Kramer, 'Turkey and the European Union', pp. 210–11 and Meltem Müftüler-Baç, 'The Never-Ending Story: Turkey and the European Union', *Middle Eastern Studies*, Vol. 34 (1998), p. 241.

69. Meltem Müftüler, 'Turkish Economic Liberalization and European Integration', *Middle Eastern Studies*, Vol. 31 (1995), pp. 92–5. On the last point, see Mükerrem Hiç, *Turkey's Customs Union with the European Union: Economic and Political Prospects*, (Ebenhausen, Germany, Stiftung Wissenschaft und Politik, 1995), pp. 17–19.

70. Müftüler-Baç, *Turkey's Relations*, pp. 90–1, and Heinz Kramer, 'The EU–Turkey Customs Union: Economic Integration Amidst Political Turmoil', *Mediterranean Politics*, Vol. 1 (1996), pp. 60, 67.

71. Kramer, 'EU–Turkey Customs Union', pp. 68–69.

72. Ibid., pp. 70–1 and Müftüler-Baç, *Turkey's Relations*, p. 94.

73. 'Decision 1/95 of the EC–Turkey Association Council of 22 December 1995', *Official Journal of the European Communities*, Vol. 39 L35 (13 February 1996) Articles 4–6, 13, 25, 31–2.

74. See *Briefing*, 13 March 1995, p. 19, and Hale, 'Turkey and the EU', p. 249. In 1996 Greece lifted its veto on Turkey's access to funds under the Mediterranean policy, although the budgetary assistance as well as the Fourth Financial Protocol remained blocked.

75. See for example, Canan Balkır, 'Turkey and the European Community: Foreign Trade and Direct Foreign Investment in the 1980s', in Canan Balkır and Allan M.

Williams, eds, *Turkey and Europe* (London and New York, NY, Pinter, 1993), p. 129.

76. In the first five months of 1999 Turkey's imports from the EU grew by 3.2 per cent over the same period of 1998, while its exports rose by 21.2 per cent. On this basis, it could be expected that the deficit in merchandise trade with the EU for the whole of 1999 would be reduced to around US$5.5 billion. Data for 1995–97 from *Statistical Yearbook of Turkey 1998* (Ankara, State Institute of Statistics, 1999), p. 512: for 1998, from *Briefing*, 8 March 1999, p. 36, and for 1999 from ibid., 2 August 1999, p. 29.
77. Quoted in *Milliyet*, 17 December 1995.
78. Welfare Party 1995 election manifesto, pp. 6–7, 29.
79. See *Milliyet*, 14 December, 17 December 1995.
80. Robins, 'Foreign Policy under Erbakan', p. 86.
81. Quoted in Müftüler-Baç, 'Never-Ending Story', p. 240.
82. Aybet, 'Turkey and European Institutions', p. 107.
83. 'Statement by the Turkish Government on 14 December 1997, Concerning the Presidency Conclusions of the European Council Held on 12–13 December 1997 in Luxembourg', reprinted in *Perceptions* (Ankara), Vol. 2, No. 4 (1997–98), pp. 154–6.
84. Kirişci, 'Kurdish Question'.
85. Aybet, 'Turkey and European Institutions', pp. 107–8.
86. During the first five months of 1999, Turkey's imports from Italy fell by 32.2 per cent compared with the same period in 1998, but this was part of a general fall in imports, caused by a slump in demand in the domestic market. As an example, Turkey's imports from Germany during the same period also fell by 32.6 per cent, although Germany was not the object of a boycott. Data from *Briefing*, 2 August 1999, p. 30. Italy remained Turkey's third biggest trading partner, after Germany and the United States. An official boycott would of course have been contrary to Turkey's obligations under the customs union agreement.
87. This was suggested by Bülent Ecevit, in an interview for *Milliyet*, 20 February 1999.
88. *Briefing*, 7 June 1999, pp. 24–6.
89. *Milliyet*, 23 July 1999.
90. See for instance, the comments by Sami Kohen, 'Asıl yardım', in ibid., 20 August 1999.
91. *Financial Times*, 7 September 1999.
92. Reuters, 20 October 1999.
93. Ibid., 3 December 1999 and *Milliyet*, 3 December 1999.
94. Reuters, 10 December 1999.
95. Associated Press, 10 December 1999.
96. Reuters, 11 December 1999.
97. Hugh Poulton, 'The Turkish State and Democracy', *International Spectator* (Rome), Vol. 34 (1999), p. 62.
98. Heinz Kramer, 'The Institutional Framework of German–Turkish Relations', paper presented to conference on 'The Parameters of Partnership: Germany, the United States and Turkey', American Institute for Contemporary German Studies, Johns Hopkins University, Washington, DC, 23–24 October 1997, p. 5. 'Turks' here includes Turkish citizens, whether or not of Turkish ethnicity, plus former Turkish citizens, or their descendants, who have acquired German nationality.
99. Heinz Kramer cites an estimate of 'about a quarter' (ibid., p. 12), whereas estimates cited by Robert Olson suggest a proportion of around 10 per cent. See Robert Olson,

'The Kurdish Question and Turkey's Foreign Policy, 1991–1995: From the Gulf War to the Incursion into Iraq', *Journal of South Asian and Middle Eastern Studies*, Vol. 19 (1995), p. 28.

100. Kramer, 'Institutional Framework', p. 13.
101. There is a vast specialist literature on this subject, mostly in German. For references, see the footnotes to Dr Kramer's paper, ibid., and the work of Dr Faruk Şen and others published by the Essen-based Zentrum für Türkeistudien. For a fairly recent summary in English, see also Faruk Şen, 'Turkish Communities in Western Europe', in Mastny and Nation, eds, *Turkey between East and West*.
102. See Kramer, 'Institutional Framework', pp. 6–7.
103. *Briefing*, 15 March 1999, p. 5.

8

Turkey and Regional Politics after the Cold War: (I) Greece, Cyprus, the Balkans and Transcaucasia

TURKEY, GREECE AND CYPRUS

In a rapidly changing world, Turkey's relations with its Greek neighbours seems to have been the theatre of foreign policy which was least affected by the end of the Cold War. The tensions and conflicts which had built up since the late 1950s continued unresolved, as the 1990s turned out to be a decade of false starts, which failed to unblock what appeared to be a condition of permanent stalemate. It was not until 1999 that reconciliation began to seem possible, as part of Turkey's moves towards possible eventual accession to the European Union (EU). As in previous years, the clash of interests and emotions over Cyprus lay at the heart of Greek–Turkish conflicts: with no progress registered on this score, there seemed to be little hope of any important improvement in the broader relationship.

Following his election as president of Cyprus in February 1988, George Vassiliou re-started negotiations with Rauf Denktash, the Turkish Cypriot leader, in 1990. These failed to get off the ground since Denktash insisted that as a precondition both sides should be recognised as having 'sovereign status'. This was unacceptable to the Greeks, who argued that the Greek Cypriot administration, as the internationally recognised government of the island, could not concede sovereignty to what they regarded as the 'illegal' Turkish Cypriot regime. Expanding this argument, Denktash began to speak of the existence of two 'peoples', rather than 'communities' in Cyprus, implying that the Turkish Cypriots had the right of self-determination, and that they were entitled to set up an independent and internationally recognised state. In his words, 'There is no single representative government in Cyprus and no homogeneous Cypriot nation, but two sovereign peoples identified on the basis of ethnic origin, language, cultural tradition and religion'.[1]

With the two sides unable to agree even on basic principles, the 1990 talks got nowhere. However, during 1991, it appeared that a break in the log-jam might be coming from Ankara, where President Turgut Özal was anxious to improve his relations with the European Community (EC) and the Western powers generally, and saw a solution of the Cyprus problem as an important step to achieving this. The election of Constantine Mitsotakis as prime minister of Greece in April 1990, in place of the hard-line Andreas Papandreou, was another hopeful sign for Özal, since it suggested that even if the two communities in Cyprus could not agree with one another, cooperation between Ankara and Athens might induce a change. Accordingly, soon after the Gulf war of 1991, Özal proposed to President George Bush that quadripartite talks should be started between the two mainland governments, plus the Greek and Turkish Cypriot leaders. Comparing such a summit to the election of a Pope, Özal argued that an overall settlement could be hammered out in a 'marathon session'.

This idea was rejected by the Greeks, but it encouraged the UN Secretary-General Boutros Boutros-Ghali to believe that a more flexible stance on the Turkish side could lead to successful intercommunal negotiations. After talks during 1991, the Secretary-General reported to the Security Council in April 1992, somewhat optimistically, that the two sides had agreed on the shape of a federal constitution, and on the implementation of the 'three freedoms' accepted as a basis for discussion by Denktash and Makarios in 1977 (see p. 159). Meanwhile, important voices in northern Cyprus – notably that of Derviş Eroğlu, leader of the National Unity Party, and Denktash's prime minister – began to question the whole idea of negotiating a federation with the Greek Cypriots, or ceding any territory as part of the deal. The application for full membership of the then EC, which had been submitted by the Greek Cypriot government in 1990 without the support of the Turkish Cypriots, was another complicating factor. Nonetheless, Boutros-Ghali produced what was referred to as a 'Set of Ideas', designed to overcome existing differences, which were endorsed by a Security Council Resolution (No.750) of 10 April 1992. On this basis, Denktash and Vasilliou arrived in New York in June 1992 for 'proximity talks', in which they sat in separate rooms with the Secretary-General shuttling between the two. These lasted until 14 August. In spite of long discussions, the talks became deadlocked over the territorial division between Greeks and Turks in a future federation, and the right of the Greek Cypriot refugees to return to their former homes in the north. Renewed direct talks between Denktash and Vassiliou were held under Boutros-Ghali's chairmanship between 28 October and 11 November, but these failed to resolve either these or other differences over the powers of each community in a federal constitution.[2]

Following the failure of the talks in 1992, prospects became further clouded by the election of Glafcos Clerides as president of Cyprus in February 1993. During his election campaign, Clerides had attacked the 'Set of Ideas', though it later became apparent that he would accept them only with significant revision. To resolve the dispute in the Greek Cypriots' favour, he emphasised the need for Cyprus to become a full member of the EU which, he apparently hoped, would put further pressure on Turkey and the Turkish Cypriots. Rather than making another direct attempt to produce an overall settlement, Boutros-Ghali then adopted a gradualist approach by proposing a series of 'confidence-building measures', designed to produce some areas of agreement which might later develop into a general reconciliation. These included, in particular, the re-opening of Nicosia airport, closed since 1974, to both Greek and Turkish Cypriots, and the return to the Greeks of Varosha, the southern suburb of Famagusta which had been occupied by the Turkish army in 1974 but never settled by the Turkish Cypriots. These proposals were accepted in principle by both sides, but a protracted series of talks, which lasted from May 1993 until May 1994 under UN and then US auspices, broke down over the details.[3]

Meanwhile, attention was diverted to the possibility of Cyprus' admission to the EU, with or without Turkish Cypriot agreement. In June 1993, the EU Commission's official Opinion reported that Cypriot accession would not create any special problems in the social or economic field, but that 'Cyprus's integration with the Community implies a peaceful, balanced and lasting settlement of the Cyprus question'.[4] The Opinion was accepted by the EU Council of Ministers in October 1993, although the process then became stalled until March 1995. In the meantime, prospects for a constitutional settlement within Cyprus dimmed further in July 1994, when the European Court of Justice effectively banned Turkish Cypriot exports to the EU. This prompted the Turkish Republic of Northern Cyprus' (TRNC) National Assembly to delete the reference to the possibility of a future confederation with the Greeks from the TRNC constitution, and reject the idea of further talks on the confidence-building measures while the judgement was in force.[5] By the beginning of 1995 it was evident that the Greek government was determined to link its approval of the prospective customs union between Turkey and the EU to the question of the accession of Cyprus to the Union, irrespective of whether there were a settlement between the two communities first. The Greeks won their point in March 1995 when the Turkey–EU Association Council accepted the customs union agreement on the condition that accession negotiations with Cyprus would begin six months after the conclusion of the intergovernmental conference which was to review the Maastricht treaty (see p. 235–6). These negotiations duly began – though with a very uncertain outcome – in January 1998, with George Vassiliou, as the Greek Cypriots' chief negotiator, nominally accepted as the representative of both sides of the island.[6]

During 1996–98, the seemingly intractable Cyprus dispute became further complicated by renewed conflict between Greece and Turkey, Turkey's worsening relations with the EU, and contemporary upheavals in Turkish domestic politics. In 1995 Tansu Çiller's government severely cut back the economic aid from Ankara on which the TRNC was dependent, but the end of the year produced a change of heart, when a 'Joint Declaration' was issued by the two sides confirming, among other things, that the impending implementation of the Turkey–EU customs union would not hinder Turkey's economic relationship with northern Cyprus.[7] Later, the coalition led by Necmettin Erbakan which ruled Turkey between June 1995 and June 1996 failed to take any initiatives over the problem, although fears that Erbakan might come out against the official Turkish policy of working for a federation in Cyprus fortunately proved unfounded.[8] Meanwhile, a bizarre 'battle of the flags' broke out between Greece and Turkey in January 1996, following a maritime accident at the uninhabited rocky outcrop of Kardak (Imia in Greek) which lies just under four nautical miles off Turkey's Aegean coast, and about 8.8 kilometres from the Greek island of Kalymnos. The mayor of Kalymnos first planted a Greek flag on the islet, but this was then removed by a group of journalists from the Turkish daily *Hürriyet*, before a landing party from the Greek navy arrived to replace the Turkish flag with a Greek one. This incident – absurd as it seemed to outsiders – stoked up fierce nationalist passions on both sides, which were inflated by the press, since for the Turks it appeared to raise the possibility that Greece might try to claim sovereign rights over the whole Aegean. Fortunately, the risk of a direct armed clash between Greece and Turkey was avoided by rapid intervention by the US mediator, Richard Holbrooke. However, attempts to widen this into a broader agreement over territorial rights in the Aegean failed. Positions established since the 1970s were continued, as the Greek side insisted on submitting these disputes to the International Court of Justice at The Hague, while Turkey, which evidently feared that the Court's decision might go against it, proposed direct bilateral negotiations (see pp. 159–60, 168).[9]

A year later, in January 1997, tensions rose once more when the Clerides government announced that it had ordered a total of 48 S-300 air defence missiles from Russia, which would be able to hit targets on the Turkish mainland as well as in Cypriot airspace. Military experts suggested that this would not substantially alter the balance of power in the island, which was still in Turkey's favour. Nonetheless, the deal was treated as a provocative challenge by Tansu Çiller, the then foreign minister, who threatened that the Turkish airforce would destroy the missiles, if they were installed. In May 1997, exercises by the Greek and Turkish airforces over the island again threatened to produce a direct clash. This was resolved by an agreed moratorium on overflights, which was broken only six months later. However, the installation of the coalition led by Mesut Yılmaz in June 1997 meant that there was now a government in Ankara prepared to mend its fences with the Western powers, and hence with Greece. At a NATO meeting in Madrid in July 1997 the Greek and Turkish governments expressed a commitment to peaceful relations, respect for each other's sovereignty and existing international treaties. This was accompanied by renewed talks between Denktash and Clerides under UN auspices, first in Troutbeck, New York, in July 1997, and then in Glion, Switzerland, in August. Neither of these encounters resulted in any progress, mainly because Denktash objected to the expected opening of accession negotiations between Cyprus and the EU without any Turkish Cypriot representation. Meanwhile, the Turkish government reacted to the EU's 'Agenda 2000' programme, which left Turkey off the list of candidates for full membership, by signing a partial integration agreement with the TRNC on 20 July 1997. This provided for an economic and financial union between Turkey and the TRNC, and what was called a 'joint defence concept'. Any chances in the short run of a meaningful dialogue with Greece, or progress on the Cyprus issue, were further reduced by the decision of the EU's Luxembourg summit in December 1997, which confirmed Turkey's apparent exclusion from the enlargement process (see pp. 239–40).[10] As Christopher de Bellaigue suggests, 'At one ill-considered stroke, the EU had destroyed what leverage it possessed over the Turks.'[11]

It was not until 1999 that more hopeful prospects began to emerge. In December 1998, apparently under intense pressure from the United States,

Glafcos Clerides announced that the planned S-300 missile detachment would not, after all be deployed in Cyprus, but would instead be based in Crete, thus neutralising a potential point of explosion. The Greek government's murky role in the Öcalan affair, made clear after his capture by the Turks in Nairobi in February 1999, also produced a change of heart by Greece in its attitude to Turkey, illustrated by the dismissal of the hard-line and unpredictable foreign minister, Theodore Pangalos, as well as the ministers of the interior and public order, immediately afterwards. The Greek prime minister, Costas Simitis, seemed anxious to turn over a new leaf in relations with Turkey. On the other side of the Aegean, Turkey's general elections of April 1999 resulted in the formation of a new government, led by Bülent Ecevit, which could take some more decisive and difficult decisions than its predecessors. In May 1999 the new Greek foreign minister, George Papandreou, took up an offer made by his Turkish opposite number, İsmail Cem, for a dialogue on bilateral issues between the two countries. This developed with a series of meetings during the summer and autumn. The agenda was mainly limited to uncontroversial questions, such as trade, tourism and environmental protection, but included 'cooperation against terrorism' (a reference to the Turkish demand for a definite end to Greek support for the PKK). Controversial issues, such as sea-bed rights and territorial waters in the Aegean, were postponed until a later date, assuming that the preliminary discussions went well.[12]

External and unexpected events also gave a boost to the détente. The Turkish earthquake of 17 August 1999, to which the Greek people and government responded rapidly and generously, and the despatch of a Turkish aid team to help with rescue operations after an earthquake in Athens on 7 September, led to a dramatic reversal of hostile attitudes in the press and public opinion. Of the various substantive obstacles to be overcome, Cyprus was still the most intractable. At the prompting of a meeting of the Group of Eight (G-8) group of industrialised countries including Russia in June 1999, the UN Secretary-General, Kofi Annan, tried to bring about renewed talks between Clerides and Denktash. This endeavour was strongly supported by President Clinton, in talks with Bülent Ecevit in Washington in October 1999. The main difficulty still was that Denktash was reluctant to re-start talks unless the TRNC's 'sovereignty' was first recognised – a demand which seemed to be quite unacceptable to the Greeks.[13] This stand appeared to be supported by Ecevit, who insisted that 'the fact that there are two completely independent states on the island should be recognised', even though he admitted that 'diplomatic recognition may not be given'.[14]

Fortunately, an apparent change in the Turkish position took place near the end of 1999. On 13 November 1999 Rauf Denktash, who was evidently under strong pressure from the US and the UN on this point, agreed to join Clerides in proximity talks in New York, even though he was not invited as the 'President of the TRNC' but merely as the 'Turkish Cypriot leader'.[15] After the talks had begun on 3 December, it was hard to know whether any advance had been achieved, since the two Cypriot leaders accepted a ban on talking to the media about the details, although on 11 December Rauf Denktash was reported as saying that good progress had been made.[16] Nevertheless, the two sides still had to overcome the wide gap between them, with the Turks pressing for a 'confederation', or a looser form of reunion than the 'federation' demanded by the Greeks, who feared that the 'confederal' formula might give the Turkish Cypriots the right to opt out of a future Cypriot state.[17]

Some EU spokesmen had optimistically suggested in 1995 that the prospect of Cypriot accession to the EU might act as a catalyst to bring the two communities together. However, all the evidence suggested that until late 1999, the EU's role in both the Aegean and Cyprus disputes had been counter-productive, since it had alienated the Turks, inducing them to dig in their heels, without producing greater flexibility on the Greek side. The turning-point only appeared in December 1999, with the decision of the Helsinki summit to admit Turkey as a candidate for EU membership, in which the Greek government appeared to back down on its previous position that this could not be accepted unless there were prior progress in settling the Cyprus and Aegean problems (see p. 242). Greece was none-theless able to insist that, as part of the accession process Greece and Turkey would, like the other candidate countries, have to 'make every effort to resolve any outstanding border disputes. Failing this, they should within a reasonable time bring the dispute to the International Court of Justice'.[18] According to this formula, the European Council would review progress by 2004, after which there could be a recourse to the Inter-national Court of Justice if the negotiations were unsuccessful. In accept-ing this condition, Turkey appeared to have backed off from its previous refusal to submit its disputes with Greece over offshore oil rights and terri-torial waters to arbitration by the Court. Equally crucially, the Council emphasised that 'a political settlement will facilitate the accession of Cyprus to the European Union', but that 'if no settlement has been reached by the completion of accession negotiations, the Council's deci-sion on accession will be made without the above being a precondition'.[19]

The suggestion that Cyprus might be admitted to the EU even if there were not a prior internal settlement was strongly opposed by the Turks on the grounds that the Treaty of Guarantee of 1960 prevented the participation of Cyprus 'in whole or in part, in any political or economic union with any State whatsoever'. While Turkey did not reject the principle of Cypriot accession, it insisted that this could not precede an internal settlement, and should be simultaneous with the accession of Turkey. Against this, it was argued that the EU was not a 'State' within the meaning of the treaty, which was in any case drawn up in quite different conditions, and was designed to prevent either union of Cyprus with Greece, or partition, not membership of the EU.[20] Irrespective of these legal arguments, it seemed unlikely that the EU would readily accept Cyprus without an internal settlement, since this would set the *de facto* partition of the island in concrete. It was also doubtful whether the Greek Cypriot government could carry out all its commitments as an EU member, if it still claimed sovereignty over the whole of Cyprus, but did not control the north. Given this situation, France and Germany in particular seemed reluctant to accept Cypriot accession if this were negotiated purely with the Greek Cypriots. Even though they did not fully support the Turkish position, they did not want the EU to import an intractable and possibly explosive problem.[21] Given these considerations, there were serious doubts as to whether the EU would actually admit Cyprus as a member in advance of an internal settlement. As an unnamed French diplomat quoted in the Istanbul daily *Milliyet*, immediately after the Helsinki summit pointed out, the final decision would be up to the European Council, which could still refuse to allow a divided Cyprus into the EU if it saw fit.[22]

In view of the Helsinki decision, it was clear that the need to resolve the Cyprus problem was a pressing one for Turkey, since this was the main point at which its policies clearly conflicted with those of its broader foreign policy interests to develop and maintain its links with the Western powers, and avoid involvement in regional conflicts. It was the only important foreign policy issue in which it had virtually no external support. While the Turkish Cypriots might argue that, as a separate 'people' they had the right to self-determination, the international community was reluctant to back such claims, since they conflicted with the perceived need to preserve agreed international frontiers and the territorial integrity of states.[23] Upholding the claim also conflicted with Turkish policy on other issues, which rejected the Kurdish claim to self-determination, or the Armenian claim to Nagorno-Karabakh. No other state recognised the TRNC, including those with which Turkey had particularly close and cooperative relations, like Israel and Azerbaijan. Admittedly, between

1997 and 1999, the EU had temporarily removed the main incentive for Turkey to settle its quarrels with Greece and the Greek Cypriots. After December 1999, however, the prospect of light at the end of the tunnel in Turkey's bid for EU membership suggested that some hard decisions on both these issues would eventually have to be taken if Turkey were to exploit its new opportunities.

TURKEY AND THE BALKANS

While Turkey's policies towards Cyprus and Greece clearly conflicted with the interests of its NATO allies, the developing ethnic conflicts in the Balkans during the 1990s – especially in the former Yugoslavia – had the opposite effect. The Turks were closely concerned with the developing Western military role, first in Bosnia-Herzegovina, beginning in 1993, and then in Kosovo in 1999. Far from opposing it in principle, their main complaint, especially before 1995, was that it was not speedy or effective enough. Once NATO had become heavily involved in these and the neighbouring republics, Turkey was usually enthusiastic and active in its support: in fact, by the end of the decade, it had itself acquired a fairly important role in NATO and UN operations in the region. Its position was also related to its relations with Greece, since Turkey could point to the fact that while Greece was at best a reluctant and uncooperative member of NATO on Balkan issues, Turkey was generally in full support of alliance policies, at least after 1995.

This is not to suggest that formulating policies towards the Balkans was all plain sailing for Turkish policy-makers, since they faced a classic dilemma of reconciling internal political pressures with external realities. On the one hand, domestic public opinion strongly favoured the Muslim side in the bloody conflict in Bosnia, and later in Kosovo. Although the Bosnian Muslims are not ethnically Turkish, Turks saw Muslim Bosnia as the last remnant of a once-powerful Muslim presence in south-east Europe. During the nineteenth century, Ottoman attentions had been concentrated on the Balkans, as the primary zone of conflict between Islam and the Christian West. Although Turkish government spokesmen frequently emphasised that they regarded the Bosnian conflict as a humanitarian issue, not a battle between two religions, and that the Ottoman empire was firmly in the past, historical memories had not been eradicated. Banners carried at a meeting protesting against Western policy over Bosnia (or lack of one) held in Istanbul's Taksim Square in February 1993, and addressed by President Özal, carried the message 'Bosnia will not become a second Andalusia' – a reference to the massacres and expulsion of the Muslim and Jewish communities of Spain in the fifteenth century.[24] In Turkey, the public impression – which, indeed, was hard to deny – was that the international community was standing idly by, in the face of massacres and expulsion of an important Muslim community, much as they had done in the nineteenth century. Islamist and ultra-nationalist parties did their best to stoke up such feelings, which were reinforced by the fact that a claimed total of four million Turkish citizens were said to be of Bosnian origin, the descendants of refugees of the nineteenth and early twentieth centuries.[25] On the other hand, successive Turkish governments recognised that they could not intervene unilaterally or independently in Bosnia, partly because of its distance from Turkish territory, and partly because Turkey could not afford to step too far out of line with the policies of its Western allies, primarily the United States. Operating from bases in Turkey, Turkish aircraft would only have had five minutes flying time over Bosnia, and Turkey could not have sustained a military presence in the former Yugoslavia except as part of an international force.[26] Hence, Turkish governments concentrated their efforts on drawing international attention to the plight of the Bosnian Muslims, and pressing their allies to intervene on their behalf.

The Bosnian problem became particularly acute for Turkey between 1992 and 1995, as the Western powers failed to take effective measures to protect the Bosnian Muslims. In 1992 Turkey strongly supported the NATO decision to deploy a naval task force in the Adriatic to monitor the application of economic sanctions against Serbia, and the force was at one point commanded by a Turkish officer. Later, in April 1993, it sent a detachment of F-15 jets to join the NATO force, based in Italy, which was to enforce the no-fly zone over Bosnia, although in practice the Turkish aircraft were kept on permanent standby rather than actively taking the field. Turkish diplomats and politicians were meanwhile making it clear that, in their view, these efforts did not go far enough. At the Helsinki summit of the Conference on Security and Cooperation in Europe (CSCE) in July 1992, Prime Minister Demirel tried to mobilise a pressure group including the central Asian republics and Azerbaijan in support of the Bosnian government, and urged President Bush to launch a major military intervention, similar to that against Iraq in 1991. In August 1992 the government also attempted to persuade the permanent members of the UN Security Council to adopt an 'Action Plan' calling for limited air strikes against the Serbs, though with no involvement of ground forces. Rebuffed by the Western powers, Turkey turned to fellow Muslim countries, a campaign in which President Özal played a prominent role. In December 1992 Turkey joined other members of the Organisation of the Islamic Conference (OIC) in threatening to send arms to the Bosnian Muslims after 15 January 1993 if the UN had not taken adequate measures to protect them by then, although when the time came this threat was not implemented. At subsequent OIC meetings in April and July 1993 Turkey sponsored resolutions demanding the lifting of the arms embargo against Bosnia-Herzegovina and proposing the despatch of a special force from Muslim countries to defend the 'safe havens' around Bosnian-Muslim areas which had been declared by the UN in April–May 1993. In all these efforts, Turkey was evidently concerned to prevent independent initiatives by radical Muslim states like Iran, and to persuade the Western powers that it would be better to have Turkey, as an officially democratic, secular and pro-Western state, to head reactions by the Muslim world.[27]

Although these attempts to mobilise the Muslim countries proved quite unavailing, events during 1994–95 suggested that Turkey was beginning to succeed in its bid to play a more active role in the crisis, and that, in the face of appalling tragedies and atrocities, the Western powers were slowly coming round to a more robust view of their responsibilities in Bosnia. Once the UN had set up a special protection force for Bosnia (UNPROFOR) Turkey pressed to be included in it, but its approaches were initially turned down, on the grounds that countries with cultural or historical links with either side should be excluded. The force of this argument was weakened in early 1994 when Russia, which had strong links with the Serbs, was allowed to participate. Accordingly, in March 1994 the UN Secretary-General announced that a Turkish detachment would be accepted. Consisting of about 1,500 troops, it arrived in Bosnia in July 1994, and was stationed at the town of Zeneca, in the western part of the country, where its main task was to monitor the ceasefire between the local Croat and Bosnian-Muslim forces. Its presence was strongly attacked by Greece, but welcomed by both the Croat and Bosnian Muslims, besides helping to reassure Turkish opinion that Turkey was playing a direct and positive role in Bosnia.[28] Diplomatically, Turkey also enhanced its image as a helpful ally to the West by brokering an entente between the Croats and Bosnian Muslims, resulting in the establishment of a Muslim–Croat Federation under the Washington agreement of March 1994. Turkey and Croatia developed close relations, mainly due to their common hostility to Serbia, but the entente also underlined the Turkish argument that the conflict in Bosnia-Herzegovina was not a straightforward war between

Christians and Muslims. Meanwhile, it was reported that Turkey was covertly supplying arms to the Bosnian Muslims (presumably with US compliance) via Croatia, although these accounts could not officially be confirmed.[29]

The most critical turning-point in the Bosnian story came in 1995, following the capture by the Serbs of Srebenica and Zepa, two of the supposedly 'safe havens' in eastern Bosnia, in July and the massacre and flight of their inhabitants. On 30 August, NATO air forces at last launched all-out air attacks on Serbian ground positions in an operation known as 'Deliberate Force', which lasted until 14 September. Following these attacks, Croat forces recaptured large areas of Croatia previously taken by the Serbs, and the Belgrade government was forced to the conference table. Under the agreements signed at Dayton, Ohio, on 21 November 1995, Bosnia-Herzegovina was reconstituted, nominally as a single state, consisting of the Muslim–Croat federation and the Bosnian Serb republic, or 'Republika Serbska', These events effectively removed the Bosnian problem as a source of potential conflict between Turkey and the Western powers, since NATO had now intervened effectively to protect the Bosnian Muslims. The Turkish peacekeeping force stayed on in Bosnia-Herzegovina as a useful part of the international implementation force (IFOR: reconstituted as the 'stabilisation force', or SFOR, in 1996). During 1996, Turkey also joined the United States in playing a significant part in the US-led programme to train and equip the army of the Muslim–Croat federation, besides joining the Italian-led peacekeeping intervention in Albania in 1997 known as 'Operation Alba', and sending a military contingent to help rebuild the Albanian forces.[30]

Following the Dayton agreement, conflicts in the Balkans seemed to have stabilised, up to the time of the eruption of the crisis in Kosovo in 1998–99. As the Serbian campaign against the Kosovar Albanians built up during the winter of 1998–99, representatives of the Kosovar Albanians and the Yugoslav (in effect, Serbian) government met in Rambouillet, near Paris, in February–March 1999, for two rounds of talks under the auspices of the six-nation Contact Group. The Kosovar Albanians accepted an agreement calling for the cessation of violence, the withdrawal of all Yugoslav military, police and paramilitary forces from Kosovo, the stationing of an international military force led by NATO in the province, the unconditional return of refugees, and a political settlement providing for the autonomy of Kosovo within the Federal Republic of Yugoslavia. However, the agreement was rejected by the Belgrade government, which stepped up its campaign of ethnic cleansing of the Kosovar Albanians, in clear violation of a cease-fire agreement reached the previous October, and UN Security Council resolutions. Although the Security Council had not specifically authorised the use of force in Kosovo, NATO began a campaign of intensive air strikes against Serbian targets in Kosovo and in Serbia itself on 23 March, triggering the expulsion of almost a million Kosovar Albanians into the neighbouring republics of Macedonia, Albania and Montenegro. The campaign lasted until 10 June, when Serbian forces were withdrawn from Kosovo, and an international peace-keeping force, known as KFOR, was installed in the province.[31]

At the outset, it appears that the Turkish foreign ministry was not enthusiastic about the prospect of a NATO intervention in Kosovo, since (unlike the conflict in Bosnia-Herzegovina) the crisis did not arise from aggression by one state against another, and appeared to conflict with the now-disputed principle that states had unrestricted sovereignty within their own frontiers. In principle, such action could theoretically be used to justify international intervention on behalf of the Turkish Kurds.[32] In the Balkan context, the official detachment of Kosovo from Yugoslavia – either as an independent state or as part of Albania – could have acted as a precedent for the territorial break-up of Macedonia, with its large Albanian minority, which Turkey strongly opposed. At worst, it could even have threatened to provoke a much wider Balkan war, in which Greece and Turkey could have been dragged in on opposite sides. Fortunately, these worries were shared by the other NATO countries, who were committed to upholding the territorial integrity of all states in the region, including Yugoslavia, at least as a legal principle.[33] More immediately, the sheer scale and brutality of the Serbian action against the Kosovar Albanians meant that Turkey, as a fellow-Muslim nation, could hardly stand aside. As prime minister, Bülent Ecevit took a hawkish line against the Serbs, whom he depicted as part of a grand alliance of the Orthodox Christian nations, including Greece and Russia, against the Balkan Muslims. The fact that Greece dragged its heels over the NATO action in Kosovo, if it did not actively obstruct it, also gave Turkey the opportunity to show that it was a much more reliable member of the alliance, especially from the US viewpoint. As President Demirel claimed, 'the people who have been subjected to cruelty in Kosovo are our brethren', and the crisis presented Turkey with the opportunity to demonstrate that it was a 'first-class' member of NATO.[34]

On these grounds, Turkey strongly supported the NATO action in Kosovo, providing a detachment of F-16 fighters, based in Italy which, according to the Turkish press, played an active role in the operation.

Around 8,000 refugees from Kosovo were accommodated in Turkey, and substantial aid was sent to those taking temporary refuge in Albania.[35] Towards the end of the air operation, in May 1999, the United States sought the use of air bases in Turkey, as well as in Hungary, as a means of increasing the pressure on the Serbs. The Ecevit government rapidly agreed to this, although in the event the bases were not needed.[36] Following the Serbian withdrawal from Kosovo, Turkey sent a detachment of around 1,000 troops to join KFOR, who arrived in July 1999. They were stationed in the town of Prizren, which is largely inhabited by Kosovo's minority of ethnic Turks.[37] In all this, it was nevertheless noticeable that the war in Kosovo failed to provoke as much public excitement or controversy within Turkey as the earlier crisis in Bosnia had done. This may partly have been due to the fact that it coincided with the period of the general elections of 1999 and their aftermath, when media attention was naturally focused on domestic affairs, but partly also because the government's policy had broad support both in Turkey and in the rest of NATO, and hence failed to stir up a strident public debate.

Elsewhere in the Balkans, the end of communism had its most dramatic effects for Turkey in the fall of the Zhivkov regime in Bulgaria in November 1989, which ended the Bulgarian campaign against the Turkish minority (see pp. 168–9). Subsequent Bulgarian governments recognised the cultural rights of the Turks, and allowed them to play a full part in Bulgaria's new democratic system. As a result, at least half of the 312,000 Turkish refugees from Bulgaria returned to their homes in 1990 and afterwards, while the 'Movement for Rights and Freedoms' (in effect, the Turkish ethnic party in Bulgaria) supported the first two Bulgarian governments which followed the fall of communism. As a sign of this dramatic improvement in attitudes and policies, the two countries signed a Treaty of Friendship, Neighbourly Relations and Security in 1992. Although Bulgaria's small size and the poor state of its economy obviously restricted this, economic collaboration was also developed. By 1999, Turkey was lobbying in Washington for Bulgaria's admission to NATO, stressing Bulgaria's supportive role in the NATO action in Kosovo, as well as supporting its eventual accession to the EU, for which Turkey hoped to be a joint candidate.[38] In this as in other respects, Turkey's generally cautious approach in the Balkans appeared to have paid good dividends, since it had helped to prevent Bulgaria as well as Macedonia from slipping into an anti-Muslim or anti-Turkish Slavic bloc led by Greece, and had strengthened its standing in NATO. Thanks to its earlier hostility towards Macedonia and its friendship with Serbia, Greece had been on the losing side in Balkan conflicts and the odd man out in NATO – in contrast to Turkey. These points seem to have been recognised by the Simitis government, which revised Greek policies in the Balkans, and softened Greek attitudes towards the Turks. In fact, as part of the dramatic thaw in relations between Ankara and Athens during 1999, the two governments even agreed to discuss joint projects on rebuilding Kosovo, and a common approach to Balkan security problems.[39]

TURKEY, RUSSIA AND TRANSCAUCASIA

For Turkey, as for the other NATO countries, the end of the Cold War had been a gradual process. Mikhail Gorbachev's accession to power in the Soviet Union in 1985 had brought about a notable decline in Soviet–Turkish tensions, and impressive progress in economic cooperation between the two countries (see p. 167). This process was sealed in March 1991, when Presidents Gorbachev and Özal finally signed a Treaty of Friendship and Good Neighbourliness. Had conditions remained unchanged, Turkey might have continued this as a long-term entente with its northern neighbour, as it had in the 1920s and 1930s. This failed to emerge, mainly because the disintegration of the Soviet Union in 1991 opened up a Pandora's box of regional conflicts – notably in the new Transcaucasian republics of Georgia, Armenia and Azerbaijan, in which Turkey and Russia were on opposite sides politically. At the same time, Turkey had important reasons, both strategic and economic, for seeking to avoid a head-on collision with Moscow. As a result, it had to walk a delicate tightrope in its relations with Russia, balancing its sympathies for the Muslim and predominantly Turkic nations of the Caucasus and central Asia, and its desire to prevent Moscow from regaining a monopoly of power in Russia's 'near abroad', with its need to promote its economic interests in Russia and avoid a direct clash with Russian military power. The uncertain and apparently changing directions of Russian foreign policy – shifting between cooperation with the West and the attempted reassertion of national power – added to the difficulties faced by Turkish foreign policy-makers and their counterparts in Western capitals.

In both military and economic terms, the Russian Federation was a far weaker state than the Soviet Union had been, but it was still an important power to be reckoned with. In spite of the end of the Warsaw Pact, it still had huge conventional armed forces, besides nuclear missiles and a permanent seat in the UN Security Council. Within the former Soviet Union, now nominally regrouped as the Commonwealth of Independent

States, or CIS, Russia was still the dominant player. Hence, in their policies towards Moscow, the Turks still had to tread warily. The risk of a direct attack by Russia on Turkey might now be remote, but Turkey still had to avoid potentially violent conflicts with Russia wherever possible, especially in situations where it could not be certain that the rest of NATO would support it. More immediately, Turkey's economic interests in maintaining cooperative relations with Moscow had continued to grow. As already noticed, by 1998 Turkey's trade with the CIS had risen to about 12.7 per cent of its total foreign merchandise trade, boosted by the growth of unofficial 'suitcase' exports (see p. 210). Within the CIS total, Russia was easily Turkey's most important trading partner. In spite of the economic crisis in Russia of 1998, Turkey's exports to Russia in that year, including an estimate for 'suitcase' trade, came to just over US$3 billion, or around 11 per cent of its total exports. This made Russia Turkey's second largest overseas market – still a long way behind Germany, at 20.3 per cent, but ahead of the United States, at 8.3 per cent. By 1997, Turkish construction companies had also won about US$5 billion worth of contracts in Russia, putting them in first place among foreign contractors working in the country. As a result, some of Turkey's biggest companies were identified by the Turkish press as part of a pro-Russian business lobby in Turkey, anxious to prevent political conflicts from undermining their position. On the imports side, Turkey's trade with Russia was far lower, at US$2.2 billion, or 4.7 per cent of total imports.[40] However, a large part of this was accounted for by natural gas, delivered through the pipeline via Bulgaria inaugurated in 1987. This provided around eight billion cubic metres per year, or about 60 per cent of Turkey's total supply of natural gas.[41] Without these imports, Turkey would have been left seriously short of a vital source of pollution-free energy.

Although Turkey has been urgently seeking to diversify its sources of natural gas, it is likely that Russia will continue to be a major supplier. Under an agreement signed in April 1997, the two governments agreed to upgrade the existing pipeline to a capacity of 14 billion cubic metres per year by 2002. More ambitiously, in December of the same year they launched a project referred to as 'Blue Stream', under which a gas pipeline would be laid directly from Russia under the Black Sea to the Turkish port of Samsun, and thence to Ankara. 'Blue Stream' would have an initial capacity of three billion cubic metres per year, rising to 16 billion cubic metres within ten years, with an estimated cost of between US$2.5 and US$3.3 billion. By late 1999 it was still doubtful whether it would ever be built, owing to serious technical problems and expected financing difficulties, as well as some political reservations on the Turkish side, which were reportedly supported in Washington. As a sign of these obstacles, Russia's renewed onslaught in Chechnya in October–November 1999 apparently helped to put the project on hold: during a visit to Moscow on 6 November, Bülent Ecevit delayed signing a further agreement on 'Blue Stream', though he stated that an agreement would be reached by the end of the year.[42]

The Russian campaigns in Chechnya during 1994–96 and 1999 also brought out a clear point of potential conflict between Turkey and Russia, in that Turkish popular sympathies were generally with the Chechens, as fellow-Muslims. It is estimated that there are around 25,000 Turkish citizens of Chechen descent, and a claimed total of around five million inhabitants of Turkey whose families originate from the north Caucasus and Transcaucasian regions as a whole (that is, Chechens, Circassians, Abkhazians, Azeris and others). These groups support a number of solidarity and cultural organisations in Turkey, with links to ultra-nationalist and Islamist parties, and are reported to have collected money and sent unofficial volunteers to fight in Chechnya. They drew particular attention to their cause in January 1996 when a group of Turkish citizens of north Caucasian origin hijacked the ferry, *Avrasya*, in the port of Trabzon. In the same year, Turkey also accepted an unofficial 'Representation of the Chechen Republic of Ichkeria'. However, successive Turkish governments have been very careful not to give substantial or open support to any of these groups, mainly for fear that this might tempt Russia into giving full financial or logistical backing to the PKK.[43] As a statement of intent, in February 1995 the two countries signed a security protocol providing for cooperation against terrorism and organised crime, with the implication that they would abstain reciprocally from involvement in either the Kurdish or Chechen conflicts.[44] This commitment was one which went right back to the original Turkish–Soviet treaty of 1921, albeit in somewhat changed circumstances (p. 51).

Subsequently, the Turks could reasonably suspect that Moscow had not strictly abided by this agreement since, like the pro-Chechen groups in Turkey, the PKK evidently enjoyed a degree of official tolerance in Russia. More dramatically, Abdullah Öcalan was periodically sheltered in Russia and Belarus in the course of his international wanderings between October 1998 and February 1999, although the Russians never openly acknowledged his presence or gave him political asylum (see p. 201). On the other hand, both sides were careful to avoid open involvement in the other's internal affairs, and neither ever became the main sponsor of rebel movements in the other's territory. The issue came to a head in November 1999 when Bülent Ecevit paid an official visit to Moscow just as the Russians were intensifying their attacks during their second campaign in Chechnya. Although Turkish public opinion was clearly sympathetic to the Chechens, and Ecevit admitted that the war was causing 'serious humanitarian worries', he stuck to the line that the war was still 'Russia's internal problem'.[45] For both Russia and Turkey, respect for international frontiers and the territorial integrity of existing states was too important a principle to be openly abandoned, whatever the temptations to infringe it.

At the beginning of the 1990s, Turgut Özal attempted to exploit and expand Turkey's growing economic links with neighbouring ex-communist states by launching a regional organisation, in the shape of the Black Sea Economic Cooperation (BSEC) project. This took official status at a meeting held in Istanbul in June 1992, which was attended by the heads of state or government of Turkey, Bulgaria, Romania, Moldova, Ukraine, Russia, Georgia, Armenia, Azerbaijan, Greece and Albania: (although the last four are not strictly speaking Black Sea states, it was evidently thought politically inexpedient to exclude them). At the Istanbul summit, the 11 countries committed themselves to 'reduce or progressively eliminate obstacles [to trade] of all kinds', and to develop joint projects in the fields of transport, energy, mining, tourism and environmental protection.[46] Institutionally, the BSEC project has a permanent secretariat in Istanbul with a rotating chair, and an annual meeting of the foreign ministers of the member states. At a meeting in Sofia in December 1993 it was decided to set up a Black Sea Foreign Trade and Development Bank, based in Salonika. After long delays, this was eventually inaugurated in June 1999.[47] In the economic sphere, it is hard to estimate whether the project had had any significant or independent effect. By 1998, Turkey's trade with the other BSEC states had risen to about 12 per cent of its total exports, and 9 per cent of its imports, but almost half of this was accounted for by Russia alone, and the growth in trade might well have occurred anyway, with the opening up of markets in the region, regardless of the BSEC objectives.[48] To criticise the project on these grounds was, however, to ignore the argument that it had political, rather than purely economic aims, being based on the idea that if the regional countries developed economic inter-dependence, they would become politically more cooperative. This ambition may well have been too optimistic, since the complex contests between almost all the members – between Greece and Turkey, between Russia and Moldova, between Ukraine and Georgia, and between Azerbaijan and Armenia – proved too obdurate for any real sense of community to emerge. As a senior member of the Turkish foreign ministry admitted, the BSEC project was not entrusted with a peace-keeping mission, and was not equipped with the mechanisms for preventive diplomacy or regional disarmament.[49] Nonetheless, it did at least provide a forum for member states to try to settle their differences, if they were minded to do so, and to enhance Turkey's image as a cooperative neighbour.

Of the various disputes between the regional states, that between Armenia and Azerbaijan was by far the most critical for Turkey, since it was the only one which produced a direct war between two independent countries and, as in the case of the conflict in Bosnia-Herzegovina, created the difficult task of reconciling domestic political pressures with external realities. While Turkish public opinion strongly favoured the Azeris, as fellow-Muslims of Turkic ethnicity, the government could not afford to give much more than moral or economic support to Azerbaijan, for fear of provoking a direct military conflict with Armenia, which might broaden into a Russian–Turkish war. Meeting in Tashkent in May 1992, Russia, Tajikistan, Uzbekistan, Kirghizstan, Kazakhstan and Armenia signed the CIS collective security treaty, under which they promised to support one another if they were attacked by any country which was not a member of the CIS. This allowed Russia to station troops in Armenia, and later Georgia, so that if Turkey had been involved in direct hostilities with Armenia it would also have found itself fighting Russia.[50]

The contest gained added international importance from the fact that the end of Soviet rule opened up the large oil and gas reserves of the Caspian basin to international exploitation. Although earlier expectations that the region could come to rival the Middle East as a source of energy have now been scaled down, the Caspian basin's proven reserves, as of the end of 1998, are put at 16.1 billion barrels of oil (about the same as those of the North Sea) and 7.4 trillion cubic metres of gas (about double those of the North Sea).[51] Possible reserves have been put at 160 billion barrels and 17.6 trillion cubic metres respectively which, if proven, would amount to 15 per cent of the world's proven oil reserves, and 12 per cent of its gas reserves.[52] Azerbaijan, like the other Caspian basin states of Kazakhstan and Turkmenistan, was anxious to develop its oil and gas industry without continuing its dependence on Russia, but could not do so without building new overland pipelines, which in turn required stable and cooperative relations with its neighbours. Equally, the prospect that the Caspian basin states might acquire extra resources and export pipelines outside their control faced Russian leaders with the expectation that these states could slip out of Moscow's sphere on influence, to the benefit of the Western powers, as well as Turkey. In this way, pipeline projects acquired the role played by railways in late nineteenth-century diplomacy, as weapons in a struggle for political power as well as economic penetration.[53]

The violent conflict between Azerbaijan and Armenia began in January 1990, before the dissolution of the Soviet Union, when Soviet troops killed several hundred Azeris while occupying Baku, the capital of Azerbaijan, following attacks on the local Armenian minority. At this stage, Turkey still hoped and expected that the Soviet Union would survive as a territorial unit. It supported Gorbachev's reform programme, and adhered to the view that the conflict was an internal Soviet problem.[54] However, events soon made this policy obsolete. On 30 August 1991 Azerbaijan declared its independence, to be followed by Armenia on 21 September. Meanwhile, on 2 September, Nagorno-Karabakh, the predominantly Armenian enclave within Azerbaijan, proclaimed itself a separate republic. On 26 November the Azeri parliament withdrew the autonomous status which Nagorno-Karabakh had previously enjoyed under the Soviet constitution. In the euphoria of independence, the Azeris and Armenians had clearly set themselves on a collision course. In Ankara, the outgoing Motherland Party administration of Mesut Yılmaz recognised Azerbaijan as an independent state on 9 November, and the succeeding government under Süleyman Demirel extended this recognition to all the former Soviet republics on 19 December 1991.

In the long run, Turkey needed peace and stability in Transcaucasia, and the chance to develop economic opportunities in all the countries of the region. In an ideal world, it would also have liked to act as a regional power-broker and arbiter. This ambition proved impossible to achieve, since it went beyond its political, economic and military resources, and the regional disputes proved far too intractable. Initially, attempts were made by Turkey to open up contacts with Armenia, and to persuade the Azeris to restore the autonomy of Nagorno-Karabakh,[55] but by February 1992 full-scale fighting in and around the enclave had erupted. Although the government of Armenia claimed that the war was being prosecuted by the Nagorno-Karabakh Armenians, rather than itself, this claim could not be taken seriously, since the Armenian fighters in the enclave were heavily dependent on supplies and other support from Armenia proper, which was in turn supported by Russia. On 26 February Armenian forces in Stepanakert, the capital of Nagorno-Karabakh, captured the Azeri-inhabited suburb of Khojali, massacring some 500 civilians, and causing widespread public protests in Turkey. President Özal apparently supported a hawkish line, suggesting that 'we should frighten [the Armenians] a little', but he was not supported by Demirel, who still stressed the need to find a peaceful settlement between the Azeris and Armenians.[56] These hopes proved unavailing. On 28 February 1992, at Turkish prompting, the CSCE condemned the alteration of frontiers by force and confirmed that Nagorno-Karabakh is part of Azerbaijan. This did not deter the Armenians, who by 11 May had captured the whole of Nagorno-Karabakh and opened up a corridor between the enclave and Armenia proper, through Lachin, besides shelling the western end of Nakhichevan, the geographically detached province of Azerbaijan which abuts onto Turkish territory.

The Armenian attack on Nakhichevan raised critical questions for Turkey, since the fighting had now moved close to its borders. An Armenian invasion of Nakhichevan would have been a clear infraction of the Turkish–Soviet Treaty of Friendship of 1921, declaring that Nakhichevan was part of Azerbaijan and could not be handed over to any other state (see p. 74, n. 14). Whether Turkey could have claimed treaty rights to intervene militarily in Nakhichevan to protect the status quo was an open question,[57] but the Commander of Land Forces, General Mühittin Fisunoğlu, announced that 'all necessary preparations' had been made for possible military action.[58] In Moscow, the commander of the armed forces of the CIS, General Yevgeny Shaposhnikov, warned that any intervention by a third country (read Turkey) could lead to a major war, and a similar warning was issued by the Russian ambassador in Ankara, Albert Chernishev. Apparently, this was the closest Turkey and Russia came to a direct armed collision.[59] Fortunately, the cautious Demirel decided to attempt a diplomatic solution, by making a direct approach to Moscow. This proved successful. After emergency talks between Demirel and Russian President Boris Yeltsin on 25–26 May, the two leaders issued a declaration condemning the occupation of Lachin and the fighting on the border between Armenia and Nakhichevan, inducing the Armenians to break off their attacks two days later.[60]

This outcome reduced the tension between the two sides. Shortly afterwards, Turkey was able to increase its influence in Baku in June 1992 when Abulfez Elchibey, who was strongly favoured in Ankara, was elected president of Azerbaijan. In March 1993 an outline agreement was signed between Turkey and Azerbaijan to construct an oil pipeline between Baku and the Turkish Mediterranean port of Ceyhan, near İskenderun. This was to become a centre-piece of Turkish policy in Transcaucasia, since, if realised, it would give Turkey an important role in the Caspian oil game, and significantly reduce Russia's leverage over the Caspian states, by avoiding Azerbaijan's existing export pipeline running through Russian territory. At this stage, Armenia's President Levon Ter Petrossian also seemed keen to soften Armenian policies towards both Turkey and Azerbaijan: in June 1992 he closed down the headquarters of the ultra-nationalist Dashnakzoutian party in Armenia, and on 16 October he dismissed his outspokenly anti-Turkish foreign minister, Raffi Hovanissian.[61] In response, Turkey sent a diplomatic mission to Armenia in August 1992, pointing out the economic advantages which Armenia could enjoy by establishing normal relations with Turkey, while the foreign minister, Hikmet Çetin, suggested that Turkey could open full diplomatic relations with Armenia if the Armenians withdrew from the Lachin corridor and other areas of Azerbaijan, without leaving Nagorno-Karabakh itself. In November 1992 Tansu Çiller's government agreed to deliver wheat to Armenia, as well as electric power through a connection of the two countries' electricity grids, but this was soon cancelled, under strong pressure from Azerbaijan.[62]

In spite of these peace feelers by Turkey, the war between the Azeris and the Armenians dragged on during 1992–93, with the Armenians clearly gaining the upper hand. By September 1993 they had captured virtually all the territory between Nagorno-Karabakh and Armenia proper, as well as the land south of the enclave as far as the Azeri–Iranian border, forcing around 100,000 Azeris to become refugees in their own country, and occupying about 20 per cent of the total land area of Azerbaijan.[63] In June 1993 Turkey joined ten other nations, including the United States, Germany, Russia, Armenia and Azerbaijan, in the so-called 'Minsk Group', set up by the CSCE as an attempt to resolve the conflict. Early in 1993, Russia appeared to be willing to join Turkey in a joint approach to secure a settlement, but then abandoned this in a bid to become the sole arbiter in Transcaucasia, and to re-establish Moscow's former monopoly of power in the region. Following a UN Security Council resolution of 6 April calling for the withdrawal of Armenian forces, Turkey joined Azerbaijan in imposing a full economic embargo on Armenia. In July 1993 Turkey also proposed that a UN peacekeeping force, including its own troops, should be sent to Azerbaijan, but this proposal was turned down by Armenia, Russia and Iran.[64] Meanwhile, the new Russian policy was demonstrated by a violent change of regime in Baku. On 4 June 1993 one of Abulfez Elchibey's rivals, ex-Colonel Suret Husseinov, who was evidently acting with covert Russian support, took over large quantities of arms and ammunition from departing Soviet forces. He seized the town of

Ganja, in northern Azerbaijan, from where he marched to Baku, and overthrew Elchibey's government. He failed to gain personal political power in Azerbaijan, however, which was taken over by Haydar Aliev, a former member of the Soviet Politburo and president of Nakhichevan since 1991.[65]

At first, Turkey reacted sharply to these events, by joining Britain and the United States in announcing that it would continue to recognise Elchibey as the legitimately elected president of Azerbaijan. However, Süleyman Demirel, who had now succeeded Turgut Özal as the Turkish president, recognised that there was nothing effective which Turkey could do to bring Elchibey back to power.[66] Hence, by the end of August, Turkey and the Western powers had been obliged to accept the *fait accompli*. This change of direction was made easier by the fact that, once he had been established in power, Haydar Aliev's actions suggested that he would not be a Russian puppet. Although Azerbaijan officially joined the CIS in September 1993, Aliev refused to allow Russian troops to be stationed in his country. Initially, Aliev had announced that he would cancel the outline agreement with Turkey for the construction of the planned Baku–Ceyhan pipeline, in favour of the development of the existing route between Baku and the Russian Black Sea port of Novorossiisk, but he then changed his stance by confirming his approval of the Turkish route.[67] In effect, he had met most of Turkey's main objectives, short of a settlement with the Armenians, in that he had prevented Azerbaijan from becoming a Russian satellite, and was prepared to allow Turkey an important indirect role in the development of Caspian oil. From Turkey's viewpoint, Aliev's presidency also had an important advantage over that of Elchibey, in that Aliev was more circumspect in his diplomacy. In particular, he was less likely to be provocatively hostile to Russia, or to Iran, with which Turkey could not afford a serious conflict (see pp. 312–13).[68] More importantly, by late 1993 both the Azeris and the Armenians seem to have realised that they had fought one another to a standstill. Hence, in May 1994 Russia was able to induce the defence ministers of Azerbaijan, Armenia and Nagorno-Karabakh to sign a cease-fire, which was also signed by the Russian minister of defence, Pavel Grachev.[69] Russia had thus emerged as the effective peace-broker in the region. The cease-fire at least stabilised the situation, although it left the Armenians in a dominant position on the ground. Since then, Turkey has continued to insist that if a political settlement of the Nagorno-Karabakh conflict could be reached, then it should be policed by a peacekeeping force under the auspices of the Organisation for Security and Cooperation in Europe (OSCE), the successor to the CSCE, in which Turkish forces would participate, rather than a purely CIS force which would be dominated by Russia.[70]

With the apparent end of the shooting war over Nagorno-Karabakh in May 1994, international attention shifted to the future development of the Caspian oil fields, and the question of securing pipeline routes for oil and gas to world markets. In this complex battle for influence, Russia, Georgia, and Iran, as well as Turkey and the main regional producing states – that is Azerbaijan, Kazakhstan and Turkmenistan – were important actual or potential players. Since most of the multi-national companies which would develop these resources were wholly or partly US-based, the US government and the oil companies themselves were also vital decision-makers. At the time of his overthrow in June 1993, Elchibey's government was about to sign an agreement with an international consortium, led by the British company BP, to develop part of Azerbaijan's offshore oil reserves. In Moscow, hard-line nationalists led by Yuri Primakov (at the time the director of Russia's Foreign Intelligence Service) and the then foreign minister, Andrei Kozyrev, urged that Russia should prevent Azerbaijan from signing separate oil exploration agreements with Western companies. Their position was based on the argument that the Caspian Sea should be considered as an inland lake, in which all littoral states should have joint rights to exploit submarine resources, rather than an international sea, geographically divided into offshore zones belonging separately to each country. However, they were opposed by moderates, led by the then prime minister, Viktor Chernomyrdin, who backed the second approach, provided Russia could get a share in the Azerbaijan consortium.[71] Chernomyrdin's view appeared to have carried the day in September 1994, when Aliev's government signed an agreement with the Azerbaijan International Oil Consortium (AIOC) to develop the country's offshore fields. The two leading partners in the consortium were the British company BP, the US company, Amoco (later merged as BP Amoco) plus a group of other US, Norwegian and Japanese companies, the Turkish state petroleum company, TPAO, and its Azeri equivalent, SOCAR. For Moscow, the significant advance was that the Russian company, Lukoil, was allowed a 10 per cent share in the consortium.[72] Russia was thus left in the paradoxical position that, while it opposed Western penetration into Transcaucasia, it had itself gained a stake in the Western-led consortium which was to develop Azeri oil, and could not effectively oppose the Western oil companies.

From 1992 until the end of the decade, the choice of the route of a main export pipeline from Baku to world markets (linked possibly to other oil-producing countries in central Asia, notably Kazakhstan) remained an open and hotly contested question.[73] Essentially there appeared to be five main options. First was the existing pipeline from Baku to the Russian Black Sea port of Novorossiisk, which passes through Chechnya. This had the advantage that it could be based on existing facilities, would be relatively cheap to develop, and was clearly supported by Russia. Its main disadvantages, from the viewpoints of Azerbaijan and the AIOC was that any route through Chechnya would obviously be insecure, that the present pipeline would need a good deal of modernisation, and that (for the Azeris) it would increase rather than reduce their dependence on the Russians. Moreover, a large increase in tanker traffic passing from the Black Sea to the Mediterranean would create serious environmental hazards in the Bosphorus, and might be prevented by Turkey. A re-routing of the pipeline across Russian territory, passing through Daghestan and thus avoiding Chechnya (which was suggested by Russia), might reduce the first hazard, but would not remove the other objections.

As a second option, the pipeline dating originally from Tsarist days, from Baku to the Georgian port of Soupsa could be reconstructed and expanded. This had the advantage that it would be relatively inexpensive to build, and (from the Azeri viewpoint) would be relatively free of Russian control. The problem of transit through the Bosphorus would remain, however, for tankers sailing to ports outside the Black Sea. To avoid the Bosphorus bottleneck, Russia, supported by Greece, proposed a cut-off pipeline running from the Bulgarian port of Burgas to Alexandroupolis, on the Greek Aegean coast. Tankers would load oil in Novorossiisk or Soupsa and discharge in Burgas. Other tankers would then re-load in Alexandroupolis, to carry the oil to world markets. The disadvantages of this route were that it would be time consuming and cumbersome, and that there was no clear sign that the finance would be available. Hence, it did not seem to attract much support from the international oil companies.

To avoid the Black Sea route altogether, a fourth option would be a pipeline passing across Iran, linking Baku with the Persian Gulf. This would be shorter, and thus cheaper to build and operate than the proposed Baku–Ceyhan pipeline. By delivering oil to the Gulf, it would also shorten the route for tankers sailing to east Asian markets. The overwhelming objection to this option was political, and came from the United States. In 1996 President Clinton issued two Executive Orders making it illegal for US oil companies to operate in Iran, and laying down penalties for any US company or individual doing business in the country. This embargo was extended by the Iran–Libya Sanctions Act (ILSA) signed by the president in August 1996, imposing penalties on any foreign corporation investing more than US$20 million in the Iranian oil and gas sector.[74] Admittedly, some US oil companies, such as Mobil, opposed Washington's hard-line policy on Iran, and western European countries contested the legality of the ILSA, but the Clinton administration remained unmoved.[75] In 1995, Haydar Aliev was also persuaded to drop support for the trans-Iranian project by a telephone call from President Clinton.[76] Given that Iran would have great difficulty in financing and constructing the pipeline on its own, or with the help of third parties, US opposition appeared to rule out any trans-Iranian pipeline, unless or until there were a radical and lasting change in Iran's regime and its foreign policies. Even then, oil companies might be reluctant to become over-dependent on an unpredictable Iran.

The Baku–Ceyhan route, passing through Georgia,[77] which was strongly promoted by Turkey, and favoured by Azerbaijan, Georgia and the United States, was thus the fifth option. For Turkey, the revenues to be derived from the pipeline – which would be about US$100 million per year – were far less important than the political role which it would acquire as an important actor in the Caspian oil industry, increasing its strategic value for the Western powers as well as the producing states. Since Turkey was a firm member of NATO, it could argue that this project carried the lowest political risk for the other parties. For Azerbaijan, and possibly Kazakhstan, the project would also significantly reduce their dependence on Russia. The main obstacle to it was economic since, with a length of 1,730 kilometres and an estimated cost of between US$2.4 billion and US$3.3 billion, it would be longer and more expensive than any of the alternatives. To be economically viable, it would need to have a through-put of at least one million barrels per day (b/d), whereas the AIOC only expected to reach a peak production of around 700,000 b/d by 2007, of which some would pass through other routes, or be consumed internally. To fill the pipeline, around 400,000 b/d would have to found from other sources – probably from Kazakhstan. However, this would require an extension under the Caspian Sea to reach the Kazakh oilfields, and in 1996 Kazakhstan had anyway signed an agreement to construct an alternative pipeline to Novorossiisk, with a capacity of 560,000 b/d. As Kazakhstan's president, Nursultan Nazarbeyev, put it, 'there will be no main export pipeline without Kazakh oil', but it was quite uncertain whether it would go through Baku–Ceyhan.[78]

Admittedly, Turkey has clear political and economic reasons for urging the construction of a Baku–Ceyhan pipeline, but Turkish arguments to the effect that unrestricted passage for tankers through the straits would lead to unacceptable environmental risks are not without foundation. The Bosphorus is 31 kilometres long, with an average width of 1.6 kilometres and a minimum width of only 700 metres. It is very twisty, with complex currents, so that a ship sailing from end to end has to alter her course at least twelve times.[79] Under Article 2 of the Montreux Convention of 1936 (see p. 64) Turkey accepted that, 'In time of peace, merchant vessels shall enjoy complete freedom of navigation in the straits, by day and night, under any flag and with any kind of cargo'.[80] At the time, this seemed acceptable, since merchant ships at the time were relatively small, and there were only about 5,000 passages through the straits per year. By the mid-1990s the figure had risen to around 50,000 passages per year, or around 140 per day, including some tankers of over 200,000 tons, and daily passages by tankers of over 100,000 tons. Besides coping with occasional poor visibility and storms, ships have to avoid collisions with local ferries making around 2,000 crossings of the straits per day. Between 1982 and 1994 the Turkish authorities counted no less than 207 accidents, of which two, in 1979 and 1994, were particularly serious, causing oil spillage, massive fires and explosions, and serious loss of life.[81] Currently, around 700,000 b/d of Russian and other oil is shipped from Novorossiisk through the Bosphorus,[82] but if this were the only export route for Azeri and Kazakh oil, then this would increase by at least one million b/d, making the risk of a disastrous accident far worse.

Whether Turkey could legally close the straits to large tankers, or limit their passage, is an open question, given the provisions of the Montreux Convention. Turkish specialists argue that Turkey would be entitled to impose such restrictions, on the grounds that Articles 19 and 21 of the United Nations Convention of the Law of the Sea of 1982 (UNCLOS) allows coastal states to regulate the 'innocent passage' of ships through their territorial waters to protect their shores and waters from pollution. As an example, in 1985 Italy closed the straits of Messina to all ships of over 50,000 tons carrying oil or otherwise dangerous cargoes, after a series of accidents, and this ban has remained in force despite protests from the United States.[83] In 1994, the Turkish authorities introduced new regulations for ships passing through the straits, under which vessels were, among other things, required to adhere to traffic separation lanes, with their speed restricted to 10 knots. At meetings of the International Maritime Organisation (IMO) in 1994, these regulations were objected to by Russia and other Black Sea countries, besides Greece, Cyprus and Oman, but in 1999 the IMO came to the conclusion that they were effective. By this stage, the other states had withdrawn their opposition, though Russia continued to raise mild objections.[84] In effect, Turkey seems to have won this argument, and might possibly develop the precedent by introducing restrictions on the number and size of tankers passing through the straits if this were necessary. In the last resort, it could try to renegotiate the Montreux Convention, or simply denounce it unilaterally, but the former would be very hard to achieve, and the latter might leave Turkey worse rather than better off.[85] Putting the case more broadly, it is clear that environmental protection is now an important item on the international agenda. The big oil companies need to be seen as behaving like good citizens, and would face serious repercussions if tankers carrying their oil caused disastrous accidents in the Bosphorus. Hence, persuasion rather than regulation is likely to be a crucial factor in inducing them to opt for alternative routes.

During 1994–95, the pipelines debate centred on the choice of a route for Azerbaijan's 'early oil' production of around 80,000 b/d, before full production was reached early in the next century. In this context, Turkey argued for adoption of the Baku–Soupsa route, since this avoided Russian territory, and could act as a precedent for eventual implementation of the Baku–Ceyhan project. Although there was a good deal of internal conflict and bureaucratic muddle in Ankara over this point, AIOC's announcement in 1995 that the 'early oil' would be delivered by both the Baku–Soupsa and the Baku Novorossiisk pipelines was seen as a limited victory for Turkey.[86] However, this still left open the choice of route for a main export pipeline, to take over once the Azeri and Kazakh fields came into full production. With oil prices at an historically low level, AIOC was evidently in no hurry to make a decision. However, in October 1999, BP Amoco and other companies in the consortium, which were under strong pressure from the US government on this point, came round in support of the Baku–Ceyhan project. BP Amoco also said it would take a lead in helping companies and governments to find the necessary finance.[87] According to James Wolf, President Clinton's special energy adviser, 'the pipeline is commercially viable on the basis of throughput guarantees', although he added that 'for that to happen … it would need to include not only the companies that are part of the AIOC but also other shippers in the Caspian'.[88] Effectively, the decision by Kazakhstan would still be the crucial factor. This obstacle seemed to be on the way to a resolution in November 1999, on the sidelines of the OSCE summit held in Istanbul, when the leaders of Turkey, Georgia, Kazakhstan and Azerbaijan signed an intergovernmental agreement for construction of the Baku–Ceyhan pipeline, which they hoped to complete by 2004. The economics of the project would also be improved if it were accompanied by a parallel gas pipeline between Turkmenistan and Turkey, for which an outline agreement was simultaneously signed in Istanbul (see p. 296). Securing the finance and throughput guarantees remained to be achieved, but the project now seemed to be nearer realisation than it had been earlier.[89]

The improved prospects for the Baku–Ceyhan project could also be seen as part of a significant shift in US policy towards the region, as well as some basic political realignments within the former Soviet Union which would have important implications for Turkey. In the early 1990s, the Bush and Clinton administrations were still under strong pressure from the powerful Armenian lobby in Congress, and seemed reluctant to adopt policies which would be seen as hostile in Moscow, for fear that this could lead to the overthrow of Boris Yeltsin, and his replacement by a more anti-Western leadership. In October 1992, Congress passed the Freedom Supports Act 907(a) under which Azerbaijan was denied all forms of US government aid unless it 'respects international human rights acts, abandons its blockade of Armenia, ceases its use of force against Armenia and Nagorno-Karabakh and searches a peaceful solution to the conflict'.[90] Subsequent attempts by the Clinton administration to get this blatantly partisan law lifted were of no avail. By the late 1990s a pro-Armenian and pro-Russian approach was clearly inconsistent with the United States' emerging interests in Caspian oil, and its growing worries about Russian policy in Chechnya and elsewhere. This paralleled the apparent reduction of the power of the Armenian lobby in Turkish–US relations (see p. 228). Hence, the US administration switched to giving full support to the Baku–Ceyhan pipeline project, which was promoted as part of an ambitious 'east–west energy corridor' by-passing both Russia and Iran. It also took a neutral position on the Nagorno-Karabakh dispute, by pressing the two sides to reach a peaceful settlement. On all these points, there was an almost total coincidence of policies between Ankara and Washington. At the end of October 1999 it was reported that Haydar Aliev and the Armenian president, Robert Kocharian, were probably close to an agreement on Nagorno-Karabakh, and there were unrealised hopes that a compromise might be reached at the OSCE summit held in Istanbul in November 1999. At the same time, Ecevit and Demirel continued to stress that Russia would still have to be an important player in securing peace.[91]

Were the conflict between Armenia and Azerbaijan to be ended, then Turkey could expect to build up its economic ties with both countries, and perhaps replace Russia as Armenia's main economic partner. More broadly, by 1998–99 it appeared that the CIS might be separating into two distinct camps, consisting of those countries seeking to break away from Moscow's influence, notably Georgia, Ukraine, Azerbaijan and Moldova (referred to from their initials as GUAM) and those which, for whatever reasons, preferred to align with Russia, such as Belarus, Kazakhstan, Armenia, Kirghizstan and Tajikistan. In April 1999, Uzbekistan also became a member of the first alignment, turning GUAM into GUUAM. Meanwhile, Haydar Aliev was elected chairman of the organisation, with a permanent secretariat in prospect, and the GUUAM countries refused to adhere to a new version of the CIS security pact.[92] By late 1999, it thus appeared that while Russia was still pushing hard to re-establish its power within its own frontiers (notably in Chechnya) an important bloc of states in the former Soviet periphery was gradually re-orienting itself towards the West. While Turkish policy in Transcaucasia, as in central Asia, had suffered some severe upsets and rebuffs in the previous six years, it seemed reasonable to expect that this evolution would redound to its benefit.

NOTES

1. Clement H. Dodd, *The Cyprus Imbroglio* (Hemingford Grey, Eothen Press, 1998), pp. 42–3, 46–7. The quotation is from ibid., p. 43.

2. Ibid., pp. 44–51. See also Suha Bölükbaşı, 'Boutros-Ghali's Cyprus Initiative in 1992: Why Did it Fail?', *Middle Eastern Studies,* Vol. 31 (1995), pp. 469, 471–6, and Keith Kyle, *Cyprus: In Search of Peace* (London Minority Rights Group International, 1997), pp. 27–9. For the text of Boutros-Ghali's 'Set of Ideas' and his 'non-map', see Dodd, *Cyprus Imbroglio,* pp. 141–61.

3. Dodd, *Cyprus Imbroglio,* pp. 53–59; Bölükbaşı, 'Boutros-Ghali's', pp. 474–5; Kyle, *Cyprus,* p. 30 and Suha Bölükbaşı, 'The Cyprus Dispute in the Post-Cold War Era', *Turkish Studies Association Bulletin,* Vol. 18 (1994), p. 18.

4. Quoted in Heinz Kramer, 'Turkey and the European Union: A Multi-Dimensional Relationship with Hazy Perspectives', in V. Mastny and R. Craig Nation, eds, *Turkey between East and West: New Challenges for a Rising Regional Power* (Boulder, CO, Westview, 1996), p. 217. See also Dodd, *Cyprus Imbroglio,* pp. 62–3.

5. Dodd, *Cyprus Imbroglio,* pp. 67–8, and Kyle, *Cyprus,* p. 31.

6. Christopher de Bellaigue, 'Conciliation in Cyprus?', *Washington Quarterly,* Vol. 22 (1999), pp. 189–90.

7. For the text of the Joint Declaration, see Dodd, *Cyprus Imbroglio,* pp. 181–3: this misprints the date as 'December 1955' (for 'December 1995').

8. Philip Robins, 'Turkish Foreign Policy under Erbakan', *Survival,* Vol. 39 (1997), pp. 87–8.

9. See Ekavi Athanassopoulou, 'Blessing in Disguise? The Imia Crisis and Turkish–Greek Relations', *Mediterranean Politics,* Vol. 2 (1997), pp. 77, 85–7. For a statement by the Turkish Foreign Ministry on the Kardak/Imia dispute, see 'Turkish Documents Regarding Issues between Turkey and Greece', *Turkish Review of Balkan Studies,* Vol. 3 (1996–97), pp. 143–7.

10. Athanassopoulou, 'Blessing in Disguise?', p. 90, and Dodd, *Cyprus Imbroglio*, pp. 101–7, 190–2.
11. De Bellaigue, 'Conciliation', p. 190.
12. *Milliyet*, 26, 29 June 1999; *Briefing*, 2 August 1999, pp. 12–13, and *Financial Times*, 10 September 1999. On the last point, see also the interview with Bülent Ecevit in *Newsweek*, 1 November 1999.
13. *Briefing*, 30 August 1999, p. 15.
14. Interview with Ecevit in *Newsweek*, 1 November 1999.
15. *Briefing*, 15 November 1999, pp. 12–13.
16. *Milliyet*, 11 December 1999.
17. Oliver P. Richmond, 'Ethno-Nationalism, Sovereignty and Negotiating Positions in the Cyprus Conflict: Obstacles to a Settlement', *Middle Eastern Studies*, Vol. 35 (1999), p. 48.
18. Quoted in *Briefing*, 13 December 1999, p. 10.
19. Ibid.
20. Dodd, *Cyprus Imbroglio*, pp. 82–90, 193–6.
21. Kyle, *Cyprus*, p. 35 and De Bellaigue, 'Conciliation', p. 192. On the last point see the statements by the French and former German foreign ministers cited in Hansjorg Brey, 'Turkey and the Cyprus Question', *International Observer* (Rome), Vol. 24 (1999), p. 119.
22. *Milliyet*, 11 December 1999.
23. Richmond, 'Ethno-Nationalism', pp. 43, 48. To illustrate the point, under Article VIII of the Helsinki Final Act of 1975 the signatory states bound themselves 'to respect the equal rights of peoples and their right to self determination, acting at all times in conformity with ... the relevant norms of international law, including those relating to territorial integrity of states'. Articles III and IV also oblige them to respect the 'inviolability of frontiers' and the 'territorial integrity of states'. Text reprinted in Ian Brownlie, ed., *Basic Documents on Human Rights* (Oxford, Clarendon Press, 2nd edn, 1981), pp. 321–7.
24. Author's observation at the meeting.
25. Estimate by the director of the Society of Solidarity and Assistance to the Refugees from Yugoslavia [in Turkey], cited in Kemal Kirişci, 'New Patterns of Turkish Foreign Policy Behavior', in Çiğdem Balım, ed., *Turkey: Political, Social and Economic Challenges in the 1990s* (Leiden, Brill, 1995), p. 7.
26. Philip Robins, 'Coping with Chaos: Turkey and the Bosnian Crisis', in Richard Gillespie, ed., *Mediterranean Politics*, Vol. 1 (1994) (annual, London, Pinter), p. 112 and Duygu Bazoğlu Sezer, 'Turkey in the New Security Environment in the Balkan and Black Sea Region', in Mastny and Nation, eds, *Turkey between East and West*, p. 82.
27. Robins, 'Coping with Chaos', pp. 122–4 and Kirişci, 'New Patterns', pp. 7–10.
28. *The Independent*, 2 July 1994 and *The Times* (London) 9 July 1994.
29. Robins, 'Coping with Chaos', pp. 125–6; John Roper, 'The West and Turkey: Varying Roles, Common Interests', *International Observer* (Rome), Vol. 24 (1999), p. 94, and Miomir Zuzul, 'Croatia and Turkey: Toward a Durable Peace in Southeastern Europe', *Perceptions* (Ankara), Vol. 3 (1998), pp. 82–8.
30. Gülnur Aybet, *NATO's Developing Role in Collective Security* (Ankara, Ministry of Foreign Affairs, Center for Strategic Research, 1999), pp. 18–20, and Roper, 'The West and Turkey', p. 95.

31. Aybet, *NATO's Developing Role*, pp. 32–4.
32. Roper, 'The West and Turkey', p. 95.
33. See the 'Statement on Kossovo' signed at the NATO summit in Washington in April 1999, paragraph 14; full text reprinted in Aybet, *NATO's Developing Role*, , pp. 63–5.
34. Quoted in *Briefing*, 24 May 1999, p. 18.
35. Ibid., 29 March 1999, pp. 14–15 and 12 April 1999, pp. 14–16.
36. Ibid., 17 May 1999, pp. 18–19. The bases concerned were at Çorlu and Bandırma, on the northern and southern sides of the Sea of Marmara, respectively.
37. Ibid., 12 July 1999, pp. 14–15.
38. See Turkish and Bulgarian reports reproduced in *Summary of World Broadcasts* (London, BBC) 15–16 October 1999.
39. See *Financial Times*, 10 September 1999, and Ekavi Athanassopoulou, 'Greece, Turkey, Europe: Constantinos Simitis in Premiership Waters', *Mediterranean Politics*, Vol. 1 (1996), p. 116.
40. Data from *Briefing*, 8 March 1999, pp. 36–7, 22 March 1999, p. 32 and *Country Report, Turkey*, 2nd Qtr 1997 (London, Economist Intelligence Unit), pp. 24, 26. In this calculation, Turkey's 'suitcase' exports to Russia have been estimated as US$1.7 billion, or 50.6 per cent of its 'suitcase' exports to the whole of the CIS – the same proportion as for normally recorded exports in the same year.
41. Pending the construction of gas pipelines from Iran and Turkmenistan, the remainder was imported as liquid natural gas (LNG) from Algeria and other countries. Data from Reuters, 5 November 1999.
42. Ibid., 6 November 1999. See also Gareth M. Winrow, 'Pipeline Politics and Turkey: a New Great Game in Eurasia?', paper presented to conference on 'Russia–China Central Asia: From Geo-politics to Geo-economics in Eurasia', Centre for Euro-Asian Studies, University of Reading, England, 23 January 1998, p. 9.
43. Gareth M. Winrow, 'Turkey and the Newly Independent States of Central Asia and Transcaucasus', *MERIA Journal* (published on internet) No. 2 (1997), and 'Turkey's Relations with the Transcaucasus and the Central Asian Republics', *Perceptions* (Ankara), Vol. 1 No. 1 (1996), pp. 129–30.
44. Suha Bölükbaşı, 'Ankara's Baku-Centered Transcaucasia Policy: Has It Failed?', *Middle East Journal*, Vol. 51 (1997), p. 90.
45. Interview on TRT television, Ankara, 4 November 1999. See also *Summary of World Broadcasts*, 6 November 1999 and *International Herald Tribune*, 29 November 1999.
46. 'Summit Declaration of Black Sea Economic Cooperation', June 1992 (copy kindly supplied by Ministry of Foreign Affairs, Ankara).
47. *Briefing*, 28 June 1999, p. 26.
48. Data from ibid., 8 March 1999, pp. 36–7.
49. Ercan Özer, 'The Black Sea Economic Cooperation and Regional Security', *Perceptions* (Ankara), Vol. 2 No. 3 (1997), pp. 100–1.
50. See Gareth M. Winrow, 'A Region at the Crossroads: Security Issues in Post-Soviet Asia', *Journal of South Asian and Middle Eastern Studies*, Vol. 18 (1994), p. 14, and Robert V. Barylski, 'Russia, the West and the Caspian Energy Hub', *Middle East Journal*, Vol. 49 (1995), pp. 220–1. Azerbaijan signed the pact in September 1993, following the takeover by Haydar Aliev (see above, p. 274) but has not allowed Russian troops to be stationed on its territory. In the same month, and under intense pressure from Russia, President Edvard Shevardnadze of Georgia also acceded to the CIS pact and allowed

Russian troops to be stationed on the Georgian–Turkish border.

51. *BP Amoco Statistical Review of World Energy, 1999* (London, BP Amoco, 1999), pp. 4, 20.

52. Patrick Clawson, 'Iran and Caspian Basin Oil and Gas', *Perceptions* (Ankara), Vol. 2, No. 4 (1998), p. 17. Clawson's percentage figures have been re-calculated according to 1998 proven reserves (see previous note). For other estimates, see Heinz Kramer and Friedemann Muller, 'Relations with Turkey and the Caspian Basin Countries', in Robert D. Blackwill and Michael Stürmer, eds, *Allies Divided: Transatlantic Policies for the Greater Middle East* (Cambridge, MA, MIT Press, 1997), pp. 192–4, and Brent Sasley, 'Turkey's Energy Politics in the Post Cold-War Era', *MERIA Journal* (published on internet), Vol. 2, No. 2.

53. This point is made by F. Stephen Larrabee, 'US and European Policy toward Turkey and the Caspian Basin', in Blackwell and Stürmer, ed, *Allies Divided*, p. 162.

54. For further details on these and subsequent events up to 1994, see the author's two earlier papers, 'Turkey, the Black Sea and Transcaucasia', in John F.R. Wright, Suzanne Goldenburg and Richard Schofield, eds, *Transcaucasian Boundaries*, (London, UCL Press, 1996), pp. 54–68, and 'Turkey and Transcaucasia', in David Menashri, ed., *Central Asia Meets the Middle East* (London, Cass, 1998), pp. 150–67. These two papers have been drawn on in preparing the following account.

55. Graham E. Fuller, 'Turkey's New Eastern Orientation', in Graham E. Fuller and Ian O. Lesser, eds, *Turkey's New Geopolitics: From the Balkans to Western China* (Boulder, CO, Westview, 1993), p. 78.

56. *Milliyet*, 6 March, 14 March 1992.

57. Bülent Ecevit claimed that this was so (*Cumhuriyet*, 25 May 1992) although the 1921 treaty appears to give Turkey far fewer rights than it had, for instance, under the 1960 Cyprus Treaty of Guarantee.

58. Quoted in *Mideast Mirror* (London, daily) 19 May 1992.

59. Ibid., 21 May 1992 and *Milliyet*, 21 May 1992.

60. *Milliyet*, 27 May 1992 and *The Independent*, 28 May 1992.

61. See Anahide Ter Minassian, 'L'Armenie, la Turquie et le marché commun de la mer Noire', *Cahiers d'Études sur la Mediterranée Orientale et le Monde Turco-Iranien* [CEMOTI] (Paris), No. 15 (1993), pp. 193, 201–4.

62. Bölükbaşı, 'Ankara's Baku-Centered Policy', pp. 84–5.

63. It is claimed that over a million Azeris have been forced to leave their homes since the start of the conflict in 1988. See Svante E. Cornell, 'Turkey and the Conflict in Nagorno Karabakh: A Delicate Balance', *Middle Eastern Studies*, Vol. 34 (1998), p. 51. See also Svante E. Cornell, 'Undeclared War: The Nagorno Karabakh Conflict Reconsidered', *Journal of South Asian and Middle Eastern Studies*, Vol. 20 (1997), p. 9.

64. Sezer, 'Turkey in the New Security Environment', pp. 88–89; Duygu Bazoğlu Sezer, *Turkey's Political and Security Interests and Policies in the New Geostrategic Environment of the Expanded Middle East* (Washington, DC, Henry L. Stimson Center, Occasional Paper No. 19, 1994), p. 13, and Stephen J. Blank, 'The Eastern Question Revived: Turkey and Russia Contend for Eurasia', in Menashri, ed., *Central Asia*, p. 172.

65. *Briefing*, 14 June 1993, p. 14, 21 June 1993, pp. 10–11.

66. *Milliyet*, 23 June 1993.

67. Ibid., 12 August 1993.

68. During his presidency, Elchibey had tactlessly stated that Iran was doomed, and that Iranian Azerbaijan would be united with his republic within five years. See Cornell,

'Undeclared War', p. 13. Statements of this kind evidently caused severe misgivings in Ankara, which fully supported Azerbaijan's independence within its existing frontiers, but did not want to stir up the cauldron by supporting vague Azeri claims to Iranian Azerbaijan.

69. Dimitry Furman and Carl Johan Asenius, 'The Case of Nagorno-Karabakh (Azerbaijan)', in Lena Jonson and Clive Archer, ed., *Peacekeeping and the Role of Russia in Eurasia* (Boulder, CO, Westview, 1996), pp. 147–9.

70. Winrow, 'Turkey's Relations', pp. 132–3. The CSCE was re-named as the OSCE in 1994. In December 1994, under heavy Western pressure, Russia appeared to change its stance, by agreeing to participate in an OSCE peace force, in exchange for co-chairing the Minsk Group. See Furman and Asenius, 'The Case of Nagorno-Karabakh', p. 150.

71. Barylski, 'Russia', p. 223.

72. For further details, including adjustments of the different companies' shares during 1995–96, see Sabit Bagirov, 'Azerbaijani Oil: Glimpses of a Long History', *Perceptions* (Ankara), Vol. 1, No. 2 (1996), pp. 40–6.

73. There is a substantial literature on this question, on which the following summary is based. See, in particular, Lowell A. Bezanis, *The Baku–Ceyhan Pipeline: Constraints to a US-Backed Central Asian/Caucasian Exit Route* (Washington, DC, Petroleum Finance Market Intelligence Service, 1998); Sasley, 'Turkey's Energy Politics': Kramer and Müller, 'Relations with Turkey': Winrow, 'Pipeline Politics'; Clawson, 'Iran and Caspian Basin'; Bülent Gökay, 'Caspian Uncertainties: Regional Rivalries and Pipelines', *Perceptions* (Ankara), Vol. 3 No. 1 (1998); and Amy Myers Jaffe and Robert A. Manning, 'The Myth of the Caspian "Great Game": The Real Geopolitics of Energy', *Survival*, Vol. 40 (1998/99).

74. For further details, see, Garry Sick, 'Rethinking Dual Containment', *Survival*, Vol. 40 (1998), pp. 9–10, 19.

75. Bezanis, *Baku–Ceyhan*, p. 19.

76. Kramer and Müller, 'Relations with Turkey', p. 196.

77. A shorter alternative route could run through the short strip of Armenian territory (the 'Zengezur corridor') separating Nakichevan from the rest of Azerbaijan, and then through Nakhichevan to Turkey. However, this appeared to be ruled out by the continuing conflict over Nagorno-Karabakh.

78. Quoted in Bezanis, *Baku–Ceyhan*, p. 13. Data from Winrow, 'Pipeline Politics', pp. 4–5, and Reuters, 19 November 1999.

79. Bayram Öztürk, 'The Istanbul Strait: A Closing Biological Corridor', in Turkish Straits Voluntary Watch Group, *Turkish Straits: New Problems, New Solutions* (Istanbul, Isis, for Foundation for Middle East and Balkan Studies, 1995), p. 145, and Saim Oğuzülgen, 'The Importance of Pilotage Services in the Turkish Straits for the Protection of Life, Property and the Environment', in ibid., p. 109.

80. For the full text of the Convention, see ibid., pp. 10–24.

81. Oğuzülgen, 'Importance', pp. 105–6, 113–26, and Gündüz Aybay and Nilüfer Oral, 'Turkey's Authority to Regulate Passage of Vessels through the Turkish Straits', *Perceptions* (Ankara), Vol. 3 No. 2 (1998), pp. 104–5.

82. Winrow, 'Pipeline Politics', p. 6.

83. Aybay and Oral, 'Turkey's Authority', pp. 94–6. Against this, UNCLOS gives more limited rights to coastal states in the case of ships in 'transit' through straits used for

international navigation. Turkish specialists argue that this does not apply in the Turkish straits since, although the English text of the Montreux Convention refers to 'freedom of transit and navigation', the original text, in French, renders this as '*la liberté de passage et de navigation*', and advance other arguments to the same effect. See ibid., pp. 97–104, and Gündüz Aybay, 'On the Power of Turkey to Regulate Free Passage through the Straits', in Turkish Straits Voluntary Watch Group, *Turkish Straits*, pp. 58–9.

84. İsmail Soysal, 'The 1936 Montreux Convention 60 Years Later', in Turkish Straits Voluntary Watch Group, *Turkish Straits*, p. 6. For the text of the 1994 regulations, see ibid., pp. 61–88. On the last point, the author is much indebted for information to Captain Gündüz Aybay and Dr Nilüfer Oral.

85. Sevin Toluner, 'Rights and Duties of Turkey regarding Merchant Vessels Passing through the Straits', in ibid., pp. 29–30.

86. See Winrow, 'Pipeline Politics', p. 8, and 'Turkey and the Newly Independent States'. See also Kramer and Müller, 'Relations with Turkey', p. 197 and Bezanis, *Baku–Ceyhan*, p. 6.

87. Reuters, 19 October 1999.

88. Ibid., 5 November 1999.

89. *Briefing*, 22 November 1999, pp. 31–2.

90. Quoted in Bölükbaşı, 'Ankara's Baku–Centered Policy', p. 57. See also Cornell, 'Undeclared War', pp. 10–11.

91. Reuters, 18 October, 31 October 1999.

92. Svante E. Cornell, 'Geopolitics and Strategic Alignments in the Caucasus and Central Asia', *Perceptions* (Ankara), Vol. 4 No. 2 (1999), pp. 108–11.

9

Turkey and Regional Politics after the Cold War: (II) Central Asia and the Middle East

Among the many effects of the disintegration of the Soviet Union on Turkey's international situation, the ending of Soviet rule in central Asia was one which attracted most attention, both in Turkey and abroad, since it suggested that Turkey might become an important regional player in a part of the world which had virtually been lifted out of international politics since the late nineteenth century. Five independent republics had now been established in the region – Kazakhstan, Uzbekistan, Kirghizstan, Turkmenistan and Tajikistan – but they all appeared to be weak and isolated. Beguiled by the precedent of the Anglo-Russian struggle for regional influence between the 1820s and the early 1900s, some writers suggested that there would be a new 'great game' in central Asia – this time, between the forces of Islamic radicalism, led by Iran, and those of secular democracy, led by Turkey and supported by the United States. Turkey, it was hoped, would be the model for the evolution of the five new republics as democratic states with free-market economies. Turkish governments at the time did nothing to discourage these ideas, but within a few years more realistic policies and expectations began to prevail. As a result, Turkey was left with an important cultural and economic role in central Asia, but without much real political power.

Turkish policies in the five ex-Soviet republics to the east of the Caspian were formed by cultural and historical legacies as well as modern political and economic realities. In a world in which ethnic identities were seen as the bedrock of modern statehood, Turkey was in a possibly unique and certainly ambiguous situation. If ethnicity were defined in terms of language, then it was unclear how far the Turkish nation extended, since many of the peoples to its east spoke languages akin to Turkish, and sharply differentiated from the other main regional languages – Russian, Persian and Chinese. This led some Turkish politicians, such as Süleyman Demirel, in February 1992, to speak of a 'Turkish world', supposedly stretching from the Adriatic to the great wall of China.[1] If this implied a strong degree of cultural homogeneity over such a vast area, it was a serious exaggeration. In practice, a distinction had to be made between 'Turkish', meaning the inhabitants of Turkey and their language, and 'Turkic' – that is, speakers of languages related to Turkish, but far from identical to it. In the linguistic sphere, the regional languages may be 'Turkic', but are not strictly 'Turkish'. The western Turkic languages like Azeri and Turkmen can be understood, albeit with some difficulty, by speakers of the Turkish of Turkey. However, the Turkic languages spoken in most of central Asia – Uzbek, Kazakh, Kirghiz and Uighur – are different, though related, and the Turks of Turkey have to learn them as virtually foreign languages. When people from different central Asian nations speak to one another or to outsiders, they will normally do so in Russian, since there is no 'standard' Turkic language, similar to Mandarin Chinese or modern literary Arabic.

This linguistic complexity is reinforced by ethnic and historical ones. Within central Asia, there is one important indigenous non-Turkic nation, the Tajiks, speaking a dialect of Persian, plus numerous smaller ones. More importantly, the period of Tsarist and then Soviet rule saw a substantial immigration of Russians and the other Slavic peoples of the Soviet Union, besides Koreans and other ethnic groups. According to Soviet data of 1990–91, ethnic Russians accounted for about 38 per cent of the population of Kazakhstan and 22 per cent of that of Kirghizstan, with smaller proportions in the other three republics. Similarly, the indigenous peoples stretched across inter-state boundaries so that, for instance, ethnic Uzbeks accounted for 23 per cent of the population of Tajikistan, and 13 per cent of that of Kirghizstan.[2] Historically, the connections between the Turkic peoples of central Asia and those of modern Turkey have been slight. According to Turkish nationalist mythology, the people of Turkey are the descendants of Turkish tribes who migrated westwards from central Asia, but in fact it is likely that the majority of the inhabitants of modern Turkey are the descendants of the original populations of Anatolia, who adopted Islam and became Turkified over the centuries, or of relatively recent immigrants from the Balkans, the Crimea and the Caucasus (see p. 16). There has been no single state including all the Turkic peoples since the days of Timur Leng, in the late fourteenth and early fifteenth centuries. In

1569 the Ottomans made an unsuccessful attempt to capture Astrakhan, just north of the Caspian, from the Russians, but this was their sole serious foray into the region, and afterwards they only retained fitful contacts with central Asia.[3] The historical break has been reinforced by geographical ones, since Turkey only has direct territorial contact with one Turkic state, the Azeri enclave of Nakhichevan, which is in turn separated from the rest of Azerbaijan by Armenian territory. The main roads and railways run from central Asia to Russia, not the west, and the overland journey from, say, Istanbul to Tashkent is long and arduous. Thanks to these geographical factors, central Asia never came to have the critical position in Turkish foreign policy occupied by Transcaucasia, where Turkish interests were far more direct, and there was a greater risk of a head-on collision with Russia.

In the early twentieth century, Turkish ethnic nationalism developed a distinctly pan-Turkish bias, calling for the union of all the Turkic peoples, but the failure of Enver Pasha's ill-advised advance into the Caucasus in 1918 and the establishment of Soviet rule throughout the region during 1920–22 made the pan-Turkist project completely unrealistic (see pp. 36, 50). Atatürk's government needed the cooperation of Moscow in opposing the entente powers, and pan-Turkism continued only as the attachment of ultra-nationalists on the political fringes.[1] It may have enjoyed a brief and tentative revival in some official circles during 1941–42, with the German invasion of the Soviet Union, but it was apparently never supported by İnönü, and was rapidly dropped after the Soviet victory at Stalingrad (p. 91). After 1991, it seemed for some to have come back onto the political agenda, as Alparslan Türkeş, the most prominent pan-Turkist in Turkish politics, was brought in from the cold, by accompanying high-level delegations to central Asia.[5]

The main effect of the change was probably in Turkish self-confidence. After years of cold-shouldering by the western Europeans, and uneasy relations with their Middle Eastern neighbours, Turks suddenly realised that in central Asia there were hitherto little-known nations with whom they could claim kinship, and who seemed to be looking for friendship with Turkey. However, it was far from clear what this would mean in political terms. At one end of the scale of possibilities, the construction of a single pan-Turkic state never looked like practical politics, and the idea was not seriously pursued. At the opposite end, Turkey could merely hope to construct good relations with the separate states, enjoying no special position in the region. Actual aims lay somewhere between these two positions, though they were not always achieved. As Philip Robins remarked, by

1993 'hard decisions based on interests rather than fanciful notions of ethnic solidarity are informing decisions on both sides'.[6] In all this, it was noticeable that while there are also substantial Turkic minorities in Iran, China and Afghanistan,[7] Turkey veered away from any support for them, effectively limiting its official contacts with the 'Turkic world' to the territories of the former Soviet Union. For broad political reasons, it was important for Ankara to maintain correct relations with both Iran and China, while Afghanistan was simply too remote and chaotic to be a focus for Turkish policy.[8]

Prior to the disintegration of the Soviet Union, Turkish policy did nothing to encourage it, and much of the Turkish political élite appeared to accept the Soviet view that the indigenous peoples of central Asia were good Soviet citizens who would probably be Russianised gradually.[9] In March 1991, as Mikhail Gorbachev was trying to restructure the Soviet Union, Turgut Özal paid an official visit to the country, including trips to the Ukraine, Azerbaijan and Kazakhstan, in which agreements on technical and economic cooperation were signed. Nevertheless, Turkey still found itself ill-prepared to deal with the end of Soviet rule in central Asia. In September 1991, President Nursultan Nazarbayev became the first central Asian head of state to visit Turkey, but two Turkish fact-finding missions sent to the region at about this time did not recommend that Turkey should recognise the self-declared independence of the central Asian republics. It was not until 16 December 1991, following Turkey's recognition of Azerbaijan, that the government decided to grant recognition to all of them in principle, and only some time after that that it opened embassies in the region. Meanwhile, the Turkish foreign ministry was internally re-organised, so that the previous department dealing with eastern Europe, the Soviet Union and the rest of Asia was divided into two, with one sub-section dealing with the Turkic republics. This recognition was hastened by a round of visits to Ankara by Sepermurad Niyazov, Islam Kerimov and Askar Akayev, the presidents of Turkmenistan, Uzbekistan and Kirghizstan respectively, in December 1991.[10]

After this hesitant start, Turkish policy then seemed to jump to the opposite extreme of expectations. During 1992, this was encouraged by Western policy, particularly that of the United States, which looked to Turkey to thwart the emergence of any radical Iranian-backed Islamic movements seeking to take advantage of the power vacuum left by the end of Soviet rule in central Asia. When Süleyman Demirel, as prime minister, visited Washington in February 1992, President Bush told him that 'Turkey is a model for the countries in the region, and especially to those

newly independent republics of central Asia'.[11] Meanwhile, during a trip
to several capitals in the region, US Secretary of State James Baker urged
the new republics to adopt the 'Turkish model' of economic and political
development. This rhetoric was supported by the British government and
parts of the Western media.[12] Initially, it was warmly received by the
central Asian leaders: for instance, in his visit to Turkey in December
1991, President Kerimov declared that he looked up to Turkey as an 'elder
brother', while President Akayev compared Turkey with the 'morning
star' guiding the Turkic republics.[13] Demirel's visit to all the central Asian
states except Tajikistan in April–May 1992, in which he claimed, among
other things, that Turkey and the Turkic republics 'share the same blood,
religion and language', is seen as marking the 'high point of this period of
euphoria'.[14] Spurred on by exaggerated expectations, and without
adequate prior consultation with the central Asian governments, the Turks
prepared an ambitious agenda for the first 'Turkic summit' of the heads of
government of all the Turkic states, to be held in Ankara in October 1992.
During his central Asian tour, Demirel had referred to the idea of a sort of
'Turkic commonwealth' or 'association of independent Turkic states',
although this would not be 'dominated' by Turkey. Other models
suggested were that of the Nordic Union of Scandinavian countries. The
summit was expected to produce an 'Ankara Political Declaration' and an
'Economic Declaration'. On the latter score, President Özal hoped to
work for a 'Turkic Common Market', with the gradual removal of all
barriers to free trade and the development of new transport systems.[15]

    In the event, the outcome of the first Turkic summit poured cold water
on many of these ambitions, since by the autumn of 1992 the central Asian
leaders had evidently come round to a more realistic assessment of their
connection with Turkey, and the realisation that adoption of anything like
a pan-Turkist programme could create serious problems for them in their
relations with Russia. The Russian government, in turn, had a legitimate
concern for protecting its economic interests in central Asia, and those of
the substantial Russian ethnic community in the region, especially in
Kazakhstan. However, this could be extended into the aim of making
Russia the 'political and military guarantor of stability on all the territory
of the former USSR', reinforced by the fear that Turkey was bent on constructing a pan-Turkic union, aimed against Russia.[16] Once the leaders of
the new republics had assembled in Ankara, President Nazarbayev
made it clear that he was against any grouping based on religious or ethnic
criteria, and that Kazakhstan could only participate in regional cooperation schemes on condition that they did not harm its commitments to

other members of the CIS – a fairly clear sign that Russia should not be shut out. For Uzbekistan, Islam Kerimov broadly supported this position, since he had an interest in supporting Russian policy in neighbouring Tajikistan, which was aimed at preventing the victory of Islamist and other opposition forces in the Tajik civil war. The other regional republics, such as Turkmenistan, were also suspicious of any 'Turkic Commonwealth' project for fear that this would lead to domination by Uzbekistan, rather than Turkey, given that Uzbekistan was the biggest state in central Asia in terms of population. Nor did any of the central Asian delegations support the Azeri cause over Nagorno-Karabakh, as Turkey had hoped. The result was that the two 'Ankara Declarations' had to be abandoned, and the summit merely produced a bland communiqué on political relations and another on economic cooperation. All this committed the participants to very little, beyond an agreement to hold regular future summits.[17]

A second Turkic summit had been scheduled to be held in Baku in January 1994, but this was postponed, partly due to Russian pressure on President Haydar Aliev of Azerbaijan. When the meeting was eventually held in Istanbul in October 1994, the heads of government confined themselves to calling for the implementation of UN resolutions which urged the peaceful settlement of the Nagorno-Karabakh dispute, and agreeing that the region's oil and natural gas should be exported through pipelines running via Turkey. By the time a third summit was convened in Bishkek, the capital of Kirghizstan, in August 1995, it appeared that the central Asian states themselves, rather than Turkey, were setting the agenda, as the meeting merely lauded separate regional cooperation efforts by Kazakhstan, Kirghizstan and Uzbekistan.[18] Within Turkey, the pan-Turkist movement led by Alparslan Türkeş organised four meetings of the Turkic States and Communities Assemblies, sponsored by the Turkic States and Communities Friendship, Brotherhood and Cooperation Foundation (TUDEV). These seemed to have a semi-official status, as they were attended on occasion by Demirel, Özal and Tansu Çiller, although they were not sanctioned by the Turkish foreign ministry. Türkeş himself continued to call for the establishment of a 'Turkic Commonwealth' headed by a 'High Council of Turkic Republics', but this kind of rhetoric was apparently addressed mainly to his own followers in Turkey, and ceased to be a serious item in Turkey's foreign policy. The Turkish government also became more aware of the need to avoid clashes with Russia – a concern primarily focused on the conflicts in Transcaucasia, but also affecting its policies in central Asia. As a result, it was suggested that Russia and Turkey might have complementary rather than conflicting interests in maintaining the regional status quo, particularly against Islamic radicalism.[19]

The result of these re-assessments was reflected in Turkish official statements in 1993 and after. The metaphor of Turkey as the 'elder brother' – paradoxically, originally coined by Islam Kerimov – was carefully avoided, as it was realised that the central Asian states did not want to exchange one patron in Moscow for another in Ankara. Rather than develop a common 'Turkic' identity, the regional republics preferred to promote separate state-anchored identities – Uzbek, Turkmen, Kazakh and so on – which would legitimate the existing state system. Turkish leaders and spokesmen accepted this, by emphasising that Turkey simply sought to promote the development of the republics as independent, democratic and secular states, with liberal market economies.[20] Once the idea of some sort of political or economic union had been abandoned, the Turks concentrated their efforts on developing cultural and educational links with the region, as well as trade and investment. On the first score, 10,000 scholarships were given each year to enable central Asian students to attend Turkish high schools and universities. Technical assistance, training and cultural cooperation, and the development of small industries in the region were conducted under the aegis of the Turkish International Cooperation Agency (TICA), which was affiliated to the foreign ministry and established in 1992.[21] The ministry of education also opened schools in central Asia, teaching in Turkish and English besides the national languages, though these were outnumbered by privately owned Turkish schools, notably those run by the 'Fethullahcı' religious brotherhood led by Fethullah Gülen, which by 1999 was reported to have 73 schools in all the central Asian republics bar Tajikistan.[22] The newspaper *Zaman*, supporting an Islamist-cum-nationalist line, which was owned by the brotherhood and printed in Turkish and the national languages, was also distributed throughout the region. While the Turkish state tried to present itself as strictly secularist, it was apparent that part of the attempted Islamic revival in central Asia was also being sponsored from Turkey by private initiatives, causing some embarrassment to Turkey's official representatives. In the official sphere, the Turkish state broadcasting corporation TRT broadcast TV programmes in Turkish via satellite on the special 'Avrasya' channel, although some of the regional states were not happy about allowing a foreign broadcaster to have direct access to their citizens, and there were complaints that the viewers found the language hard to understand. Turkey also supported the adoption of the Latin alphabet for writing the regional languages, as an alternative to the existing Cyrillic, or the Arabic script urged by Iran and other Muslim countries. This campaign was successful, to the extent that by 1996, Azerbaijan, Uzbekistan and Turkmenistan had officially adopted the Latin alphabet, although many of their citizens will probably continue to use Cyrillic for some time to come.[23]

At the multilateral level, Turkey, Iran and Pakistan inherited the Economic Cooperation Organisation, or ECO, which had officially been set up in 1985, but did not become operational until 1991 (p. 172). In 1992, Azerbaijan, Turkmenistan, Uzbekistan, Tajikistan, Kirghizstan, Kazakhstan and Afghanistan were added to the membership list, so that it effectively became a combination of the old 'northern tier' alignment of the Cold War era, plus the Muslim nations of central Asia and Transcaucasia. The ECO established a secretariat in Tehran, with periodic meetings of a council of the foreign ministers of member states, a Council of Permanent Representatives in Tehran, and a Regional Planning Council. Its main aims were to implement a protocol on preferential tariff arrangements, signed by the three original members in 1991, and to develop transport links between the member countries, among other activities.[24] As in the case of the Black Sea Economic Cooperation (BSEC) project, it was hard to say how much effect it had in encouraging regional cooperation, and critics would argue that it amounted to little more than a talking-shop. However, given that Iran was an important member, it was a useful way of maintaining relations with Tehran, with which Ankara did not have any other formal institutional links.

In developing its economic relations with central Asia, the Turkish government started off by claiming that it would launch an aid programme worth US$3 billion to the Turkic states, but it soon became apparent that this vastly outran Turkey's resources. Nonetheless, by 1997, the Turkish Eximbank had provided about US$1.1 billion in programme and investment credits to the new republics. Meanwhile, private Turkish firms were reported to have invested over US$6 billion in the region, and Turkish construction companies had important contracts for building hotels, airports and industrial projects. While Turkey was hardly emerging as an economic giant in central Asia, Turkish firms were particularly active in telecommunications, with small and medium-sized Turkish businesses, often working with local partners, prominent in food processing and textiles.[25] On the other hand, the expectation that central Asia would become a major focus for Turkey's total foreign trade proved wide of the mark. Although there was a substantial growth in Turkey's trade turnover with the five republics, from US$147 million in 1992 to US$939 million in

1997, the simultaneous rise in Turkey's total foreign trade meant that the 1997 figure still represented only 1.3 per cent of Turkey's total exports plus imports. By comparison, recorded trade with the whole of the rest of the CIS (excluding 'suitcase trade') came to almost US$6.2 billion, with Russia easily Turkey's biggest trade partner in the former Soviet Union.[26]

The relative success in Turkey's more modest programme in central Asia was not without its political setbacks, however. These particularly affected relations between Uzbekistan and Turkey. After a series of earlier complaints by President Kerimov that Turkey had been harbouring or encouraging movements opposed to his authoritarian regime, tensions between the two countries came to a head in 1999, following an unsuccessful attempt to murder the president in Tashkent with a massive car bomb on 16 February. Two Uzbeks who were suspected of the crime fled to Turkey via Iran, and were only extradited back to Uzbekistan after some delay. One of the suspects then claimed that the attempt had been financed by Necmettin Erbakan, the Turkish Islamist leader. In response, the Uzbek government forced Turkey to recall its ambassador in Tashkent, closed Uzbek airspace to the Turkish state airline THY, and withdrew Uzbek students from Turkish schools and universities. Uzbek official anger was also directed against the 'Fethullahcis' in Uzbekistan, and six of their schools in the country, together with six Turkish state schools, were closed down. Coincidentally, investigations were opened in Turkey against Fethullah Gülen, on the grounds that he had aimed to set up a fundamentalist Islamic state in Turkey, so that President Demirel was able to claim that both Turkey and Uzbekistan were the victims of the same underground Islamist movement. As prime minister, Bülent Ecevit assured the Uzbek ambassador that Turkey would not permit any activities against Uzbekistan to operate on its soil. Although Turkish firms continued to express interest in investing in Uzbekistan, the diplomatic stand-off seemed set to continue for some time, and indicated that, thanks to its important presence in central Asia, Turkey would have to work hard to avoid suspected involvement in the internal politics of the region.[27]

By the late 1990s, pipeline projects were also coming to play an important role in Turkish policies in the region, as in Transcaucasia. As related earlier, oil from Kazakhstan, and thus a pipeline between Kazakhstan and Azerbaijan, would almost certainly be essential, if the Baku–Ceyhan pipeline were to be made commercially viable (p. 277). Apart from this, the possible construction of a natural gas pipeline between Turkmenistan and Turkey, to meet Turkey's own demand and perhaps supply European markets via Turkey, was also the subject of protracted negotiations. On the one side, Turkmenistan favoured the idea, since it had little oil but abundant gas deposits, for which it needed to find new markets and export routes not dependent on Russia. On the other side, Turkey was anxious to diversify its own supplies of natural gas. As in the case of the Baku–Ceyhan project, the main obstacles to the scheme were distance and cost, with the additional complication of deciding whether the pipeline should pass across northern Iran (an idea opposed by the United States), or under the Caspian to Azerbaijan, from where it could be laid alongside the Baku–Ceyhan pipeline, reducing the cost of both. At the ECO ministerial meeting in Askhabad in May 1997 the two governments agreed in principle to construct an addition to the planned gas pipeline between Turkey and Iran from Turkmenistan, to allow initial deliveries of three billion cubic metres per year rising eventually to 15 billion cubic metres per year.[28] Later, this project appeared to have been shunted aside, in preference for the northern route via Azerbaijan, which had US support. On the sidelines of the OSCE summit held in Istanbul in November 1999 the presidents of Turkey, Georgia, Azerbaijan and Turkmenistan signed a declaration pledging to conclude intergovernmental agreements for the construction of the 2,000 kilometre pipeline, which would run from Turkmenistan under the Caspian to Azerbaijan, and thence to Georgia and Turkey. The plan was to complete construction by 2002, at which point the pipeline would deliver 5 billion cubic metres per year, with an eventual increase to 30 billion cubic metres per year. Of this, 16 billion cubic metres would be used in Turkey, and the remainder transferred to European markets through a pipeline running across either Greece or Bulgaria. However, the parties still seemed some way off making financial arrangements for the project, which was expected to cost around US$2.3 billion.[29]

TURKEY, ISRAEL AND THE MIDDLE EAST

During the 1990s, it appeared to some observers that Turkey was abandoning its traditional policy of strict neutrality in the Arab–Israeli contest, by developing an entente with Israel. Regional and global changes helped to explain this change of line. On the one hand, the removal of the Soviet Union as an important player in Middle Eastern politics left the radical Arab states, especially Syria, in a more exposed and isolated position, and meant that tensions with the Arab countries would not impact on Turkey's relations with Moscow, as they had done during the Cold War. There was widespread disillusionment in Turkey with the Arab countries, which had failed to support the Turkish cause over Cyprus and, in the case of Syria, gave active support to the PKK. Conflicts over the waters of the Tigris and Euphrates added to these tensions. More positively, the beginning of the Arab–Israeli peace process in 1991, followed by the signing of the 'Declaration of Principles' by Yitzhak Rabin and Yasser Arafat in September 1993, made it possible for Turkey to develop much closer relations with Israel without provoking a rupture in its relations with the PLO and the main Arab states. Strategically, the prospective gains for Turkey from closer links with the Israelis derived mainly from the fact both countries had a common interest in opposing Syria, although the Turkish foreign ministry steadfastly denied that Turkey's agreements with Israel were directed against any other state. The expectation that good relations with Iseael would increase Turkish influence in Washington, and that both countries stood to gain from technical, military and economic cooperation, were additional incentives for the construction of a Turkish Israeli entente.[30]

The new trend in Turkish policy began in December 1991, when the Demirel government upgraded its relations with both Israel and the PLO to ambassadorial level. Following the signature of the 'Declaration of Principles', Hikmet Çetin, Demirel's foreign minister, visited Israel in November 1993, to be followed by Tansu Çiller, now the prime minister, one year later, and by Demirel, as president, in March 1996. Significantly, both Tansu Çiller and Demirel took in visits to Gaza and the Palestinian authorities in east Jerusalem as part of their trips. These visits were reciprocated by those of the Israeli president, prime minister and foreign minister to Turkey.[31] According to later Turkish press reports, subsequent moves for military collaboration between the two countries originated from a defence pact between Israel and the United States proposed by Washington in 1995 which was supposed to be linked to 'a chain of regional alliances for defence of the Middle East'.[32] In the event, the Turkish–Israeli agreement on 'Military Training and Cooperation' which was signed in February 1996 was more modest than this. Valid for five years, with subsequent renewal at annual intervals, it provided for mutual military visits and the acquisition of military know-how, besides joint exercises in which Israeli and Turkish pilots would train in one another's countries. There would be Turkish–Israeli cooperation in the manufacture of surface-to-air missiles and other advanced weapons systems, and the exchange of intelligence. An Israeli firm also contracted to modernise Turkey's 102 ageing F-4 and F-5 fighter 'planes.[33] In the civilian sphere, it was accompanied by a free trade agreement between the two countries,

which was originally signed in March 1996, and eventually ratified by the
Turkish parliament in April 1997.

The Turkish–Israeli military agreement was evidently reached
primarily on the initiative of the Turkish armed forces chiefs, and was
signed at a time when there was effectively no government in Turkey
(officially, the country was under a caretaker government headed by
Tansu Çiller). However, shortly afterwards, in June 1996, Turkish policy
towards the Middle East became a domestic political football, as the coalition government headed by Necmettin Erbakan took over, with Mrs Çiller
playing an awkward role as foreign minister. In opposition, Erbakan and
his party had strongly denounced Israel, and Turkey's links with it. Once
installed in office, he bowed to military pressure by reluctantly accepting
the military cooperation and free trade agreements, much as he had done
in the case of 'Operation Provide Comfort' (see p. 226). However, he also
tried to steer an independent course, by keeping Israel at arm's length, and
supporting militant Palestinians who opposed the peace process

In pursuit of his programme to develop an 'Islamic' foreign policy,
Erbakan made a well-publicised trip to Iran, Pakistan, Singapore, Malaysia
and Indonesia in August 1996, followed by a swing through Africa, taking
in Egypt, Libya and (partly Muslim) Nigeria, in the following October. His
visit to Libya was a political fiasco, as Muammer Qaddafi treated him
to a public dressing-down over Turkey's developing links with Israel, and
openly called for the establishment on an independent Kurdish state.
Having pushed forward his project at the level of bilateral contacts,
Erbakan was then quick to develop it in the multilateral dimension, by
setting up what was known as the D-8 ('developing-8') group of mainly
Muslim nations, as an Islamic response to the G-7 and other Western
economic groupings. Nevertheless, a large number of Muslim countries –
in particular, all the Arab countries bar Egypt, and all the central Asian
republics – were notable by their absence from 'D-8'. The probable reason
was that they did not wish to be associated with what could have been
interpreted as a pro-Iranian grouping, or did not take Erbakan's project
seriously.[34] Against this, secularist opinion, particularly in the military and
the foreign ministry, strongly opposed Erbakan's policies, mainly because
they alienated Turkey from the West, but also because Turkey need to
preserve a balance in its relations between Israel and the Arabs, and an
'Islamic' foreign policy conflicted with their Kemalist commitments. The
military in particular, saw positive benefits from developing the relationship with Israel. In the event, the alignment of Erbakan's party with Iran
and the militant Palestinians played a part (though probably not a decisive

one) in Erbakan's fall from power in June 1997 (see p. 198).[35] This left the following Yılmaz administration with the task of having to pick up the pieces, and give a more logical and effective direction to foreign policy.

Clearing up the uncertainties and embarrassments created by Erbakan was not the only problem faced by the Yılmaz government in developing its policies towards the Middle East. The main Arab governments may have distrusted Erbakan, but they were unlikely to welcome the developing entente between Ankara and Tel Aviv. At a meeting in Damascus in June 1996, the leaders of Egypt, Syria and Saudi Arabia issued a communiqué demanding that Turkey reconsider the military agreement with Israel. This call was repeated at an Arab summit meeting held in Cairo later in the same month, though an outright condemnation of Turkey, proposed by Syria, was vetoed by Jordan. Reportedly, the Iranian government offered Syria a 'Syrian–Iranian Military Pact' against Israel and Turkey, although nothing came of this.[36] On the other side, the US government apparently viewed the Turkish–Israeli agreement as the first building-block of wider regional coalitions, embracing other pro-US Middle Eastern states, an idea on which Turkey was evidently unenthusiastic. Meanwhile, the right-wing government under Benjamin Netanyahu which came to power in Israel in April 1996 pressed for the conclusion of an outright military pact with Turkey as the main 'axis' of a 'regional security framework'. This was rejected by the Turks in the absence of a general Arab–Israeli peace settlement, which Netanyahu appeared to oppose except on terms quite unacceptable to the Arabs. The fate of the Baghdad Pact was perhaps at the back of Turkish thinking when the Turkish ambassador in Tel Aviv responded to Netanyahu's suggestion by saying that 'if axis signifies a military alliance, then I would object because this could only mean to divide this region into "us" and "them"'.[37] Some commentators referred to the Turkish–Israeli entente as a 'military alliance',[38] but the phrase seemed something of an exaggeration, given that there was no commitment by either side to wage a joint war on any third parties.[39] In effect, it was clear that Turkey wanted to get what it could out of its relationship with Israel, without driving the Arab states into united opposition, creating extra problems in other theatres, and without taking on military commitments in the Middle East which would have had little support at home.

Apart from its disagreements with the Netanyahu government over the basic aims and scope of the relationship, Turkish and Israeli policies did not entirely overlap on all the other issues confronting them. While secularist governments in Turkey did not support Erbakan's embrace of

Iran, they still needed to preserve correct relationships with the Iranians, and refused Israeli suggestions that they should denounce the Iranian regime, on the grounds that the nature of the Iranian government was purely a domestic affair for Iran. When the Israelis warned them of the danger that Iran might acquire nuclear weapons, they replied that they opposed nuclear proliferation in any part of the Middle East – implicitly a criticism of Israel as much as of Iran.[40] Until May 1997, Israel refused to support Turkey against the PKK, but Netanyahu then broke with this principle by denouncing Abdullah Öcalan's organisation. In response, the PKK threatened to launch attacks against Israeli targets, though it failed to carry this out.[41] Even so, there does not seem to have been any active Israeli involvement in the Turkish army's campaign against the PKK, which remained a purely Turkish affair.

On the positive side, the Turkish military certainly gained from access to advanced weaponry and intelligence, which could have been blocked in western Europe or the United States because of the Kurdish issue. Whether the existence of the Turkish–Israeli link was influential in inducing the Syrian president, Hafiz al-Assad, to expel Abdullah Öcalan from Syria in October 1998 must remain an open question, since the Israeli government stated at the time that it was neutral on this question, but the possibility is still there (see pp. 304–6). In the economic sphere, both countries almost certainly gained from the free trade agreement, as the annual volume of trade between them grew from US$407 million in 1995 to US$761 million in 1998. However the latter figure only represented about 1 per cent of Turkey's total foreign trade. Economically, Turkey was still far more dependent on trade with the Arab countries, mainly because of its imports of oil and natural gas, though it also had important markets for foodstuffs and light industrial products in the Arab states.[42]

In the broader political sphere, the most significant gain for Turkey from its entente with Israel was that it cemented its relationship with the United States. In particular, the powerful pro-Israeli lobby in Washington now came to Turkey's aid, helping to cancel out the power of the pro-Armenian and other pressure groups which were critical of Turkey. According to one account, the Israeli lobby in Congress helped to tone down criticism of Turkey on the Kurdish and human rights issues, and helped with Turkey's campaign against the stationing of Russian-made S-300 missiles in southern Cyprus (see pp. 256–7). It also helped to sway US opinion in favour of Azerbaijan (and thus indirectly of Turkey) over the Azeri–Armenian contest. Although Israel's effect on European opinion was likely to be weaker, Shimon Peres is said to have been influential in persuading his European colleagues in the Socialist International to shelve their objections to the Turkey–EU customs union.[43] In effect, Turkey was able to make up for the fact that there was virtually no Turkish ethnic lobby in the United States or Europe, by riding on the back of the pro-Israeli one.

While the Turks got what they could out of their entente with Israel, they were also careful to maintain contacts with, and support for, the PLO, and the Arab–Israeli peace process in general. Although nothing came of this proposal, in 1991 Turgut Özal suggested that Turkey should host an Arab–Israeli dialogue, and urged the Israelis to accept the principle of an exchange of land for peace.[44] Later, Tansu Çiller confirmed Turkey's support for UN Security Council Resolutions 242 and 338, and 'a solution that would safeguard all rights of the people of Palestine, including the right to establish their own state'.[45] When visiting Israel, both she and her successors were careful to pay equally official visits to Gaza and the Palestinian authorities. Turkey promised a US$50 million credit to the Palestinians, although it apparently failed to make good on this. Its failure to send more than six of the promised 60 Turkish monitors to oversee the Palestinian elections in January 1996 was also criticised by the Palestinian envoy in Turkey. On the other hand, Yasser Arafat paid an official visit to Turkey in 1995: he opposed strong Arab criticism of Turkey over the Turkish–Israeli agreement and refused to support the PKK. There was even an alignment between the secularist forces in Turkey and the PLO against the Turkish Islamists, since Erbakan's party opposed the peace process, and invited representatives of the Palestinian Hamas movement and the Lebanese Hizbullah to its party congress. Similarly, when he visited Cairo in October 1996 Erbakan alienated the Egyptian president, Hosni Mubarak, by telling him to tolerate the Egyptian Islamists of the Muslim Brotherhood, to which Mubarak responded that Erbakan could 'have them in Turkey if he liked them so much'.[46] The overall effect of these complications was that while Turkey only played a minimal role in bringing the Arabs and Israelis together, it succeeded in continuing its entente with Israel without provoking the Arab states into united or effective opposition to its policies on other vital issues, such as its confrontation with Syria over Abdullah Öcalan. This approach was naturally made easier by the return of the Labor Party to power in Israel in 1999, and the re-launch of the peace process.

TURKEY, SYRIA AND THE EUPHRATES

In the overall pattern of Turkey's relationships with its Arab neighbours in the 1990s, its relations with Syria were arguably the most critical, since they posed the greatest risk of armed confrontation with another state. The collapse of the Soviet Union and Turkey's entente with Israel increased the balance of power in Turkey's favour, but these changes did not by themselves solve the conflicts between the two countries, or ensure that Ankara would have it all its own way in its confrontation with Damascus. The tensions derived from disputes which had antedated the end of the Cold War, and aroused strong feelings in both countries. They derived mainly from Syrian support for the PKK and, on the other side, Syria's determination to prevent unlimited Turkish use of the waters of the Euphrates, which threatened to deprive Syria of a vital resource. Syrian calls for the return of the province of Alexandretta, or Hatay, annexed by Turkey in 1939 (see p. 67) could still produce ruptures between the two countries, but by the 1990s it appeared that the Syrian government was placing this issue lower down on its list of priorities, apparently recognising that the return of Alexandretta was probably an unachievable aim for Syria.

In theory, the agreement reached between Turgut Özal and President Hafiz al-Assad in 1987 should have provided the basis for the settlement of both the Euphrates waters dispute and Syrian support for the PKK (see p. 174). It failed to do so, partly because the Syrian government could not believe that the Turks would not in fact restrict or cut off the supply of water in the Euphrates. On the other hand, Syria also failed to honour its undertaking to 'prevent the activities of organisations … threatening or undermining the security and stability of the other party'[47] – in fact, when pressed by the Turks on this issue, the Syrian government flatly but unconvincingly denied that it gave support to the PKK, and even that Abdullah Öcalan was on its territory. As a result, in 1989 Özal threatened that if Syria did not stick to its side of the bargain of 1987, then Turkey might not adhere to its promise to maintain the cross-border flow of the Euphrates at 500 cusecs (cubic metres per second).[48]

Although a full discussion of this issue lies outside the scope of this book, it can be said in summary that the Euphrates problem – which affects Turkey's relations with Iraq as well as with Syria – derives essentially from the fact that water resources in the Middle East are becoming increasingly scarce. This is due to a fixed and relatively limited supply which combined with rising populations and living standards, have escalated the demand for water both for agriculture and for non-agricultural uses. Turkey's increased use of the Euphrates waters, especially after the completion of the Atatürk dam in 1990, is only one aspect of this complicated problem, which centres around the fact that if the three countries through which the river flows drew off all the water which they claim they need, then their total demands would exceed the total supply of water in the river by a margin of about 60 per cent.[49] One Turkish writer on this issue recognises that Turkey would not be entitled under international law to cut off the cross-border flow as a political weapon,[50] and the international Convention on the Law of Non-Navigational Use of International Watercourses adopted by the UN General Assembly in May 1997 confirms, among other things, that upstream states have the obligation not to disadvantage those downstream.[51] However, Turkey, along with China and Burundi, voted against the Convention, and has not officially accepted any legal obligation to limit its use of the Euphrates. Instead, it has sometimes argued that the water is its own natural resource, just as oil is that of the Arabs, and can claim sovereign rights over it, with 'priority of usage'. Against this, Syria and Iraq claim 'acquired' or 'historical' rights over the Euphrates waters, based on long historical sharing between the three countries. While differing on points of detail, the two Arab countries essentially argue that the Euphrates waters should be shared according to a mathematical formula, based on the total flow of the river and each country's demands. They both claim that the Syrian acceptance of the 500 cusecs figure in 1987 was valid only while the Atatürk dam was being completed, and that subsequently Turkey should supply at least 700 cusecs.[52] In response, the Turkish authorities argue that the two downstream states should not be allowed to put forward large claims to the Euphrates waters, based on unrealised and unrealistic irrigation projects. Instead, Turkey proposes a complicated 'three-stage plan' under which the three countries would first share the relevant hydrological and meteorological information, followed by an inventory study of land resources. In the third stage, they would agree on a distribution of the waters, bearing in mind, among other things, the adoption of irrigation systems which would minimise water losses and (in the Iraqi case) the availability of water from other sources, notably the Tigris.[53]

Tension over the Euphrates question reached a critical point in January 1990, when the Turkish authorities interrupted the flow of the river to fill the storage reservoir behind the Atatürk dam. During this operation, which lasted for one month, the cross-border flow was reduced to 22 cusecs, according to Turkish figures. However, during the previous 51-day period the flow had been maintained at about 770 cusecs, or well above the 500 cusecs obligation, allowing Syria and Iraq to accumulate extra water in their reservoirs. Nonetheless, this did not satisfy the downstream states, who won wide verbal support (though no positive action) from other Arab countries on this issue. Iraq, in particular, was vociferous in its protests: when the then Turkish prime minister, Yıldırım Akbulut, visited Baghdad in May 1990, the Iraqi government refused to renew the cross-border security agreement of 1984, allowing Turkey to enter Iraqi territory in pursuit of the PKK, which had lapsed in 1988 (see p. 172). Meanwhile, in April 1990 Iraq and Syria agreed that, in any overall settlement, Syria would be entitled to 42 per cent of the Euphrates waters entering from Turkey, and Iraq to the remaining 58 per cent. Subsequently, the Gulf crisis of 1990–91 and the resultant international embargo on Iraq, virtually removed the Iraqis as effective players in the dispute. Nonetheless, sporadic talks between Turkey and Syria over the following six years failed to produce any progress.[54]

Like the Euphrates dispute (and partly because of it) arguments between Turkey and Syria over the latter's role in supporting the PKK dragged on fruitlessly between 1990 and 1998. Progress seemed to have been made in 1992, when the Syrian General Adnan Badr al-Hassan, and General Esref Bitlis, the then Commander of the Turkish Gendarmerie, signed an agreement to engage in a 'joint struggle against terrorism', and prohibit shelter or other support to organisations outlawed in both countries: simultaneously the Syrian side declared the PKK to be an 'outlawed organisation' in its territory.[55] During 1993–94, as part of Turkey's attempt to put together a common policy between the three countries on the Iraqi Kurdish question (see p. 309) Turkey and Syria, joined later by Iran, further agreed not to support organisations hostile to either of the others. Although Turkey again made it clear that it would not undertake serious negotiations with Syria on the Euphrates issue if Syria continued to support the PKK and shelter Abdullah Öcalan, it was clear that Syria was actually continuing to do both these things. During 1994–95 there were attempts by both sides to develop bilateral trade links, but these failed to produce important political results, in the absence of any progress on the Euphrates or PKK disputes.[56]

It was not until the autumn of 1998 that any advance became visible. By this stage, the Turkish army had clearly gained the upper hand in its war against the PKK within Turkey, and had limited the PKK's ability to operate from northern Iraq (see p. 200). Hence, elimination of the PKK presence in Syria seemed to be the one remaining obstacle to its overall defeat as a paramilitary organisation. During September 1998 Turkey mounted a strong campaign against Syria, backed up by military force, in a bid to force Hafiz al-Assad to carry out his commitments under the 1987 and 1992 agreements. As Turkish troops and armour were moved towards the border, the Turkish Commander of Land Forces, General Atilla Ateş, visited Reyhanlı, just north of the Syrian frontier, and announced that 'if Turkey's expectations are not met we will earn the right to take any sort of precaution. Our patience has run out'.[57] Prime Minister Mesut Yılmaz added his voice to the campaign, saying that Syria had to end its support for the PKK, now that the latter had been defeated in Turkey. There was speculation that even if Turkey did not attack Syria by land, it might launch punishing air strikes against Syrian missile batteries or assumed PKK bases in Syria and the Lebanon.[58]

This stung other Middle Eastern states – especially Egypt and Iran – into intense diplomatic activity. Egypt's president, Hosni Mubarak, had a clear interest in preventing a military collision between Turkey and Syria, given that Syria was a fellow-Arab state, while Turkey was an ally of the United States, with which Egypt also had good relations. His mediation was evidently supported by Washington, which wished to draw Syria towards accepting a peace agreement with Israel. Iran, meanwhile, was Syria's closest friend in the Middle East, but could not afford to get dragged into an armed confrontation with Turkey (or vice versa). Fortunately, the Turks and Syrians were apparently ready to accept mediation by Egypt and Iran. Both Mubarak and the Iranian foreign minister, Kemal Kharrazi, paid emergency visits to Ankara and Damascus, which succeeded in defusing the crisis. On 7 October Abdullah Öcalan was reported to have left Syria for Russia. Later, on 19–20 October Uğur Ziyal, the Deputy Under-Secretary at the Turkish foreign ministry, held talks in Adana with General Adnan Badr al-Hassan (who had also signed the 1992 agreement for Syria). The two negotiators signed an agreement on 20 October 1998. This confirmed that 'Öcalan is no longer in Syria and permission will definitely not be given for him to re-enter the country'. Syria declared that it had closed down all PKK camps in its territory, and that the PKK would not be allowed to re-establish itself in Syria. A direct hotline to prevent future clashes would be established between Ankara and Damascus, and there would be joint inspection of security measures on both sides of the frontier.[59] Apparently, Turkey had come out of the crisis with its main objectives realised (except that Öcalan had not actually been returned to Turkey) and without having had to make good its military threats.

This left open the question as to why Hafiz al-Assad had conceded virtually all Turkey's demands without securing some concessions over the Euphrates waters, which had previously appeared to be the likely quid pro quo for his abandonment of the PKK. One cannot be certain that Turkey would have launched a military strike against Syria if he had not backed down, or what form this would have taken, but there is no clear evidence that it would not have done so – rather the reverse. Certainly, Assad himself could not have ignored the possibility, and could expect to be defeated if Turkey had attacked. The Israelis had carefully distanced themselves from the dispute, but Syria could not have afforded to denude its forces on the Golan front or the Lebanon, reducing its ability to defend itself against Turkey. Although none of the other Middle Eastern states would have supported Turkey in a war against Syria, it is unlikely that they would have been willing to come to Syria's aid militarily. For Assad, the main priorities were probably to regain Syrian sovereignty over the Golan and expel pro-Israeli forces from southern Lebanon. To induce the United States to put pressure on Israel to withdraw from the Golan, he needed to make himself more acceptable in Washington, and thus move towards settling his differences with Turkey. Given his age and ill health, he needed to clear up both these problems, so as to prepare for a smooth succession by his son, Bashar, and could not have afforded a war with the Turks. Furthermore, Öcalan probably had a relatively low ranking on his agenda, and could be sacrificed if need be – especially since the PKK was now a waning force within Turkey.[60] There is also the unproven possibility that Öcalan had himself previously decided to leave Syria, in an attempt to convert his movement into an internationally acceptable political force, so that he did not take much persuading, although it is unlikely that the Turks could have been sure of this.[61] At the same time, Turkey had been lucky in that it had not had to resort to military action against Syria, as there was no knowing where this could have ended, especially if Assad had proved obdurate. On the positive side, the fact that it had cultivated good relations with Egypt, and correct ones with Iran, enabled these two countries to act as effective mediators.

With this important obstacle out of the way, Turkey was able to cultivate something of a *rapprochement* with Syria. In March 1999, delegations headed by Hikmet Çetin, now the speaker of the Turkish parliament, and Salim Yassin, the deputy prime minister of Syria, met in Ankara to discuss the improvement of trade and transport links between the two countries, although sensitive issues, such as the Euphrates, were carefully left off the agenda. In the same month, the border between the two countries was opened on the occasion of the Muslim Festival of the Sacrifice (*Kurban*

Bayrami) to allow long-separated relatives to greet one another.[62] The opening of a new border crossing point was announced in October. More critically, after talks in October 1999 between the Governors of Raqqah and Urfa provinces, on the Syrian and Turkish sides of the border respectively, it was reported that the Turkish government had declared its readiness to enter into 'serious talks on the water issue'.[63] This left it uncertain as to whether such talks would actually take place, or when. Even if they did, it would probably require substantial concessions on both sides to reach agreement. On the other hand, there were strong arguments on the Turkish side for exploiting the opportunity to settle the dispute. Among other things, there had for some time been worries in Turkey that if Syria reached a peace agreement with Israel, this would make it much less flexible in its contests with Turkey.[64] This increased the incentive for resolving the Euphrates dispute with Syria in advance of a Syrian Israeli deal, and the possible ending of Iraq's isolation on the international stage.

TURKEY, IRAQ AND THE IRAQI KURDS

As has been seen, after the Gulf crisis of 1990–91, Western policies towards the Kurds of northern Iraq, and towards Saddam Hussein's regime in Baghdad, had become a thorny issue in Turkish–US relations, since many Turks were suspicious that the Western powers aimed to create an independent Kurdish state in Iraq (see p. 225). However, Turkey's own relations with the Iraqi Kurds also raised problems for Ankara. Encouragement of any Kurdish ambition to independent statehood would have been quite contrary to Turkish interests, as most Turks saw them. Ideally, Turkey would have liked the Iraqi Kurds to reach an accommodation with Saddam, so as to restore Baghdad's authority in northern Iraq. Unfortunately, there was no chance of achieving this, partly because the United States would have opposed it, but also because Saddam Hussein's treatment of the Kurds in the recent past hardly encouraged confidence in his good faith. For Turkey, there was thus a strong argument for building bridges with the Iraqi Kurdish leaders. Like it or not, they were effectively in power in northern Iraq, and Turkey could not seriously contemplate permanent occupation of the region as an alternative. Given that Turkey's main enemy was the PKK, and that the Iraqi Kurds did not necessarily see eye to eye with Abdullah Öcalan and his organisation, there was even the possibility that they might be co-opted into a common front against the PKK. The struggle for power and territory between the rival Iraqi Kurdish leaders, which erupted in 1994, also presented Turkey with a dilemma. On the one hand, Kurdish disunity in Iraq was an advantage for Turkey, since it badly undermined the credibility of the Kurdish nationalist project. On the other hand, if intra-Kurdish fighting resulted in general chaos in northern Iraq, the PKK would find it easier to extend its presence there, and thus strengthen its campaign in Turkey. Essentially, Turkey had to try to control the internal conflict if it could, but did not necessarily want it to be ended entirely.[65]

Similar problems affected Ankara's relationship with the Iraqi government. Historically, Turkey's relationship with Iraq had usually been co-operative, in spite of frequent changes of regime in Baghdad, and both countries had a common interest in opposing Kurdish nationalism. Whether or not Saddam Hussein's regime survived (and it seemed increasingly likely that it would) Iraq as a state would probably do so, and Turkey could not afford to create a long-run conflict with it. Above all, Turkey needed to ensure that Saddam did not form an alliance with the PKK – an aim in which it apparently succeeded.[66] Nor did it have any interest in continuing the economic blockade against Iraq, quite the reverse. Against this, Turkey could not have struck out on its own – by for instance ignoring the sanctions regime, or developing a political entente with Saddam Hussein. Its overall foreign policy interests and traditions demanded respect for the UN, of which it had been a founding member. Since its external relations were based on its membership of NATO and a broad alignment with the Western powers, the most it could reasonably expect to do was to try to influence Western policy in accordance with its own interests, not break with it entirely.

The first set of problems and policies worked themselves out gradually between 1991 and 1995. During the 1980s, Turkish governments had generally held both the main Iraqi Kurdish parties – that is, the Kurdistan Democratic Party (KDP) led by Masud Barzani, and Jelal Talabani's Patriotic Union of Kurdistan (PUK) – at arm's length. These suspicions were mutual: in fact, between 1983 and the end of 1987, the KDP and PKK were in alliance, until attacks by the PKK on innocent civilians and even on members of the KDP itself created a rupture. After this, Öcalan's organisation formed an alliance with the PUK.[67] The situation was radically changed by the aftermath of the Gulf war of 1991. In March 1991, while the brief Kurdish rebellion against Saddam Hussein was still raging, Turgut Özal broke with Turkish tradition by sanctioning a secret visit to Ankara by Jelal Talabani and a representative of the KDP, Mohsin Dizai. The two Iraqi Kurdish factions were keen to establish this link, since it gave Turkish approval for direct contacts between themselves and the

United States. This interest obviously continued after Saddam Hussein's ruthless suppression of the rebellion, and the subsequent establishment of the 'safe haven' in northern Iraq, since the Iraqi Kurds were dependent on Turkey for food and other supplies through 'Operation Provide Comfort' (see pp. 222-3). On the other side, Turkey needed to gain first-hand information about the situation in northern Iraq, and to exercise some influence over events there – notably by preventing a renewed alliance between the PKK and either the KDP, the PUK, or both. The need to protect the position of the Iraqi Turcomans, said to number as many as one million, some of whom were living within the 'safe haven' and were seen as fellow-Turks, was another reason for Ankara's new engagement with the Iraqi Kurds.[68]

By October 1992 the Turkish forces were receiving help from the Kurdish leaders in northern Iraq in operations against the PKK, which had earlier tried to place an embargo on trade between the Kurdish region and Turkey. In December 1992 the Iraqi Kurdish leaders reached an agreement on border security with the Turks, although the PUK forces subsequently refused to hand over PKK militants who had surrendered to them. In May 1994 full-scale fighting broke out between the KDP and PUK, further complicating the situation, and allowing the PKK to establish bases near the border with Turkey, in territory nominally controlled by the KDP. This prompted the Turks to launch further cross-border operations in March and July 1995, the first being a massive operation involving some 35,000 soldiers, which was said to have been the biggest military operation outside its own borders which the Turkish army had launched since the start of the republic.[69] Meanwhile, in November 1992, Turkey had begun to hold a series of tripartite meetings with Iran and Syria, designed to express the three countries' determination to prevent the territorial break-up of Iraq (implicitly, a criticism of US policy) which lasted until 1995.[70] These talks were evidently aimed at overcoming Arab and Iranian suspicions that the aim of Turkey's military interventions in northern Iraq was not just to destroy PKK bases, but to take over the province of Mosul, with the Kirkuk oilfield – an aim frequently denied by Turkey.[71] However, the three countries could effectively agree only on a negative, without being able to produce a common policy on the Iraqi Kurdish question.

Although Turkey supported the peace talks between the KDP and PUK sponsored by the United States and held in Dublin in 1995, these failed to produce a settlement (see p. 227). In May 1996, and with the support of the KDP, the Turkish army launched further attacks against the PKK near the border. An agreement with Barzani was easier to achieve, and more important for Turkey, since he held power in the northern part of Iraqi Kurdistan, along the border with Turkey, whereas Talabani's power-base was in the south. The civil war between the two Iraqi Kurdish factions resumed in August 1996, as Barzani formed a brief alliance with Saddam Hussein against the PUK. Iran also became involved in the struggle, as it cooperated with the PUK against anti-government Iranian Kurdish forces of the Kurdistan Democratic Party of Iran (KDPI) who were allied with the Iraqi Kurds of the KDP.[72] Initially, with Iraqi help, Barzani's forces captured the PUK strongholds of Irbil and Suleymaniya, but in October the PUK recovered, apparently with Iranian assistance, and had recaptured the ground it had lost by the end of the month. The result was that by 1996 there appeared to be an informal alliance between Iran, the PUK and the PKK on the one side, and Turkey, the KDP and the KDPI on the other. At the same time, the failure of both the KDP and PUK to eliminate the other had at least stabilised the situation, and prompted Turkey to announce in September 1996 that it would establish what looked like a semi-permanent 'security zone' along the frontier region, extending several miles into Iraqi territory. In May and October 1997, Turkish forces carried out further operations in northern Iraq – apparently, even bigger than those of 1995 – in which the Turkish air force bombed PUK as well as PKK positions. At one point Turkish ground forces approached the cities of Irbil and Kirkuk, causing protests from Iran. As a result, and thanks to its continued cooperation with the KDP, Turkey had secured a significant decline in the PKK's ability to operate from northern Iraq by 1997–98. This formed the background to the Turkish pressure on Syria in September–October 1998, and a general re-focusing of the Kurdish question on the position in Turkey itself.[73]

The struggle for power in Iraqi Kurdistan also affected Turkey's relations with Baghdad after the Gulf war of 1991. Although Turgut Özal strongly opposed Saddam Hussein, in line with US policy, Bülent Ecevit, then in opposition, paid a private visit to Baghdad shortly after the war, allowing Saddam Hussein to attack the US policy of supporting the UN economic embargo on Iraq, and Turkey's support for 'Operation Provide Comfort'.[74] While Ecevit's visit had no official status, it was also clear that Turkey was anxious to have the sanctions lifted if it could, granted the serious economic losses it was suffering from the embargo (see pp. 224–5) and wished to maintain diplomatic and economic contacts with Baghdad. In the diplomatic sphere, Iraq maintained its embassy in Ankara throughout the period, while Turkey re-opened its embassy in Baghdad in 1993, at the level of chargé d'affaires. Although Turkey's official foreign trade statistics show only limited imports from Iraq after 1991, and virtually no exports to it, cross-border trade with Iraq was in fact resumed, with Turkish trucks crossing the Habur border crossing point carrying food and other supplies to Iraq and the Iraqi Kurds, and returning with diesel fuel from the refinery at Kirkuk. The UN was evidently prepared to allow this, since the Iraqi Kurds were heavily dependent on these supplies, as well as the revenues from customs duties, which were said to amount to US$150,000 per day. The Habur crossing point was officially re-opened in August 1994.[75] In the following month, a high-level Turkish trade mission visited Baghdad, and signed an economic protocol with the Iraqi government, although it was emphasised that Turkey could not resume normal economic relations with Iraq until the UN lifted the embargo. Meanwhile the foreign ministry stressed that the negotiations with Iraq were 'conducted in close consultation with our Western allies'.[76]

Clearly, Turkey's main objective was to try to persuade Saddam Hussein to comply with UN conditions for the lifting of sanctions, and to press the Western powers on the same issue. On this score, it was aware that France and Russia were also anxious to have the sanctions removed, if possible. A step forward in this direction was achieved in December 1996, when Saddam Hussein accepted UN Security Council Resolution 986 of April 1995, allowing Iraq to export oil to the value of US$2 billion in each six-month period. About 65 per cent of the proceeds were to be used to buy food and medical supplies, and the remainder used to cover the costs of the UN's inspection operation, plus compensation and war reparation payments to other Middle Eastern countries, including Turkey. Since about half the oil was to be exported via the Kirkuk–Yumurtalık pipeline, which was partially re-opened, Turkey was a particular beneficiary. Although the implementation of Resolution 986 was periodically interrupted, owing to Saddam Hussein's refusal to allow UN weapons inspectors full access, the new arrangements were estimated to bring in about US$500 million per year to Turkey, going some way to compensate it for the costs of the embargo.[77] Nonetheless, Turkey continued to press for the overall lifting of sanctions. As an incentive to Saddam Hussein, in February 1998 the Turkish foreign minister İsmail Cem visited Baghdad after consultation with the UN. During his visit, he submitted concrete proposals to end the sanctions, restore Iraq's sovereignty over its Kurdish regions and to ensure Iraq's participation in regional cooperation schemes, in return for full Iraqi compliance with UN resolutions.[78]

TURKEY AND IRAN

During the 1990s, relations with Iran continued to be a difficult test for Turkish diplomacy. Essentially, problems in the relationship were the product of the Iranian Revolution of 1979, uncertainties in the direction of Iran's internal politics, and of the two countries' conflicting relations with the Iraqi Kurds, rather than the end of the Cold War. As in the 1980s, Turkey's commitment to state secularism, and its links with the West, could have put it on a collision course with the Islamic Republic. Nonetheless, Turkey needed to create a reasonably cooperative relationship with Iran if it could, for pragmatic political and economic reasons. Outright hostility could have induced the Iranians to give all-out support to the PKK. Had this happened, it could have had the most serious effects for Turkey, given the length of the Turkish–Iranian border in a remote and mountainous area. A carefully tuned approach was also needed, giving encouragement where possible to moderate elements in Iranian politics. This incentive was substantially increased after the victory of Mohammad Khatami in the Iranian presidential elections of May 1997, and the new president's subsequent attempt to re-build bridges with the West. If the impasse in Iranian–US relations could be overcome, then Turkey could expect to be a substantial beneficiary since, apart from economic benefits, it was Iran's only neighbour which was also an ally of the United States. Economically, there was a substantial degree of actual or potential economic interdependence between the two countries. Even in difficult times, Turkey's annual trade volume with Iran ran at an average of US$908 million during 1992–98,[79] and Iran had the potential to become an important supplier of natural gas as well as crude oil to Turkey.

While there were evident advantages for Turkey from a cooperative relationship with Iran, the obstacles to achieving it were also clear. In broad political terms, the rulers in Tehran were bound to regard Turkey with grave suspicion, as the United States' main ally in the Middle East alongside Israel. While the Iranian government might periodically sign mutual security agreements with Turkey, there were reciprocal suspicions on the Turkish side that militant sections of the Iranian regime were not above aiding ultra-Islamist terrorists active in Turkey, and that the PKK was able to use some bases in Iran, even though this support was not so important or consistent as that given by Syria. The Turkish military, in particular, took a strong line against the Iranians – partly because of its strongly secularist commitments, and partly because it had to deal with periodic incursions by the PKK from Iranian territory. These apparent differences of emphasis within the circle of Turkish policy-makers concerning Turkish–Iranian relations strained Turkey's relations with the United States – in particular, over Turkey's opposition to US economic sanctions against Iran under the Iran–Libya Sanctions Act , or ILSA (see pp. 276–7).[80]

For all this, the widely predicted clash between Turkey and Iran in central Asia failed to materialise. Admittedly, Iran's apparent alignment with Armenia and Russia over the Nagorno-Karabakh dispute caused some frictions with Turkey, but this does not seem to have reached critical proportions (see pp. 284–5, n. 68). In central Asia, Iran held back from overtly sponsoring the cause of Islamic revolution in the new republics, preferring to exploit such economic opportunities as it had (in particular, the central Asian states' need for transit routes to the outside world) by cultivating relations with the existing governments. Some differentiation between each of the republics was also apparent. Iran attached importance to Tajikistan, but Turkey did not, while Kirghizstan was of minor importance to both, so these two states were lifted out of the zone of potential conflict. Equally, Kazakhstan was closer to Russia, both geographically and politically, than it was to either Turkey or Iran. In Turkemistan, Turkey and Iran had a generally cooperative relationship, though Iran had the advantage of geographical contiguity. This left Uzbekistan as the only state where Turkish and Iranian interests conflicted. However, in spite of its occasional arguments with Turkey, Islam Kerimov's government clearly favoured Turkey over Iran, and the Iranians were apparently prepared to accept this. Moreover, both countries had an interest in preventing the central Asian or Transcaucasian states from reverting to the status of satellites of Russia.[81] Consequently, as John Calabrese concludes, 'prospects for Iran and Turkey in Central Asia and the Caucasus depend[ed] more on developing a *modus vivendi* with Moscow than in out-duelling one another'.[82]

Turkish suspicions that Iran was involved in sponsoring ultra-Islamist terrorism in Turkey came to the surface in 1993, following the murder of the widely respected and strongly pro-secularist journalist Uğur Mumcu, on 24 January. Four days later, an unsuccessful attempt was made on the life of Jak Kamhi, one of Turkey's leading businessmen, and a prominent member of Istanbul's Jewish community. Investigations were also launched into the murders of two other pro-secularist journalists, Çetin Emeç and Turan Dursun, who had been killed some two years previously. Although no one was charged in connection with Mumcu's murder, the minister of the interior, İsmet Sezgin, told a press conference on 4 February that 19 people had been arrested for these crimes, of whom the majority had confessed that they had been trained for terrorism in Iran.[83] Predictably, the Iranian government denied any such involvement, while Süleyman Demirel, as prime minister, stressed that Turkey would adopt a 'cool-headed approach', and hoped that relations with Iran would not be disrupted.[84]

In the aftermath, the Turks decided to develop the joint approach towards the Iraqi Kurds which they were trying to establish with both Iran and Syria, by reaching an agreement with Tehran designed to prevent the PKK using bases in Iran, and prevent Iranian sponsorship of Islamist terrorism in Turkey. In return, Turkey would promise not to allow attacks on Iran by the *Mujahiddin-i Khalq*, the Iranian organisation of anti-regime Iranian militants, some of whose members had taken refuge in Turkey.[85] Accordingly, in November 1993 the two governments signed a security protocol stipulating that neither would allow any terrorist organisation hostile to the other to operate from its territory. In May 1994, this agreement appeared to be working, as Iran turned over a number of members of the PKK, plus the corpses of others, to the Turkish authorities. The 1993 agreement was backed up by another one in June 1994, under which the Iranians promised to prevent the passage of PKK members from Iraq to Iran, or from Iran to Armenia, and thence to Russia. As part of the *rapprochement*, Demirel paid an official visit to Tehran in July 1994 – the first Turkish president to do so since before the Iranian Revolution.[86] Nonetheless, it appeared that by the spring of 1995, relations had again deteriorated: in fact, it seems that in May 1995 Tansu Çiller, as prime minister, proposed launching air attacks on assumed PKK bases in Iran, but was overruled on this by President Demirel.[87] This renewed tension evidently stemmed from Turkish military offensives in northern Iraq, which were opposed by Iran, and had evidently forced some of the PKK militants to take refuge in Iranian territory.

During 1996–97, Turkey's relations with Iran became an important item in Necmettin Erbakan's attempt to re-orient Turkey's foreign relations towards the Muslim countries, and secularist resistance to it. The high point of Erbakan's project came with his visit to Tehran in August 1996, in the course of which he signed an agreement with the Iranians for the construction of a natural gas pipeline from Tabriz, in north-western Iran, to the eastern Turkish city of Erzurum, with a future extension westwards to Sivas and Ankara. This was expected to deliver three billion cubic metres of gas per year to Turkey, rising to ten billion cubic metres per year by 2003. It was also envisaged that the Iran–Turkey connection might become the middle segment in a gas pipeline between Turkmenistan and Turkey (see p. 280). There were actually strong economic reasons for pushing ahead with the project from the Turkish viewpoint: in fact, an out-line agreement on the proposal had been signed the previous year, by Tansu Çiller's government. Nonetheless, Erbakan was happy to stress the 'Islamic' aspect of his policies, in the knowledge that it would cause severe misgivings in Washington. These were only to be expected, given that the signature of the agreement came only a few days after the passage of the ILSA. The Turkish authorities argued that the agreement did not infringe the ILSA, since this was a government-to-government deal, which did not involve any direct Turkish investments in Iran (the cost of building the pipeline on the Iranian side was to be met by the Iranians). At the time, the Clinton administration seemed prepared to accept this, though Washington was clearly unhappy with the project.[88] Within Turkey, the conflict over relations with Iran became still more acute in December 1996, when the then Iranian president, Hashemi Rafsanjani, visited Ankara and Erbakan apparently tried to negotiate a defence cooperation agreement with Iran. This idea was hotly opposed by the Turkish military, which saw Iran as far more of an enemy than an ally, and was vetoed by the General Staff, indicating the severe ruptures over foreign policy at the time.[89]

As in other policy theatres, the Yılmaz administration was left with the job of re-adjusting Turkey's relations with Iran, after the fall of the Erbakan–Çiller coalition in June 1997. Turkey's links with Israel, as well as conflicts over policy towards the Iraqi Kurds, were still serious points of friction, and caused Demirel to walk out of a meeting of the OIC held in Tehran in December 1997.[90] There was another clash between the two countries in July 1999, when the Iranians claimed that Turkish air-craft had bombed two Iranian border villages (the Turks claimed that they were PKK camps on the Iraqi side of the Iraqi–Iranian border). On the other side Turkey alleged that there were as many as 50 PKK camps in Iran, and the Turkish press suggested that Turkey might launch direct air raids against them. In the event, the two countries signed another security agreement on 13 August under which they would carry out 'simul-taneous operations' against insurgent bases on both sides of the border. These succeeded in improving the atmosphere, and on 17 October Korkmaz Haktanır, the under-secretary at the Turkish foreign ministry and a former Turkish ambassador in Tehran, announced that the two countries had 'normalised their relations'.[91] Meanwhile, prospects for the planned gas pipeline remained uncertain. In November 1999, the Iranian petroleum minister stated that Iran's section of the pipeline would be completed by the end of the year: the Turkish pipeline company, Botaş, had meanwhile virtually completed the first part of its section, between the Iranian frontier and Erzurum, but finance to extend it to Ankara had been obstructed by the ILSA legislation. The Turkish minister of energy meanwhile expressed doubts as to whether Iran would have enough gas production to meet its commitments under the deal: even if the project did go ahead, it was unlikely to be completed by 2001.[92] In fact, it seemed that by this stage Turkey would have been happier to import gas from Azerbaijan or Turkmenistan, via a trans-Caspian connection, rather than Iran, in accordance with US preferences, but could not officially cancel the agreement. More broadly, the two countries seemed to have drawn back from a direct conflict over northern Iraq. At the same time, prospects were, as ever, heavily dependent on the outcome of the internal struggle for power in Iran between radical and moderate Islamists, which would almost certainly continue.

NOTES

1. Gareth M. Winrow, *Turkey in Post-Soviet Central Asia* (London, Royal Institute of International Affairs, 1995), p. 17.
2. Gareth M. Winrow, 'Regional Security and National Identity: The Role of Turkey in former Soviet Central Asia', in Çiğdem Balım, ed., *Turkey: Political, Social and Economic Challenges in the 1990s* (Leiden, Brill, 1995), p. 31 (citing Soviet data of 1990–91).
3. Winrow, *Turkey in Post-Soviet Central Asia* , pp. 6–7.
4. See Jacob M. Landau, *Pan-Turkism: From Irredentism to Cooperation* (London, Hurst, 1995) Ch 3.
5. On Türkeş's pan-Turkist ideas, and their relationship to Islamism, see Hugh Poulton, *Top Hat, Grey Wolf and Crescent: Turkish Nationalism and the Turkish Republic* (London, Hurst, 1997), pp. 147–50, 155–8.
6. Philip Robins, 'Between Sentiment and Self-Interest: Turkey's Policy toward Azerbaijan and the Central Asian States', *Middle East Journal*, Vol. 47 (1993), p. 592.
7. That is, the Azeris and Turkmen of northern Iran, the Turkmen, Uzbeks and Kirghiz of northern Afghanistan, and the Uighurs, Kazakhs and Kirghiz of the province of Xinjiang, in the extreme west of China.
8. General Dostum, the then Uzbek warlord in northern Afghanistan, did however visit Turkey in 1996, and requested Turkish government aid for his forces, apparently unsuccessfully. See Gareth M. Winrow, 'Turkey and the Newly Independent States of Central Asia and Transcaucasus', *MERIA Journal* (published on internet), No. 2 (1997). With regard to Iran, the fact that Abulfez Elchibey, the president of Azerbaijan during 1992–93, was prone to call for 're-union' with the Azeris of north-western Iran was also a cause of embarrassment for Turkey (see above, pp. 284–5, n. 68). On the Uighurs of Xinjiang and their connections with Turkey, see Graham E. Fuller, 'Turkey's New Eastern Orientation', in Graham E. Fuller and Ian O. Lesser, eds,

Turkey's New Geopolitics: From the Balkans to Western China (Boulder, CO, Westview, 1993), pp. 73–4. Turkey has been careful not to interfere with the internal affairs of China, although there are some representatives of the Kazakh, Kirghiz and Uighur minorities of China in Turkey who continue to call for the 'liberation of eastern Turkestan'. Gareth M. Winrow, 'Turkey's Relations with the Transcaucasus and the Central Asian Republics', *Perceptions* (Ankara), Vol. 1, No. 1 (1996), p. 138.

9. Paul B. Henze, *Turkey: Toward the Twenty-First Century* (Washington, DC, Rand Corporation, n.d.), p. 31.
10. Winrow, *Turkey in Post-Soviet Central Asia*, pp. 11–12 and Philip Robins, 'Turkey's Ost-politik: Relations with the Central Asian States', in David Menashri, ed., *Central Asia Meets the Middle East* (London, Cass, 1998), pp. 131–3.
11. Quoted in Robins, 'Turkey's Ostpolitik', p. 135.
12. Ibid., p. 135 and Heinz Kramer, 'Options for Turkish Foreign Policy: Central Asia and Transcaucasus', unpublished paper (1997), p. 3.
13. Winrow, *Turkey in Post-Soviet Central Asia*, p. 13.
14. Robins, 'Turkey's Ostpolitik', p. 133.
15. Ibid., pp. 136–7, and Winrow, *Turkey in Post-Soviet Central Asia*, p. 19.
16. Winrow, 'Regional Security', pp. 32–3. The quotation is from ibid., p. 32, quoting the Foreign Affairs Committee of the Russian parliament in 1992.
17. Ibid., pp. 33–8; Robins, 'Turkey's Ostpolitik', pp. 137–40 and Gareth M. Winrow, 'A Region at the Crossroads: Security Issues in Post-Soviet Asia', *Journal of South Asian and Middle Eastern Studies*, Vol 18 (1994), pp. 16–17.
18. Winrow, *Turkey in Post-Soviet Central Asia* , pp. 28–30, and Winrow, 'Turkey and the Newly Independent States'.
19. Winrow, 'Turkey and the Newly Independent States', and Winrow, 'Regional Security', p. 40
20. Robins, 'Between Sentiment and Self-Interest', p. 600; Winrow, 'Regional Security', p. 34, and Heinz Kramer, 'Will Central Asia Become Turkey's Sphere of Influence?', *Perceptions* (Ankara), Vol. 1, No. 1 (1996), p. 116.
21. Kramer, 'Options', pp. 11–12.
22. *Briefing* (Ankara, weekly), 28 June 1999, p. 10.
23. Robins, 'Turkey's Ostpolitik', p. 144, and Winrow, *Turkey in Post-Soviet Central Asia*, p. 47.
24. For further details, see Selim İlkin, 'The Economic Cooperation Organisation (ECO): a Short Note', *Journal of Economic Cooperation among Islamic Countries* (Ankara), Vol. 15 (1994), pp. 31–43, and Önder Özar, 'Economic Co-operation Organisation: A Promising Future', *Perceptions* (Ankara), Vol. 2 No. 1 (1997), pp. 15–23.
25. Winrow, *Turkey in Post-Soviet Central Asia* , pp. 32–3; Kramer, 'Options', pp. 11–12 and the author's observations in Uzbekistan.
26. Data for 1992 from Winrow, *Turkey in Post-Soviet Central Asia*, p. 37; for 1997, from *Statistical Yearbook of Turkey 1998* (Ankara, State Institute of Statistics, 1999), pp. 515–16.
27. *Briefing*, 21 June 1999, pp. 14–15, 12 July 1999, p. 15.
28. Ibid., 19 May 1997 p. 16, 30 June 1997 p. 17.
29. Ibid., 22 November 1999, p. 22.
30. Ayşegül Sever, 'The Arab–Israeli Peace Process and Turkey since the 1995 Interim Agreement', *Turkish Review of Middle East Studies* (Istanbul), Vol. 9 (1996/97), pp. 121, 125, and M. Hakan Yavuz, 'Turkish–Israeli Relations through the Lens of the Turkish

Identity Debate', *Journal of Palestine Studies*, Vol. 27 (1997), pp. 26–7.

31. Mahmut Bali Aykan, 'The Palestinian Question in Turkish Foreign Policy from the 1950s to the 1990s', *International Journal of Middle East Studies*, Vol. 25 (1993), p. 106; Bülent Aras, *Palestinian–Israeli Peace Process and Turkey* (Commack, NY, Nova Science Publishers, 1998), p. 134, and Kemal Kirişci, 'Post Cold-War Turkish Security and the Middle East', *MERIA Journal* (published on internet), No. 2 (1997).

32. Mahmut Bali Aykan, 'The Turkey–US–Israel Triangle: Continuity, Change and Implications for Turkey's Post-Cold War Middle East Policy', *Journal of South Asian and Middle Eastern Studies*, Vol. 22 (1999), pp. 6–7.

33. For further details, see Amikam Nachmani, 'The Remarkable Turkish–Israeli Tie', in Amikam Nachmani, *Turkey and the Middle East* (Tel Aviv, Begin-Sadat Center for Strategic Studies, Bar Ilan University, 1999: reprinted from *Middle East Quarterly*, Vol. 5 [1998]), pp. 24–6.

34. Besides Turkey, the members of the 'D-8' were Bangladesh, Egypt, Indonesia, Iran, Malaysia, Nigeria and Pakistan. The title was changed to 'D-8' from 'M-8' or 'Muslim-8', apparently because the latter sounded too provocative. See Philip Robins, 'Turkish Foreign Policy Under Erbakan', *Survival*, Vol. 39 (1997), pp. 93–4, and Sabri Sayarı, 'Turkey and the Middle East in the 1990s', *Journal of Palestine Studies*, Vol. 26 (1997), p. 52.

35. In particular, on 2 February 1997, the Welfare Party mayor of Sincan, an outer suburb of Ankara, organised 'Jerusalem Night' celebrations, which were addressed by the Iranian ambassador, and calls for a *jihad* against Israel were issued from the platform. In response, on 4 February, the army rolled its tanks down the main street of Sincan during the morning rush-hour, and the mayor was arrested. This marked the start of the military's open campaign against Erbakan, although there were many other factors, mainly domestic, which led to the fall of his government. See Yavuz, 'Turkish–Israeli', pp. 22, 29–31.

36. Sayarı, 'Turkey and the Middle East', p. 50 and Aykan, 'Turkey–US–Israel', pp. 22–5.

37. Quoted in Aykan, 'Turkey-US–Israel', pp. 10–11.

38. Alain Gresh, 'Turkish–Israeli–Syrian Relations and their Impact on the Middle East', *Middle East Journal*, Vol. 52 (1998), p. 189. Gresh is reporting an interview with the former Israeli defence minister, Moshe Arens.

39. On 26 April 1997 the then Israeli defence minister, Yitzhak Mordechai, was quoted in the Turkish newspaper *Yeni Yüzyıl* as saying, 'There is no agreement between us [Turkey and Israel] to use or defend our territories in the event of attack. But if countries like Iran, Iraq or Syria want to resort to violence against Turkey they should know that they would be facing a united force' (quoted in ibid., p. 192, n.17). What the second sentence meant precisely was unclear. Mordechai denied the statement on the following day, although Gresh states that its 'authenticity ... is not in question' (ibid.).

40. Aykan, 'Turkey–US–Israel', p. 18. Nachmani remarks that Israel 'desists from criticizing Turkish ties with Iran and Iraq', but this does not seem to have been true of private contacts. See Nachmani, 'Turkish–Israeli Tie', pp. 20–1.

41. Nachmani, 'Turkish–Israeli Tie', pp. 19–20, and Gresh, 'Turkish–Israeli–Syrian', pp. 193–4.

42. By comparison, Turkey's trade volume with Saudi Arabia in 1998 was US$1,141 million, with Algeria US$1,128 million and with Egypt US$865 million. Data for 1998

from *Briefing*, 8 March 1999, p. 37; for 1992 from *Statistical Yearbook of Turkey 1998*, p. 525.

43. Nachmani, 'Turkish–Israeli Tie', p. 27.
44. Aras, *Palestinian–Israeli*, p. 130.
45. Quoted in ibid., p. 130.
46. Kirişci, 'Post Cold-War'. See also Sayarı, 'Turkey and the Middle East', p. 50, and Aras, *Palestinian–Israeli*, p. 134.
47. In the words of Article 5 of the 1987 agreement. For the full text, see H. Fahir Alaçam, 'Turkish–Syrian Relations', *Turkish Review of Middle East Studies* (Istanbul), Vol. 8 (1994/95), pp. 12–14.
48. Suha Bölükbaşı, 'Turkey Challenges Iraq and Syria: The Euphrates Dispute', *Journal of South Asian and Middle Eastern Studies*, Vol. 16 (1993), pp. 22–3.
49. According to figures cited by Ayşegül Kibaroğlu and the Turkish foreign ministry, the total annual average supply of water in the river (including the relatively small supply from tributaries within Syria) is around 1,130 cusecs. On the other hand, total demand within Turkey (including the Southeast Anatolia Project, or GAP) is put at around 580 cusecs, that of Syria at 490 cusecs, and of Iraq at 730 cusecs, making a total of around 1,800 cusecs. See Ayşegül Kibaroğlu, 'Prospects for Cooperation in the Euphrates–Tigris River Basin', *Turkish Review of Middle East Studies* (Istanbul), Vol. 8 (1994/95), p. 143 and Turkish Ministry of Foreign Affairs, (hereafter abbreviated as 'MFA'), 'Water Issues between Turkey, Syria and Iraq', *Perceptions* (Ankara), Vol. 1, No. 2 (1996), p. 87. (Figures converted from billion cubic metres per year.)
50. Alaçam, 'Turkish–Syrian', p. 9.
51. See Gresh, 'Turkish–Israeli–Syrian', p. 196.
52. Against this, the Turks point out that the relevant section (Article 6) of the 1987 agreement provided that Turkey would maintain an average flow of 500 cusecs '[D]uring the filling up period of the Atatürk Dam reservoir and until the final allocation of the waters of [the] Euphrates among the three riparian countries'. The Atatürk dam (though not all the associated irrigations work) was completed in 1990, but the second condition has not been fulfilled; hence it is implied that the 1987 agreement is still binding on both parties. See MFA, 'Water Issues', p. 102.
53. Ibid., pp. 100–5, 109–12. See also Ali Çarkoğlu and Mine Eder, 'GAP: The Water Conflict', *Private View* (Istanbul), Autumn 1998, pp. 63–4, and Gün Kut, 'Burning Waters: The Hydropolitics of the Euphrates and Tigris', *New Perspectives on Turkey*, Fall 1993, pp. 12–13. On the last point, the Tigris could in principle be a point of conflict between Turkey and Iraq, since its upper reaches are included in the GAP project. However, its total flow is around 1,550 cusecs, of which 48 per cent originates in Iraq. Turkey's demand on its waters (including the uncompleted GAP project) only amounts to 220 cusecs, and that of Iraq to 725 cusecs, so that in theory Iraq should be able to transfer around 500 cusecs from the Tigris into the Euphrates (allowing for some use of the Tigris waters by Syria. Figures converted from billion cubic metres per year.) See MFA, 'Water Issues', pp. 89–91.
54. Bölükbaşı, 'Turkey Challenges', pp. 23–5, and MFA, 'Water Issues', pp. 98–100.
55. For the English text of the relevant parts of this agreement (Articles 1 and 2) see *Briefing*, 26 October 1998, p. 11.
56. See Alaçam, 'Turkish–Syrian', pp. 15–17, and Robert Olson, 'The Kurdish Question and Turkey's Foreign Policy, 1991–95: From the Gulf War to the Incursion into Iraq',

Journal of South Asian and Middle Eastern Studies, Vol. 19 (1995), pp. 4–7.

57. Quoted in *Briefing*, 21 September 1998, p. 10.

58. Ibid., 12 October 1998, pp. 16–17. See also Kemal Kirişci, 'The Kurdish Question and Turkish Foreign Policy', in Lenora Martin, ed., *The Future of Turkish Foreign Policy* (forthcoming).

59. *Briefing*, 12 October 1998, pp. 16–17, 19 October 1998, pp. 11–12, 26 October 1998, pp. 11–12. For the text of the agreement, see ibid., 26 October 1998, p. 12, from which the quotation is taken.

60. The author is much indebted to Dr Bill Harris for advice on these points.

61. According to later reports, Ramon Mantovani, of the Italian Communist Refoundation Party, visited Damascus in early September 1998, to plan Öcalan's flight to Italy, among other things. This suggests that Öcalan had been contemplating the move before the tension between Turkey and Syria reached its height. Mantovani later played an instrumental role in bringing Öcalan from Russia to Italy on 12 November, although evidently without the knowledge of the Italian foreign ministry. See *Briefing*, 22 February 1999, p. 20.

62. Ibid., 29 March 1999, pp. 4–5.

63. Reported in the London-based Arabic daily, *al-Hayat*, 26 October 1999; translation in *Summary of World Broadcasts* (BBC, London) 29 October 1999.

64. See, Alaçam, 'Turkish–Syrian', p. 6, and Sayarı, 'Turkey and the Middle East', p. 50. There were also suggestions that Israel would put pressure on Turkey to release more water in the Euphrates, so as to induce Syria to accept a deal over the Golan. However, Israeli officials denied that Israel would try to link the Arab–Israeli peace process with the Euphrates issue, and the suggestion was naturally strongly opposed by Turkey. See Aykan, 'Turkey–US–Israel' pp. 20–1.

65. On these points, see Michael M. Gunter, 'The Foreign Policy of the Iraqi Kurds', *Journal of South Asian and Middle Eastern Studies*, Vol. 20 (1997), p. 10: Kemal Kirişci, 'Turkey and the Kurdish Safe Haven in Northern Iraq', *Journal of South Asian and Middle Eastern Studies*, Vol. 19 (1996), pp. 35–7, and Gresh, 'Turkish–Israeli–Syrian', pp. 194–5.

66. There were occasional reports in the Turkish press that the PKK had in fact established bases in Iraq in government-controlled territory, and Saddam Hussein was reported to have received Öcalan in June 1992. However, Saddam Hussein maintained that he had never supported the PKK, and if there was any arrangement between the two it does not seem to have had more than a marginal effect. See İhsan Gürkan, 'Turkish–Iraqi Relations: The Cold War and its Aftermath', *Turkish Review of Middle East Studies* (Istanbul), Vol. 9 (1996–97), pp. 59–60, 62.

67. Michael M. Gunter, *The Kurds and the Future of Turkey* (London, Macmillan, 1997), pp. 115–16.

68. Ibid., p. 117 and Gunter, 'Foreign Policy', p. 10. On the last point, Suha Bölükbaşı, claims that there are 'about one million ethnic Turks in Mosul'. See Bölübasi, 'Turkey Challenges', p. 11. See also Gürkan, 'Turkish–Iraqi Relations', p. 58, who claims that the Turcomans number as many as 2.3 million. Their main original homes were in Mosul and Kirkuk, both of which were still controlled by Saddam Hussein, but it appears that in 1991 many of them had re-established themselves within the 'safe haven'.

69. Gunter, *Kurds and the Future*, pp. 120–1; Mahmut Bali Aykan, 'Turkey's Policy in

Northern Iraq, 1991–95', *Middle Eastern Studies,* Vol. 32 (1996), p. 352 and Kirişci, 'Turkey and the Kurdish Safe Haven', p. 21.

70. Mahmut Bali Aykan, 'Turkish Perspectives on Turkish–US Relations concerning Persian Gulf Security in the Post-Cold War Era: 1989–1995', *Middle Eastern Studies,* Vol. 50 (1996), p. 354; Aykan, 'Turkey's Policy', p. 357; Gunter, 'Foreign Policy', pp. 12–13 and Michael M. Gunter, 'Turkey and Iran Face Off in Kurdistan', *Middle East Quarterly,* Vol. 5 (1998), p. 35. For the text of the agreement reached in August 1994, see Alaçam, 'Turkish–Syrian', pp. 15–17.

71. In May 1995 President Demirel proposed that the Iraqi–Turkish frontier be altered in Turkey's favour, but quickly withdrew this suggestion in the face of strong opposition from the Arab states and Iran. See Gunter, 'Turkey and Iran', p. 36. As General İhsan Gürkan concludes, Turkey 'cannot file a claim to the region' unless 'northern Iraq is separated from Iraq in any way' (presumably, as part of a general partition of the country). Gürkan, 'Turkish–Iraqi Relations', p. 62.

72. John Calabrese, 'Turkey and Iran: Limits of a Stable Relationship', *British Journal of Middle Eastern Studies,* Vol. 25 (1998), p. 89.

73. Gunter, 'Foreign Policy', pp. 14–19; 'Turkey and Iran', pp. 36–8; and Kirişci, 'Kurdish Question'.

74. Gürkan, 'Turkish Iraqi Relations', p. 59.

75. Aykan, 'Turkey's Policy', p. 358; Olson, 'Kurdish Question', pp. 14–15 and Gunter, *Kurds and the Future,* p. 117.

76. Statement by Özdem Sanberk, then the Under-Secretary at the foreign ministry, quoted in Olson, 'Kurdish Question', p. 16. For the details of the protocol, see ibid., p. 15.

77. Gürkan, 'Turkish Iraqi Relations', pp. 68–9, and Amikam Nachmani, 'Turkey in the Wake of the Gulf War: Recent History and its Implications', in Nachmani, *Turkey and the Middle East,* p. 11. Iraq's permitted oil exports under Resolution 986 were put at 700,000 barrels per day (b/d). Half of this would be 350,000 b/d, which is well below the full capacity of the Kirkuk–Yumurtalık pipeline of 1.5 million b/d.

78. Aykan, 'Turkey–US–Israel', p. 27.

79. Data for 1992–97 from *Statistical Yearbook of Turkey 1998,* p. 525; for 1998 from *Briefing,* 8 March 1999, p. 37.

80. On the last point, see Aykan, 'Turkish Perspectives', p. 353.

81. Calabrese, 'Turkey and Iran' pp. 90–3.

82. Ibid., p. 93.

83. Ankara Radio, 4 February 1993, in *Summary of World Broadcasts,* (BBC, London), 6 February 1993. See also *Milliyet,* 3 February 1993, and Hugh Pope, 'Pointing Fingers at Iran', *Middle East International,* 5 February 1993. For other connections between ultra-Islamist political movements in Turkey and Iran, see Calabrese, 'Turkey and Iran', pp. 84–5.

84. Ankara Radio, 8 February 1993, in *Summary of World Broadcasts,* (BBC, London), 10 February 1993.

85. In the spring of 1996, the Iranians claimed that the Turkish authorities had allowed members of the *Mujahiddin-i Khalq* to stage an anti-Iranian demonstration. See Gunter, *Kurds and the Future,* pp. 96–7. However, there is no other evidence known to the author that members of the organisation were actually active in Turkey, even though the Iranian government was evidently suspicious that they might be.

86. Ibid., p. 96; Olson, 'Kurdish Question', pp. 8–10, and Gunter, 'Turkey and Iran', p. 35.
87. Kirişci, 'Kurdish Question' and Gunter, *Kurds and the Future,* p. 96. The author is also indebted to Sedat Ergin for information on this point.
88. *Briefing,* 19 August 1996 pp. 4–5; Calabrese, 'Turkey and Iran', pp. 83–4 and Robins, 'Turkish Foreign Policy', pp. 90–1.
89. Kirişci, 'Kurdish Question'. Needless to say, the prospect of a military agreement between Turkey and Iran also provoked profound misgivings in Israel. See Aykan, 'Turkey–US–Israel', pp. 17–19.
90. See Gunter, 'Turkey and Iran', p. 40.
91. *Milliyet,* 27, 28 July 1999; *Briefing,* 9 August 1999, pp. 13–14, 16 August 1999, p. 9 and Anatolia Agency, 17 October 1999 in *Summary of World Broadcasts,* (BBC, London), 19 October 1999.
92. *Briefing,* 15 November 1992, p. 22, 22 November 1999, pp. 32–3 and Reuters, 15 December 1999.

10

Conclusions and Prospects

In an attempt to draw conclusions from a long and tangled story, this chapter is divided into three sections. The first tries to assess the effects of historical changes on the foreign policy options of the late Ottoman empire and the Turkish republic, and to identify the continuities as well as reorientations of their policies in successive periods. The second summarises the effects of domestic political changes, and varying self perceptions of the identity of the state, on the way it conducted its foreign policy. The final section offers some speculative suggestions as to what challenges Turkish foreign policy-makers seem likely to face in the first few decades of the new century, in the light of their historical experiences and policies.

HISTORICAL CHANGES AND POLICY OPTIONS

An underlying assumption of this book is that there have been some important elements of continuity, as well as change, in Turkish foreign policy since the days of the late Ottoman empire. For most of the period surveyed (that is, from the late eighteenth century until 1914, and from 1939 until the 1980s) Turkey was a state under threat from other powers, normally Russia, and, during the nineteenth century, from internal ethnic rebellions. Between 1914 and 1918 it was unnecessarily embroiled in the First World War, and between 1919 and 1922 it was locked in a basic struggle for survival. During these periods, the dominant question for foreign policy-makers was whether they should seek an alliance with a major power, and if so with whom. During the remaining periods, between 1923 and 1939, and again after 1990, the external threat was reduced. Nonetheless, the policy options adopted during the two periods were quite different.

Looking back at the nineteenth century, it seems fairly safe to say that Ottoman foreign policy was essentially defensive. Its main purpose was to protect the territory, primarily in Europe, which the empire retained, and to secure a period of peace in which the state could reconstruct its institutions and strengthen its resources. The main threat which the empire faced was the challenge posed by the rise in power of Russia, and the emergence of nationalist movements among the Christian societies of the Balkans, though there were also threats from other directions, notably from the Sultan's nominal vassal, Mehmet Ali Pasha, between 1831 and 1841. Given that they could not rely on their own resources to defeat these enemies, the Ottoman rulers had either to form an alliance with one or more of the European powers, or remain outside alliances, and hope that the rivalries between the powers would deter any of them from destroying the empire. During the confused period of the Napoleonic wars, the empire switched sides no less that four times, forming periodic alliances with Britain, France and Russia. Faced with the challenge from Mehmet Ali, it constructed a brief entente with Russia in 1833 and then a successful alliance with Britain, Austria, Prussia and Russia in 1840. Its participation in great-power politics reached its peak with the alliance with Britain and France signed in 1854, which led to the Crimean war. The alignment with Britain nonetheless withered away after the treaty of Berlin of 1878, under which the empire lost most, but not all, of its territories in the Balkans. Under Abdul Hamid, the Ottomans first sought an alliance with Germany but, when this attempt failed, moved back to the second policy of uneasy neutrality. Although the Young Turk regime of 1908 investigated the possibility of alliances with all the main European powers except Russia, the formation of the two great alliances of the First World War made it more difficult to maintain the balancing act between them, and the empire had no formal alliances until it fatefully joined Germany in 1914.

The period between 1918 and 1923 marked the nadir of Turkish power, in which the survival of a Turkish state was most in doubt. That Turkey managed to survive it was mainly due to the stubborn determination of its people and leaders to resist occupation and partition. However, the war-weariness of the entente powers, and the divisions between them also played an important part. By reaching separate settlements with France and Italy, and an entente with the new Soviet state, the founders of the republic showed themselves adept at exploiting the remnants of the old balance-of-power system. Through it, they were effectively able to isolate the Greeks, and belatedly convince the British that supporting Greek ambitions was a losing game. After the signature of the treaty of Lausanne in 1923, they reverted to a policy of neutrality between all the main European powers. This was partly because an alliance was unnecessary. The events of 1918–23 had ended the mis-match between the state's resources and its territorial commitments. Turkey had no important *terra irridenta* to recover, and Russia's power had temporarily been reduced by its internal turmoils, so that it was not a serious threat to Turkey for the first time in over a century. Apart from this, alliances were simply unavailable at the time. In the world of the 1920s, the expectation was that collective security agreements under the League of Nations would suffice to keep the peace. By the mid-1930s, however, this hope was evaporating as Turkey began to see a new security threat, first from Italy and then from Germany. After a rare and unsuccessful attempt to forge an alliance with the minor powers of the Balkans in 1934, the Turks began to look for agreements with the Soviet Union, and with Britain and France, as a means of obtaining security in the Mediterranean and the Balkans. The first quest proved unavailing, and was abruptly blocked by the signature of the Nazi–Soviet pact in August 1939, but the second was eventually achieved in October 1939, as the tripartite treaty between Britain, France and Turkey.

At the beginning of the Second World War, it appears that İsmet İnönü's government was fully prepared to undertake its commitments to the British and French – in effect, to join them in operations against Italy if Mussolini joined the war. However, the unexpectedly rapid collapse of France in the early summer of 1940 changed the external dimensions drastically. Henceforth, the Turks were determined to stay out of the war, and successfully resisted pressure from both sides to break their *de facto* neutrality – first by Germany, during 1940–41, and then by Britain and the United States, during 1942–44. That İnönü's tactic succeeded was partly due to adroit diplomacy and foot-dragging by Turkey, and partly to sheer good luck – in particular, Hitler's decision to invade the Soviet Union rather than the Middle East in 1941, and subsequent disagreements between Britain and the United States about the wisdom of trying to bring Turkey into the war. Nonetheless, by 1945, Turkey was still in a position of great international danger, as the victorious Stalin demanded concessions from Ankara which, if realised, would probably have converted Turkey into a Soviet satellite, and it was as yet unclear that the Western powers would resist him.

In the post-war world, and faced with the classic choice between alliance and non-alignment, Turkey was almost bound to take the first option. In effect, it was in the same position as most of the medium and small powers of western Europe, which preferred a defensive alliance with the United States to active non-alignment. Unlike say, India, it was in the middle of a zone of intense rivalry between the superpowers, and if unaided, it could not expect to hold off a direct attack by the Warsaw Pact for more than a limited time – especially if, as expected, this was launched against the straits. In the words of a former Chief of the Turkish General Staff, Turkey's military doctrine during the Cold War 'could only be defensive', and depended on alliance with the Western powers.[1] As a result, the principle obstacle to forging the alliance was not reluctance on the Turkish side, but misgivings on the part of the United States, which was initially anxious not to disperse its resources over too many potential fronts. The Korean war changed Western perceptions, and resulted in the admission of Greece and Turkey into NATO in 1952.

Thereafter, Turkey's alliance with the West was fairly unproblematic, until the Cyprus crisis brought about a serious clash of perceived interests between Turkey and the United States in 1964. In the succeeding phase, there were some calls in Turkey for a reconsideration of the alliance, and in 1978–79 the government, led by Bülent Ecevit, tried to follow a more independent line. However, the arguments in favour of remaining in NATO proved conclusive, and were strengthened during the period of the 'second Cold War' of the early 1980s. At the same time, Turkey avoided becoming a mere satellite of the United States and was, for instance, able to follow a quite independent policy towards Cyprus and the Middle East. Interference in Turkey's domestic affairs by the United States was also minimal, although periodic economic crises meant that Turkey had to pay attention to the prescriptions of the IMF and other international financial institutions in determining macro-economic policy. The formation of the EEC, and Turkey's associate membership of it beginning in 1963, added a new dimension to its relationships with the Western powers, besides a new set of actual or potential dependencies.

At first glance, the end of the Cold War might seem to have given Turkey the option of abandoning its alliance with the West, since the main cause of its original formation – the direct threat from the Soviet Union – had now been removed. That this did not happen was partly the result of the redefinition of the alliance, which was now seen as having a general mission to protect peace and democratic values throughout Europe and (more vaguely) in the Middle East, and partly because the alliance had acquired value for its members quite outside the limited field of national defence. Given this remit, Turkey was still of substantial value to NATO, thanks to its geographical position at the crossroads between the Balkans, the Middle East, and the southern regions of the former Soviet Union. This preference was reciprocated on the Turkish side, since the NATO connection has now greatly broadened by the formation of institutionalised links in other fields – notably with the EU. In effect, the original military alliance had been extended into a host of diverse theatres, and underpinned by Turkey's integration into a global economy dominated by the Western powers and Japan. This added to the Kemalist vision of making Turkey a modern Westernised nation, which vastly outweighed alternative projects, such as the Islamist one. In effect, the previous determinants of middle-power strategies, which had been based almost entirely on crude considerations of power and security, had arguably been overtaken by a much wider range of concerns.

How well did Turkish foreign policy cope with the problems it faced after 1990? An answer to this question means making a judgement about policy performance in a number of different theatres, since one of the features of the new environment was that it presented a range of regional problems more diverse than at any previous period in the history of the republic. In fact, for a state of its size and strength, Turkey had to deal with an extraordinarily wide range of international questions, mainly due to its geographical position. In the central theatre of relations with the United States, and with the NATO alliance as a whole, the balance sheet was generally positive. This was a huge advantage for Turkey in virtually all the other theatres in which it was engaged, since the knowledge that Turkey had strong links with Washington vastly increased the seriousness with which other regional countries regarded it. The Bush and Clinton administrations put a high premium on preserving their links with Turkey. For their part, the Turks normally took care to cultivate the relationship, although it passed through a severe test during the period of the Erbakan-led government in 1996–97. Relations with Washington were further strengthened by Turkey's new entente with Israel. The Greek and Armenian lobbies in Washington also seemed to be weaker than they had been in the 1960s and 1970s, removing a previous source of friction. In operations in which NATO was actively involved, notably in the former Yugoslavia, Turkey was a cooperative and useful member of the alliance, though certainly not a major player. For the United States, Turkey's main strategic importance derived from its important role in Western policies in the Middle East, beginning with the Gulf crisis of 1990–91, and especially in Iraq. This was also the most problematic feature of the Turkish–US relationship, however, since policy towards Iraq (and sometimes towards Iran) was the only important point to which Turkish and US attitudes seemed to be in conflict. Nonetheless, the Turks kept their commitments to the West, and were apparently able to influence Western policy in northern Iraq in accordance with their own interests.

In Turkey's relationship with western Europe, the record was far more mixed. The faults lay partly on the European side, since until the end of 1999 the EU nations never really decided what their approach to Turkey should be. On the one hand, they did not want to alienate the Turks entirely, since EU member states (some more than others) attached value to Turkey's strategic importance, and realised that an uncooperative or hostile Turkey could seriously damage their own interests, both political and economic. On the other hand, they were very reluctant to admit Turkey as a full member of the EU, given its poor human rights record, its conflicts with Greece, the Kurdish problem, and the potential budgetary costs of Turkish accession, besides outright religious and racial prejudice, in some cases. Hence, they hoped to postpone a decision for as long as possible. On their side, the Turks initially underestimated the obstacles to accession, and tended to resent European criticism of human rights and the treatment of the Kurds as unwarranted intrusions into their internal affairs. Conflicts with Greece and the Cyprus question exacerbated the tensions, since many Turks (not always without justification) felt that European attitudes were prejudiced against them by allowing Greece too big a role in determining EU policies. Although the blame for Greek–Turkish tensions could be laid at Greek as well as Turkish doors, Turkish policy was generally inflexible towards the Greeks. Turkey had been able to save the Turkish Cypriots from disaster in 1974, but its attempts to win international support for its case over Cyprus were quite unsuccessful. It was not until the end of the 1990s that a resolution seemed possible, as Greeks and Turks began to see the advantages of renouncing hostility, and the EU at last officially ranked Turkey as a candidate for possible accession.

Although the dissolution of the Soviet Union and the Warsaw Pact removed the main threat to Turkey's security, handling its relations with Russia was a tricky problem. While Russian policies in the Balkans and Transcaucasia brought Ankara into conflict with Moscow, Turkey needed to preserve a workable relationship, since the two countries had important mutual economic interests, and Turkey could not afford to run the risk of a head-on military clash with Russia. Hence, the Turks were critical of Russia's policies in its 'near abroad', but carefully steered clear of supporting oppositional movements within the Russian Federation, notably in Chechnya. The fear that, if provoked, Russia might give all-out support to the PKK was another reason for caution. Until the end of the 1990s, this policy seemed to have been successful. Turkey had protected its own interests, and prevented Russia from establishing a monopoly control of the oil and gas resources of the Caspian basin, while avoiding dangerous collisions with Moscow, and developing the economic relationship. In Transcaucasia, Turkish governments had to performing a similar balancing act, and state interests normally won out over natural Turkish sympathies with Azerbaijan in its struggle with the Armenians. At the same time, Turkey was too weak to play the role of arbiter in the region, and had very little leverage over Armenia. The overthrow of Abulfez Elchibey in 1993 was also seen at the time as a serious setback for Turkish policy, although Elchibey's downfall was as much a product of his deficiencies as president, and Azerbaijan's internal divisions, as outright intervention by Russia and Turkey's inability to prevent it. In central Asia, also, expectations that Turkey would emerge as a regional power failed to materialise, but this was probably because Turkish policy-makers had set themselves too ambitious an agenda in the first place. On the other hand, Turkey had won itself a useful economic and cultural role in central Asia, and avoided damaging collisions with either Russia or Iran.

In the Middle East, the most striking change in Turkish policy was the emergence of the entente with Israel. On the positive side, this strengthened Turkey's influence in Washington, and helped to tip the balance of power in favour of Turkey in its confrontation with Syria, besides giving it access to advanced military hardware which might not have been available otherwise. On the other hand, the idea that there was now an Israel–Turkey axis sharpened longstanding Arab suspicions of the Turks, especially on such issues as the Euphrates waters. That this did not have seriously damaging effects for Turkey was mainly due to rivalries and divisions between the Arab states themselves, and the fact that a number of them, such as Egypt, Jordan and Saudi Arabia, were crucially dependent on the United States. Turkey's position in the Middle East would almost certainly have been far weaker if the Arab states had united, or had been uniformly anti-Western. A significant demonstration of this was Hafiz al-Assad's climb-down in his confrontation with Turkey in the autumn of 1998 over Abdullah Öcalan, which showed both an impressive degree of Turkish regional power, and the anxiety of Egypt to play the role of mediator, rather than give full support to Syria. In Iraq, also, Turkish policy showed both a degree of flexibility – for instance by constructing an unwritten, and probably uncertain, alliance with the Iraqi Kurds of the KDP – and a powerful military presence, which severely weakened the PKK's ability to operate from northern Iraq. The fact that the United States effectively turned a blind eye to its military incursions was also an advantage for Turkey. Finally, Turkey managed to preserve a working relationship with Iran which was of value both politically and (potentially) economically. The problems in the relationship derived more from internal struggles for power within Iran, over which Turkey had virtually no influence, than any inherent or inevitable clash of interests between the two countries. In this, as in most other theatres (with the arguable exception of Cyprus) realism and pragmatism was the dominant theme in Turkish policy in the post-Cold War era, as it had been throughout most of Turkish diplomacy since the late eighteenth century.

DOMESTIC POLITICAL CHANGES AND SELF-PERCEPTIONS

The effects of changes in the domestic political structure on Turkish foreign policy are hard to categorise. Except for two brief periods in 1876–78 and 1908–14, which saw unsuccessful attempts to establish parliamentary government, the Ottoman empire was a patrimonial autocracy, in which power was wielded by the Sultan, his ministers and generals. After 1918, authority was briefly divided by the contest between the occupying entente forces, the Sultan's government in Istanbul, and the nationalist resistance based in Ankara, which lasted until 1922. From then until 1946 Turkey was, for the most part, a single-party state in which power was monopolised by a statist élite of politicians, bureaucrats and army officers. After 1950, it became a multi-party parliamentary republic, with three intervals of military or quasi-military rule. However, until the mid-1960s, the transition to pluralism had relatively little effect on its foreign policies – partly because most Turks apparently continued to accept the idea that foreign policy required special expertise, available only to the state élite, but also because Turkey's attachment to the West in the Cold War was almost universally accepted domestically and the country had few other outstanding foreign policy problems.

After 1964, with the emergence of the Cyprus conflict as a major item on the external agenda, domestic political pressures began to have more effect on foreign policy. Nonetheless, as Ferenc Vali suggested in the early 1970s, on most foreign policy issues 'the interest of the average Turkish citizen remained skin deep', and only 'questions affecting national feeling or religious sentiment are more likely to arouse deeper interest'.[2] Besides Cyprus, the list of such questions came to include the conflicts in Bosnia, Kosovo and between Armenia and Azerbaijan or, for instance, the fracas between Turkey and Italy over the fate of Abdullah Öcalan in 1998–99. However, public interest even in these questions tended to be rather sporadic and unsustained. In general election campaigns, the competing parties usually devoted little attention to foreign policy questions, restricting themselves to vague generalities. Except during the period of the Erbakan–Çiller government of 1996–97, inter-party consensus was maintained on most foreign policy issues, at least between the mainstream parties. The establishment of the military regime of 1980–83 coincided with (though was not necessarily the cause of) a shift towards a more pro-Western foreign policy, but the other two military interventions had few discernible foreign policy effects. Probably, the most important indirect result of the liberalisation of the political regime was the fragmentation of the party system, especially during the period 1973–80, and again after 1991. During both these periods Turkey experienced serious governmental instability, with power switching frequently from one weak coalition government to another, and long hiatuses under caretaker governments. With foreign ministers changing with dizzying rapidity (to be precise, ten times between 1990 and 1999) and attention concentrated on the search for a viable government, it was much more difficult to establish effective or sustained initiatives abroad.

Nor has Turkey's transition to political pluralism supported the contention that democratic governments are less likely to go to war than autocratic ones.[3] The Ottoman empire was an autocracy, but it generally tried to avoid war when it could, with the significant exception of its participation in the First World War in 1914. Once it had defeated the Greeks in 1922, the authoritarian Kemalist regime was firmly in favour of peace, and skilfully avoided joining either side in the Second World War. Since 1923, the only occasions on which the Turkish army has been involved in serious fighting on foreign territory (the Korean war, the invasion of Cyprus in 1974, and repeated forays into northern Iraq against the PKK) all occurred after the transition to a multi-party system. In other words, decisions to use force appear to have derived from external circumstances, not the nature of the internal regime.

As in other states, the national self-perceptions of foreign policy-makers have also had important effects, although these are not always easy to define. The Ottoman government based its legitimacy on its attachment to Islam, at least so far as its Muslim citizens were concerned, but it recognised that it had a large number of Christian subjects, and had to operate in an international system dominated by nominally Christian states. For the reformist Ottoman statesmen of the *Tanzimat* era, the Islamic attachment was less important than the simple need to secure the survival and strengthening of the state, and to win recognition as a member of the comity of European powers – a status supposedly conceded by the treaty of Paris in 1856. Between 1878 and 1908, under the autocratic rule of Sultan Abdul Hamid II, greater emphasis was put on the Islamic identity of the state. The Sultan tended to be suspicious of all the European powers, but he was generally pragmatic in his foreign policies, and was not averse to seeking European alliances, if he could secure them on favourable terms. After the Young Turk revolution of 1908, the political élite was divided in its attachments between the multi-ethnic 'Ottoman' identity, and ethnic Turkish nationalism, with loyalty to the Islamic community still a lingering commitment. Although the ethnic Turkish identity came to be dominant, the result was a wavering foreign policy, ending in the disastrous alliance with Germany of 1914.

After 1923, the state's self-definition, and its foreign policy directions, became far more clear cut. With the establishment of an officially secular republic, any idea that Turkey should act primarily, or even partially, as a Muslim state was definitely abandoned. Atatürk's clear aim was to establish Turkey as a respected nation state, on the Western model, with sufficient economic and military strength to sustain that role. As a result, Turkey sought to establish good relations with all the main European powers, and to avoid international conflicts wherever possible. Although Turkish foreign policy during the Second World War was arguably less straightforward than is sometimes supposed, Atatürk's approach was continued by İsmet İnönü. At the end of the Second World War, İnönü tried to re-define Turkey as a secular democracy as well as a nation state. Unfortunately, the effects of this attempted reorientation are hard to establish with certainty. On the one hand, Turkey would almost certainly have opted for an alliance with the West, even if had not been trying to become more democratic, out of simple considerations of national security. On the other hand, the fact that the Western powers were clearly more concerned than the Soviet Union to protect the interests of small or medium powers must have been an important factor in Ankara's decision. Moreover, the alliance with the Western powers, once it was secured, was an additional reason for attempting to maintain democratic government at home.

Since the 1960s, the widening of the circle of domestic political debate, and changing world conditions, have produced new or revived identities which have complicated further the difficulties of national self-definition. During the 1970s, there was an attempt by the Turkish left to redefine Turkey as a socialist, or at least more of a 'Third World' state, but this largely evaporated during the following decade. Domestic changes after 1987 also resulted in the revival of political Islamism for the first time since the Young Turk era. At the same time, the aim of making Turkey a full member of the EU gave a potential institutional dimension to Turkey's Western identity which had previously been lacking. At the extreme, this resulted in the classification of Turkey as the prototype of what Samuel Huntington, in a much-criticised proposal, defined as a 'torn society', in which the élite defined Turkey as a Western society, although the élite of the West (according to Huntington) refused to accept Turkey as such, while 'elements in Turkish society' argued that Turkey was basically a Middle Eastern Muslim nation. As a result, he suggested, Turkey might opt for identity with the newly independent Turkic republics of central Asia.[4]

While Turkish identities are certainly more pluralist than they used to be, the idea that this would make a coherent foreign policy impossible seems quite exaggerated. At one end of the spectrum, there is admittedly an Islamist minority, probably supported by around 15 per cent of the population, which would support an Islamic identification in external relations, but its ideas are very poorly worked out, and there has only been one partial attempt to achieve them, in 1996–97. At the opposite end of the spectrum, there is another militantly secularist minority. In between, the majority of Turks and the mainstream parties make an accommodation between attachment to Islam as a religion, and alignment with the West for pragmatic considerations of defence and economics. Huntington's prediction that Turkey would move towards a 'pan-Turkic' identity has also proved to be wide of the mark. Instead, most Turkish governments have sought to identify with the West politically, while maintaining good relations with fellow-Muslim nations where possible, for pragmatic reasons.

INTO THE TWENTY-FIRST CENTURY

Not surprisingly, predicting Turkey's future foreign policy is far more difficult than analysing its past, thanks to the near-impossibility of accurately forecasting global changes. Nonetheless, some important shifts are evident, and Turkish policy-makers would need to consider how they would cope with them. In the late 1990s, a common expectation was that China would emerge as a major power over the next 50 years, rivalling the United States and western Europe. However, unless this resulted in a clash between Russia and China, or a new Cold War – this time between China and the Western powers – it was hard to see how this would affect Turkey's international position. Admittedly, China might try to establish its dominance over the rest of east Asia, but Turkey would simply be too remote to be deeply or directly affected by this. Like those of other middle powers, its policy horizons would probably continue to be essentially regional rather than global. With China established as a major economic power, Turkish businessmen would be presented with new opportunities, but would be no better placed to exploit them than their competitors in the United States, western Europe, and the other east Asian countries.

In this situation, the most critical questions for Turkey related, first, to possible shifts in the basic orientation of US policy; second, to the evolution of the EU and its member states; third, to domestic political and economic trends in Russia and the rest of the former Soviet Union, and their foreign-policy implications; and fourth, to the likely pattern of future politics in the Middle East. On the first score, there was the possibility that the United States might withdraw into isolationism, by ending its military presence in western Europe, and its involvement in European security and defence. For most NATO members, this would be most unwelcome, but governments had to consider how they would cope with it, if it happened. In all probability, the western European countries would be forced to develop independent security structures – a project on which there had been much talk, but little action, in the 1990s. If the project did achieve concrete shape, then it would be essential for both sides that Turkey, along with several other NATO members which were not yet part of the EU, should be incorporated in the new structures – if necessary before they acquired EU membership, or even in conditions of uncertainty as to whether they would do so. Pending that outcome, Turkey would have to do what it could to prevent a US withdrawal, if this were threatened, or the limitation of European security horizons to central or northern Europe. More broadly, the ending of a US security role in Europe would rob Turkey of an important balancing element in its relations with the western European countries. The possibility that the United States might also lose its interest in Middle Eastern security seemed much more remote, however, thanks to the US connection with Israel, and the expectation (given the size of Middle Eastern reserves compared with those of other regions) that Middle Eastern oil would become more rather than less important in the world economy. Accordingly, Turkey would probably continue to be an important regional ally for Washington, even if the United States gave up the aim of trying to ensure global security.

The future of the EU, and Turkey's position in it, was a related and equally critical area of uncertainty. On the central question which had hung over Turkey's relations with western Europe for more than three decades, as to whether Turkey would ever gain accession to the EU, the decision taken at the Helsinki summit of December 1999 meant that the outlook was distinctly more hopeful. Arguments that Turkey was simply 'non-European' (itself a vague term) and would thus be permanently barred from membership, seemed to have been abandoned.[5] Provided Turkey could meet the Copenhagen criteria, and settle its differences with Greece, there seemed to be a fairly good prospect that it could gain accession at some not too distant point in the future. To cope with this enlargement, the EU would have to reform many of its internal structures and policies: in particular, there would need to be further reforms of its agricultural and regional policies, so as to avoid unacceptable budgetary costs – arising not only from prospective Turkish accession, but also from the accession of the other eastern European candidates. Establishing free movement of labour in the short term would also create unacceptable problems for Germany and other countries, and Turkey and the other applicants would almost certainly have to face delays in the full implementation of this provision To get the best terms they could, there seemed to be a case for wider collaboration in policy towards the EU between Turkey and the eastern European candidates than they had shown so far. Finally, as the Helsinki decision also made clear, an overall settlement with Greece of bilateral disputes, and a solution to the Cyprus problem, would almost certainly be a *sine qua non* for Turkish accession. The Turkish government obviously needed to pay urgent attention to both these issues, though it was also entitled to expect Greece and the Greek Cypriots to be reasonably flexible, and to press the other EU countries on this point if they were not.

While the Turkey–EU relationship was still full of problems, it was at least reasonably clear which policy paths Turkey would have to follow if it were to realise its ambitions. Unfortunately, this was not true of its relations with Russia and the rest of the CIS, mainly because it was virtually impossible to give a reliable prediction of future Russian policies. The most optimistic expectation was that Russia would succeed in liberalising its economy, and establish a stable and reasonably liberal democracy. If, as part of this process, pro-Western forces in Russia dominated, and Russia established cooperative relations with the Western powers, then Turkey could expect to benefit. A more prosperous Russia would also be a more powerful one, but Turkey probably had more to gain than to lose from this, since it would have additional opportunities for trade and investment. In these conditions, it could also expect Russia to seek a stable and non-conflictual relationship with its southern neighbours, including Turkey. If, on the other hand, Russia turned inwards or, worse still, tried to take over the rest of the CIS, then Turkey would face severe challenges. The best it could probably hope to do was to continue the policies of the 1990s by avoiding direct conflicts with Russia where possible, and by enlisting the help of other states – including, quite possibly, Iran – to oppose Russian revisionism. The signs are that Russia would in any case face severe problems in implementing such an agenda. This is suggested, in particular, by the emergence of the GUUAM group within the CIS, and the prospect that the Caspian basin countries would be able to break out of their economic dependence on Russia by developing their oil and gas resources, and building export pipelines avoiding Russian territory. On the last point, Turkey could probably expect US support, barring a dramatic reversal of US policies.

This left the Middle East as another problematic theatre for Turkish policy. By the end of 1999, it seemed possible that Israel might be able to hammer out a peace settlement with Syria, embracing also the Lebanon. Previously, the Turks had been somewhat worried by this prospect, suspecting that the Syrians and Israelis might make a deal at their expense, perhaps over the Euphrates waters. Even if Israeli assurances that this would not be the case were genuine, the removal of its security threat from Israel might make Syria more aggressive towards Turkey, it was feared. Against this, two points could be urged. First, Syria might sign a truce with Israel, but this would not necessarily make the two nations friends. Twenty years after the peace settlement between Israel and Egypt, Egyptian–Israeli relations were still far from close, and there was no reason to expect that the Syrian–Israeli relationship would be substantially different. Mutual suspicions, built up by half a century of hostility, could be expected to carry on for some time to come, and Israel would probably continue to look to Turkey as a balancing power. Second, peace between Israel and the Arabs would make it easier for Turkey to reach its basic policy objective of securing cooperative relations with both sides. This would naturally be reinforced by a lasting agreement between Israel and the Palestinians, and would make it important for Turkey to show that it fully supported the peace process. In the Middle East, as elsewhere, international politics was not a zero-sum game, and the fact that its southern neighbours had overcome their differences would not necessarily mean an overall loss for Turkey.

Elsewhere in the Middle East, the most significant change to be hoped for was that Iran and Iraq would eventually come in from the cold, and re-establish normal relations with the Western powers. 'Dual containment' was an important part of US policy, but it seemed unlikely that it could last indefinitely. Saddam Hussein would either die or be overthrown eventually, and there was at least some prospect that even if Iran continued to be an 'Islamic republic' in name, liberal forces would be able to establish themselves in power, and to re-build Iran's bridges with the West. If this happened, then the two countries could expect to increase their regional power impressively. By the end of the century, Iran already had a bigger population than Turkey, with a much higher birth-rate, and taken together Iran and Iraq could expect to have a combined population of over 100 million within a few decades. If they were able to make full use of their immense reserves of oil and gas, and settle their mutual rivalries so as to avoid wasting their resources on an arms race, then they could substantially expand their economies, and increase their international influence accordingly. For Turkey, there were both dangers and opportunities in this prospect. A revival of Iraqi and Iranian power could pose a serious security threat to Turkey, especially if either or both countries acquired nuclear weapons. To cope with it, Turkey would probably need the help of Israel, and further security guarantees from the United States, as well as the rest of NATO. On the other hand, if this result were avoided, and Turkey continued its generally non-provocative policies towards both the Iranian and Iraqi governments, then it stood to gain substantially from the development of revived export markets, which might help to offset economic downturns elsewhere in the world.

Finally, a notable feature of Turkish foreign policy up to the end of the Cold War was that Turkey seldom, if ever, sought to exploit its status as a middle power to act as a mediator in regional or global disputes, as several similarly ranked states tried to do. Though the issue is seldom discussed, it seems likely that Turkey rejected this role mainly because it might have weakened US support, on which its defence critically depended, and contradicted its regional concerns, such as those over Cyprus. The end of the Cold War, and the break-up of the Soviet Union have altered this perspective, and increased the number of regional contests in which Turkey might act as a mediator and peacemaker. During the 1990s, Turkey began to set up regional cooperation initiatives, notably that in the Black Sea, and started to play a more active role in such projects as the OSCE, the NATO interventions in Bosnia and Kosovo, and the Italian-led operation to restore stability in Albania. In 1999, as part of an operation to mend its fences with Greece, it began to plan a multilateral project for increasing security among the Balkan states. Admittedly, there were serious limitations to these initiatives. On the one side, they did not seem to have provoked much declared support from public opinion, which still appeared to emphasise the protection of narrowly defined national interests. On the other, Turkey's ability to act as a mediator in some of these conflicts was quite limited, partly because it lacked the power to tempt or cajole several of its neighbours, notably Russia and Armenia. Nonetheless, the fact that this role was at least being considered more widely was another potential signpost to the future.

NOTES

1. Necip Torumtay, 'Turkey's Military Doctrine', *Foreign Policy* (Ankara, Foreign Policy Institute), Vol. 15, Nos 1–2 (1990), p. 21.
2. Ferenc A. Vali, *Bridge across the Bosporus: The Foreign Policy of Turkey* (Baltimore, MD, and London, John Hopkins University Press, 1971), p. 100.
3. The reference here is to the proposal that 'democracies do not go to war' (at least with one another). For a summary of debates on this issue, see Laura Neack, 'Linking State Type with Foreign Policy Behavior', in Laura Neack, Jeanne A.K. Hey and Patrick J. Haney, *Foreign Policy Analysis: Continuity and Change in its Second Generation* (Englewood Cliffs, NJ, Prentice-Hall, 1995), pp. 218–24.
4. Samuel P. Huntington, 'The Clash of Civilizations?', *Foreign Affairs*, Vol. 72 (1993), p. 42.
5. As Andrew Mango puts it, 'the question whether the Turks are European or not does not admit of a clear answer, since the concept of "European" is itself vague'. Andrew Mango, 'European Dimensions', *Middle Eastern Studies*, Vol. 28 (1992), p. 398.

Bibliography

OFFICIAL PUBLICATIONS AND DOCUMENTS

Britain

Treaty of Peace with Turkey and other Instruments signed at Lausanne on July 24, 1923 (London, HMSO, 1923: Cmd 1929)
Cyprus, (London, HMSO, Cmnd 1093, 1960)

EC/EU

Official Journal of the European Communities: Information and Notices, Vol. 16, No. C 113 (texts of Association Agreement of 1963 and Additional Protocol of 1970)
Commission des Communautés Européennes, Sec (89) 2290, 'Avis de la Commission sur la demande d'adhésion de la Turquie à la Communauté' (Brussels, December 1989)
'Decision 1/95 of the EC–Turkey Association Council of 22 December 1995', *Official Journal of the European Communities,* Vol. 39, L35 (13 February 1996)
'Press Conference by Mr Matutes on Membership of Turkey to the Community' (Brussels, Commission of the European Communities, December 1989: ref BIC/89/393)

Turkey

'Statement by the Turkish Government on 14 December 1997, Concerning the Presidency Conclusions of the European Council Held on 12–13 December 1997 in Luxembourg', reprinted in *Perceptions* (Ankara), Vol. 2, No. 4 (1997–98)
'Turkish Documents Regarding Issues between Turkey and Greece', *Turkish Review of Balkan Studies,* Vol. 3 (1996–97)

SERIAL PUBLICATIONS

Country Report: Turkey (London, Economist Intelligence Unit, quarterly)
Middle East Contemporary Survey (Boulder, CO, Westview Press, annual)
Statistical Yearbook of Turkey / Türkiye İstatistik Yıllığı (Ankara, State Institute of Statistics, normally annual, in English and Turkish)
The Military Balance (London, Oxford University Press for International Institute of Strategic Studies, annual)
Turkey Almanac (Ankara, Turkish Daily News, annual: now discontinued)
BP Amoco Statistical Review of World Energy (London, BP Amoco [previously BP], annual)

BOOKS AND ARTICLES

Ahmad, Feroz, 'Great Britain's Relations with the Young Turks, 1908–1914', *Middle Eastern Studies*, Vol. 2 (1965–66).
——, *The Young Turks: The Committee of Union and Progress in Turkish Politics, 1908–1914* (Oxford, Oxford University Press, 1969).
——, *The Turkish Experiment in Democracy, 1950–1975* (London, Hurst, for Royal Institute of International Affairs, 1977).
——, 'The Late Ottoman Empire', in Marian Kent, ed., *The Great Powers and the End of the Ottoman Empire* (London, Cass, 2nd edn, 1996).
Akbayar, Nuri, 'Tanzimat'tan Sonra Osmanlı Devleti Nüfusu', *Tanzimat'tan Cumhuriyet'e Türkiye Ansiklopedisi* (Istanbul, İletişim Yayınları, 1985), Vol. 5.
Akşin, Aptülhat, *Atatürk'ün Dış Politika İlkeleri ve Diplomasisi* (Ankara, Türk Tarih Kurumu, 1991).
Alaçam, H. Fahir, 'Turkish–Syrian Relations', *Turkish Review of Middle East Studies* (Istanbul), Vol. 8 (1994/95).
Albright, David E., 'The USSR and the Third World in the 1980s', *Problems of Communism*, Vol. 38 (1989).
Anderson, M.S., *The Eastern Question, 1774–1923: A Study in International Relations* (London, Macmillan, 1966).
Aras, Bülent, 'The Impact of the Palestinian–Israeli Peace Process in Turkish Foreign Policy', *Journal of South Asian and Middle Eastern Studies*, Vol. 20 (1997).
——, *Palestinian–Israeli Peace Process and Turkey* (Commack, NY, Nova Science Publishers, 1998).
Ataöv, Türkaya, *Turkish Foreign Policy, 1939–1945* (Ankara University, Political Science Faculty, 1965).

Atatürk, Kemal, *Speech Delivered by Ghazi Mustapha Kemal, President of the Turkish Republic, October 1927* (Leipzig, K.F. Koehler, 1929).

Athanassopoulou, Ekavi, 'Ankara's Foreign Policy Objectives after the End of the Cold War: Making Policy in a Changing Environment', *Orient*, Vol. 36 (1995).

——, 'Greece, Turkey, Europe: Constantinos Simitis in Premiership Waters', *Mediterranean Politics*, Vol. 1 (1996).

——, 'Western Defence Developments and Turkey's Search for Security in 1948', *Middle Eastern Studies*, Vol. 32 (1996), reprinted in Sylvia Kedourie, ed., *Turkey: Identity, Democracy, Politics* (London, Cass, 1996).

——, 'Blessing in Disguise? The Imia Crisis and Turkish–Greek Relations', *Mediterranean Politics*, Vol. 2 (1997).

——, *Turkey – Anglo-American Security Interests 1945–1952: The First Enlargement of NATO* (London, Cass, 1999).

Ayata, Sencer, 'Perceptions of International Relations and Turkish Foreign Policy in the Islamist Press', paper presented to the Conference on 'The Domestic Context of Turkish Foreign Policy', The Washington Institute for Near East Policy, Washington, DC, July 1997.

Aybay, Gündüz, 'On the Power of Turkey to Regulate Free Passage through the Straits', in Turkish Straits Voluntary Watch Group, *Turkish Straits: New Problems, New Solutions* (Istanbul, Isis, for Foundation for Middle East and Balkan Studies, 1995).

——, and Nilüfer Oral, 'Turkey's Authority to Regulate Passage of Vessels through the Turkish Straits', *Perceptions* (Ankara), Vol. 3, No. 2 (1998).

Aybet, Gülnur, 'NATO's New Missions', *Perceptions* (Ankara), Vol. 4, No. 1 (1999).

——, 'The CFE Treaty: The Way Forward for Conventional Arms Control in Europe', *Perceptions* (Ankara), Vol. 1, No. 1 (1996).

——, 'Turkey and European Institutions', *International Spectator* (Rome), Vol. 34 (1999).

——, *NATO's Developing Role in Collective Security* (Ankara, Ministry of Foreign Affairs, Center for Strategic Research, 1999).

Aykan, Mahmut Bali, 'The Palestinian Question in Turkish Foreign Policy from the 1950s to the 1990s', *International Journal of Middle East Studies*, Vol. 25 (1993).

——, 'Turkey's Policy in Northern Iraq, 1991–95', *Middle Eastern Studies*, Vol. 32 (1996).

——, 'Turkish Perspectives on Turkish–US Relations Concerning Persian Gulf Security in the Post-Cold War Era: 1989–1995', *Middle East*

Journal, Vol. 50 (1996).

——, 'The Turkey–US–Israel Triangle: Continuity, Change and Implications for Turkey's Post-Cold War Middle East Policy', *Journal of South Asian and Middle Eastern Studies,* Vol. 22 (1999).

Bağcı, Hüseyin, *Demokrat Parti Dönemi Dış Politikası* (Ankara, İmge Kitabevi, 1990).

Bagirov, Sabit, 'Azerbaijani Oil: Glimpses of a Long History', *Perceptions* (Ankara), Vol. 1, No. 2 (1996).

Bahceli, Tozun, *Greek–Turkish Relations since 1955* (Boulder, CO, Westview, 1990).

Bailey, Frank Edgar, *British Policy and the Turkish Reform Movement: A Study in Anglo-Turkish Relations, 1826–1853* (Cambridge, MA, Harvard University Press, 1942).

Balkır, Canan, 'Turkey and the European Community: Foreign Trade and Direct Foreign Investment in the 1980s', in Canan Balkır and Allan M. Williams, eds, *Turkey and Europe* (London and New York, NY, Pinter, 1993).

Barchard, David, *Turkey and the West* (London, Routledge & Kegan Paul for Royal Institute of International Affairs, 1985).

Barkey, Henri J., 'The Silent Victor: Turkey's Role in the Gulf War', in Efraim Karsh, ed., *The Iran–Iraq War: Impact and Implications* (London, Macmillan, in association with Jafee Center for Strategic Studies, Tel Aviv University, 1989).

——, 'The People's Democracy Party (HADEP): The Travails of a Legal Kurdish Party in Turkey', *Journal of Muslim Minority Affairs,* Vol. 18 (1998).

——, and Graham E. Fuller, 'Turkey's Kurdish Question: Critical Turning Points and Missed Opportunities', *Middle East Journal,* Vol. 51 (1997).

——, and Graham E. Fuller, *Turkey's Kurdish Question* (Lanham, MD, Rowman and Littlefield, 1998).

Barylski, Robert V., 'Russia, the West and the Caspian Energy Hub', *Middle East Journal,* Vol. 49 (1995).

Beck, Peter J., ' "A Tedious and Perilous Controversy": Britain and the Settlement of the Mosul Dispute, 1918–1926', *Middle Eastern Studies,* Vol. 17 (1981).

Bellaigue, Christopher de, 'Conciliation in Cyprus?' *Washington Quarterly,* Vol. 22 (1999).

Bernstein, Barton J., 'The Cuban Missile Crisis: Trading the Jupiters in Turkey?', *Political Science Quarterly,* Vol. 95 (1980).

——, 'Reconsidering the Missile Crisis: Dealing with the Problem of the American Jupiters in Turkey', in James A. Nathan, ed., *The Cuban Missile Crisis Revisited* (New York, NY, St Martin's Press, 1992).

Bezanis, Lowell A., *The Baku–Ceyhan Pipeline: Constraints to a US-Backed Central Asian/Caucasian Exit Route* (Washington, DC, Petroleum Finance Market Intelligence Service, 1998).

Bilge, A. Suat, *et al.*, *Olaylarla Türk Dış Politikası (1919–1965)* (Ankara University, Political Science Faculty, 1969).

——, 'The Cyprus Conflict and Turkey', in Kemal H. Karpat *et al.*, *Turkey's Foreign Policy in Transition* (Leiden, Brill, 1975).

——, *Güç Komşuluk: Türkiye–Sovyetler Birliği İlişkileri, 1920–1964* (Ankara, Türkiye İş Bankası Kültür Yayınları, 1992).

Birand, Mehmet Ali, *30 Hot Days* (London, Nicosia and Istanbul, Rustem, 1985) (originally published in Turkish as *30 Sıcak Gün*, Istanbul, Milliyet Yayınları, 1975).

——, 'Turkey and the European Community', *World Today*, Vol. 38 (1978).

——, trans. M.A. Dikerdem, *The Generals' Coup in Turkey: An Inside Story of 12 September 1980* (London, Brassey's Defence Publishers, 1987).

Bishku, Michael M., 'Turkey and its Middle Eastern Neighbours since 1945', *Journal of South Asian and Middle Eastern Studies*, Vol. 15 (1992).

Blackwell, Stephen, 'A Desert Squall: Anglo-American Planning for Military Intervention in Iraq, July 1958–August 1959', *Middle Eastern Studies*, Vol. 35 (1999).

Blank, Stephen J., 'The Eastern Question Revived: Turkey and Russia Contend for Eurasia', in David Menashri, ed., *Central Asia Meets the Middle East* (London, Cass, 1998).

Blight, James G., and David A. Welch, *On the Brink: Americans and Soviets Reexamine the Cuban Missile Crisis* (New York, NY, Noonday Press, 1989).

Bölükbaşı, Suha, *Turkish–American Relations and Cyprus* (Lanham, MD, University Press of America, for White Burkett Miller Center of Public Affairs, University of Virginia, 1988).

——, 'Turkey Copes with Revolutionary Iran', *Journal of South Asian and Middle Eastern Studies*, Vol. 13 (1989).

——, 'The Turco-Greek Dispute: Issues, Policies and Prospects', in C.H. Dodd, ed., *Turkish Foreign Policy: New Prospects* (Wistow, Eothen Press, for Modern Turkish Studies Programme, SOAS, 1992).

——, 'The Johnson Letter Revisited', *Middle Eastern Studies*, Vol. 29 (1993).

——, 'Turkey Challenges Iraq and Syria: The Euphrates Dispute', *Journal of South Asian and Middle Eastern Studies*, Vol. 16 (1993).

——, 'The Cyprus Dispute in the Post-Cold War Era', *Turkish Studies Association Bulletin*, Vol. 18 (1994).

——, 'Boutros-Ghali's Cyprus Initiative in 1992: Why Did it Fail?', *Middle Eastern Studies*, Vol. 31 (1995).

——, 'Ankara's Baku-Centered Transcaucasia Policy: Has It Failed?', *Middle East Journal*, Vol. 51 (1997).

Bourguignon, Roswitha, 'The History of the Association Agreement between Turkey and the European Community', in Ahmet Evin and Geoffrey Denton, eds, *Turkey and the European Community* (Opladen, Leske and Budrich, 1990).

Brey, Hansjorg, 'Turkey and the Cyprus Question', *International Observer* (Rome), Vol. 24 (1999).

Bridge, F. R., 'The Hapsburg Monarchy and the Ottoman Empire, 1900–18', in Marian Kent, ed., *The Great Powers and the End of the Ottoman Empire* (London, Cass, 2nd edn, 1996).

Brownlie, Ian, ed., *Basic Documents on Human Rights* (Oxford, Clarendon Press, 2nd edn, 1981).

Buzan, Barry, 'The Status and Future of the Montreux Convention', *Survival*, Vol. 18 (1976).

Calabrese, John, 'Turkey and Iran: Limits of a Stable Relationship', *British Journal of Middle Eastern Studies*, Vol. 25 (1998).

Campany, Richard C., Jnr, *Turkey and the United States: The Arms Embargo Period* (New York, NY, Praeger, 1986).

Campbell, John C., *Defense of the Middle East: Problems of American Policy* (New York, NY, Praeger, 1960).

Çarkoğlu, Ali, and Mine Eder, 'GAP: The Water Conflict', *Private View* (Istanbul), Autumn 1998·

Clark, Edward C., 'The Turkish Varlık Vergisi Reconsidered', *Middle Eastern Studies*, Vol. 8 (1972).

Clawson, Patrick, 'Iran and Caspian Basin Oil and Gas', *Perceptions* (Ankara), Vol. 2 No. 4 (1998).

Cornell, Svante E., 'Undeclared War: The Nagorno Karabakh Conflict Reconsidered', *Journal of South Asian and Middle Eastern Studies*, Vol. 20 (1997).

——, 'Turkey and the Conflict in Nagorno Karabakh: A Delicate Balance', *Middle Eastern Studies*, Vol. 34 (1998).

——, 'Geopolitics and Strategic Alignments in the Caucasus and Central Asia', *Perceptions* (Ankara), Vol. 4 No. 2 (1999).

Couloumbis, Theodore A., *The United States, Greece and Turkey: The Troubled Triangle* (New York, NY, Praeger, 1983).

Davison, Roderic H., 'Turkish Diplomacy from Mudros to Lausanne', in Gordon A. Craig and Felix Gilbert, eds, *The Diplomats, 1919–1939* (New York, NY, Atheneum, 1974), Vol. 1.

——, *Reform in the Ottoman Empire, 1856–1876* (Princeton, NJ, Princeton University Press, 1963).

Dağı, İhsan D., 'Democratic Transition in Turkey, 1980 83: The Impact of European Diplomacy', *Middle Eastern Studies*, Vol. 32 (1996), reprinted in Sylvia Kedourie, ed., *Turkey: Identity, Democracy, Politics* (London and Portland, OR, Cass, 1996).

Denniston, Robin, *Churchill's Secret War: Diplomatic Decrypts, the Foreign Office and Turkey, 1942–44* (Stroud, Sutton Publishing: New York, NY, St Martin's Press, 1997).

Deringil, Selim, 'The Preservation of Turkey's Neutrality During the Second World War: 1940', *Middle Eastern Studies*, Vol. 18 (1982).

——, 'Aspects of Continuity in Turkish Foreign Policy: Abdulhamid II and İsmet İnönü', *International Journal of Turkish Studies*, Vol. 4 (1987).

——, *Turkish Foreign Policy during the Second World War: An 'Active' Neutrality* (Cambridge, Cambridge University Press, 1989).

Devereux, Robert, *The First Ottoman Constitutional Period* (Baltimore, MD, Johns Hopkins University Press, 1963).

Dodd, C.H., *The Crisis of Turkish Democracy* (2nd edn, Wistow, Eothen Press, 1990).

——, *The Cyprus Imbroglio* (Hemingford Grey, Eothen Press, 1998).

Dyer, Gwynne, 'The Turkish Armistice of 1918: 1 – The Turkish Decision for a Separate Peace, Autumn 1918', *Middle Eastern Studies*, Vol. 8 (1972).

——, 'The Turkish Armistice of 1918: 2 – A Lost Opportunity: The Armistice Negotiations of Moudros', *Middle Eastern Studies*, Vol. 8 (1972).

——, 'Turkish "Falsifiers" and Armenian "Deceivers": Historiography and the Armenian Massacres', *Middle Eastern Studies*, Vol. 12 (1976).

Earle, E.M., *Turkey, the Great Powers and the Baghdad Railway* (New York, NY, Macmillan, 1923).

Ecevit, Bülent, 'Turkey's Security Policies', in Jonathan Alford, ed., *Greece and Turkey: Adversity in Alliance* (London, Gower, for International Institute of Strategic Studies, 1984).

Eden, Sir Anthony, *Full Circle* (London, Cassell, 1960).

Ekin, Nusret, 'Turkish Labor in the EEC', in Werner Gumpel, ed., *Die Türkei auf dem Weg in die EG* (Munich and Vienna, R. Oldenbourg, 1979).

Elekdağ, Şükrü, 'Two and a Half War Strategy', *Perceptions* (Ankara), Vol. 1, No. 1 (1996), p. 57.

Ergün, İsmet, 'The Problem of Freedom of Movement of Turkish Workers in the European Community', in Ahmet Evin and Geoffrey Denton, eds, *Turkey and the European Community* (Opladen, Leske and Budrich, 1990).

Ertekün, Necati, *The Cyprus Dispute and the Birth of the Turkish Republic of Northern Cyprus* (Nicosia, Rustem, 2nd edn, 1984).

Evans, Stephen F., *The Slow Rapprochement: Britain and Turkey in the Age of Kemal Atatürk, 1919–38* (Walkington, Eothen Press, 1982).

Foreign Policy Institute, 'Turkey's Foreign Policy Objectives', *Foreign Policy* (Ankara), Vol. 17, Nos. 1–2 (1993).

Fox, Annette Baker, *The Power of Small States: Diplomacy in World War II* (Chicago, IL, University of Chicago Press, 1959).

Fuller, Graham E., 'Turkey's New Eastern Orientation', in Graham E. Fuller and Ian O. Lesser, eds, *Turkey's New Geopolitics: From the Balkans to Western China* (Boulder, CO, Westview, 1993).

Furman, Dimitry, and Carl Johan Asenius, 'The Case of Nagorno-Karabakh (Azerbaijan)', in Lena Jonson and Clive Archer, eds, *Peace-keeping and the Role of Russia in Eurasia* (Boulder, CO, Westview, 1996).

G.E.K., 'The Turco-Egyptian Flirtation of Autumn 1954', *The World Today*, Vol. 12 (1956).

Gilead, Baruch, 'Turkish–Egyptian Relations 1952–1957', *Middle Eastern Affairs*, Vol. 10 (1959).

Girgin, Kemal, *Osmanlı ve Cumhuriyet Dönemleri Hariciye Tarihimiz (Teşkilat ve Protokol)* (Ankara, Türk Tarih Kurumu, 1992).

Gökay, Bülent, 'Turkish Settlement and the Caucasus, 1918–20', *Middle Eastern Studies*, Vol. 32 (1996); reprinted in Sylvia Kedourie, ed., *Turkey; Identity, Democracy, Politics* (London and Portland, OR, Cass, 1996).

——, *A Clash of Empires: Turkey between Russian Bolshevism and British Imperialism, 1918–1923* (London, I.B. Tauris, 1997)·

——, 'Caspian Uncertainties: Regional Rivalries and Pipelines', *Perceptions* (Ankara), Vol. 3, No. 1 (1998).

Göle, Nilüfer, 'Towards an Autonomization of Politics and Civil Society in Turkey', in Metin Heper and Ahmet Evin, eds, *Politics in the Third Turkish Republic* (Boulder, CO, Westview, 1994).

Gommershall, Stephen J., 'Nato and European Defence', *Perceptions*, (Ankara), Vol. 4, No. 1 (1999).

Gönlübol, Mehmet, 'NATO, USA and Turkey', in Kemal H. Karpat *et al.*, *Turkey's Foreign Policy in Transition* (Leiden, Brill, 1975).

Gresh, Alain, 'Turkish–Israeli–Syrian Relations and their Impact on the Middle East', *Middle East Journal*, Vol. 52 (1998).

Groom, A.J.R., 'The Process of Negotiation, 1974–1993', in C.H. Dodd ed., *The Political, Social and Economic Development of Northern Cyprus* (Hemingford Grey, Eothen, 1993).

Gruen, George E., 'Ambivalence in the Alliance: US Interests in the Middle East and the Evolution of Turkish Foreign Policy', *Orbis*, Vol. 24 (1980).

——, 'Turkey Between the Middle East and the West', in Robert O. Freedman, ed., *The Middle East from the Iran Contra Affair to the Intifada* (New York, NY, Syracuse University Press, 1991).

Gunter, Michael M., *The Kurds in Turkey* (Boulder, CO, Westview, 1990).

——, 'The Foreign Policy of the Iraqi Kurds', *Journal of South Asian and Middle Eastern Studies*, Vol. 20 (1997).

——, *The Kurds and the Future of Turkey* (New York, NY, St Martin's Press, 1997).

——, 'Turkey and Iran Face Off in Kurdistan', *Middle East Quarterly*, Vol. 5 (1998).

Gürkan, İhsan, 'Turkish–Iraqi Relations: The Cold War and its Aftermath', *Turkish Review of Middle East Studies* (Istanbul), Vol. 9 (1996–97).

Hafner, Donald L., 'Bureaucratic Politics and "Those Frigging Missiles": JFK, Cuba, and US Missiles in Turkey', *Orbis*, Vol. 21 (1977).

Hale, William, *The Political and Economic Development of Modern Turkey* (London, Croom Helm, 1981).

——. 'Anglo-Turkish Trade since 1923: Experiences and Problems', in William Hale and Ali İhsan Bağış, eds, *Four Centuries of Turco-British Relations* (Walkington, Eothen, 1984).

——, 'The Traditional and Modern in the Economy of Kemalist Turkey', in J.M. Landau, ed., *Atatürk and the Modernization of Turkey* (Boulder, CO, Westview Press, 1984).

——, 'Turkey, the Middle East and the Gulf Crisis', *International Affairs*, Vol. 68 (1992).

——, 'Turkey: A Crucial but Problematic Applicant', in John Redmond, ed., *Prospective Europeans: New Members for the European Union* (New York, NY, and London, Harvester Wheatsheaf, 1994).

——, *Turkish Politics and the Military* (London, Routledge, 1994).

——, 'Turkey, the Black Sea and Transcaucasia', in John F. R. Wright, Suzanne Goldenburg and Richard Schofield, eds, *Transcaucasian Boundaries* (London, UCL Press, 1996).

——, 'Turkey and the EU: The Customs Union and the Future, *Boğaziçi Journal* (Istanbul), Vol. 10 (1997).

——, 'Turkey and Transcaucasia', in David Menashri, ed., *Central Asia*

Meets the Middle East (London, Cass, 1998).

——, 'Foreign Policy and Turkey's Domestic Politics', in David Shankland, ed., *The Turkish Republic at 75 Years* (Hemingford Grey, Eothen, 1999).

——, 'Turkey's Political Landscape: A Glance at the Past and the Future' *International Observer* (Rome), Vol. 34 (1999).

——, 'Economic Issues in Turkish Foreign Policy', in Alan Makovsky and Sabri Sayarı, eds, *Changing Dynamics in Turkish Foreign Policy* (Washington, DC, Washington Institute for Near East Policy, 2000).

——, and Julian Bharier, 'CENTO, RCD and the Northern Tier: A Political and Economic Appraisal', *Middle Eastern Studies*, Vol. 8 (1972).

Halliday, Fred, *The Making of the Second Cold War* (2nd edn, London, Verso, 1986).

——, 'The Middle East, the Great Powers and the Cold War', in Yezid Sayigh and Avi Shlaim, eds, *The Cold War and the Middle East* (Oxford, Clarendon Press, 1997).

Harris, George S., *The Origins of Communism in Turkey* (Stanford, CA, Hoover Institution, 1967).

——, *Troubled Alliance: Turkish–American Problems in Historical Perspective, 1945–1971* (Washington, DC, American Enterprise Institute for Public Policy Research and Hoover Institution, 1972).

Hart, Parker T., *Two NATO Allies at the Threshold of War: Cyprus: A Firsthand Account of Crisis Management, 1965–1968* (Durham, NC, and London, Duke University Press, 1990).

Hartley, Anthony, 'Maastricht's Problematical Future', *World Today*, Vol. 48 (1992).

Heller, Joseph, *British Policy towards the Ottoman Empire, 1908–1914* (London, Cass, 1983).

Henze, Paul B., *Turkey: Toward the Twenty-First Century* (Wasington, DC, Rand Corporation, n.d.).

——, 'Turkey: Toward the Twenty-First Century', in Graham E. Fuller *et al.*, *Turkey's New Geopolitics: From the Balkans to Western China* (Boulder, CO, Westview, 1993).

Hershlag, Z.Y., *Turkey, an Economy in Transition* (The Hague, van Keulen, 1958).

Hiç, Mükerrem, *Turkey's Customs Union with the European Union: Economic and Political Prospects* (Ebenhausen, Germany, Stiftung Wissenschaft und Politik, 1995).

Hirszowicz, Lukasz, *The Third Reich and the Arab East* (London, Routledge & Kegan Paul, 1966).

Holbraad, Carsten, *Middle Powers in International Politics* (London, Macmillan, 1984).

Hostler, Charles Warren, *Turkism and the Soviets* (London, Allen and Unwin, 1957).

Howard, Harry N., *The Partition of Turkey: A Diplomatic History, 1913–1923* (New York, NY, Fertig, 1966).

——, *Turkey, the Straits and US Policy* (Baltimore, MD, and London, Johns Hopkins University Press, 1974).

Huntington, Samuel P., 'The Clash of Civilizations?', *Foreign Affairs*, Vol. 72 (1993).

Hurewitz, J.C., ed., *Diplomacy in the Near and Middle East: A Documentary Record, 1914–1956* (Princeton, NJ, Van Nostrand, 1956).

——, 'Ottoman Diplomacy and the European State System', *Middle East Journal*, Vol. 15 (1961).

——, 'Russia and the Turkish Straits: A Revaluation of the Origins of the Problem', *World Politics*, Vol. 14 (1961–62).

İlkin, Selim, 'The Chester Railway Project', in Türkiye İş Bankası, *International Symposium on Atatürk (17–22 May 1981): Papers and Discussions* (Ankara, Türkiye İş Bankası Kültür Yayınları, 1984).

——, 'A History of Turkey's Association with the European Community', in Ahmet Evin and Geoffrey Denton, eds, *Turkey and the European Community* (Opladen, Leske & Budrich, 1990).

——, 'The Economic Cooperation Organisation (ECO): A Short Note', *Journal of Economic Cooperation among Islamic Countries* (Ankara), Vol. 15 (1994).

Issawi, Charles, *An Economic History of the Middle East and North Africa* (London, Methuen, 1982).

Jaffe, Amy Myers, and Robert A. Manning, 'The Myth of the Caspian "Great Game": The Real Geopolitics of Energy', *Survival*, Vol. 40 (1998–99).

Kaplan, Morton A., *System and Process in International Politics* (New York, NY, Wiley, 1957).

Karaosmanoğlu, Ali L., 'Turkey's Security and the Middle East', *Foreign Affairs*, Vol. 62 (1983).

Karasapan, Ömer, 'Turkey's Armaments Industries', *Middle East Report*, January–February 1987.

Karpat, Kemal H., *Turkey's Politics: The Transition to a Multi-Party System* (Princeton, NJ, Princeton University Press, 1959).

——, 'Turkish and Arab–Israeli Relations', in Kemal H. Karpat *et al.*, *Turkey's Foreign Policy in Transition* (Leiden, Brill, 1975).

——, 'Turkish–Soviet Relations', in Kemal H. Karpat *et al.*, *Turkey's Foreign Policy in Transition* (Leiden, Brill, 1975).

——, 'Turkish Democracy at Impasse: Party Politics and the Third Military Intervention', *International Journal of Turkish Studies*, Vol. 2 (1981).

Kedourie, Elie, 'Young Turks, Freemasons and Jews', *Middle Eastern Studies*, Vol. 7 (1971).

Kennedy, Robert F., *Thirteen Days: A Memoir of the Cuban Missile Crisis* (New York, NY, Norton, 1961).

Kent, Marian, 'British Policy, International Diplomacy and the Turkish Revolution', *International Journal of Turkish Studies*, Vol. 3 (1985–86).

Kibaroğlu, Ayşegül, 'Prospects for Cooperation in the Euphrates–Tigris River Basin', *Turkish Review of Middle East Studies* (Istanbul), Vol. 8 (1994–95).

Kılıç, Altemur, *Turkey and the World* (Washington, DC, Public Affairs Press, 1959).

Kinross, Lord, *Atatürk, the Rebirth of a Nation* (London, Weidenfeld and Nicolson, 1964).

Kirişci, Kemal, 'Post Second World War Immigration from the Balkan Countries to Turkey', *Turkish Review of Balkan Studies* (Istanbul, annual), Vol. 2 (1994–95).

——, 'New Patterns of Turkish Foreign Policy Behaviour', in Çiğdem Balım, ed., *Turkey: Political, Social and Economic Challenges in the 1990s* (Leiden, Brill, 1995).

——, 'Turkey and the Kurdish Safe Haven in Northern Iraq', *Journal of South Asian and Middle Eastern Studies*, Vol. 19 (1996).

——, 'Post Cold-War Turkish Security and the Middle East', *MERIA Journal* (published on internet) No. 2 (1997).

——, 'The Kurdish Question and Turkish Foreign Policy', in Lenora Martin, ed., *The Future of Turkish Foreign Policy* (forthcoming).

——, 'Turkey and the United States: Ambivalent Allies', in B. Rubin and T. Keaney, eds, *US Allies in a Changing World* (London, Cass, 2000).

——, and Gareth Winrow, *The Kurdish Question and Turkey: An Example of Trans-state Ethnic Conflict* (London, Cass, 1997).

Knatchbull-Hugessen, Sir Hughe, *Diplomat in Peace and War* (London, Murray, 1949).

Kramer, Heinz, 'Turkey and EC's Southern Enlargement', *Aussenpolitik*, Vol. 35 (1984).

——, 'The EU–Turkey Customs Union: Economic Integration Amidst Political Turmoil', *Mediterranean Politics*, Vol. 1 (1996).

——, 'Turkey and the European Union: A Multi-Dimensional Relationship with Hazy Perspectives', in V. Mastny and R. Craig Nation, eds, *Turkey between East and West: New Challenges for a Rising Regional Power* (Boulder, CO, Westview, 1996).

———, 'Will Central Asia Become Turkey's Sphere of Influence?', *Perceptions* (Ankara), Vol. 1, No. 1 (1996).

———, 'The Institutional Framework of German–Turkish Relations', paper presented to conference on 'The Parameters of Partnership: Germany, the United States and Turkey', American Institute for Contemporary German Studies, Johns Hopkins University, Washington, DC, 23–24 October 1997.

———, 'Options for Turkish Foreign Policy: Central Asia and Transcaucasus', unpublished paper (1997).

———, 'Turkey's Place and Role in the Emerging European Security Architecture', paper given to seminar series of Modern Turkish Studies Programme, SOAS, London University, 25 April 1997.

———, and Friedemann Muller, 'Relations with Turkey and the Caspian Basin Countries', in Robert D. Blackwill and Michael Stürmer, eds, *Allies Divided: Transatlantic Policies for the Great Middle East* (Cambridge, MA, MIT Press, 1997).

Kuniholm, Bruce R., 'Turkey and NATO: Past, Present and Future', *Orbis*, Vol. 27 (1983).

———, 'Turkey and the West', *Foreign Affairs*, Vol. 70 (1991).

———, *The Origins of the Cold War in the Near East* (Princeton, NJ, Princeton University Press, 2nd edn, 1994).

———, 'Turkey and the West Since World War II', in Vojtech Mastny and R. Craig Nation, eds, *Turkey Between East and West: New Challenges for a Rising Regional Power* (Boulder, CO, Westview, 1996).

Kut, Gün, 'Burning Waters: The Hydropolitics of the Euphrates and Tigris', *New Perspectives on Turkey*, Fall (1993).

Kyle, Keith, *Cyprus: In Search of Peace* (London, Minority Rights Group International, 1997).

Kyriakides, Stanley, *Cyprus: Constitutionalism and Crisis Government* (Philadelphia, PA, University of Philadelphia Press, 1968).

Landau, Jacob M., *Johnson's 1964 Letter to İnönü and Greek Lobbying of the White House* (Jerusalem, Hebrew University of Jerusalem, Jerusalem Papers on Peace Problems 28, 1979)·

———, *Pan-Turkism: From Irredentism to Cooperation* (London, Hurst, 1995).

Larrabee, F. Stephen, 'US and European Policy towards Turkey and the Caspian Basin', in Robert D. Blackwill and Michael Stürmer, eds, *Allies Divided: Transatlantic Policies for the Greater Middle East* (Cambridge, MA,

MIT Press, 1997).

Leffler, Melvin, 'The American Conception of National Security and the Beginnings of the Cold War', *American Historical Review*, Vol. 89 (1984).

Lesser, Ian O., 'Bridge or Barrier? Turkey and the West After the Cold War', in Graham E. Fuller *et al.*, *Turkey's New Geopolitics: From the Balkans to Western China* (Boulder, CO, Westview, 1993).

——, 'Turkey's Strategic Options', *International Observer* (Rome), Vol. 34 (1999).

Lewis, Bernard, *The Emergence of Modern Turkey* (London, Oxford University Press, 1961).

Macfie, A.L., 'The Straits Question: The Conference of Lausanne (November 1922–July 1923)', *Middle Eastern Studies*, Vol. 15 (1979).

——, 'The Straits Question at the Potsdam Conference: The British Position', *Middle Eastern Studies*, Vol. 23 (1987).

——, 'The Turkish Straits in the Second World War, 1939–45', *Middle Eastern Studies*, Vol. 25 (1989).

——, *The Straits Question, 1908–36* (Thessaloniki, Institute for Balkan Studies, 1993).

Mango, Andrew, 'European Dimensions', *Middle Eastern Studies*, Vol. 28 (1992).

——, *Atatürk* (London, Murray, 1999).

Marriott, J.A.R., *The Eastern Question: An Historical Study in European Diplomacy* (Oxford, Clarendon Press, 4th edn, 1940).

Marzari, Frank, 'Western–Soviet Rivalry in Turkey, 1939' (in two parts), *Middle Eastern Studies*, Vol. 7 (1971).

McCarthy, Justin, *Death and Exile: The Ethnic Cleansing of Ottoman Muslims, 1821–1922* (Princeton, NJ, Darwin Press, 1995).

McDowall, David, *A Modern History of the Kurds* (London, I.B. Tauris, 1996).

McGhee, George C., 'Turkey Joins the West', *Foreign Affairs*, Vol. 32 (1954).

——, *The US–Turkish–NATO Middle East Connection* (London, Macmillan, 1990).

Meyer, H.C., 'German Economic Relations with South-Eastern Europe, 1870–1914', *American Historical Review*, Vol. 62 (1951–52).

Milman, Brock, 'Turkish Foreign and Strategic Policy, 1934–42', *Middle Eastern Studies*, Vol. 31 (1995).

Müftüler, Meltem, 'Turkish Economic Liberalization and European Integration', *Middle Eastern Studies*, Vol. 31 (1995).

Müftüler-Baç, Meltem, 'Turkey's Predicament in the Post-Cold War Era',

Futures, Vol. 28 (1996).

——, *Turkey's Relations with a Changing Europe* (Manchester and New York, NY, Manchester University Press, 1997).

——, 'The Never-Ending Story: Turkey and the European Union', *Middle Eastern Studies*, Vol. 34 (1998).

Nachmani, Amikam, *Israel, Turkey and Greece: Uneasy Relations in the Eastern Mediterranean* ((London, Cass, 1987).

——, 'The Remarkable Turkish–Israeli Tie', in Amikam Nachmani, *Turkey and the Middle East* (Tel Aviv, Begin–Sadat Center for Strategic Studies, Bar Ilan University, 1999), reprinted from *Middle East Quarterly*, Vol. 5,1998.

——, 'Turkey in the Wake of the Gulf War: Recent History and its Implications', in Amikam Nachmani, *Turkey and the Middle East* (Tel Aviv, Begin–Sadat Center for Strategic Studies, Bar Ilan University, 1999).

Nathan, James A., 'The Heyday of the New Strategy', in James A. Nathan, ed., *The Cuban Missile Crisis Revisited* (New York, NY, St Martin's Press, 1992).

Neack, Laura, 'Linking State Type with Foreign Policy Behavior', in Laura Neack, Jeanne A.K. Hey and Patrick J. Haney, *Foreign Policy Analysis: Continuity and Change in its Second Generation* (Englewood Cliffs, NJ, Prentice-Hall, 1995).

Oğuzülgen, Saim, 'The Importance of Pilotage Services in the Turkish Straits for the Protection of Life, Property and the Environment', in Turkish Straits Voluntary Watch Group, *Turkish Straits: New Problems, New Solutions* (Istanbul, Isis, for Foundation for Middle East and Balkan Studies, 1995).

Oktar, Selim, 'The Turkish Foreign Policy Environment: A Public Opinion Perspective', paper presented to a Conference on 'The Domestic Context of Turkish Foreign Policy', Washington Institute for Near East Policy, Washington, DC, July 1997.

Ökte, Faik, trans. Geoffrey Cox, *The Tragedy of the Capital Tax* (London, Croom Helm, 1987).

Okyar, Osman, 'Turco-British Relations in the Inter-War Period: Fethi Okyar's Missions to London', in William Hale and Ali İhsan Bağış, eds, *Four Centuries of Turco-British Relations* (Walkington, Eothen Press, 1984).

Olmert, Y., 'Britain, Turkey and the Levant Question during the Second World War', *Middle Eastern Studies*, Vol. 23 (1987).

Olson, Robert, 'The Kurdish Question and Turkey's Foreign Policy, 1991–1995: From the Gulf War to the Incursion into Iraq', *Journal of South Asian and Middle Eastern Studies*, Vol. 19 (1995).

——, ed., *The Kurdish Nationalist Movement in the 1990s: Its Impact on Turkey and the Middle East* (Lexington, KY, University of Kentucky Press, 1996).

Öniş, Ziya, 'Turkey in the Post-Cold War Era: In Search of Identity', *Middle East Journal*, Vol. 49 (1995).

Orhun, Ömür, 'The Uncertainties and Challenges Ahead: A Southern Perspective', *Perceptions* (Ankara), Vol. 4, No. 1 (1999).

Ortaylı, İlber, 'Osmanlı Dipolmasisi ve Dışişleri Örgütü', *Tanzimat'tan Cumhuryet'e Türkiye Ansiklopedisi* (Istanbul, İletişim Yayınları, 1985), Vol. 1.

Öymen, Onur, *Türkiye'nin Gücü* (Istanbul, AD Kitapçilik, 1998).

Özal, Turgut, *Turkey in Europe and Europe in Turkey* (Nicosia, Rustem, 1991).

Özar, Önder, 'Economic Co-operation Organisation: A Promising Future', *Perceptions* (Ankara), Vol. 2, No. 1 (1997).

Özel, Soli, 'On Not Being a Lone Wolf: Geography, Domestic Plays, and Turkish Foreign Policy in the Middle East', in Geoffrey Kemp and Janice Gross Stein, eds, *Powder Keg in the Middle East: The Struggle for Gulf Security* (Lanham, MD, Rowman and Littlefield, 1995).

Özer, Ercan, 'The Black Sea Economic Cooperation and Regional Security', *Perceptions* (Ankara), Vol. 2, No. 3 (1997).

Öztürk, Bayram, 'The Istanbul Strait: A Closing Biological Corridor', in Turkish Straits Voluntary Watch Group, *Turkish Straits: New Problems, New Solutions* (Istanbul, Isis, for Foundation for Middle East and Balkan Studies, 1995).

Perincek, Doğu, ed., *Mustafa Kemal Eskişehir–İzmit Konuşmaları* (Istanbul, Kaynak Yayınları, 1993).

Petersen, Philip A., 'Turkey in Soviet Military Strategy', *Foreign Policy* (Ankara, Foreign Policy Institute), Vol. 13 (1986).

Polyviou, Polyvios G., *Cyprus: Conflict and Negotiation, 1960–1980* (London, Duckworth, 1980).

Pope, Hugh, 'Pointing Fingers at Iran', *Middle East International*, 5 February 1993.

Pope, Nicole and Hugh, *Turkey Unveiled: Atatürk and After* (London, Murray, 1997).

Poulton, Hugh, *Top Hat, Grey Wolf and Crescent: Turkish Nationalism and the Turkish Republic* (London, Hurst, 1997).

——, 'The Turkish State and Democracy', *International Observer* (Rome), Vol. 34 (1999).

Redmond, John, *The Next Mediterranean Enlargement of the European Community: Turkey, Cyprus and Malta?* (Aldershot, Dartmouth Publishing, 1993).

Richmond, J.C.B., *Egypt, 1798–1952* (London, Methuen, 1977).

Richmond, Oliver P., 'Ethno-Nationalism, Sovereignty and Negotiating Positions in the Cyprus Conflict: Obstacles to a Settlement', *Middle Eastern Studies*, Vol. 35 (1999).

Robins, Philip, *Turkey and the Middle East* (London, Pinter, for Royal Institute of International Affairs, 1991).

——, 'Turkish Policy in the Gulf Crisis: Adventurist or Dynamic?' in C.H. Dodd, ed., *Turkish Foreign Policy: New Prospects* (Wistow, Eothen Press, for Modern Turkish Studies Programme, SOAS, 1992).

——, 'Between Sentiment and Self-Interest: Turkey's Policy toward Azerbaijan and the Central Asian States', *Middle East Journal*, Vol. 47 (1993).

——, 'The Overlord State: Turkish Policy and the Kurdish Issue', *International Affairs*, Vol. 69 (1993).

——, 'Coping with Chaos: Turkey and the Bosnian Crisis', in Richard Gillespie, ed., *Mediterranean Politics*, Vol. 1 (1994) (annual, London, Pinter).

——, 'Turkish Foreign Policy under Erbakan', *Survival*, Vol. 39 (1997).

——, 'Turkey's Ostpolitik: Relations with the Central Asian States', in David Menashri, ed., *Central Asia Meets the Middle East* (London, Cass, 1998).

Robinson, Richard D., *The First Turkish Republic* (Cambridge, MA, Harvard University Press, 1963).

Roper, John, 'The West and Turkey: Varying Roles, Common Interests', *International Spectator* (Rome), Vol. 34 (1999).

Rothstein, Robert L., *Alliances and Small Powers* (New York, NY, and London, Columbia University Press, 1968).

Rubinstein, Alvin Z., *Soviet Policy Toward Turkey, Iran and Afghanistan: The Dynamics of Influence* (New York, NY, Praeger, 1982).

Rustow, Dankwart A., 'Transitions to Democracy: Turkey's Experience in Historical and Comparative Perspective', in Metin Heper and Ahmet Evin, eds, *State, Democracy and the Military: Turkey in the 1980s* (Berlin, de Gruyter, 1988).

Sadak, Necmeddin, 'Turkey Faces the Soviets', *Foreign Affairs*, Vol. 27 (1949).

Sanjian, Ara, 'The Formulation of the Baghdad Pact', *Middle Eastern Studies*, Vol. 33 (1997).

Sanjian, Avedis K., 'The Sanjak of Alexandretta (Hatay): Its Impact on Turkish–Syrian Relations (1939–1956)', *Middle East Journal*, Vol. 10 (1956).

Sasley, Brent, 'Turkey's Energy Politics in the Post Cold-War Era',

MERIA Journal (published on internet), Vol. 2, No. 2.

Satloff, Robert B., 'Prelude to Conflict: Communal Interdependence in the Sanjak of Alexandretta 1920–1936', *Middle Eastern Studies*, Vol. 22 (1986).

Sayarı, Sabri, 'Turkey: The Changing European Security Environment and the Gulf Crisis', *Middle East Journal*, Vol. 46 (1992).

——, 'Turkey and the Middle East in the 1990s', *Journal of Palestine Studies*, Vol. 26 (1997).

Sayılgan, Aclan, *Solun 94 Yılı, 1871–1965* (Ankara, Mars Matbaası, 1968).

Sever, Ayşegül, 'The Arab–Israeli Peace Process and Turkey since the 1995 Interim Agreement', *Turkish Review of Middle East Studies* (Istanbul), Vol. 9 (1996–97).

——, 'The Compliant Ally? Turkey and the West in the Middle East, 1954–58', *Middle Eastern Studies*, Vol. 34 (1998).

Sezer, Duygu Bazoğlu, 'Turkey's Security Policies', in Jonathan Alford, ed., *Greece and Turkey: Adversity in Alliance* (London, Gower, for International Institute of Strategic Studies, 1984).

——, 'Turkey and the Western Alliance in the 1980s', in Atila Eralp, Muharrem Tünay and Birol Yeşilada, eds, *The Political and Socioeconomic Transformation of Turkey* (Westport, CT, Praeger, 1993).

——, *Turkey's Political and Security Interests and Policies in the New Geostrategic Environment of the Expanded Middle East* (Washington, DC, Henry L. Stimson Center, Occasional Paper No. 19, 1994).

——, 'Turkey in the New Security Environment in the Balkan and Black Sea Region', in Vojtech Mastny and R. Craig Nation, eds, *Turkey Between East and West: New Challenges for a Rising Regional Power* (Boulder, CO, Westview, 1996).

Şen, Faruk, 'Turkish Communities in Western Europe', in Vojtech Mastny and R. Craig Nation, eds, *Turkey Between East and West: New Challenges for a Rising Regional Power* (Boulder, CO, Westview, 1996).

Shaw, Stanford J., 'The Ottoman Census System and Population, 1831–1914', *International Journal of Middle East Studies*, Vol. 9 (1978).

——, and Ezel Kural Shaw, *History of the Ottoman Empire and Modern Turkey* (Cambridge, Cambridge University Press, 1977).

Sick, Garry, 'Rethinking Dual Containment', *Survival*, Vol. 40 (1998).

Smith, Michael Llewellyn, *Ionian Vision: Greece in Asia Minor, 1919–1922* (2nd edn, London, Hurst, 1998).

Solana, Javier, 'NATO in Transition', *Perceptions* (Ankara), Vol. 1, No. 1 (1996).

Sönmezoğlu, Faruk, *ABD'nin Türkiye Politikası (1964–1980)* (Istanbul, Der

Yayınevi, 1995).

Sonyel, Salahi Ransdan, *Turkish Diplomacy, 1913–1923: Mustafa Kemal and the Turkish National Movement* (London and Beverly Hills, CA, Sage, 1975).

Soysal, İsmail, 'The 1936 Montreux Convention 60 Years Later', in Turkish Straits Voluntary Watch Group, *Turkish Straits: New Problems, New Solutions* (Istanbul, Isis, for Foundation for Middle East and Balkan Studies, 1995).

Spain, James W., 'The United States, Turkey and the Poppy', *Middle East Journal*, Vol. 29 (1975).

Stavrinides, Zenon, *The Cyprus Conflict: National Identity and Statehood* (Wakefield, Loris Stavrinides, 1976).

Stephens, Robert, *Cyprus, a Place of Arms: Power Politics and Ethnic Conflict in the Eastern Mediterranean* (London, Pall Mall, 1966).

Taylor, A.J.P., *The Struggle for Mastery in Europe, 1848–1918* (Oxford, Oxford University Press, 1954).

Taşhan, Seyfi, 'The Case for Turkish Membership', in Ahmet Evin and Geoffrey Denton, eds, *Turkey and the European Community* (Opladen, Leske and Budrich, 1990).

Ter Minassian, Anahide, 'L'Armenie, la Turquie et le marché commun de la mer Noire', *Cahiers d'Études sur la Mediterranée Orientale et le Monde Turco-Iranien* [CEMOTI] (Paris), No. 15 (1993).

Toluner, Sevin, 'Rights and Duties of Turkey regarding Merchant Vessels Passing through the Straits', in Turkish Straits Voluntary Watch Group, *Turkish Straits: New Problems, New Solutions* (Istanbul, Isis, for Foundation for Middle East and Balkan Studies, 1995).

Toprak, Binnaz, 'Civil Society in Turkey', in Augustus R. Norton, ed., *Civil Society in the Middle East*, Vol. 2 (Leiden, Brill, 1995).

Torumtay, Necip, 'Turkey's Military Doctrine', *Foreign Policy* (Ankara, Foreign Policy Institute), Vol. 15, Nos 1–2 (1990).

——, *Orgeneral Torumtay'ın Anıları* (Istanbul, Milliyet Yayınları, 1994).

Trumpener, Ulrich, 'Turkey's Entry into World War I: An Assessment of Responsibilities', *Journal of Modern History*, Vol. 34 (1962).

——, *Germany and the Ottoman Empire, 1914–1918* (Princeton, NJ, Princeton University Press, 1968).

——, 'Germany and the End of the Ottoman Empire', in Marian Kent, ed., *The Great Powers and the End of the Ottoman Empire* (London, Cass, 2nd edn, 1996).

Tuck, Christopher, 'Greece, Turkey and Arms Control', *Defense Analysis*, Vol. 12 (1996).

Tuncer, Baran, 'External Financing of the Turkish Economy and its

Foreign Policy Implications', in Kemal H. Karpat, ed., *Turkey's Foreign Policy in Transition* (Leiden, Brill, 1975).

Türkeş, Mustafa, 'The Balkan Pact and its Immediate Implications for the Balkan States, 1930–34', *Middle Eastern Studies*, Vol. 30 (1994).

Turkish Ministry of Foreign Affairs, 'Water Issues between Turkey, Syria and Iraq', *Perceptions* (Ankara), Vol. 1 No. 2 (1996)·

Turkish Straits Voluntary Watch Group, *Turkish Straits: New Problems, New Solutions* (Istanbul, Isis, for Foundation for Middle East and Balkan Studies, 1995).

Ulman, A.H., and R.H. Dekmejian, 'Changing Patterns in Turkish Foreign Policy', *Orbis*, Vol. 11 (1967).

Ünal, Hasan, 'Young Turks Assessments of International Politics, 1906–9', *Middle Eastern Studies*, Vol. 32 (1996); reprinted in Sylvia Kedourie, ed., *Turkey: Identity, Democracy, Politics* (London and Portland, OR, Cass, 1996).

——, 'Ottoman Policy during the Bulgarian Independence Crisis, 1908–9: Ottoman Empire and Bulgaria at the Outset of the Young Turk Revolution', *Middle Eastern Studies*, Vol. 34 (1998).

Uslu, Nazih, 'Turkey's Relationship with the United States, 1960–1975' (PhD thesis, University of Durham, England, 1994).

Vali, Ferenc A., *Bridge across the Bosporus: The Foreign Policy of Turkey* (Baltimore, MD, and London, Johns Hopkins University Press, 1971).

Vital, David, *The Inequality of States: A Study of the Small Power in International Relations* (Oxford, Clarendon Press, 1967).

Von Papen, Franz, trans. Brian Connell, *Memoirs* (London, André Deutsch, 1952).

Waterfield, Gordon, *Professional Diplomat: Sir Percy Loraine of Kirkharle Bt, 1880–1961* (London, Murray, 1973).

Weber, Frank G., *Eagles on the Crescent: Germany, Austria and the Diplomacy of the Turkish Alliance, 1914–1918* (Ithaca, NY, and London, Cornell University Press, 1970).

——, *The Evasive Neutral: Germany, Britain and the Quest for a Turkish Alliance in the Second World War* (Columbia, MO, and London, University of Missouri Press, 1979).

Weiker, Walter F., *The Turkish Revolution, 1960–1961* (Washington, DC, Brookings Institution, 1963).

——, *Political Tutelage and Democracy in Turkey: The Free Party and its Aftermath* (Leiden, Brill, 1973).

Weisband, Edward, *Turkish Foreign Policy, 1943–1945: Small State Diplomacy and Great Power Politics* (Princeton, NJ, Princeton University Press, 1973).

White, Jenny B., 'Civic Culture and Islam in Urban Turkey', in Chris Hann and Elizabeth Dunn, eds, *Civil Society: Challenging Western Models* (London, Routledge, 1996).

Wilson, Andrew, *The Aegean Dispute* (London, International Institute for Strategic Studies, Adelphi Papers No.155, 1980).

Winrow, Gareth M., 'Gorbachev's New Political Thinking and Turkey', paper delivered to conference of British International Studies Association, University of Warwick, December 1991.

——, 'NATO and the Out-of-Area Issue: The Positions of Turkey and Italy', *Il Politico* (Pavia), Vol. 58 (1993).

——, 'A Region at the Crossroads: Security Issues in Post-Soviet Asia', *Journal of South Asian and Middle Eastern Studies*, Vol. 18 (1994).

——, 'Regional Security and National Identity: The Role of Turkey in Former Soviet Central Asia', in Çiğdem Balım, ed., *Turkey: Political, Social and Economic Challenges in the 1990s* (Leiden, Brill, 1995)

——, *Turkey in Post-Soviet Central Asia* (London, Royal Institute of International Affairs, 1995).

——, 'Turkey's Relations with the Transcaucasus and the Central Asian Republics', *Perceptions* (Ankara), Vol. 1, No. 1 (1996).

——, 'Turkey and the Newly Independent States of Central Asia and Transcaucasus', *MERIA Journal* (published on internet), No. 2 (1997).

——, 'Pipeline Politics and Turkey: A New Great Game in Eurasia?', paper presented to conference on 'Russia–China–Central Asia: From Geo-politics to Geo-economics in Eurasia', Centre for Euro-Asian Studies, University of Reading, England, 23 January 1998.

Yasamee, F.A.K., 'Abdülhamid II and the Ottoman Defence Problem', *Diplomacy & Statecraft*, Vol. 4 (1993).

——, *Ottoman Diplomacy: Abdülhamid II and the Great Powers, 1878–1888* (Istanbul, Isis, 1996).

Yavuz, M. Hakan, 'Turkish–Israeli Relations through the Lens of the Turkish Identity Debate', *Journal of Palestine Studies*, Vol. 27 (1997).

——, and Mujeeb R. Khan, 'Turkish Foreign Policy Toward the Arab–Israeli Conflict: Duality and the [*sic*] Development', *Arab Studies Quarterly*, Vol. 14 (1992).

Yerasimos, Stefanos, *Türk–Sovyet İlişkileri, Ekim Devrimden Milli Mücadele'ye* (Istanbul, Gözlem Yayınları, 1979).

Zamir, Meir, 'Population Statistics of the Ottoman Empire in 1914 and 1918', *Middle Eastern Studies*, Vol. 17 (1981).

Zürcher, Erik J., *The Unionist Factor: The Role of the Committee of Union and Progress in the Turkish National Movement* (Leiden, Brill, 1984).

——, *Political Opposition in the Early Turkish Republic: The Progressive Republican Party 1924–1925* (Leiden, Brill, 1991).

——, *Turkey: A Modern History* (London, I.B. Tauris, 1993).

Zuzul, Miomir, 'Croatia and Turkey: Toward a Durable Peace in Southeastern Europe', *Perceptions* (Ankara), Vol. 3 (1998).

Index